THE FINAL NIGHT

THE FINAL NIGHT

KARL KESEL

RON MARZ
Writers

STUART IMMONEN

MIKE McKONE
Pencillers

JOSE MARZAN JR.

MARK McKENNA
Inkers

PATRICIA MULVIHILL

JOHN KALISZ

LEE LOUGHRIDGE
Colorists

GASPAR SALADINO

CHRIS ELIOPOULOS
Letterers

PROLOGUE

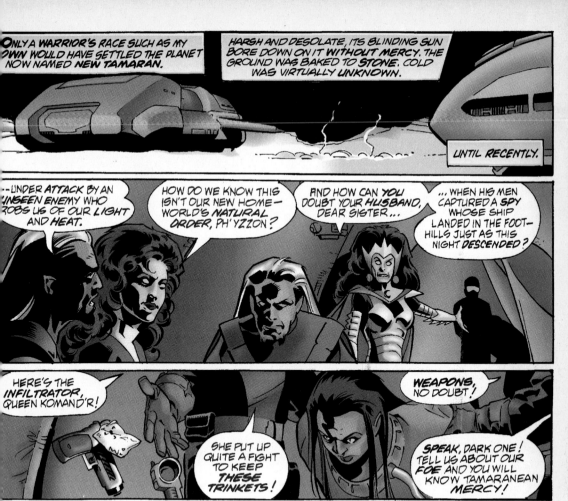

ONLY A WARRIOR'S RACE SUCH AS MY OWN WOULD HAVE SETTLED THE PLANET NOW NAMED **NEW TAMARAN.**

HARSH AND DESOLATE, ITS BLINDING SUN BORE DOWN ON IT **WITHOUT MERCY.** THE GROUND WAS BAKED TO STONE. COLD WAS VIRTUALLY UNKNOWN.

UNTIL **RECENTLY.**

--UNDER **ATTACK** BY AN UNSEEN ENEMY WHO ROBS US OF OUR **LIGHT** AND **HEAT.**

HOW DO WE KNOW THIS ISN'T OUR NEW HOME-WORLD'S **NATURAL ORDER,** PH'YZZON?

AND HOW CAN **YOU** DOUBT YOUR **HUSBAND,** DEAR SISTER...

...WHEN HIS MEN CAPTURED A SPY WHOSE SHIP LANDED IN THE FOOTHILLS JUST AS THIS NIGHT **DESCENDED?**

HERE'S THE INFILTRATOR, QUEEN KOMAND'R!

SHE PUT UP QUITE A FIGHT TO KEEP **THESE** TRINKETS!

WEAPONS, NO DOUBT!

SPEAK, DARK ONE! TELL US ABOUT OUR **FOE** AND YOU WILL KNOW TAMARANEAN **MERCY!**

WITH SUDDEN DESPERATION, THE STRANGER TWISTED **FREE!** A TAMARANEAN WOULD RATHER **DIE** FIGHTING THAN AID AN ENEMY...

...BUT IN HER EYES I SAW SOMETHING **DIFFERENT.**

SOMETHING I HADN'T SEEN SINCE MY DAYS ON **EARTH.**

FZZUM!

WHEN I WAS NOT ONLY A **PRINCESS,** BUT A TITAN... CALLED **STARFIRE!**

COMPASSION FOR A **SPY,** KORIAND'R? I ASSURE YOU SHE IS **FINE,** AND WILL TELL US ALL WE NEED TO KNOW...

EVEN IF IT IS WITH HER **DYING** BREATH!

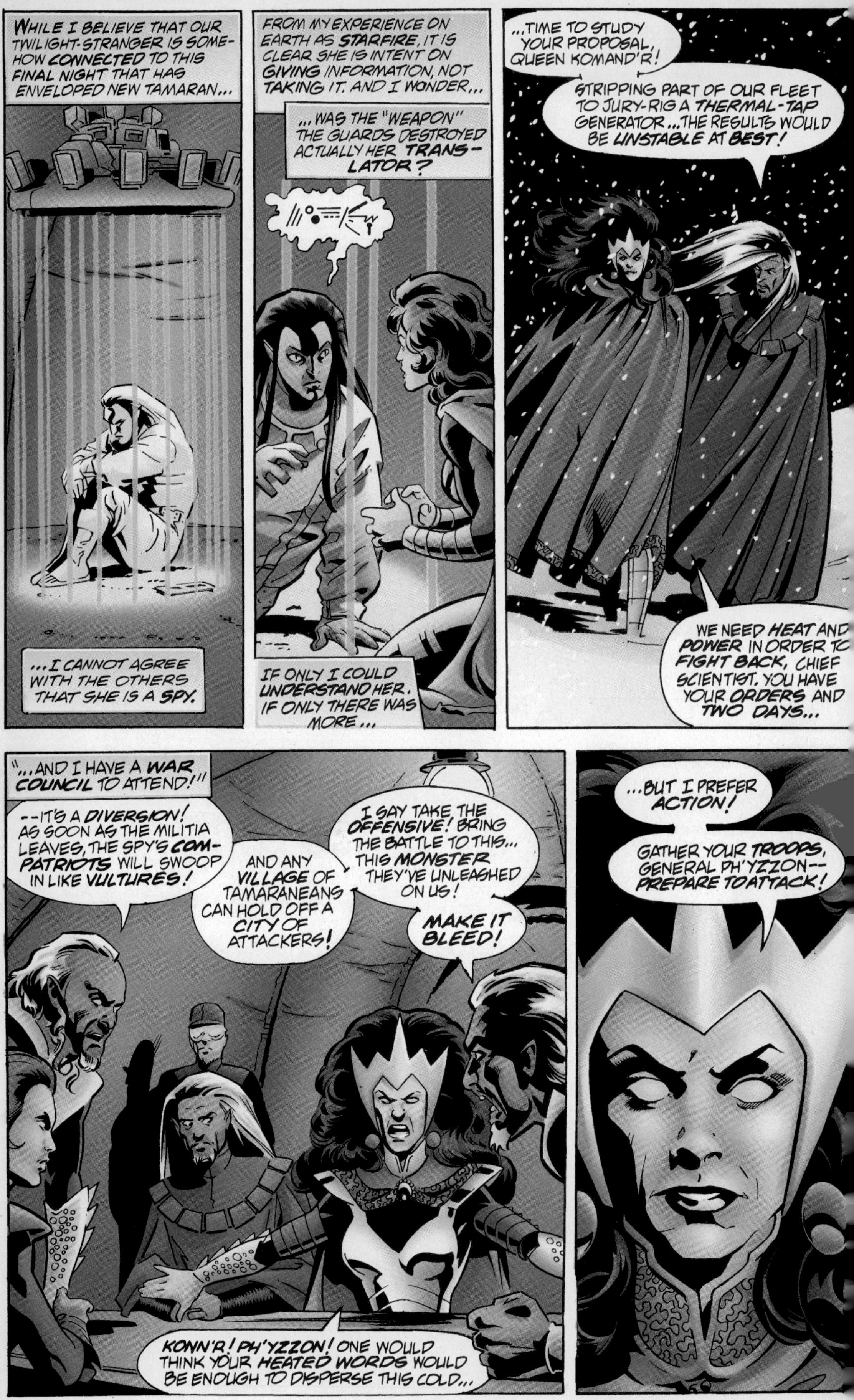
WHILE I BELIEVE THAT OUR TWILIGHT-STRANGER IS SOMEHOW CONNECTED TO THIS FINAL NIGHT THAT HAS ENVELOPED NEW TAMARAN...
...I CANNOT AGREE WITH THE OTHERS THAT SHE IS A SPY.
FROM MY EXPERIENCE ON EARTH AS STARFIRE, IT IS CLEAR SHE IS INTENT ON GIVING INFORMATION, NOT TAKING IT. AND I WONDER...
...WAS THE "WEAPON" THE GUARDS DESTROYED ACTUALLY HER TRANSLATOR?
IF ONLY I COULD UNDERSTAND HER. IF ONLY THERE WAS MORE...
...TIME TO STUDY YOUR PROPOSAL, QUEEN KOMAND'R!
STRIPPING PART OF OUR FLEET TO JURY-RIG A THERMAL-TAP GENERATOR...THE RESULTS WOULD BE UNSTABLE AT BEST!
WE NEED HEAT AND POWER IN ORDER TO FIGHT BACK, CHIEF SCIENTIST. YOU HAVE YOUR ORDERS AND TWO DAYS...
"...AND I HAVE A WAR COUNCIL TO ATTEND!"
--IT'S A DIVERSION! AS SOON AS THE MILITIA LEAVES, THE SPY'S COMPATRIOTS WILL SWOOP IN LIKE VULTURES!
AND ANY VILLAGE OF TAMARANEANS CAN HOLD OFF A CITY OF ATTACKERS!
I SAY TAKE THE OFFENSIVE! BRING THE BATTLE TO THIS... THIS MONSTER THEY'VE UNLEASHED ON US!
MAKE IT BLEED!
KONN'R! PH'YZZON! ONE WOULD THINK YOUR HEATED WORDS WOULD BE ENOUGH TO DISPERSE THIS COLD...
...BUT I PREFER ACTION!
GATHER YOUR TROOPS, GENERAL PH'YZZON-- PREPARE TO ATTACK!

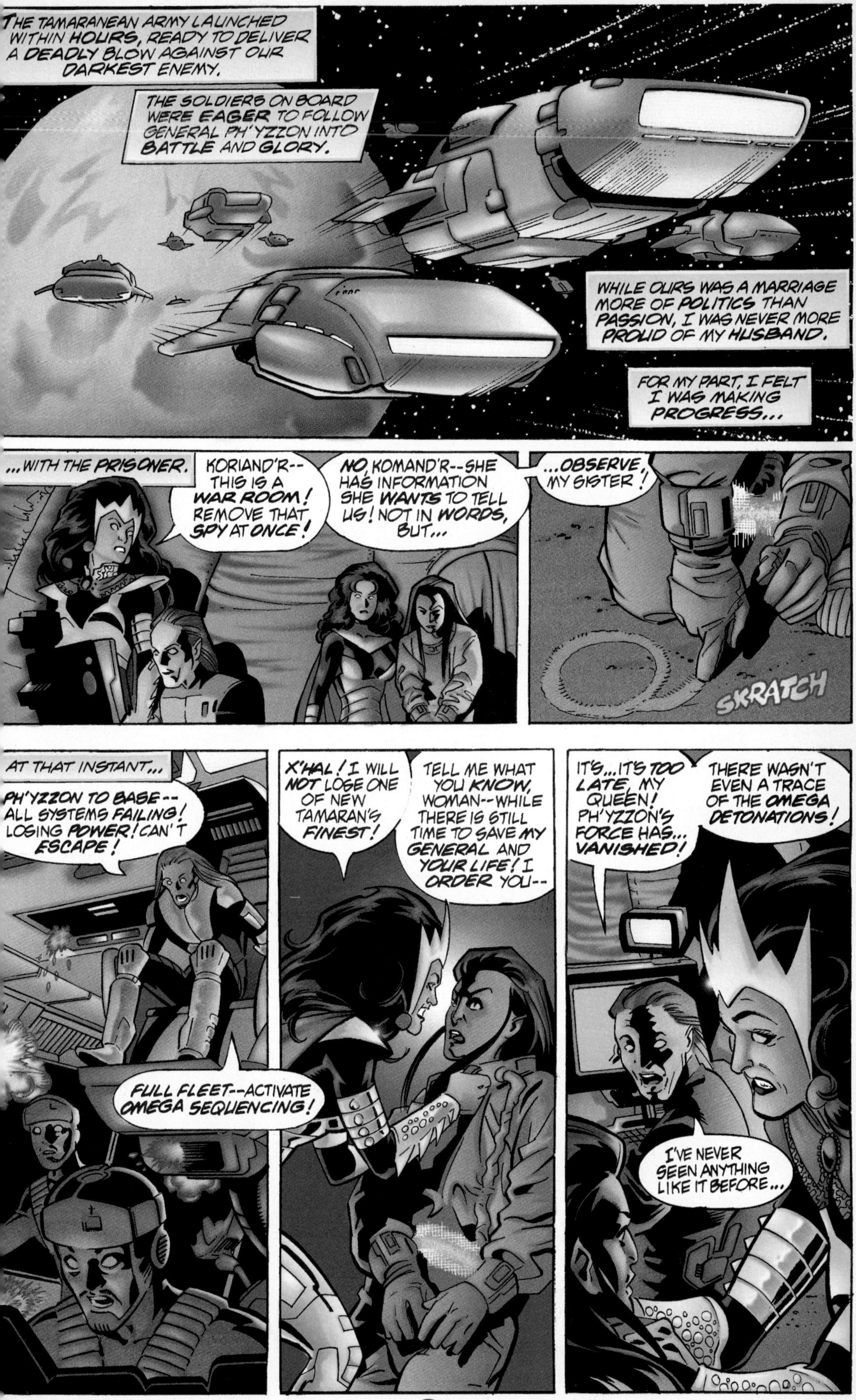
THE TAMARANEAN ARMY LAUNCHED WITHIN HOURS, READY TO DELIVER A DEADLY BLOW AGAINST OUR DARKEST ENEMY.
THE SOLDIERS ON BOARD WERE EAGER TO FOLLOW GENERAL PH'YZZON INTO BATTLE AND GLORY.
WHILE OURS WAS A MARRIAGE MORE OF POLITICS THAN PASSION, I WAS NEVER MORE PROUD OF MY HUSBAND.
FOR MY PART, I FELT I WAS MAKING PROGRESS...
...WITH THE PRISONER.
KORIAND'R-- THIS IS A WAR ROOM! REMOVE THAT SPY AT ONCE!
NO, KOMAND'R--SHE HAS INFORMATION SHE WANTS TO TELL US! NOT IN WORDS, BUT...
...OBSERVE, MY SISTER!
SKRATCH
AT THAT INSTANT...
PH'YZZON TO BASE-- ALL SYSTEMS FAILING! LOSING POWER! CAN'T ESCAPE!
FULL FLEET--ACTIVATE OMEGA SEQUENCING!
X'HAL! I WILL NOT LOSE ONE OF NEW TAMARAN'S FINEST!
TELL ME WHAT YOU KNOW, WOMAN--WHILE THERE IS STILL TIME TO SAVE MY GENERAL AND YOUR LIFE! I ORDER YOU--
IT'S...IT'S TOO LATE, MY QUEEN! PH'YZZON'S FORCE HAS... VANISHED!
THERE WASN'T EVEN A TRACE OF THE OMEGA DETONATIONS!
I'VE NEVER SEEN ANYTHING LIKE IT BEFORE...

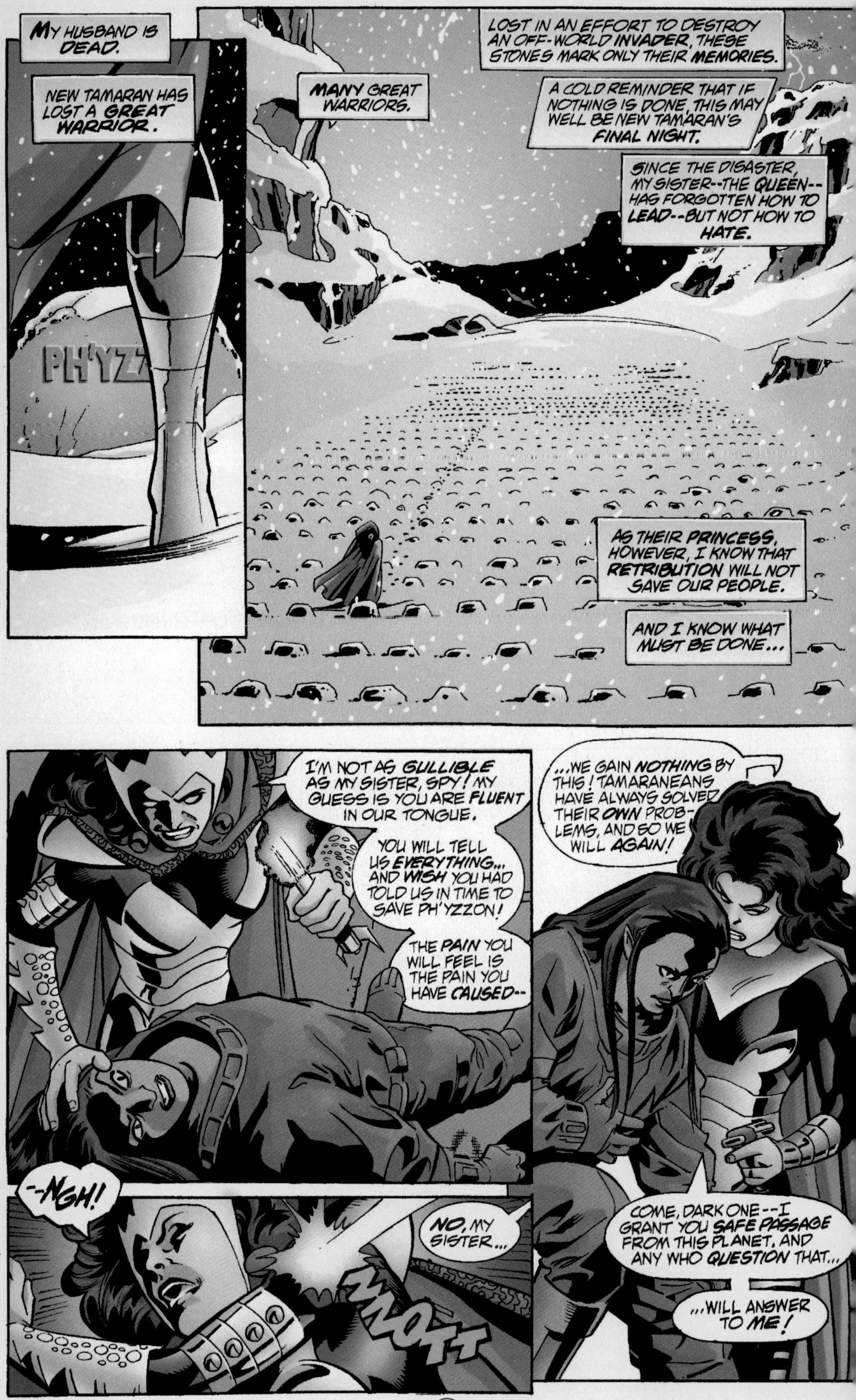

MY HUSBAND IS DEAD.
NEW TAMARAN HAS LOST A GREAT WARRIOR.
PH'YZZ
MANY GREAT WARRIORS.
LOST IN AN EFFORT TO DESTROY AN OFF-WORLD INVADER, THESE STONES MARK ONLY THEIR MEMORIES.
A COLD REMINDER THAT IF NOTHING IS DONE, THIS MAY WELL BE NEW TAMARAN'S FINAL NIGHT.
SINCE THE DISASTER, MY SISTER--THE QUEEN--HAS FORGOTTEN HOW TO LEAD--BUT NOT HOW TO HATE.
AS THEIR PRINCESS, HOWEVER, I KNOW THAT RETRIBUTION WILL NOT SAVE OUR PEOPLE.
AND I KNOW WHAT MUST BE DONE...
I'M NOT AS GULLIBLE AS MY SISTER, SPY! MY GUESS IS YOU ARE FLUENT IN OUR TONGUE.
YOU WILL TELL US EVERYTHING... AND WISH YOU HAD TOLD US IN TIME TO SAVE PH'YZZON!
THE PAIN YOU WILL FEEL IS THE PAIN YOU HAVE CAUSED--
--NGH!
NO, MY SISTER...
WNOTT
...WE GAIN NOTHING BY THIS! TAMARANEANS HAVE ALWAYS SOLVED THEIR OWN PROB-LEMS, AND SO WE WILL AGAIN!
COME, DARK ONE--I GRANT YOU SAFE PASSAGE FROM THIS PLANET, AND ANY WHO QUESTION THAT...
...WILL ANSWER TO ME!

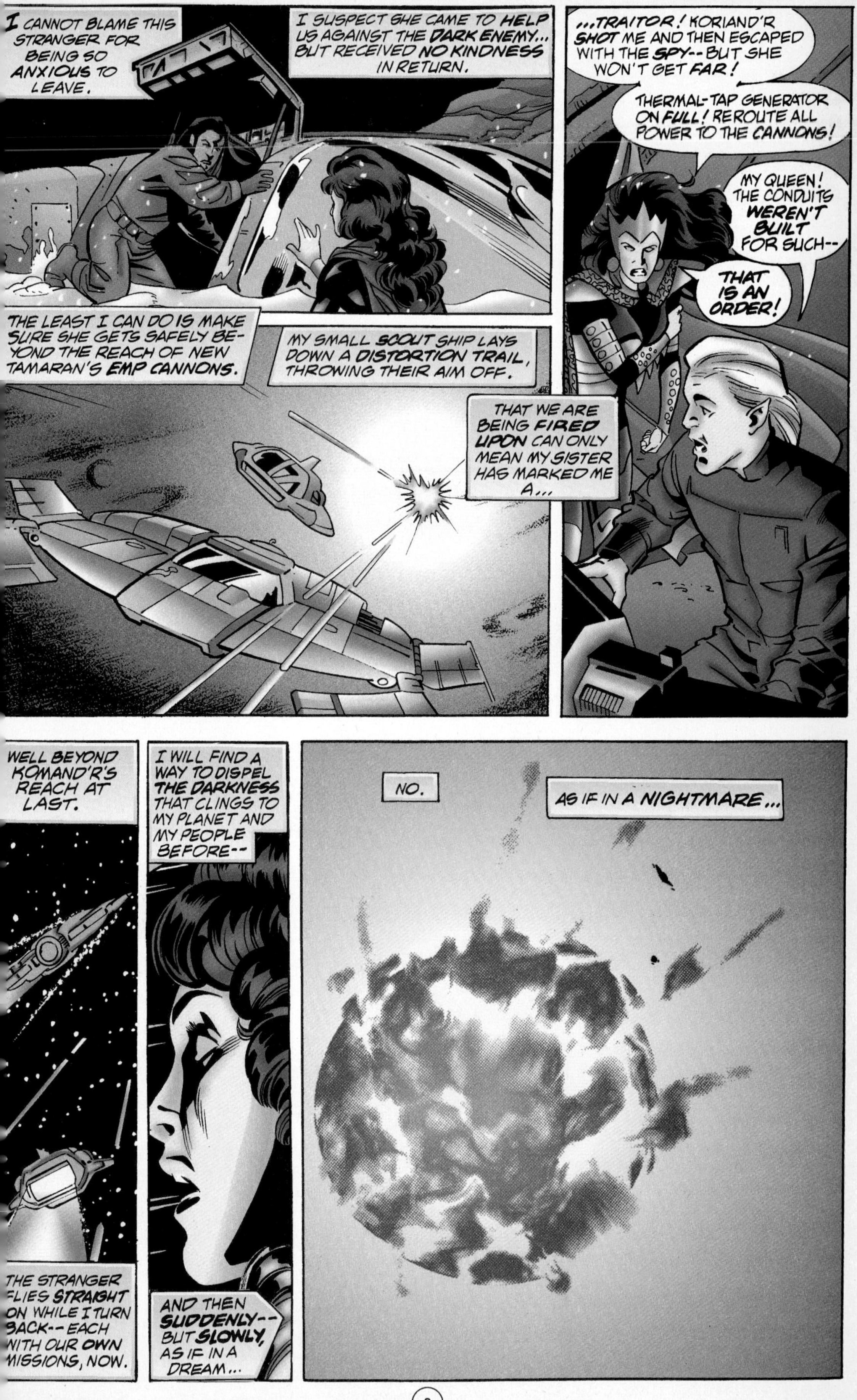
I CANNOT BLAME THIS STRANGER FOR BEING SO ANXIOUS TO LEAVE.
I SUSPECT SHE CAME TO HELP US AGAINST THE DARK ENEMY... BUT RECEIVED NO KINDNESS IN RETURN.
...TRAITOR! KORIAND'R SHOT ME AND THEN ESCAPED WITH THE SPY-- BUT SHE WON'T GET FAR!
THERMAL-TAP GENERATOR ON FULL! REROUTE ALL POWER TO THE CANNONS!
MY QUEEN! THE CONDUITS WEREN'T BUILT FOR SUCH--
THAT IS AN ORDER!
THE LEAST I CAN DO IS MAKE SURE SHE GETS SAFELY BEYOND THE REACH OF NEW TAMARAN'S EMP CANNONS.
MY SMALL SCOUT SHIP LAYS DOWN A DISTORTION TRAIL, THROWING THEIR AIM OFF.
THAT WE ARE BEING FIRED UPON CAN ONLY MEAN MY SISTER HAS MARKED ME A...
WELL BEYOND KOMAND'R'S REACH AT LAST.
THE STRANGER FLIES STRAIGHT ON WHILE I TURN BACK-- EACH WITH OUR OWN MISSIONS, NOW.
I WILL FIND A WAY TO DISPEL THE DARKNESS THAT CLINGS TO MY PLANET AND MY PEOPLE BEFORE--
AND THEN SUDDENLY-- BUT SLOWLY, AS IF IN A DREAM...
NO.
AS IF IN A NIGHTMARE...

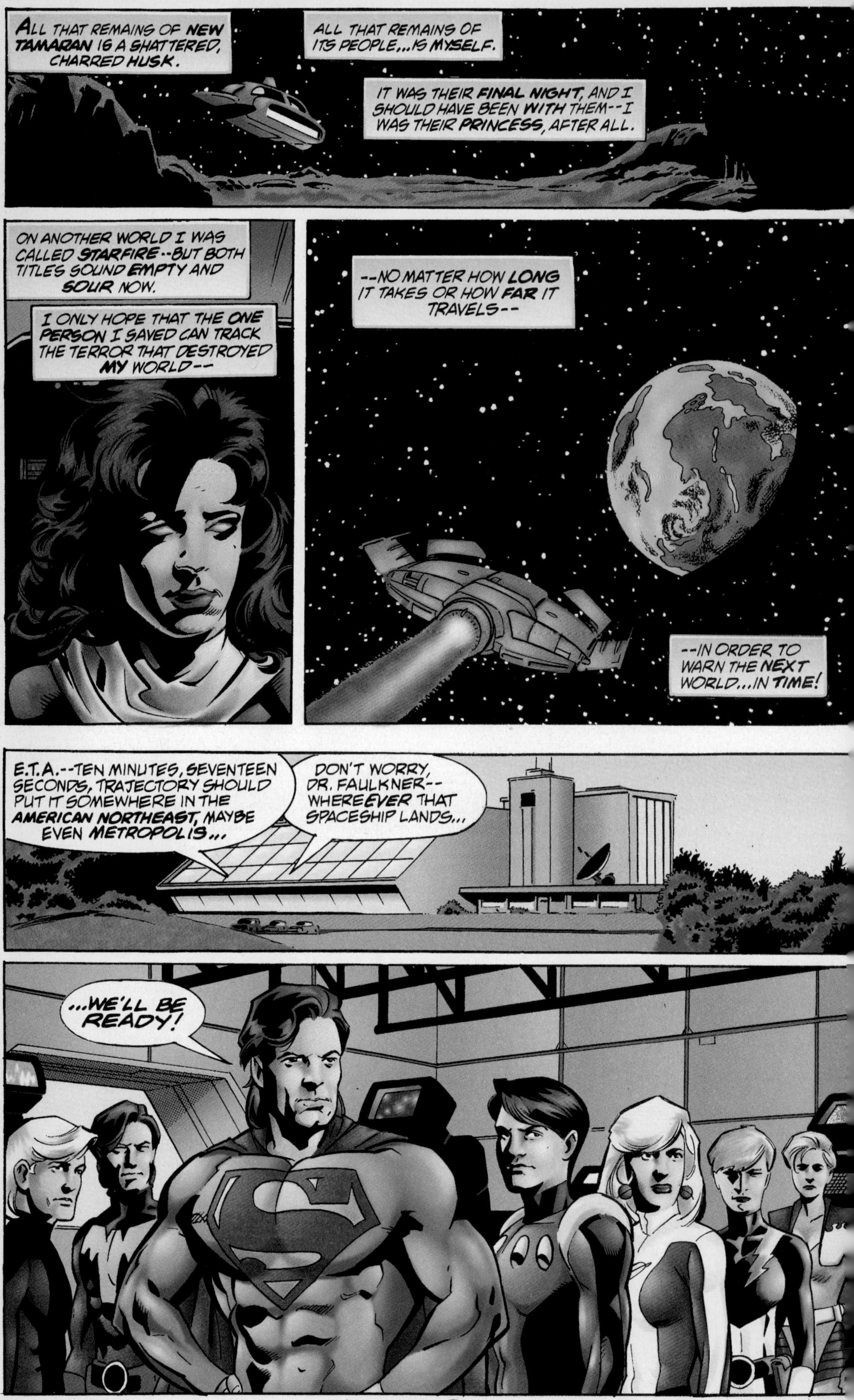
ALL THAT REMAINS OF NEW TAMARAN IS A SHATTERED, CHARRED HUSK.
ALL THAT REMAINS OF ITS PEOPLE,...IS MYSELF.
IT WAS THEIR FINAL NIGHT, AND I SHOULD HAVE BEEN WITH THEM--I WAS THEIR PRINCESS, AFTER ALL.
ON ANOTHER WORLD I WAS CALLED STARFIRE--BUT BOTH TITLES SOUND EMPTY AND SOUR NOW.
I ONLY HOPE THAT THE ONE PERSON I SAVED CAN TRACK THE TERROR THAT DESTROYED MY WORLD--
--NO MATTER HOW LONG IT TAKES OR HOW FAR IT TRAVELS--
--IN ORDER TO WARN THE NEXT WORLD...IN TIME!
E.T.A.--TEN MINUTES, SEVENTEEN SECONDS, TRAJECTORY SHOULD PUT IT SOMEWHERE IN THE AMERICAN NORTHEAST, MAYBE EVEN METROPOLIS...
DON'T WORRY, DR. FAULKNER--WHEREEVER THAT SPACESHIP LANDS...
...WE'LL BE READY!

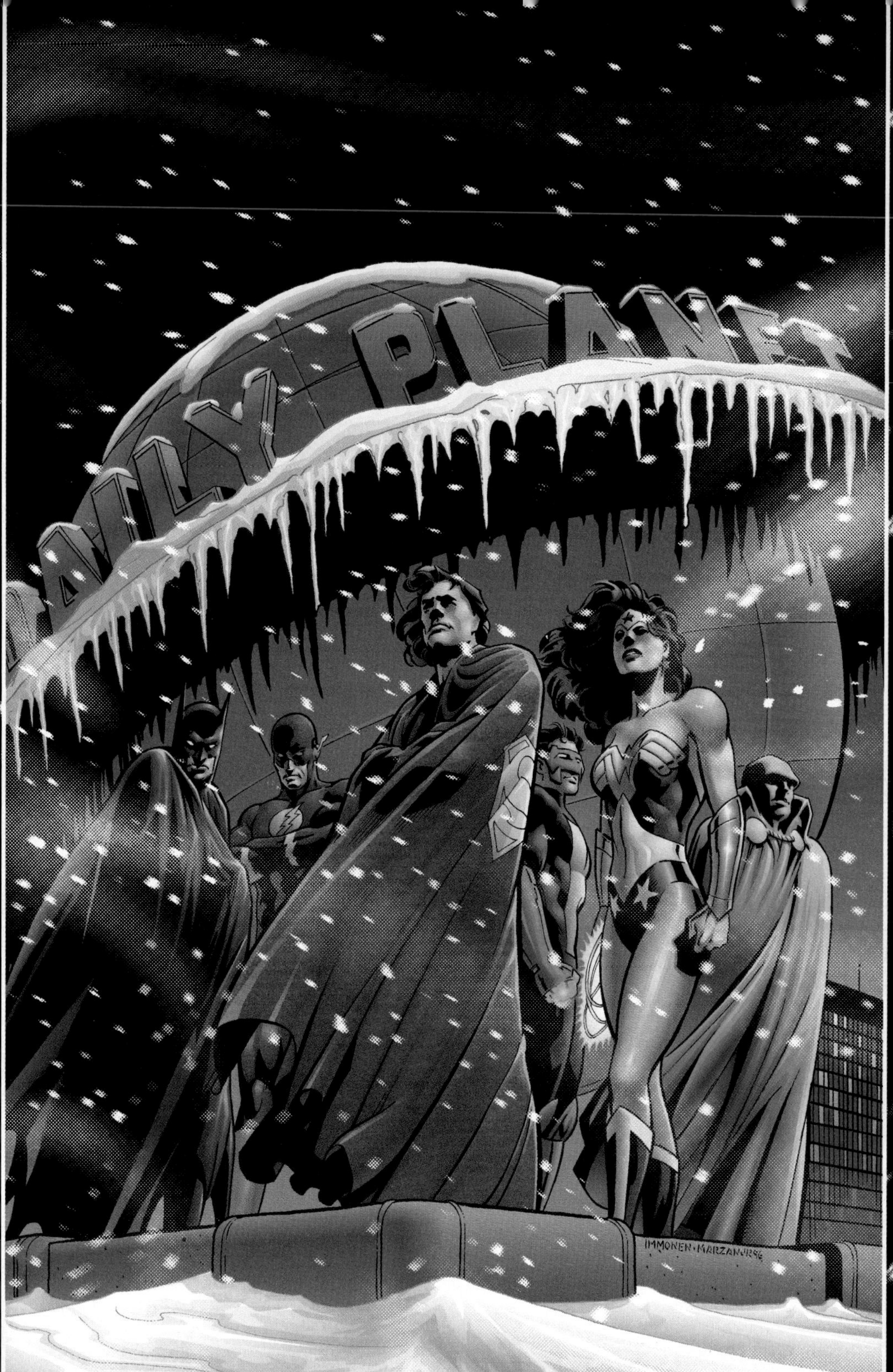

ARMAGEDDON

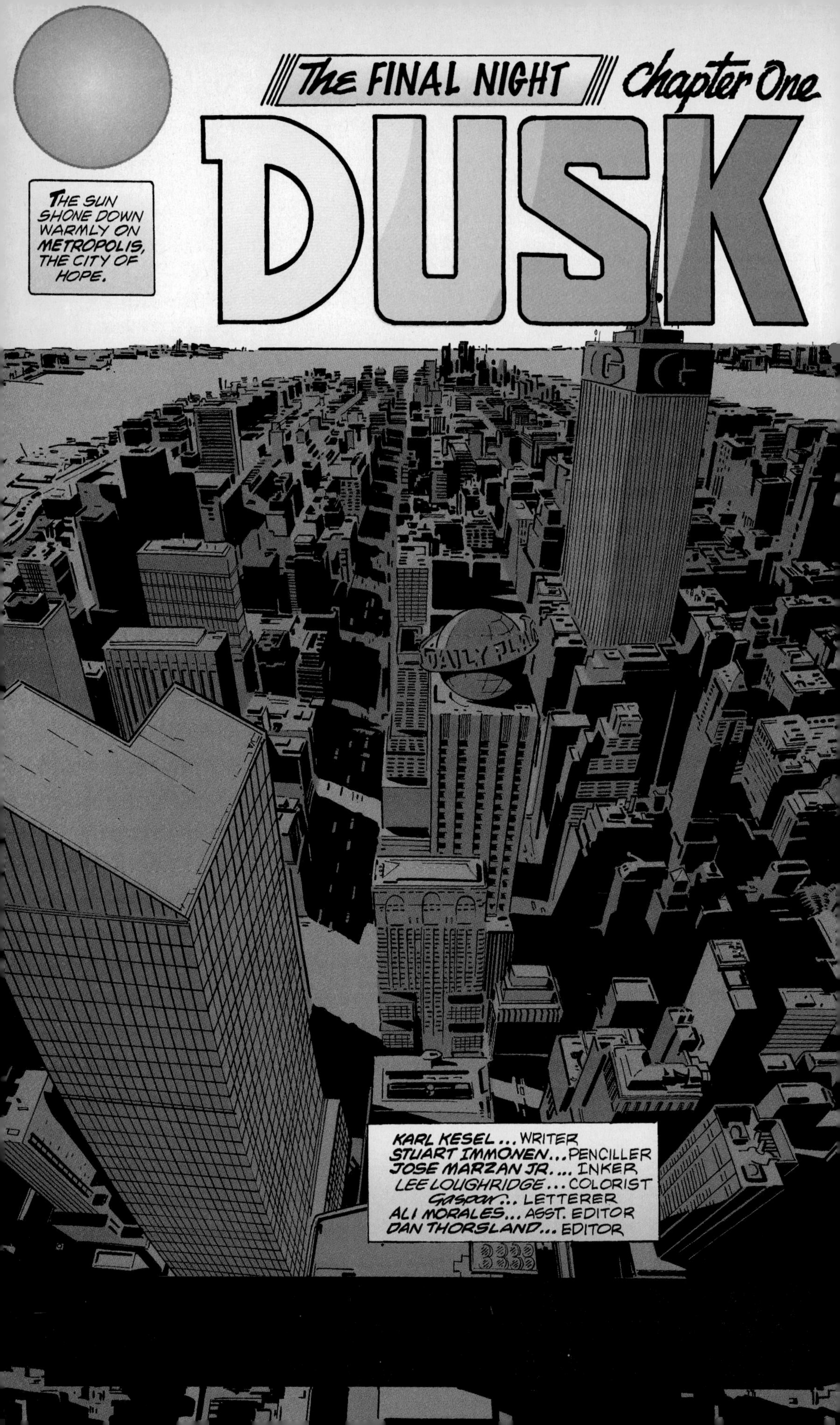
The FINAL NIGHT Chapter One
DUSK
THE SUN SHONE DOWN WARMLY ON METROPOLIS, THE CITY OF HOPE.
DAILY PLANET
KARL KESEL ... WRITER
STUART IMMONEN ... PENCILLER
JOSE MARZAN JR. ... INKER
LEE LOUGHRIDGE ... COLORIST
Gaspar ... LETTERER
ALI MORALES ... ASST. EDITOR
DAN THORSLAND ... EDITOR

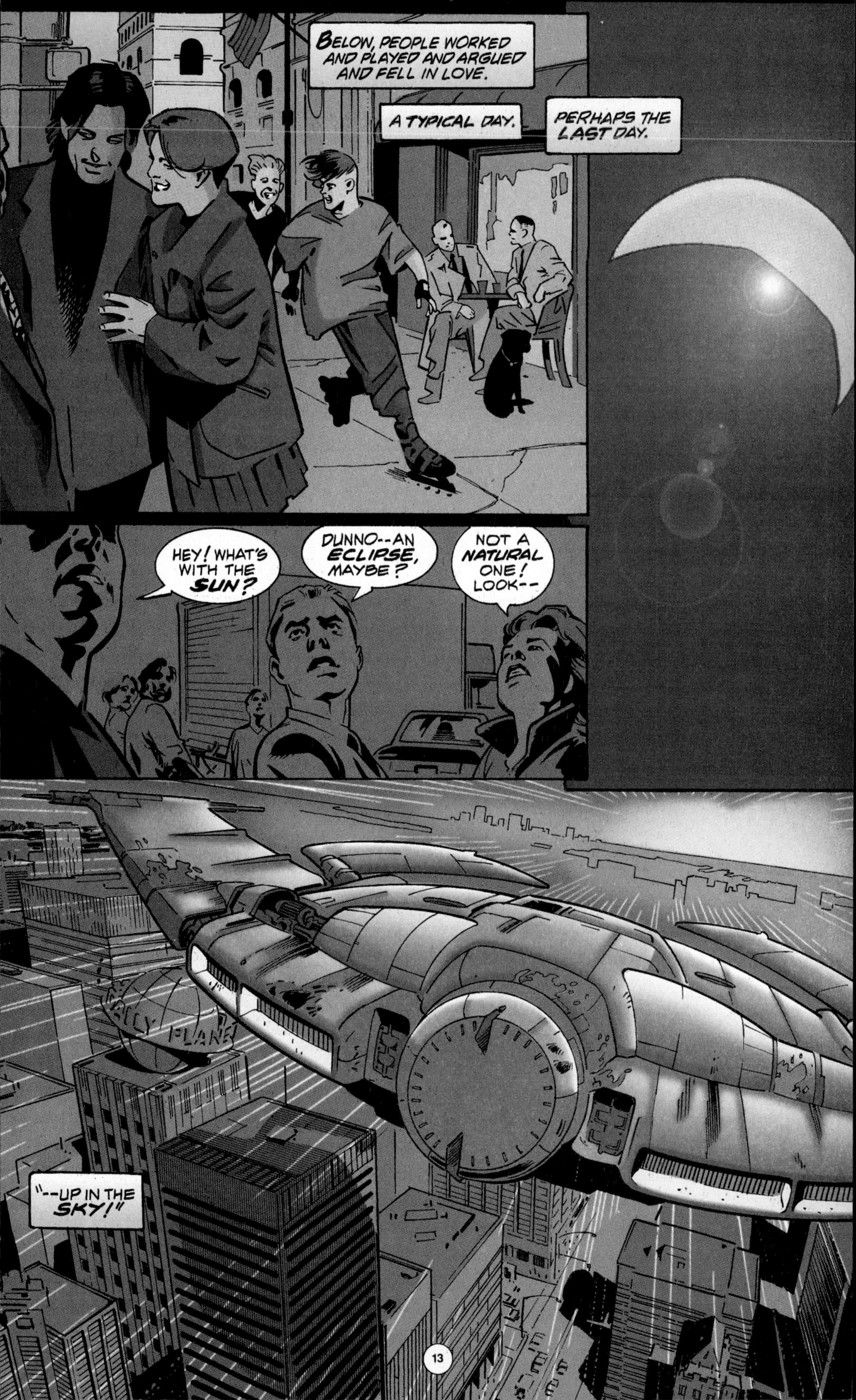
BELOW, PEOPLE WORKED AND PLAYED AND ARGUED AND FELL IN LOVE.
A TYPICAL DAY.
PERHAPS THE LAST DAY.
HEY! WHAT'S WITH THE SUN?
DUNNO--AN ECLIPSE, MAYBE?
NOT A NATURAL ONE! LOOK--
"--UP IN THE SKY!"

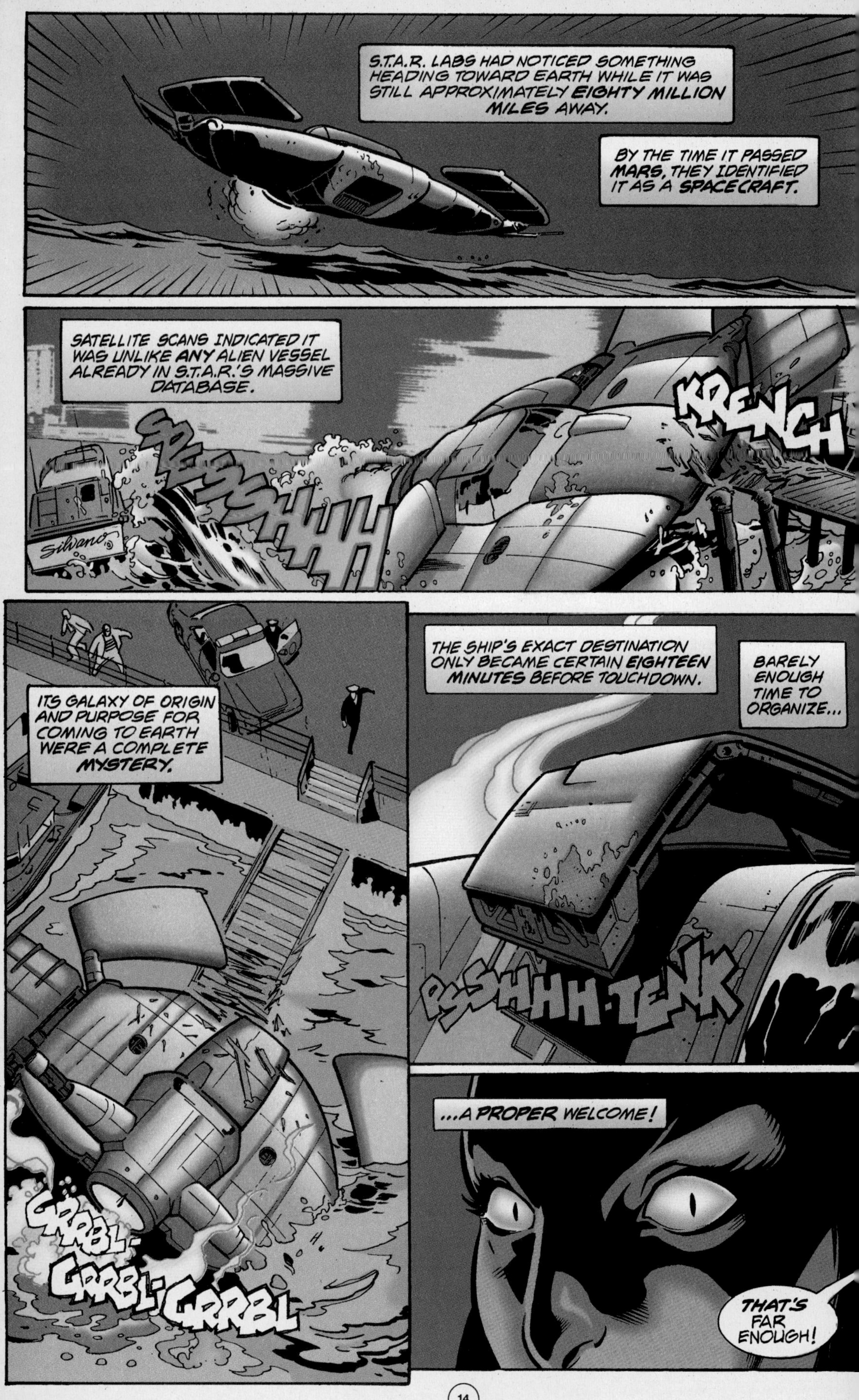
S.T.A.R. LABS HAD NOTICED SOMETHING HEADING TOWARD EARTH WHILE IT WAS STILL APPROXIMATELY EIGHTY MILLION MILES AWAY.
BY THE TIME IT PASSED MARS, THEY IDENTIFIED IT AS A SPACECRAFT.
SATELLITE SCANS INDICATED IT WAS UNLIKE ANY ALIEN VESSEL ALREADY IN S.T.A.R.'S MASSIVE DATABASE.
KRENCH
SPLASHHH
Silvano
ITS GALAXY OF ORIGIN AND PURPOSE FOR COMING TO EARTH WERE A COMPLETE MYSTERY.
GRRBL-GRRBL-GRRBL
THE SHIP'S EXACT DESTINATION ONLY BECAME CERTAIN EIGHTEEN MINUTES BEFORE TOUCHDOWN.
BARELY ENOUGH TIME TO ORGANIZE...
PSSHHH-TENK
...A PROPER WELCOME!
THAT'S FAR ENOUGH!

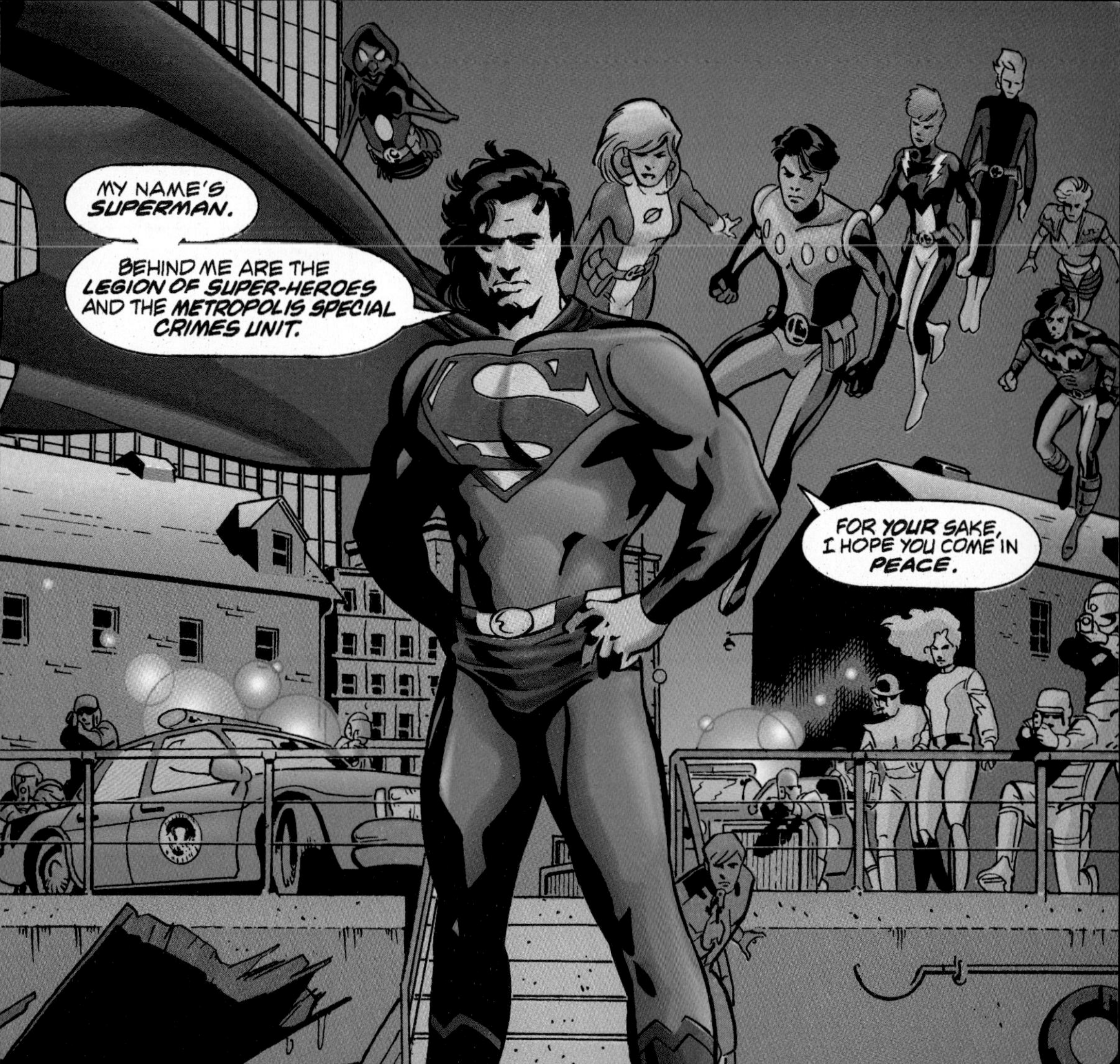
MY NAME'S SUPERMAN.
BEHIND ME ARE THE LEGION OF SUPER-HEROES AND THE METROPOLIS SPECIAL CRIMES UNIT.
FOR YOUR SAKE, I HOPE YOU COME IN PEACE.

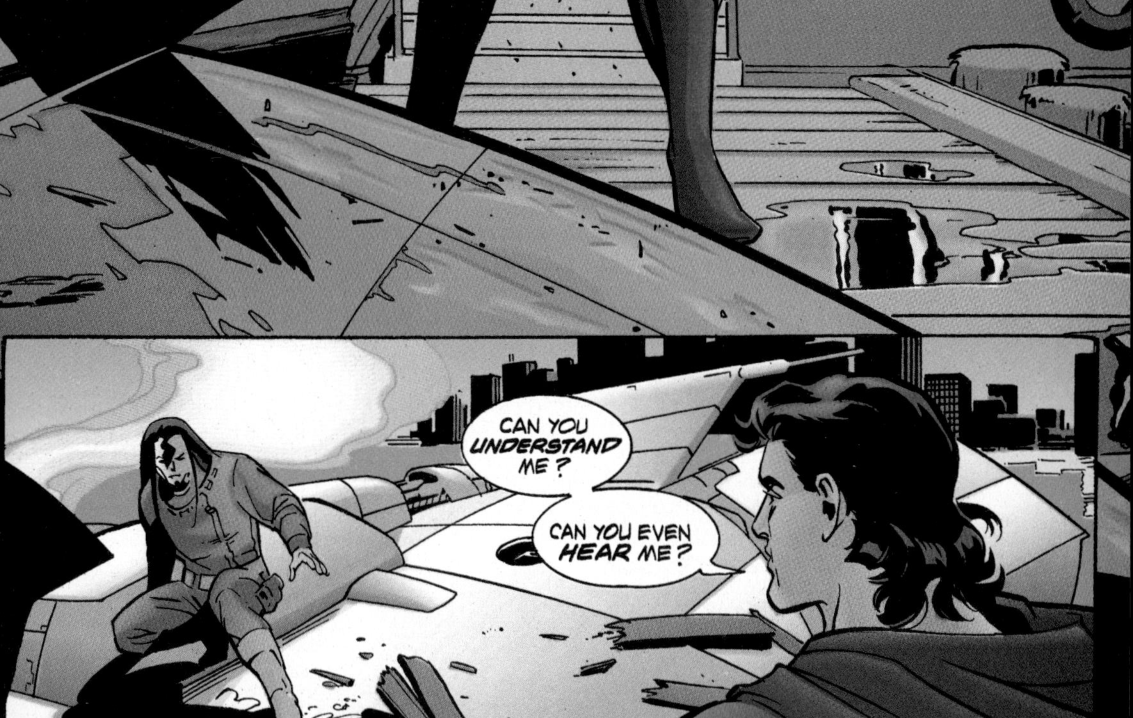
CAN YOU UNDERSTAND ME?
CAN YOU EVEN HEAR ME?

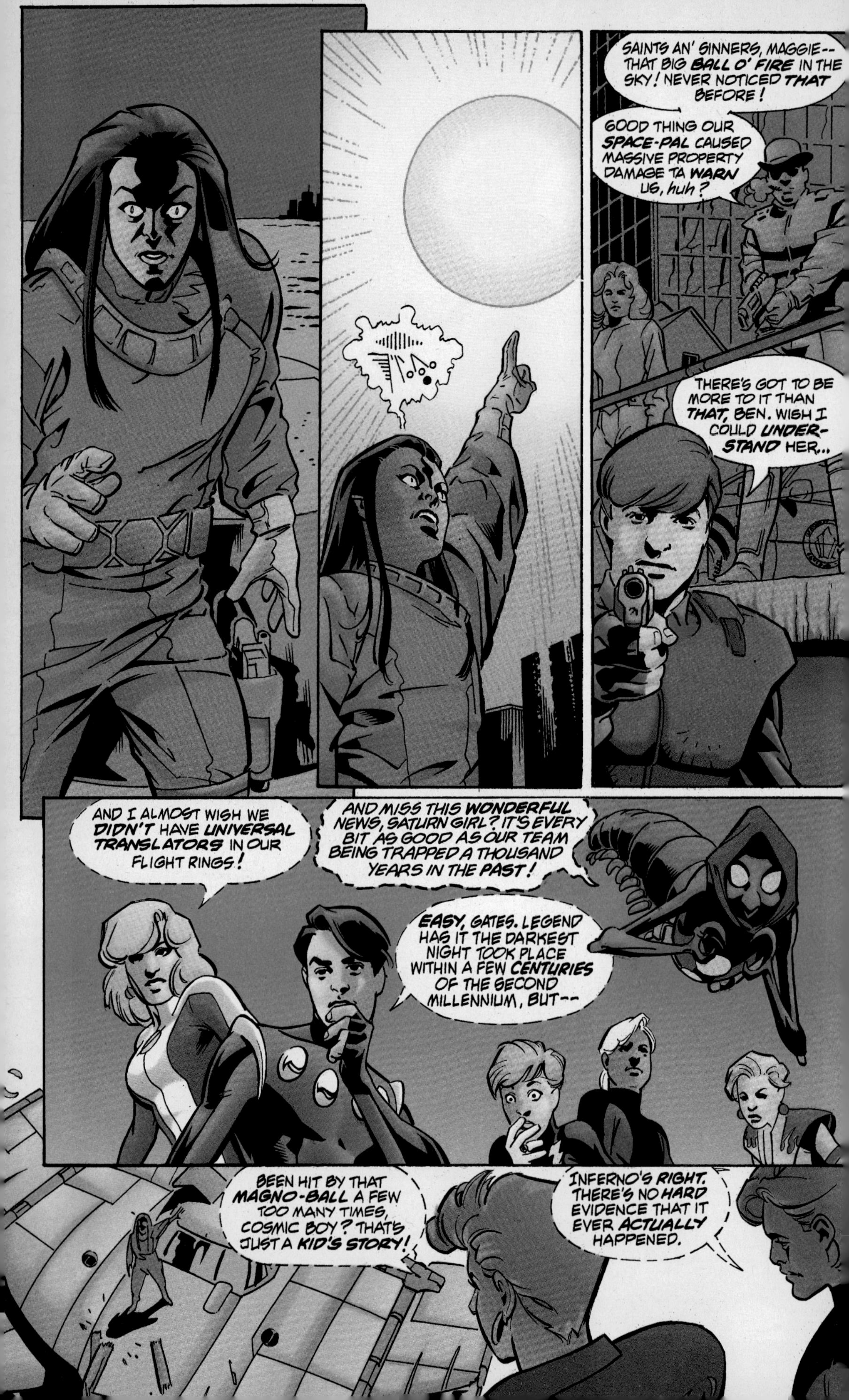
SAINTS AN' SINNERS, MAGGIE-- THAT BIG BALL O' FIRE IN THE SKY! NEVER NOTICED THAT BEFORE!
GOOD THING OUR SPACE-PAL CAUSED MASSIVE PROPERTY DAMAGE TA WARN US, huh?
THERE'S GOT TO BE MORE TO IT THAN THAT, BEN. WISH I COULD UNDER-STAND HER...
AND I ALMOST WISH WE DIDN'T HAVE UNIVERSAL TRANSLATORS IN OUR FLIGHT RINGS!
AND MISS THIS WONDERFUL NEWS, SATURN GIRL? IT'S EVERY BIT AS GOOD AS OUR TEAM BEING TRAPPED A THOUSAND YEARS IN THE PAST!
EASY, GATES. LEGEND HAS IT THE DARKEST NIGHT TOOK PLACE WITHIN A FEW CENTURIES OF THE SECOND MILLENNIUM, BUT--
BEEN HIT BY THAT MAGNO-BALL A FEW TOO MANY TIMES, COSMIC BOY? THAT'S JUST A KID'S STORY!
INFERNO'S RIGHT. THERE'S NO HARD EVIDENCE THAT IT EVER ACTUALLY HAPPENED.

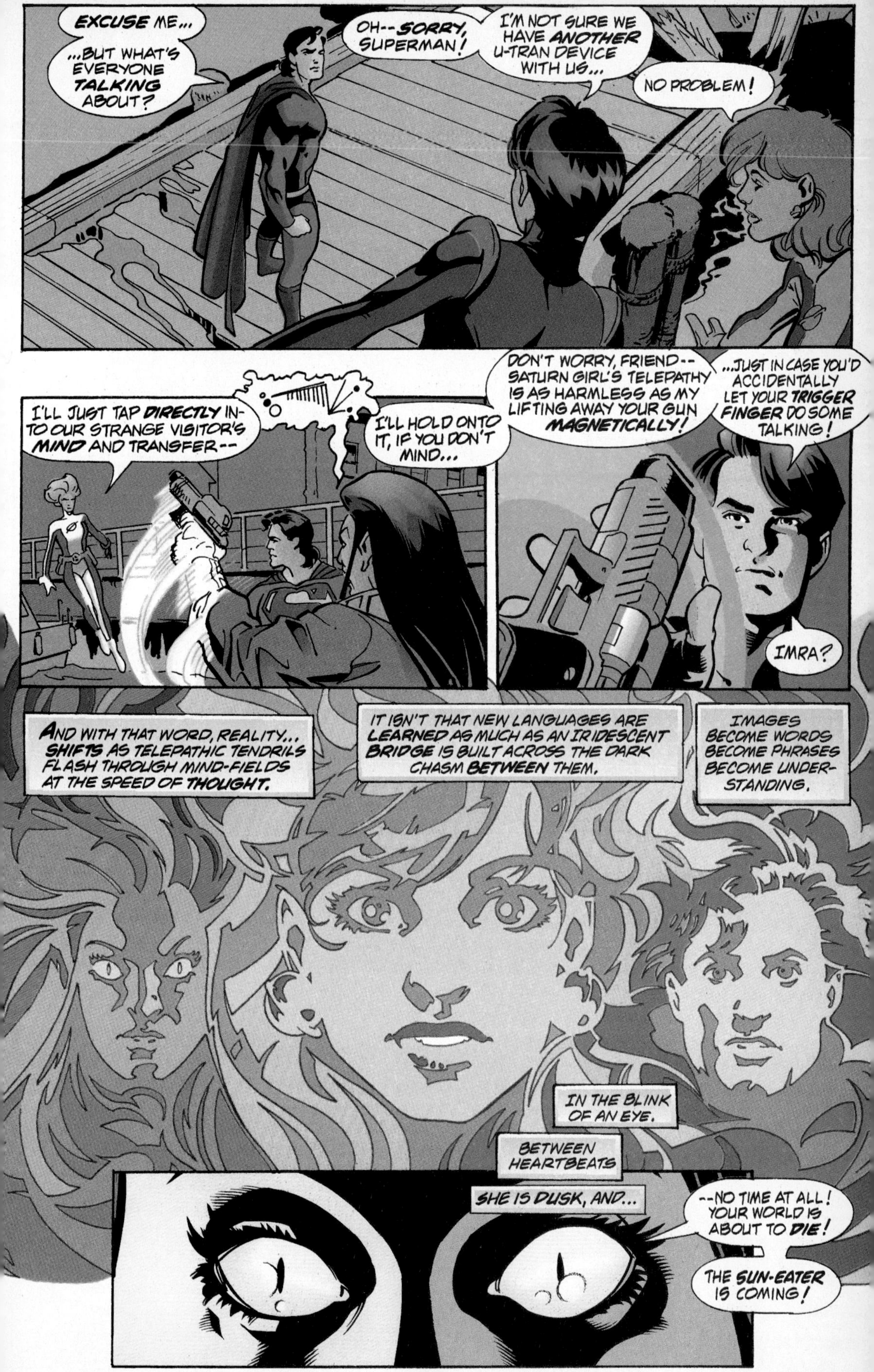
EXCUSE ME...
...BUT WHAT'S EVERYONE TALKING ABOUT?
OH--SORRY, SUPERMAN!
I'M NOT SURE WE HAVE ANOTHER U-TRAN DEVICE WITH US...
NO PROBLEM!
I'LL JUST TAP DIRECTLY INTO OUR STRANGE VISITOR'S MIND AND TRANSFER--
I'LL HOLD ONTO IT, IF YOU DON'T MIND...
DON'T WORRY, FRIEND--SATURN GIRL'S TELEPATHY IS AS HARMLESS AS MY LIFTING AWAY YOUR GUN MAGNETICALLY!
...JUST IN CASE YOU'D ACCIDENTALLY LET YOUR TRIGGER FINGER DO SOME TALKING!
IMRA?
AND WITH THAT WORD, REALITY... SHIFTS AS TELEPATHIC TENDRILS FLASH THROUGH MIND-FIELDS AT THE SPEED OF THOUGHT.
IT ISN'T THAT NEW LANGUAGES ARE LEARNED AS MUCH AS AN IRIDESCENT BRIDGE IS BUILT ACROSS THE DARK CHASM BETWEEN THEM.
IMAGES BECOME WORDS BECOME PHRASES BECOME UNDERSTANDING.
IN THE BLINK OF AN EYE.
BETWEEN HEARTBEATS
SHE IS DUSK, AND...
--NO TIME AT ALL! YOUR WORLD IS ABOUT TO DIE!
THE SUN-EATER IS COMING!

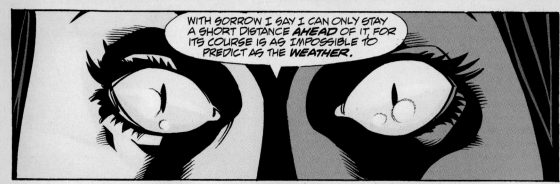

WITH SORROW I SAY I CAN ONLY STAY A SHORT DISTANCE *AHEAD* OF IT, FOR ITS COURSE IS AS IMPOSSIBLE TO PREDICT AS THE *WEATHER.*

BUT I HAVE OBSERVED ITS *DARK DEEDS* MANY TIMES, AND I CAN SAY FOR A CERTAINTY THAT IT IS COMING FOR *YOUR* SUN NOW!

IF IT IS NOT WITHIN YOUR SOLAR SYSTEM AT *PRESENT,* IT WILL BE IN A SHORT TIME.

IT WILL *ENVELOP* YOUR SUN AND *STEAL* ITS LIGHT AND HEAT FROM YOU!

YOUR CROPS WILL *WITHER.* YOUR WATERS WILL *FREEZE.* AND THAT IS ONLY THE *BEGINNING.*

THERE IS... *NO* WAY TO STOP IT!

I OFFER THIS WARNING AS I HAVE A *HUNDRED* TIMES BEFORE...

...WITH THE HOPE THAT SOME MAY *ESCAPE* THIS DOOMED WORLD.

BUT WE HAVE LOST PRECIOUS *HOURS* SINCE MY ARRIVAL, AND I FEAR MORE AND MORE THAT YOUR PEOPLE WILL SUFFER THE *SAME FATE...*

...AS MINE...

YOU'VE DONE WHAT YOU *COULD,* DUSK--WE'LL *NEVER* BE ABLE TO THANK YOU *ENOUGH.*

LIGHTS, PLEASE.

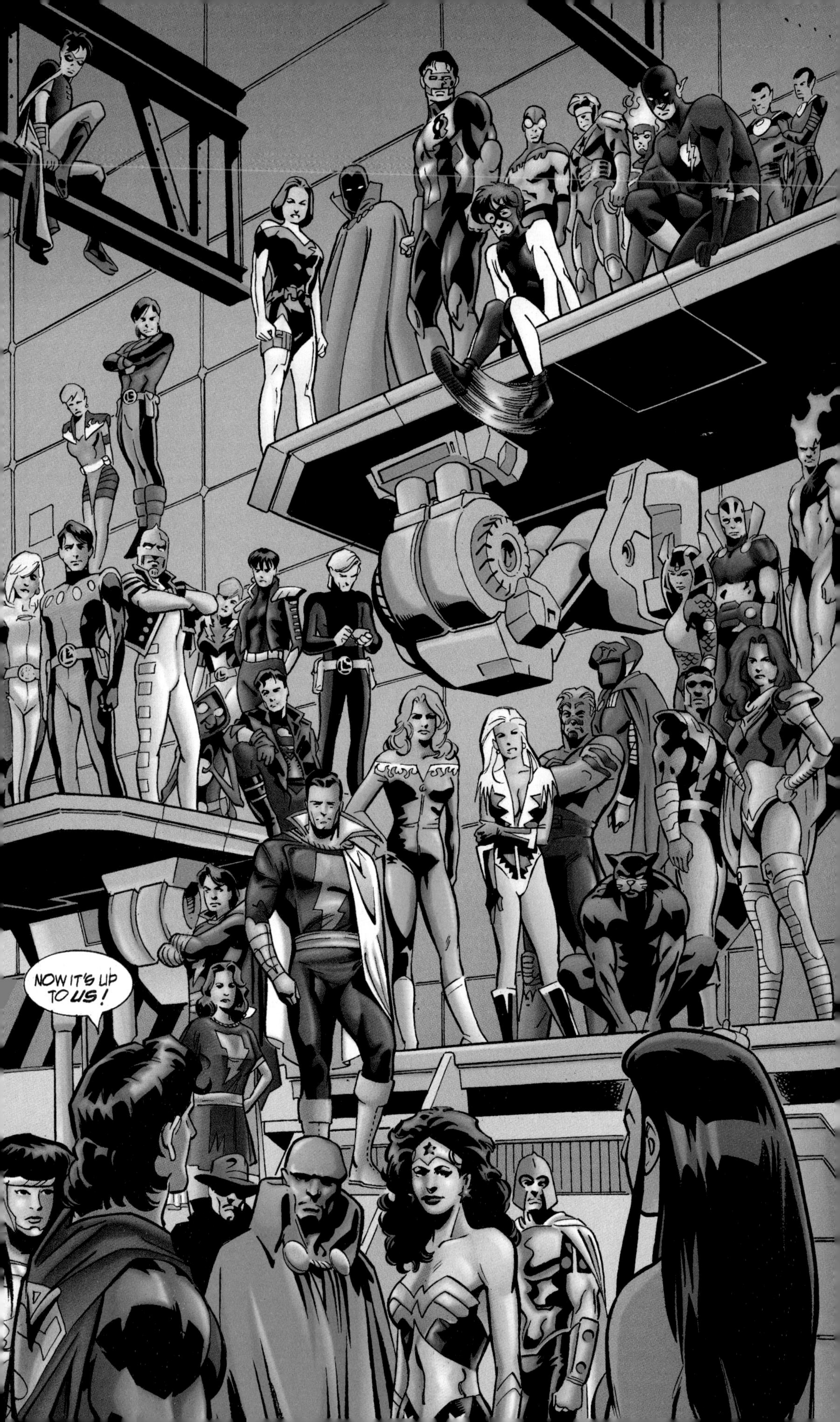
NOW IT'S UP TO US!

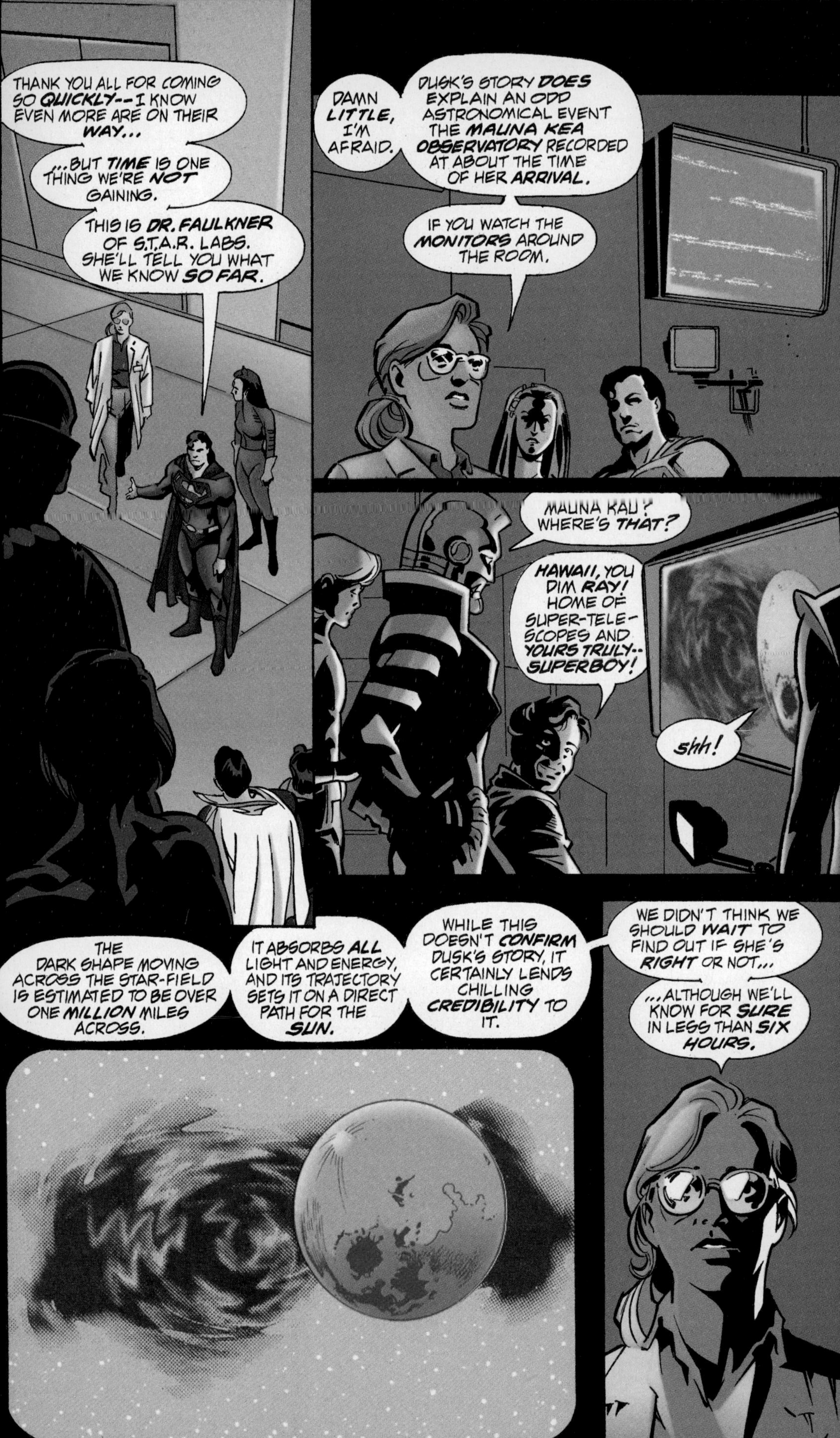

THANK YOU ALL FOR COMING SO QUICKLY--I KNOW EVEN MORE ARE ON THEIR WAY...
...BUT TIME IS ONE THING WE'RE NOT GAINING.
THIS IS DR. FAULKNER OF S.T.A.R. LABS. SHE'LL TELL YOU WHAT WE KNOW SO FAR.
DAMN LITTLE, I'M AFRAID.
DUSK'S STORY DOES EXPLAIN AN ODD ASTRONOMICAL EVENT THE MAUNA KEA OBSERVATORY RECORDED AT ABOUT THE TIME OF HER ARRIVAL.
IF YOU WATCH THE MONITORS AROUND THE ROOM.
MAUNA KAU? WHERE'S THAT?
HAWAII, YOU DIM RAY! HOME OF SUPER-TELE-SCOPES AND YOURS TRULY.. SUPERBOY!
shh!
THE DARK SHAPE MOVING ACROSS THE STAR-FIELD IS ESTIMATED TO BE OVER ONE MILLION MILES ACROSS.
IT ABSORBS ALL LIGHT AND ENERGY, AND ITS TRAJECTORY SETS IT ON A DIRECT PATH FOR THE SUN.
WHILE THIS DOESN'T CONFIRM DUSK'S STORY, IT CERTAINLY LENDS CHILLING CREDIBILITY TO IT.
WE DIDN'T THINK WE SHOULD WAIT TO FIND OUT IF SHE'S RIGHT OR NOT...
...ALTHOUGH WE'LL KNOW FOR SURE IN LESS THAN SIX HOURS.

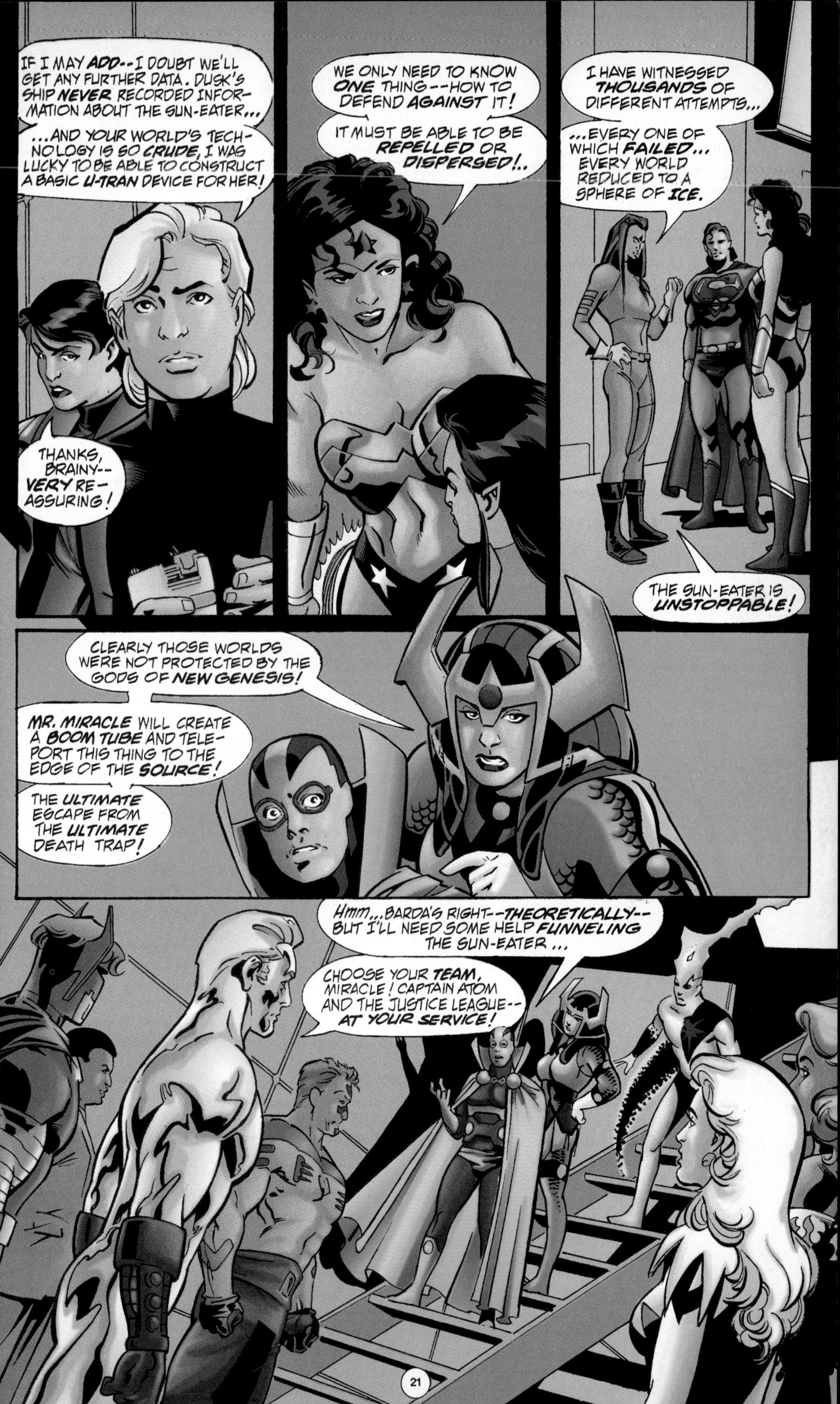
IF I MAY ADD--I DOUBT WE'LL GET ANY FURTHER DATA. DUSK'S SHIP NEVER RECORDED INFORMATION ABOUT THE SUN-EATER...
...AND YOUR WORLD'S TECHNOLOGY IS SO CRUDE, I WAS LUCKY TO BE ABLE TO CONSTRUCT A BASIC U-TRAN DEVICE FOR HER!
THANKS, BRAINY--VERY REASSURING!
WE ONLY NEED TO KNOW ONE THING--HOW TO DEFEND AGAINST IT!
IT MUST BE ABLE TO BE REPELLED OR DISPERSED!..
I HAVE WITNESSED THOUSANDS OF DIFFERENT ATTEMPTS...
...EVERY ONE OF WHICH FAILED... EVERY WORLD REDUCED TO A SPHERE OF ICE.
THE SUN-EATER IS UNSTOPPABLE!
CLEARLY THOSE WORLDS WERE NOT PROTECTED BY THE GODS OF NEW GENESIS!
MR. MIRACLE WILL CREATE A BOOM TUBE AND TELEPORT THIS THING TO THE EDGE OF THE SOURCE!
THE ULTIMATE ESCAPE FROM THE ULTIMATE DEATH TRAP!
Hmm... BARDA'S RIGHT--THEORETICALLY--BUT I'LL NEED SOME HELP FUNNELING THE SUN-EATER...
CHOOSE YOUR TEAM, MIRACLE! CAPTAIN ATOM AND THE JUSTICE LEAGUE--AT YOUR SERVICE!

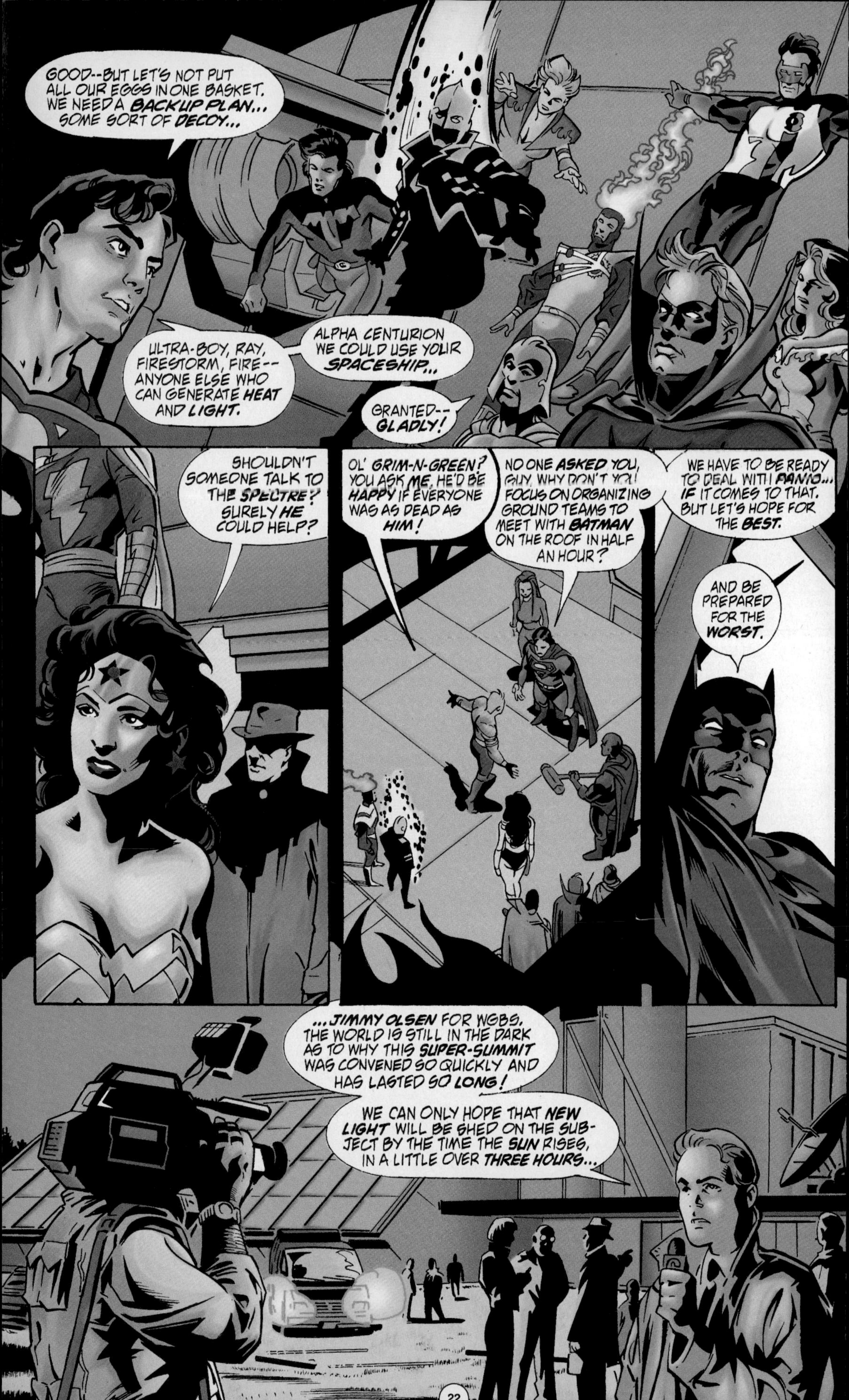
GOOD--BUT LET'S NOT PUT ALL OUR EGGS IN ONE BASKET. WE NEED A BACKUP PLAN... SOME SORT OF DECOY...
ULTRA-BOY, RAY, FIRESTORM, FIRE-- ANYONE ELSE WHO CAN GENERATE HEAT AND LIGHT.
ALPHA CENTURION WE COULD USE YOUR SPACESHIP...
GRANTED-- GLADLY!
SHOULDN'T SOMEONE TALK TO THE SPECTRE? SURELY HE COULD HELP?
OL' GRIM-N-GREEN? YOU ASK ME, HE'D BE HAPPY IF EVERYONE WAS AS DEAD AS HIM!
NO ONE ASKED YOU, GUY. WHY DON'T YOU FOCUS ON ORGANIZING GROUND TEAMS TO MEET WITH BATMAN ON THE ROOF IN HALF AN HOUR?
WE HAVE TO BE READY TO DEAL WITH PANIC... IF IT COMES TO THAT. BUT LET'S HOPE FOR THE BEST.
AND BE PREPARED FOR THE WORST.
...JIMMY OLSEN FOR WGBS. THE WORLD IS STILL IN THE DARK AS TO WHY THIS SUPER-SUMMIT WAS CONVENED SO QUICKLY AND HAS LASTED SO LONG!
WE CAN ONLY HOPE THAT NEW LIGHT WILL BE SHED ON THE SUB-JECT BY THE TIME THE SUN RISES, IN A LITTLE OVER THREE HOURS...

BOOOOOM!

ATOM TO SUPERMAN-- ALPHA COMPANY AT INTERSECTION POINT!

BACKUP TEAM'S IN PLACE, TOO, CAPTAIN! LET'S HOPE THE LAST FEW HOURS OF PREP- ARATION PAY OFF! GOOD LUCK!

REMEMBER, DR. POLARIS-- DO AS YOU'RE TOLD, WHEN YOU'RE TOLD!

I DON'T KNOW WHAT SORT OF DEAL A CON LIKE YOU CUT WITH AMANDA WALLER, BUT--

THERE'S NO DEAL, CAPTAIN. SHE OUT- LINED THE SITUATION; I VOLUNTEERED.

IF WE FAIL, IT DOESN'T REALLY MATTER IF I'M IN PRISON OR NOT... DOES IT?

MOTHER BOX IS READY. LET ME KNOW WHEN YOU SEE--

THERE--!

PING PING PING

23

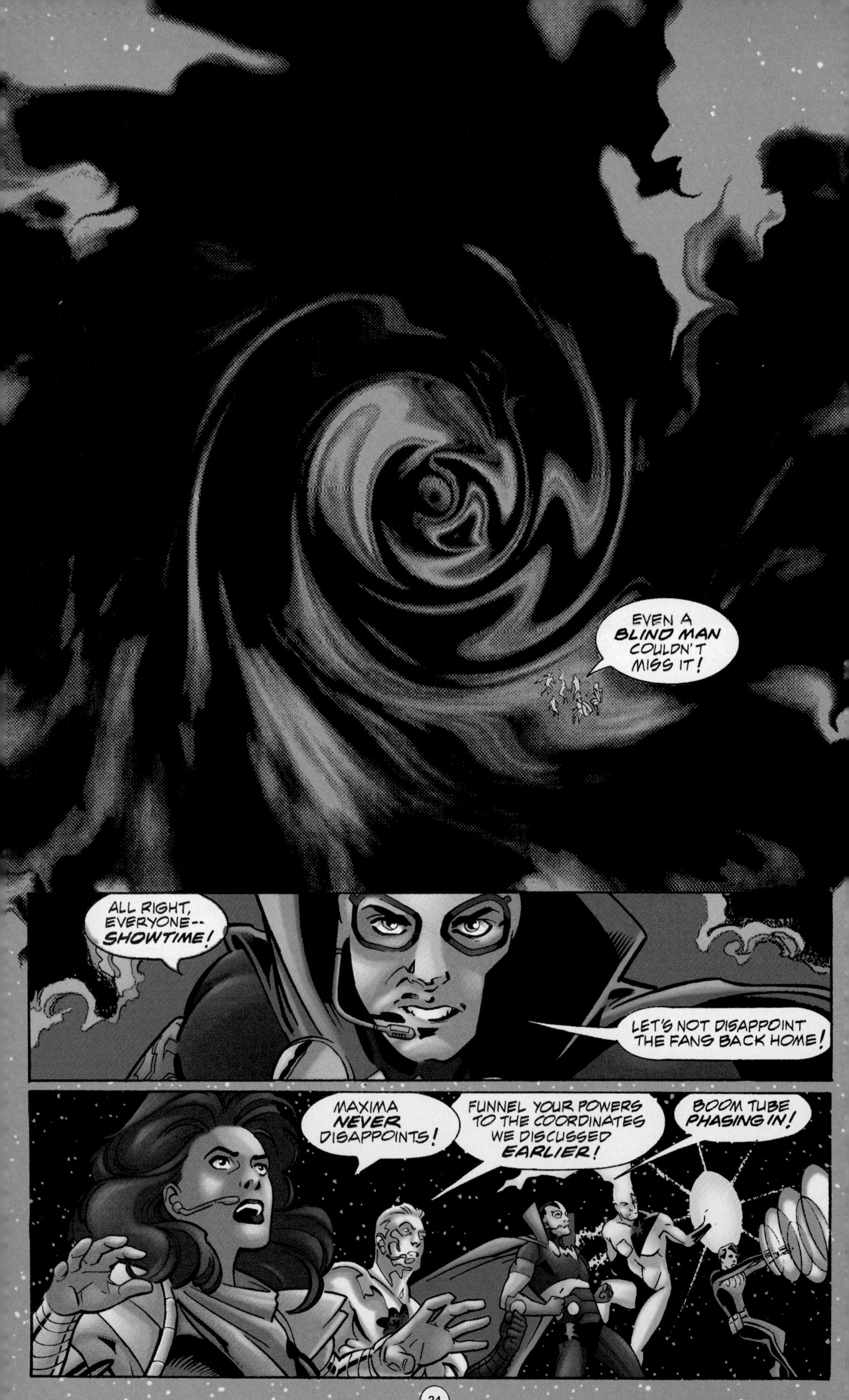

EVEN A BLIND MAN COULDN'T MISS IT!
ALL RIGHT, EVERYONE-- SHOWTIME!
LET'S NOT DISAPPOINT THE FANS BACK HOME!
MAXIMA NEVER DISAPPOINTS!
FUNNEL YOUR POWERS TO THE COORDINATES WE DISCUSSED EARLIER!
BOOM TUBE PHASING IN!

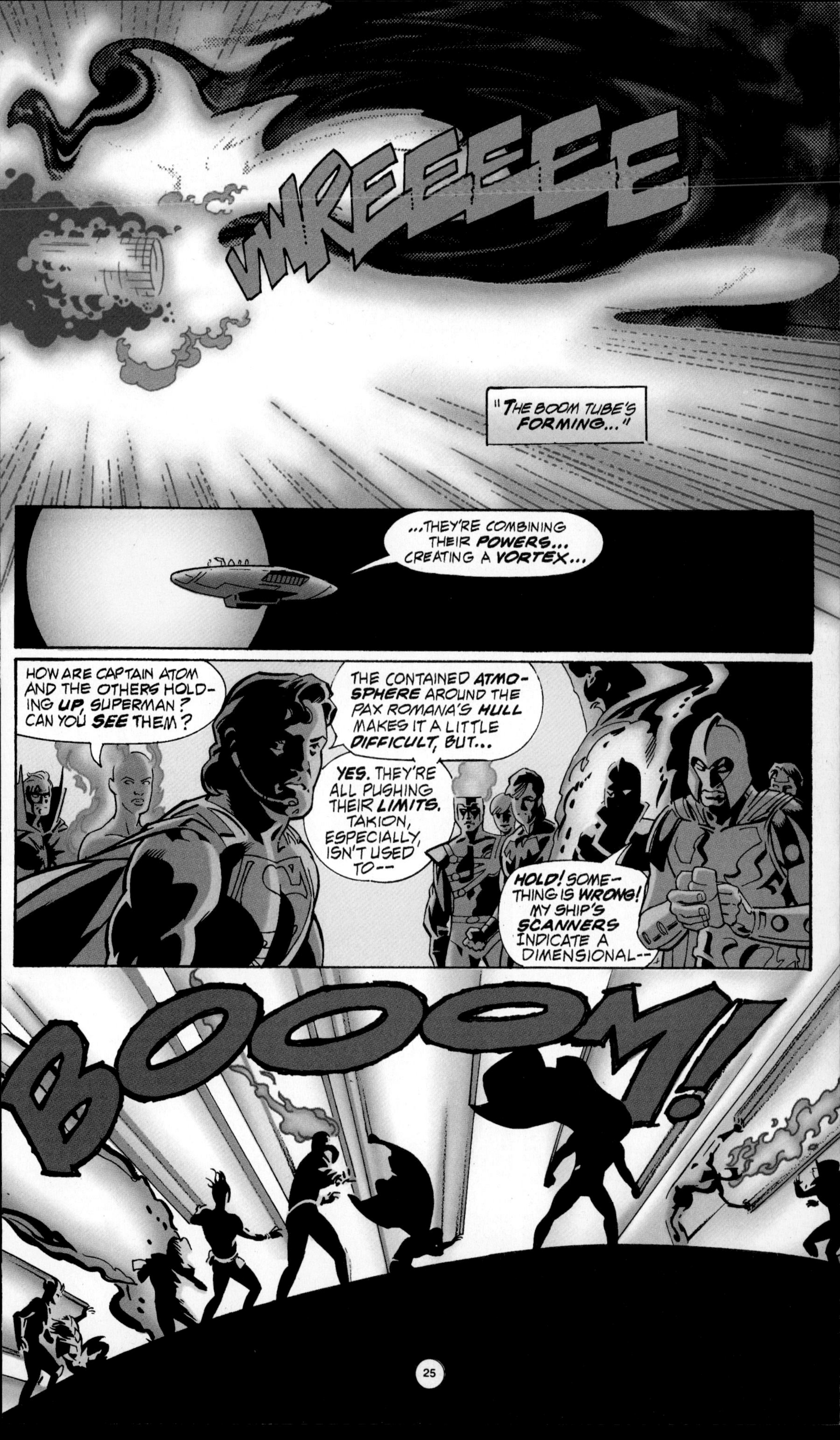

VVHREEEEEE
"THE BOOM TUBE'S FORMING..."
...THEY'RE COMBINING THEIR POWERS... CREATING A VORTEX...
HOW ARE CAPTAIN ATOM AND THE OTHERS HOLDING UP, SUPERMAN? CAN YOU SEE THEM?
THE CONTAINED ATMOSPHERE AROUND THE PAX ROMANA'S HULL MAKES IT A LITTLE DIFFICULT, BUT...
YES. THEY'RE ALL PUSHING THEIR LIMITS. TAKION, ESPECIALLY, ISN'T USED TO--
HOLD! SOMETHING IS WRONG! MY SHIP'S SCANNERS INDICATE A DIMENSIONAL--
BOOOM!

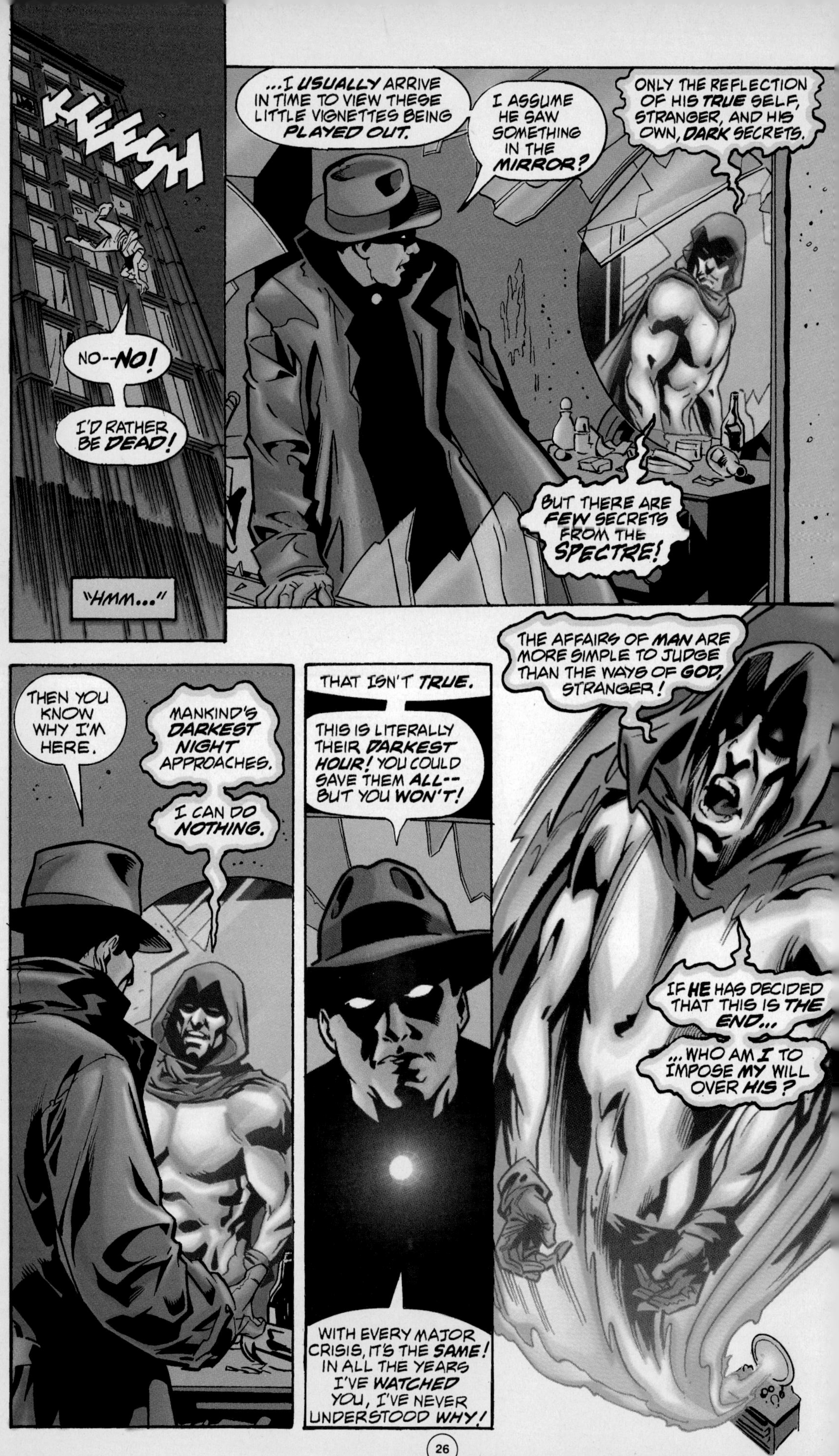
KKEESH
NO--NO!
I'D RATHER BE DEAD!
"HMM..."
...I USUALLY ARRIVE IN TIME TO VIEW THESE LITTLE VIGNETTES BEING PLAYED OUT.
I ASSUME HE SAW SOMETHING IN THE MIRROR?
ONLY THE REFLECTION OF HIS TRUE SELF, STRANGER, AND HIS OWN, DARK SECRETS.
BUT THERE ARE FEW SECRETS FROM THE SPECTRE!
THEN YOU KNOW WHY I'M HERE.
MANKIND'S DARKEST NIGHT APPROACHES.
I CAN DO NOTHING.
THAT ISN'T TRUE.
THIS IS LITERALLY THEIR DARKEST HOUR! YOU COULD SAVE THEM ALL--BUT YOU WON'T!
WITH EVERY MAJOR CRISIS, IT'S THE SAME! IN ALL THE YEARS I'VE WATCHED YOU, I'VE NEVER UNDERSTOOD WHY!
THE AFFAIRS OF MAN ARE MORE SIMPLE TO JUDGE THAN THE WAYS OF GOD, STRANGER!
IF HE HAS DECIDED THAT THIS IS THE END...
...WHO AM I TO IMPOSE MY WILL OVER HIS?

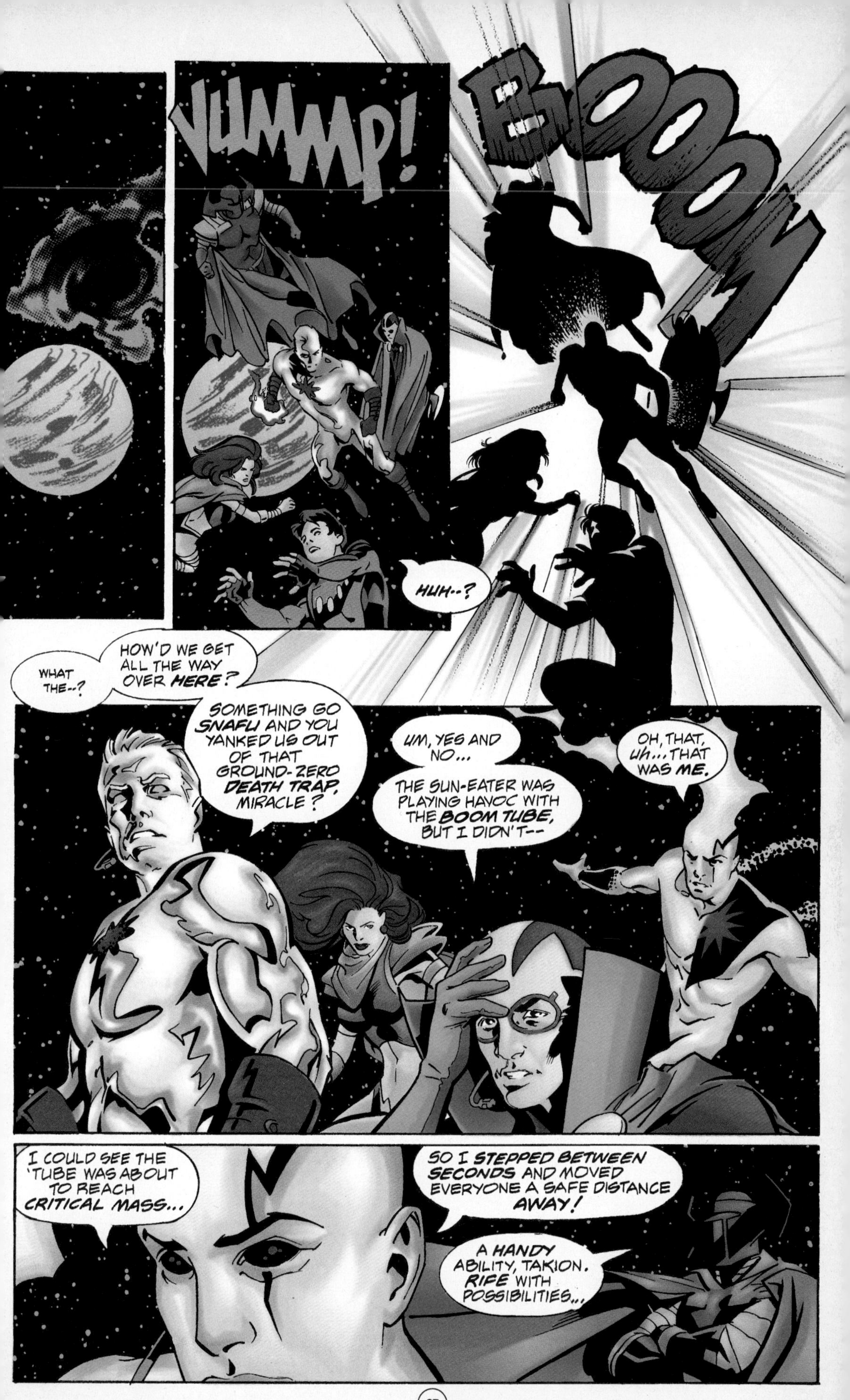
VUMMP!
BOOOOM
HUH..?
WHAT THE--?
HOW'D WE GET ALL THE WAY OVER HERE?
SOMETHING GO SNAFU AND YOU YANKED US OUT OF THAT GROUND-ZERO DEATH TRAP, MIRACLE?
UM, YES AND NO...
THE SUN-EATER WAS PLAYING HAVOC WITH THE BOOM TUBE, BUT I DIDN'T--
OH, THAT, uh... THAT WAS ME.
I COULD SEE THE 'TUBE WAS ABOUT TO REACH CRITICAL MASS...
SO I STEPPED BETWEEN SECONDS AND MOVED EVERYONE A SAFE DISTANCE AWAY!
A HANDY ABILITY, TAKION. RIFE WITH POSSIBILITIES...

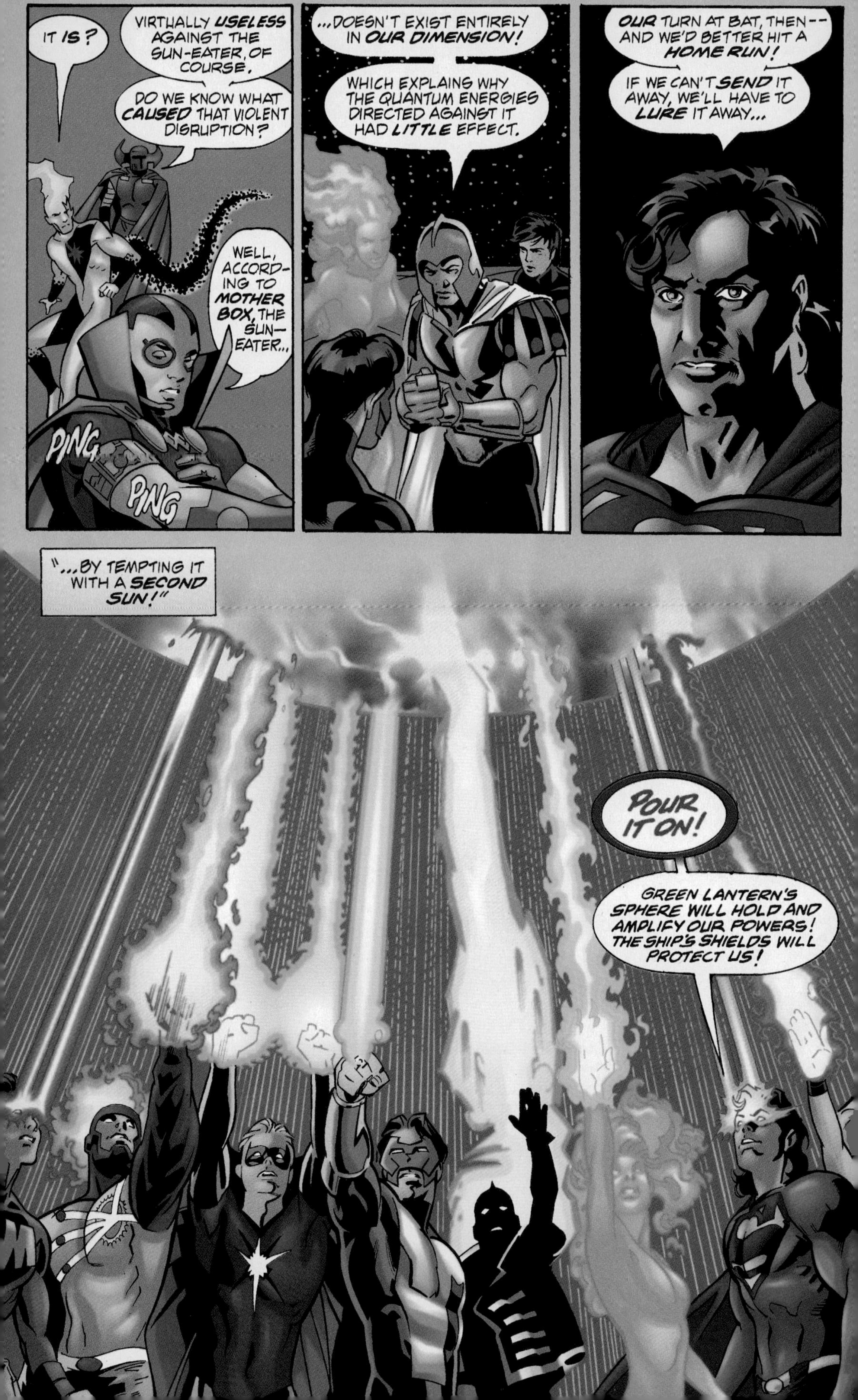
IT IS?
VIRTUALLY USELESS AGAINST THE SUN-EATER, OF COURSE.
DO WE KNOW WHAT CAUSED THAT VIOLENT DISRUPTION?
WELL, ACCORDING TO MOTHER BOX, THE SUN-EATER...
PING
PING
...DOESN'T EXIST ENTIRELY IN OUR DIMENSION!
WHICH EXPLAINS WHY THE QUANTUM ENERGIES DIRECTED AGAINST IT HAD LITTLE EFFECT.
OUR TURN AT BAT, THEN-- AND WE'D BETTER HIT A HOME RUN!
IF WE CAN'T SEND IT AWAY, WE'LL HAVE TO LURE IT AWAY...
"...BY TEMPTING IT WITH A SECOND SUN!"
POUR IT ON!
GREEN LANTERN'S SPHERE WILL HOLD AND AMPLIFY OUR POWERS! THE SHIP'S SHIELDS WILL PROTECT US!

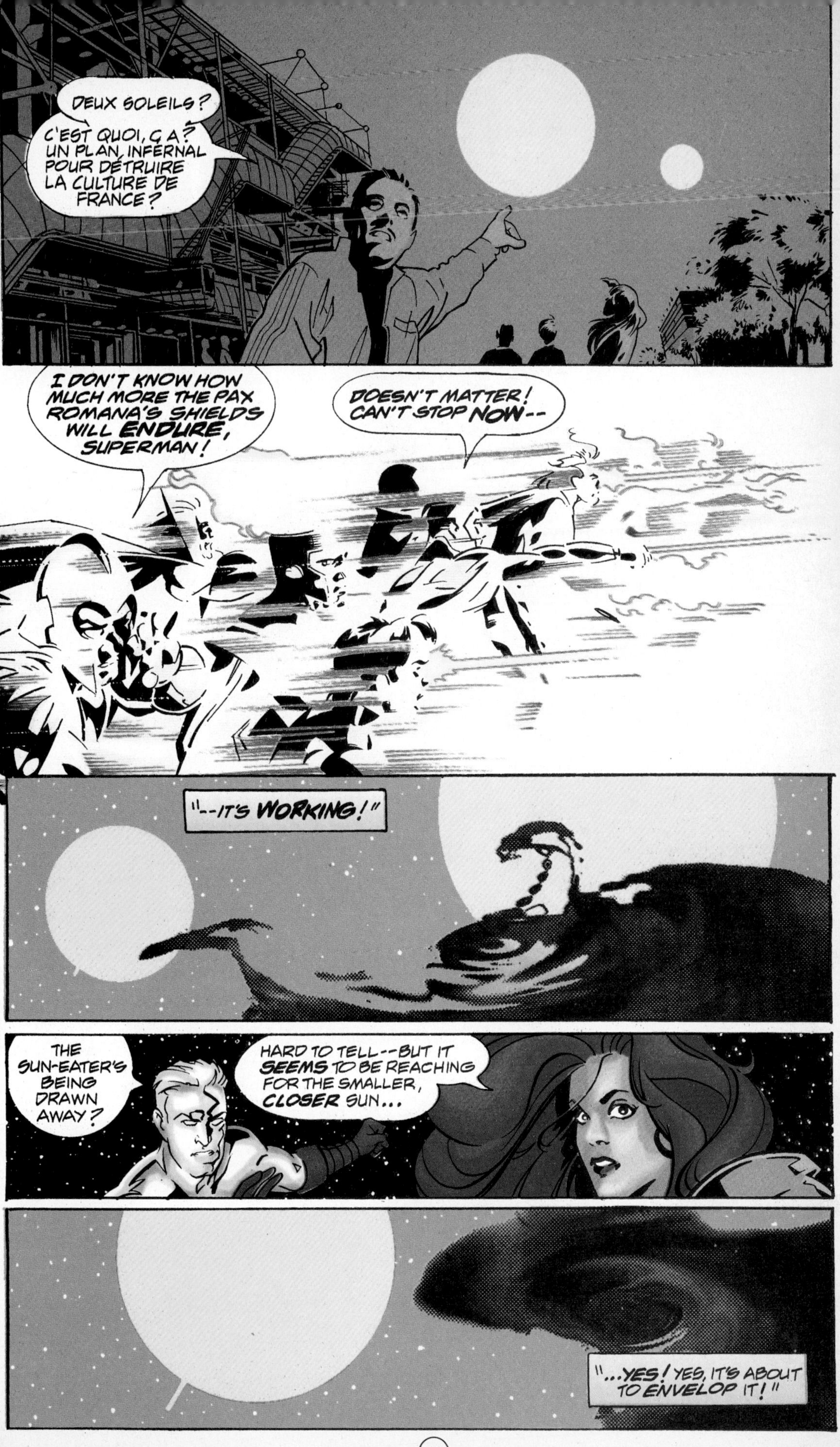
DEUX SOLEILS? C'EST QUOI, ÇA? UN PLAN INFERNAL POUR DÉTRUIRE LA CULTURE DE FRANCE?
I DON'T KNOW HOW MUCH MORE THE PAX ROMANA'S SHIELDS WILL ENDURE, SUPERMAN!
DOESN'T MATTER! CAN'T STOP NOW--
"--IT'S WORKING!"
THE SUN-EATER'S BEING DRAWN AWAY?
HARD TO TELL--BUT IT SEEMS TO BE REACHING FOR THE SMALLER, CLOSER SUN...
"...YES! YES, IT'S ABOUT TO ENVELOP IT!"

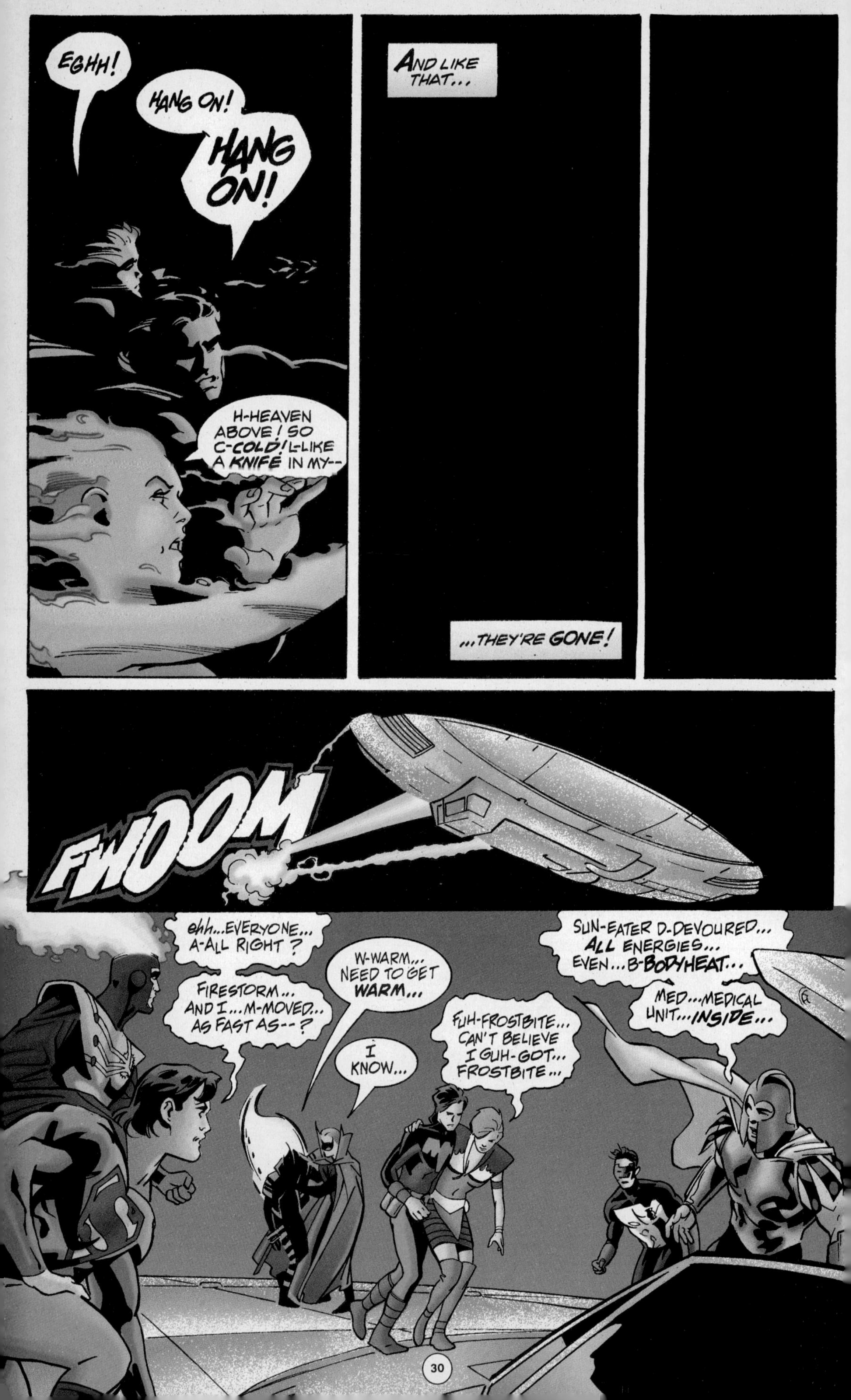
EGHH!
HANG ON!
HANG ON!
H-HEAVEN ABOVE! SO C-COLD! L-LIKE A KNIFE IN MY--
AND LIKE THAT...
...THEY'RE GONE!
FWOOM
ehh...EVERYONE... A-ALL RIGHT?
FIRESTORM... AND I...M-MOVED... AS FAST AS--?
W-WARM... NEED TO GET WARM...
I KNOW...
FUH-FROSTBITE... CAN'T BELIEVE I GUH-GOT... FROSTBITE...
SUN-EATER D-DEVOURED... ALL ENERGIES... EVEN...B-BODYHEAT...
MED...MEDICAL UNIT...INSIDE...

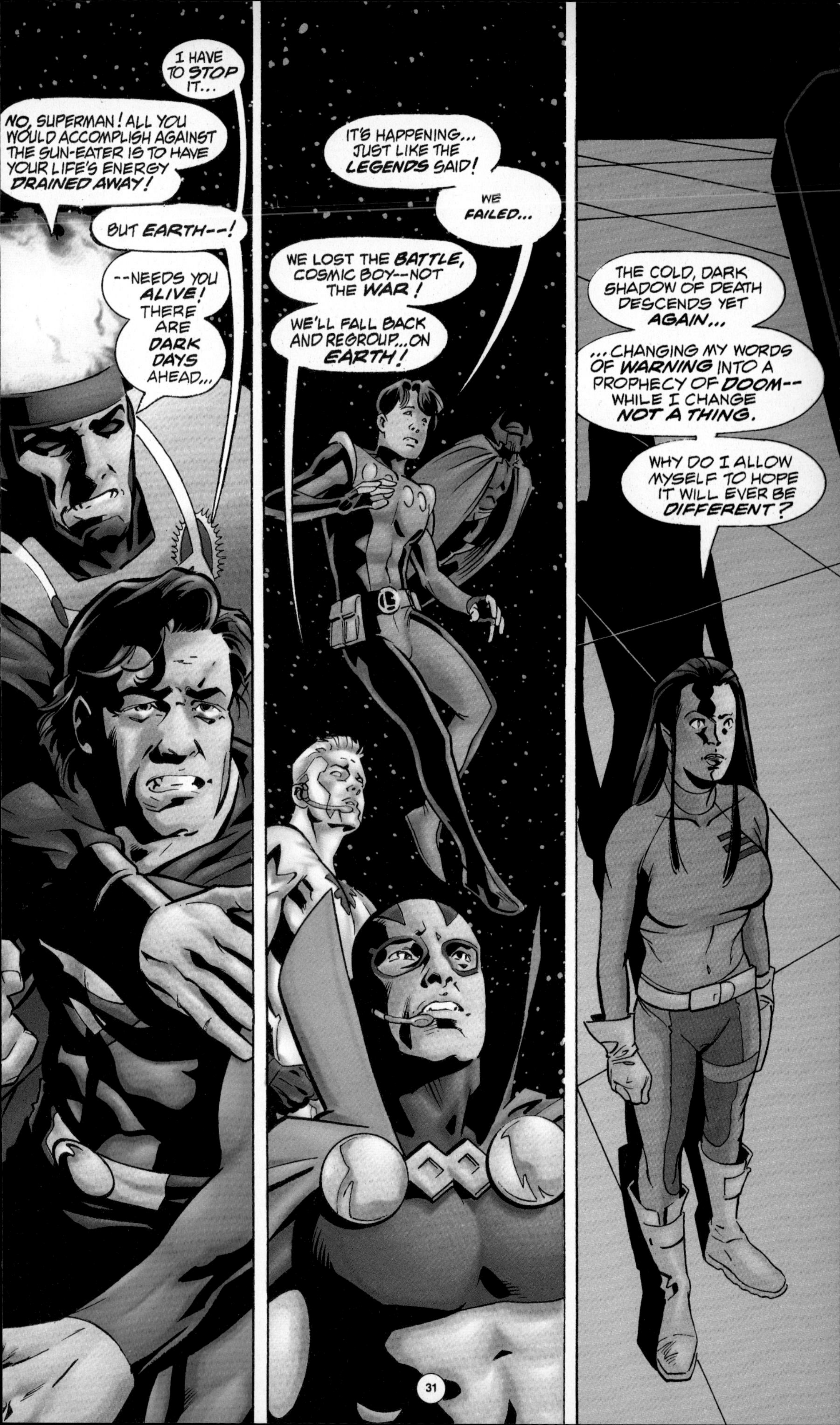
I HAVE TO STOP IT...
NO, SUPERMAN! ALL YOU WOULD ACCOMPLISH AGAINST THE SUN-EATER IS TO HAVE YOUR LIFE'S ENERGY DRAINED AWAY!
BUT EARTH--!
--NEEDS YOU ALIVE! THERE ARE DARK DAYS AHEAD...
IT'S HAPPENING... JUST LIKE THE LEGENDS SAID!
WE FAILED...
WE LOST THE BATTLE, COSMIC BOY--NOT THE WAR!
WE'LL FALL BACK AND REGROUP...ON EARTH!
THE COLD, DARK SHADOW OF DEATH DESCENDS YET AGAIN...
...CHANGING MY WORDS OF WARNING INTO A PROPHECY OF DOOM--WHILE I CHANGE NOT A THING.
WHY DO I ALLOW MYSELF TO HOPE IT WILL EVER BE DIFFERENT?

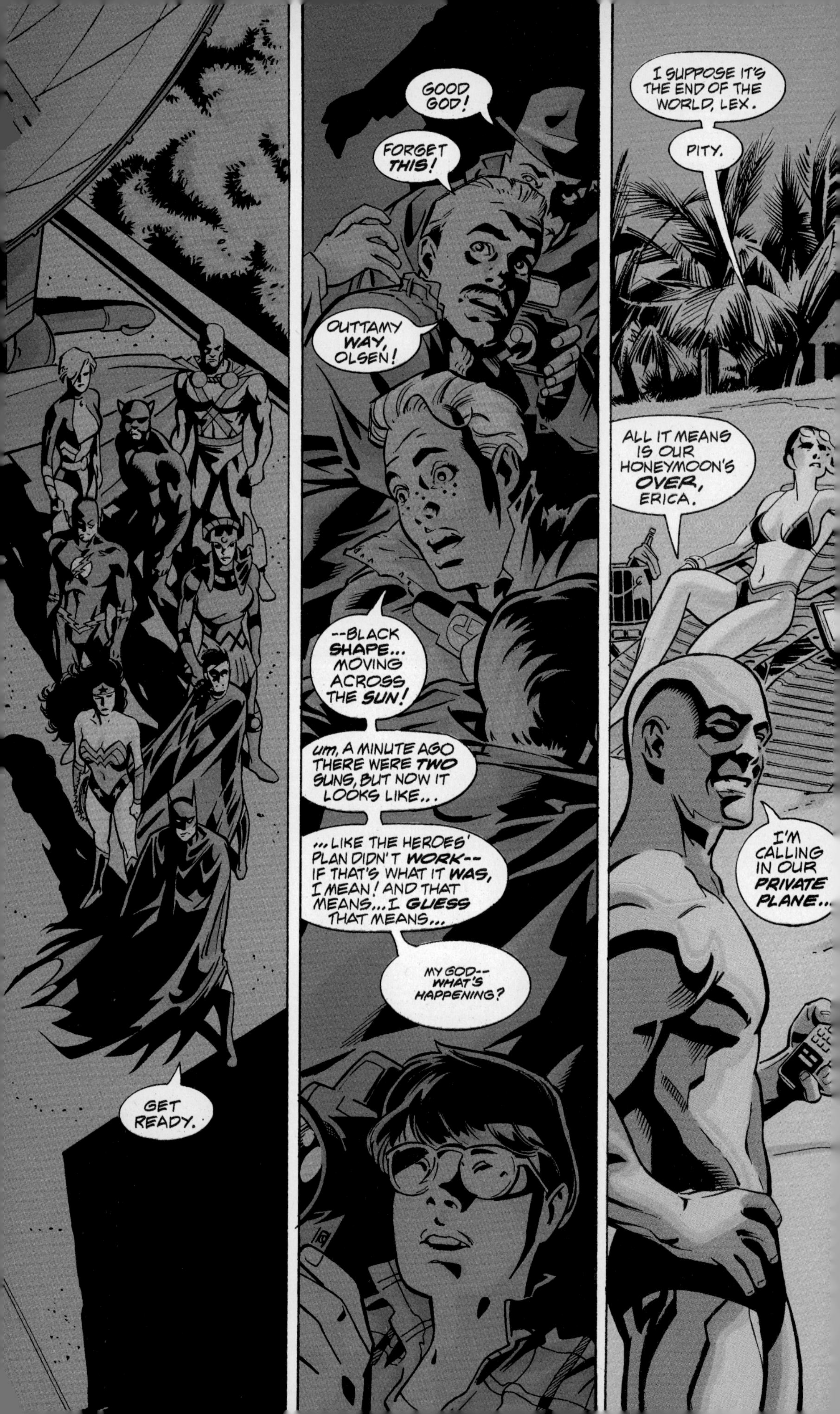
GET READY.
GOOD GOD!
FORGET THIS!
OUTTAMY WAY, OLSEN!
--BLACK SHAPE... MOVING ACROSS THE SUN!
um, A MINUTE AGO THERE WERE TWO SUNS, BUT NOW IT LOOKS LIKE...
...LIKE THE HEROES' PLAN DIDN'T WORK-- IF THAT'S WHAT IT WAS, I MEAN! AND THAT MEANS... I GUESS THAT MEANS...
MY GOD-- WHAT'S HAPPENING?
I SUPPOSE IT'S THE END OF THE WORLD, LEX.
PITY.
ALL IT MEANS IS OUR HONEYMOON'S OVER, ERICA.
I'M CALLING IN OUR PRIVATE PLANE...

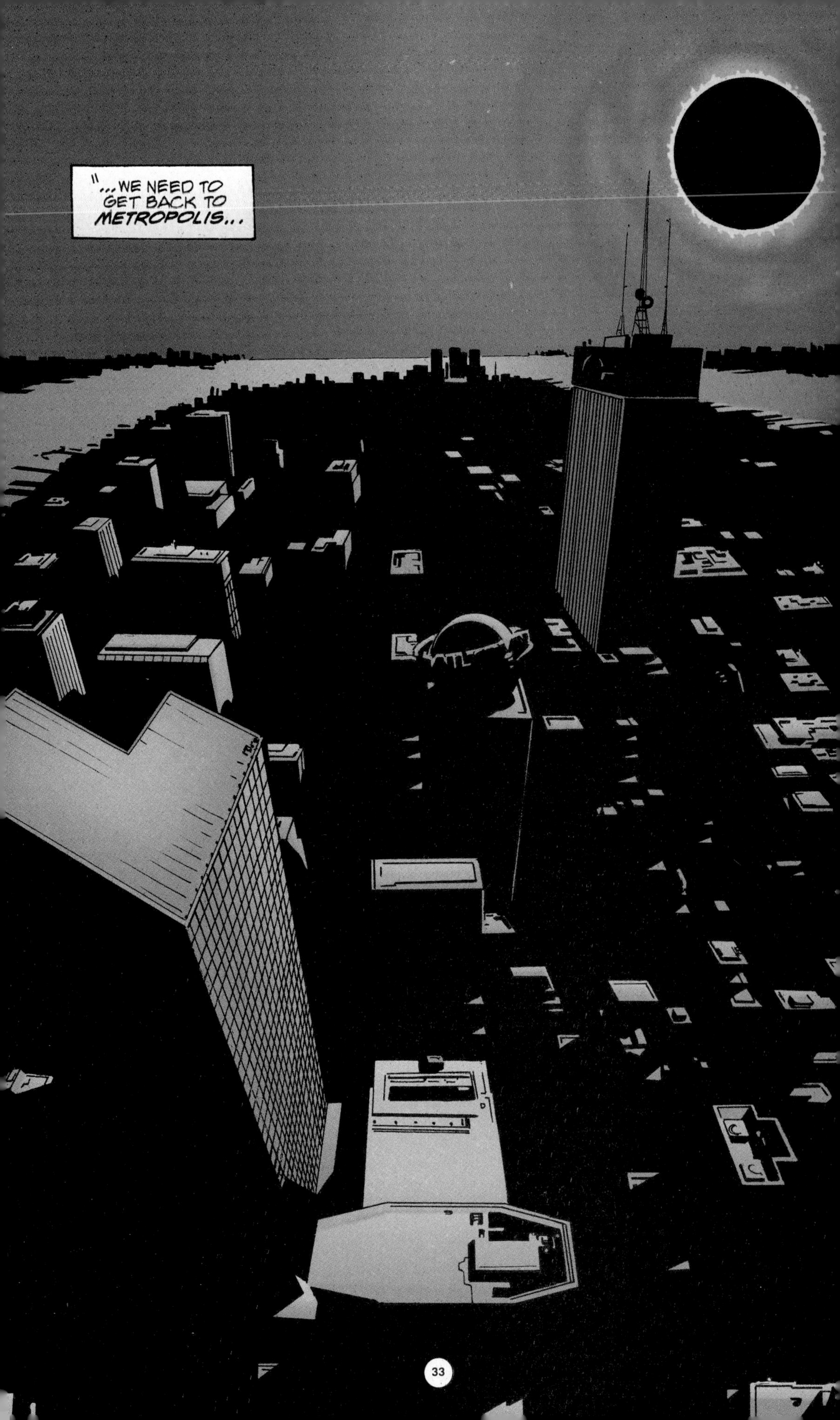
"...WE NEED TO GET BACK TO METROPOLIS...

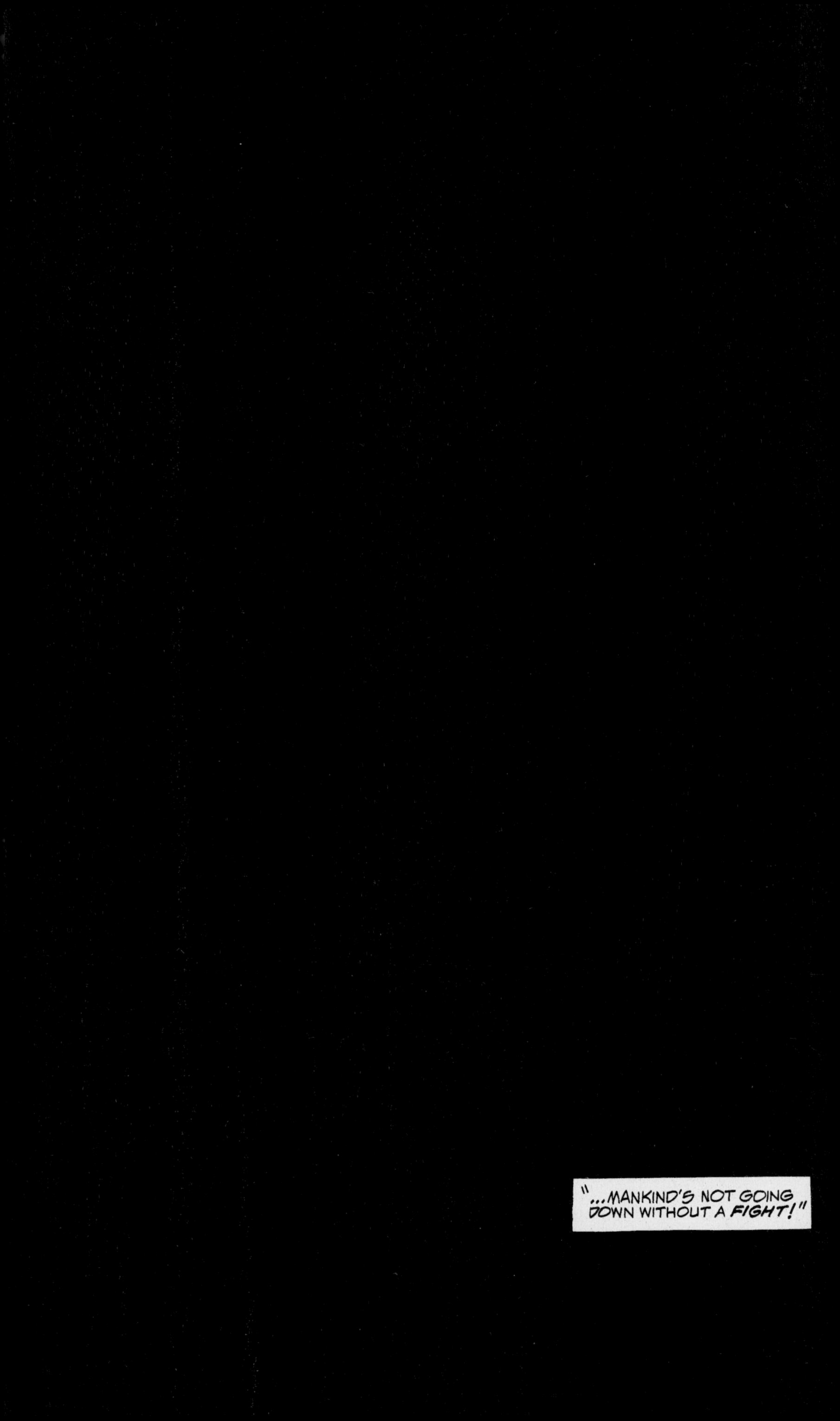
"...MANKIND'S NOT GOING DOWN WITHOUT A *FIGHT!*"

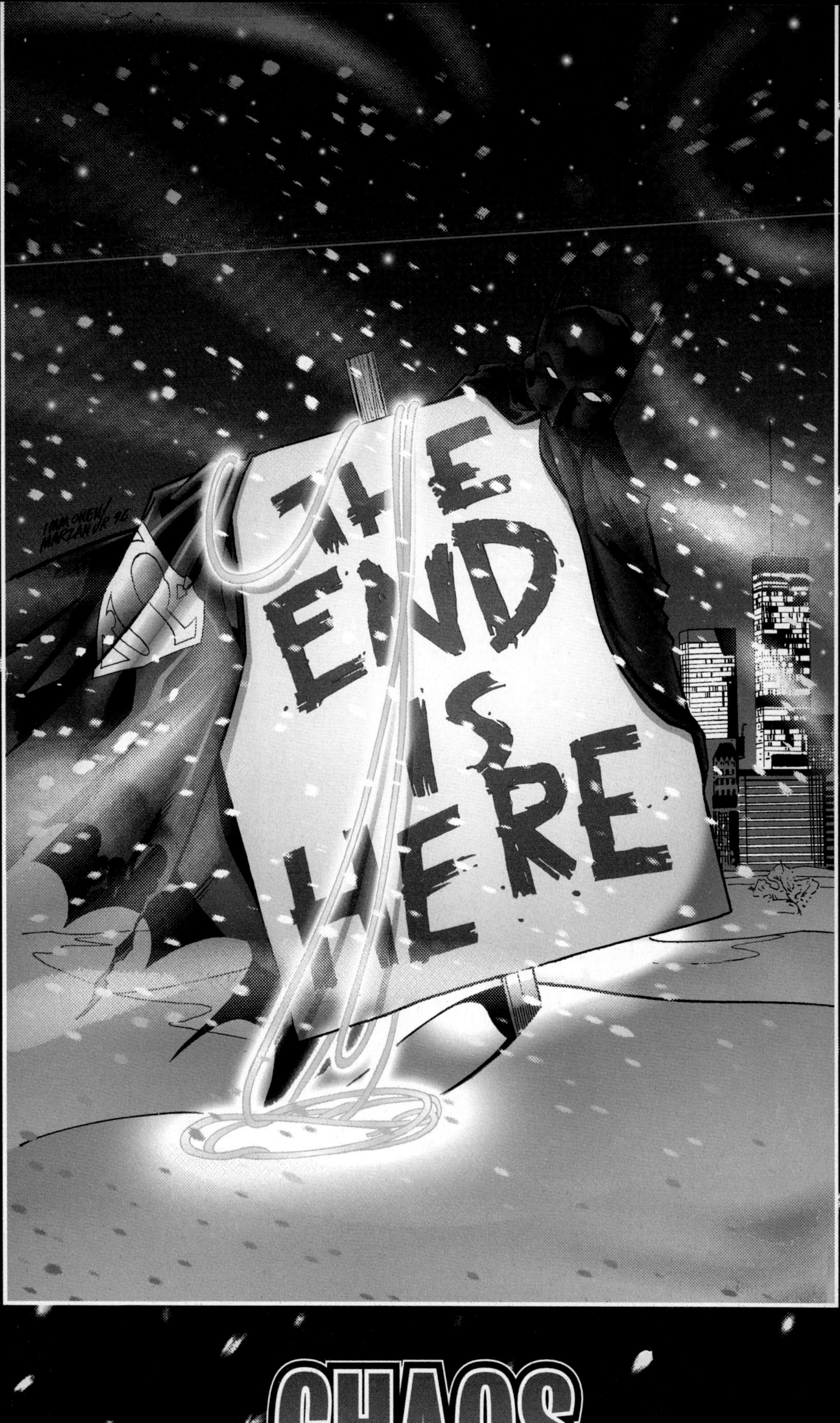
THE END IS HERE

CHAOS

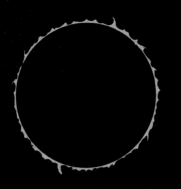

"*THIS IMAGE IS THE LAST GLIMPSE WE HAD OF THE SUN AS IT WAS ENGULFED BY THE ENERGY-DRAINING FORCE OF NATURE CALLED THE 'SUN-EATER.'*

"*IT HAS NOW BEEN OVER TWENTY-SEVEN HOURS SINCE ANY LIGHT OR HEAT REACHED THE EARTH.*

"*SOURCES INFORMED THIS STATION THAT SCIENTISTS SUSPECTED NOTHING UNTIL THE ARRIVAL OF THE MYSTERIOUS ALIEN KNOWN AS DUSK.*

"*CRASHING HER SHIP INTO THE DOCKS ALONG METROPOLIS'S WEST RIVER, SHE WARNED SUPERMAN...*

"*...AND THE YOUNG LEGION OF SUPER-HEROES ABOUT THE SUN-EATER'S IMMINENT ARRIVAL.*

"*WE UNDERSTAND TWO HEROIC ATTEMPTS WERE MADE TO AVERT THE DISASTER.*

"*BOTH WERE... UNSUCCESSFUL.*

"*BUT THERE'S STILL A LIGHT OF HOPE IN MANKIND'S DARKEST NIGHT...*"

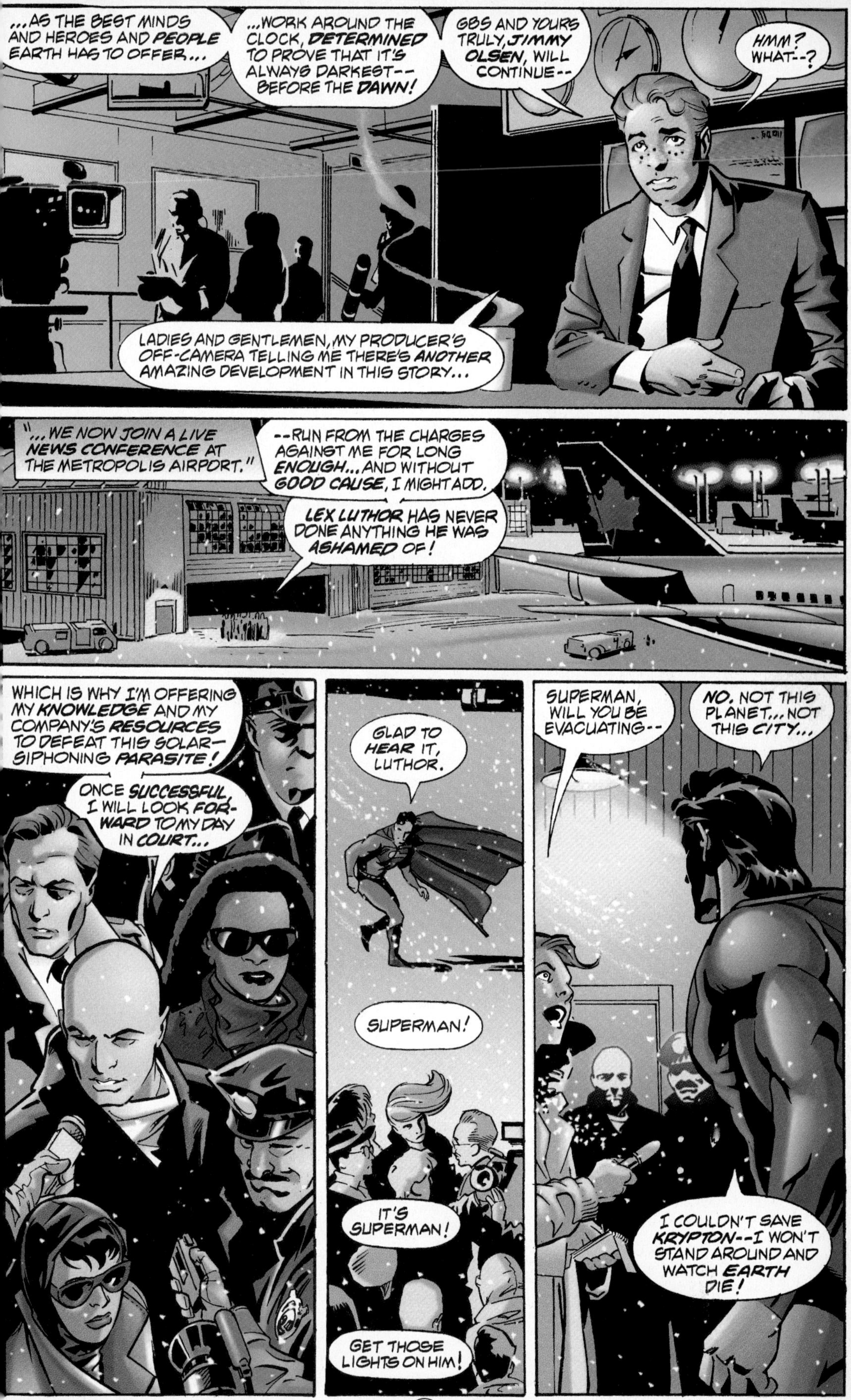
...AS THE BEST MINDS AND HEROES AND PEOPLE EARTH HAS TO OFFER...
...WORK AROUND THE CLOCK, DETERMINED TO PROVE THAT IT'S ALWAYS DARKEST-- BEFORE THE DAWN!
GBS AND YOURS TRULY, JIMMY OLSEN, WILL CONTINUE--
HMM? WHAT--?
LADIES AND GENTLEMEN, MY PRODUCER'S OFF-CAMERA TELLING ME THERE'S ANOTHER AMAZING DEVELOPMENT IN THIS STORY...
"...WE NOW JOIN A LIVE NEWS CONFERENCE AT THE METROPOLIS AIRPORT."
--RUN FROM THE CHARGES AGAINST ME FOR LONG ENOUGH... AND WITHOUT GOOD CAUSE, I MIGHT ADD.
LEX LUTHOR HAS NEVER DONE ANYTHING HE WAS ASHAMED OF!
WHICH IS WHY I'M OFFERING MY KNOWLEDGE AND MY COMPANY'S RESOURCES TO DEFEAT THIS SOLAR-SIPHONING PARASITE!
ONCE SUCCESSFUL, I WILL LOOK FORWARD TO MY DAY IN COURT...
GLAD TO HEAR IT, LUTHOR.
SUPERMAN!
IT'S SUPERMAN!
GET THOSE LIGHTS ON HIM!
SUPERMAN, WILL YOU BE EVACUATING--
NO. NOT THIS PLANET... NOT THIS CITY...
I COULDN'T SAVE KRYPTON--I WON'T STAND AROUND AND WATCH EARTH DIE!

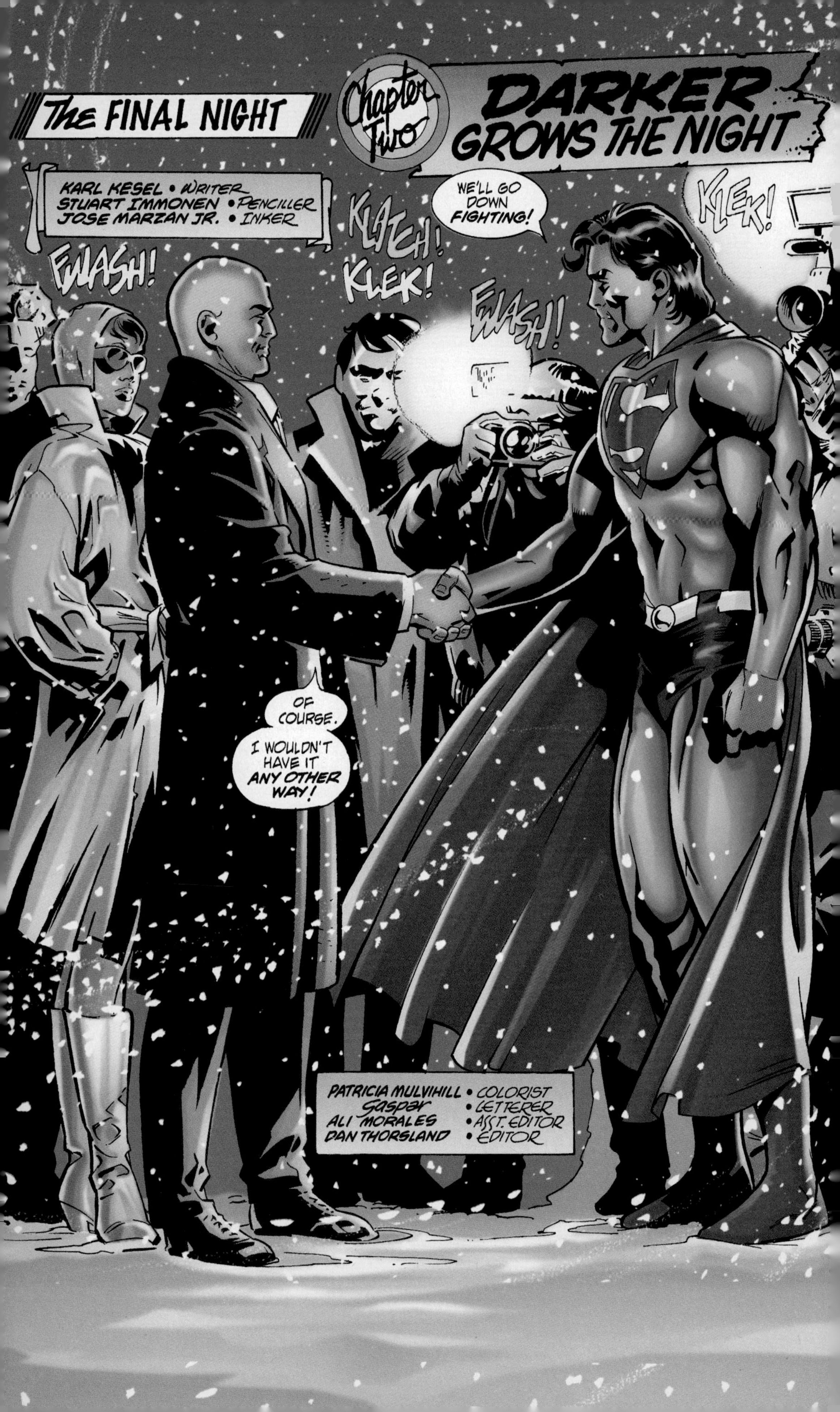
THE FINAL NIGHT
Chapter Two
DARKER GROWS THE NIGHT
KARL KESEL • WRITER
STUART IMMONEN • PENCILLER
JOSE MARZAN JR. • INKER
FWASH!
KLATCH!
KLEK!
WE'LL GO DOWN FIGHTING!
KLEK!
FWASH!
OF COURSE.
I WOULDN'T HAVE IT ANY OTHER WAY!
PATRICIA MULVIHILL • COLORIST
Gaspar • LETTERER
ALI MORALES • ASST. EDITOR
DAN THORSLAND • EDITOR

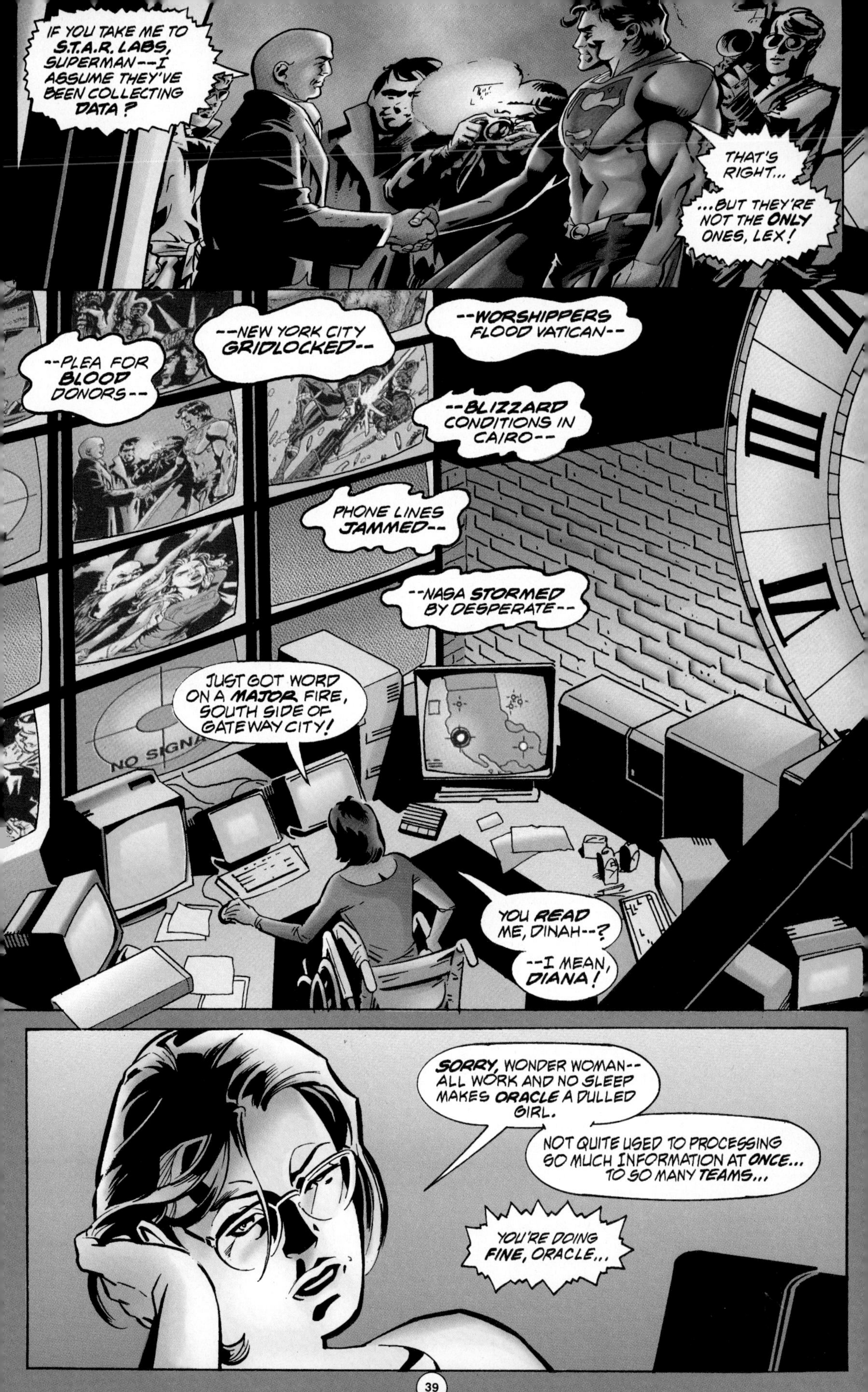
IF YOU TAKE ME TO S.T.A.R. LABS, SUPERMAN--I ASSUME THEY'VE BEEN COLLECTING DATA?
THAT'S RIGHT...
...BUT THEY'RE NOT THE ONLY ONES, LEX!
--PLEA FOR BLOOD DONORS--
--NEW YORK CITY GRIDLOCKED--
--WORSHIPPERS FLOOD VATICAN--
--BLIZZARD CONDITIONS IN CAIRO--
PHONE LINES JAMMED--
--NASA STORMED BY DESPERATE--
JUST GOT WORD ON A MAJOR FIRE, SOUTH SIDE OF GATEWAY CITY!
NO SIGNA
YOU READ ME, DINAH--?
--I MEAN, DIANA!
SORRY, WONDER WOMAN--ALL WORK AND NO SLEEP MAKES ORACLE A DULLED GIRL.
NOT QUITE USED TO PROCESSING SO MUCH INFORMATION AT ONCE... TO SO MANY TEAMS...
YOU'RE DOING FINE, ORACLE...

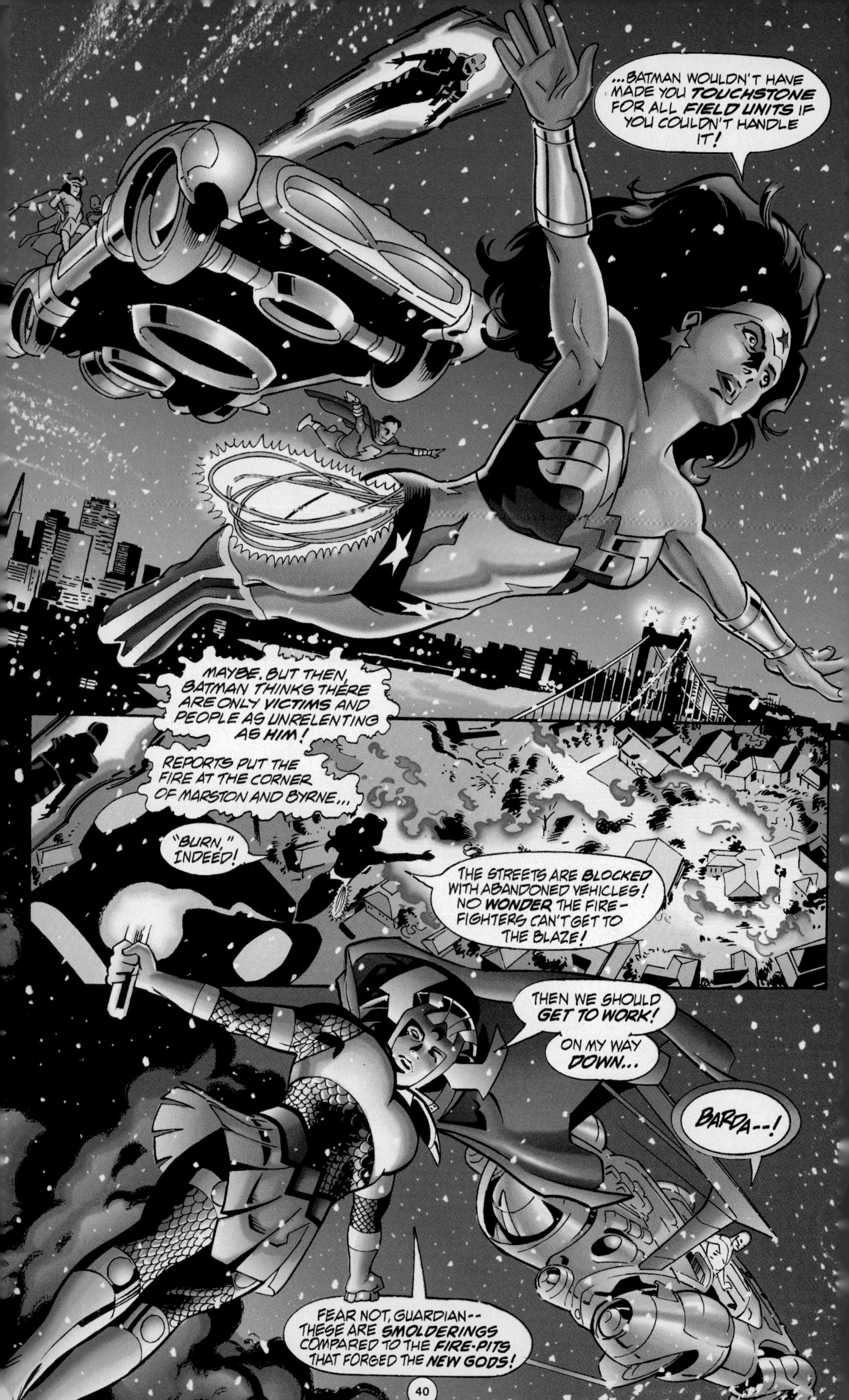
...BATMAN WOULDN'T HAVE MADE YOU TOUCHSTONE FOR ALL FIELD UNITS IF YOU COULDN'T HANDLE IT!
MAYBE. BUT THEN, BATMAN THINKS THERE ARE ONLY VICTIMS AND PEOPLE AS UNRELENTING AS HIM!
REPORTS PUT THE FIRE AT THE CORNER OF MARSTON AND BYRNE...
"BURN," INDEED!
THE STREETS ARE BLOCKED WITH ABANDONED VEHICLES! NO WONDER THE FIRE-FIGHTERS CAN'T GET TO THE BLAZE!
THEN WE SHOULD GET TO WORK!
ON MY WAY DOWN...
BARDA--!
FEAR NOT, GUARDIAN-- THESE ARE SMOLDERINGS COMPARED TO THE FIRE-PITS THAT FORGED THE NEW GODS!

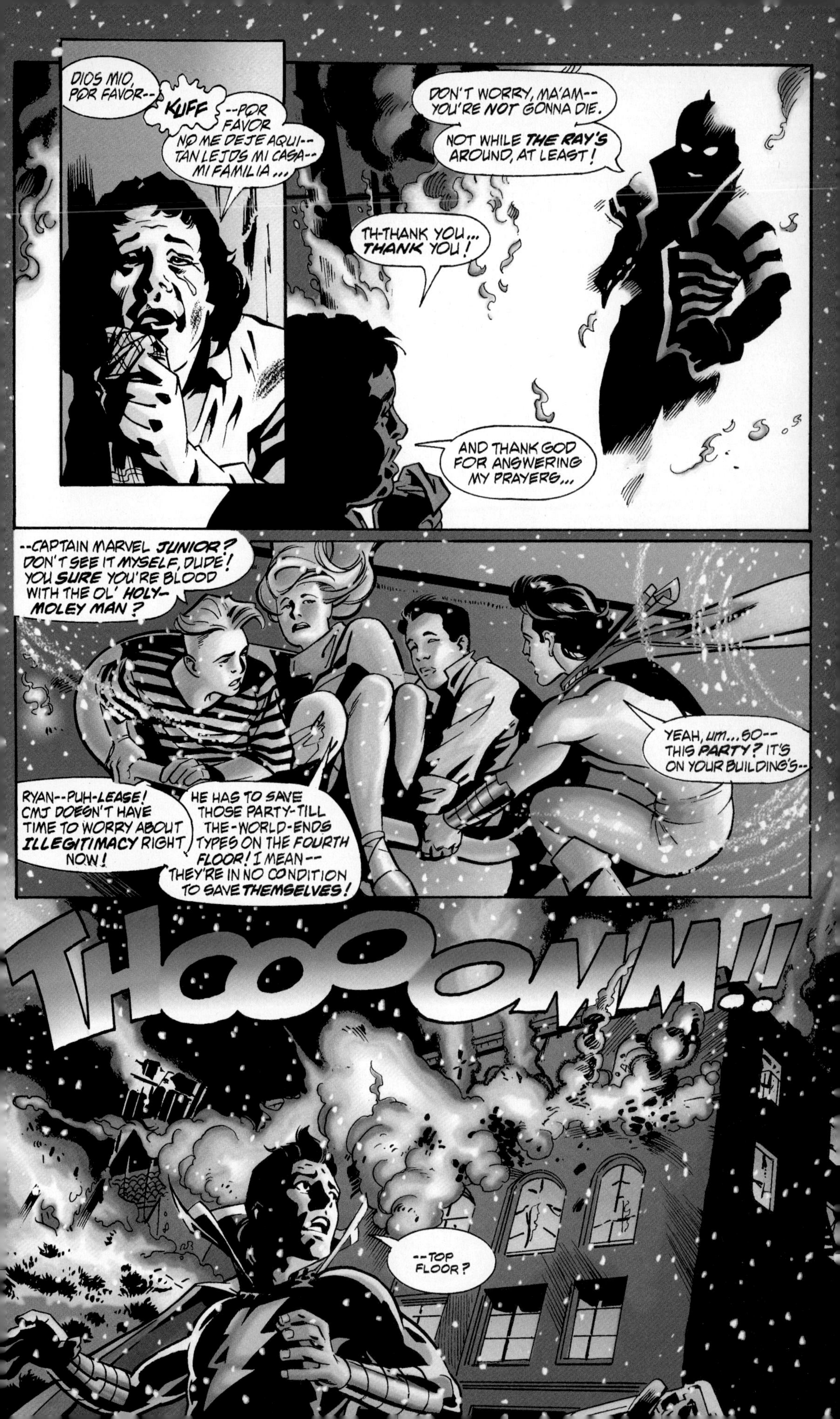
DIOS MIO, POR FAVOR--
KUFF
--POR FAVOR NO ME DEJE AQUI-- TAN LEJOS MI CASA-- MI FAMILIA...
DON'T WORRY, MA'AM-- YOU'RE NOT GONNA DIE.
NOT WHILE THE RAY'S AROUND, AT LEAST!
TH-THANK YOU... THANK YOU!
AND THANK GOD FOR ANSWERING MY PRAYERS...
--CAPTAIN MARVEL JUNIOR? DON'T SEE IT MYSELF, DUDE! YOU SURE YOU'RE BLOOD WITH THE OL' HOLY-MOLEY MAN?
YEAH, UM... SO-- THIS PARTY? IT'S ON YOUR BUILDING'S--
RYAN--PUH-LEASE! CMJ DOESN'T HAVE TIME TO WORRY ABOUT ILLEGITIMACY RIGHT NOW!
HE HAS TO SAVE THOSE PARTY-TILL-THE-WORLD-ENDS TYPES ON THE FOURTH FLOOR! I MEAN-- THEY'RE IN NO CONDITION TO SAVE THEMSELVES!
THOOOMM!!
--TOP FLOOR?

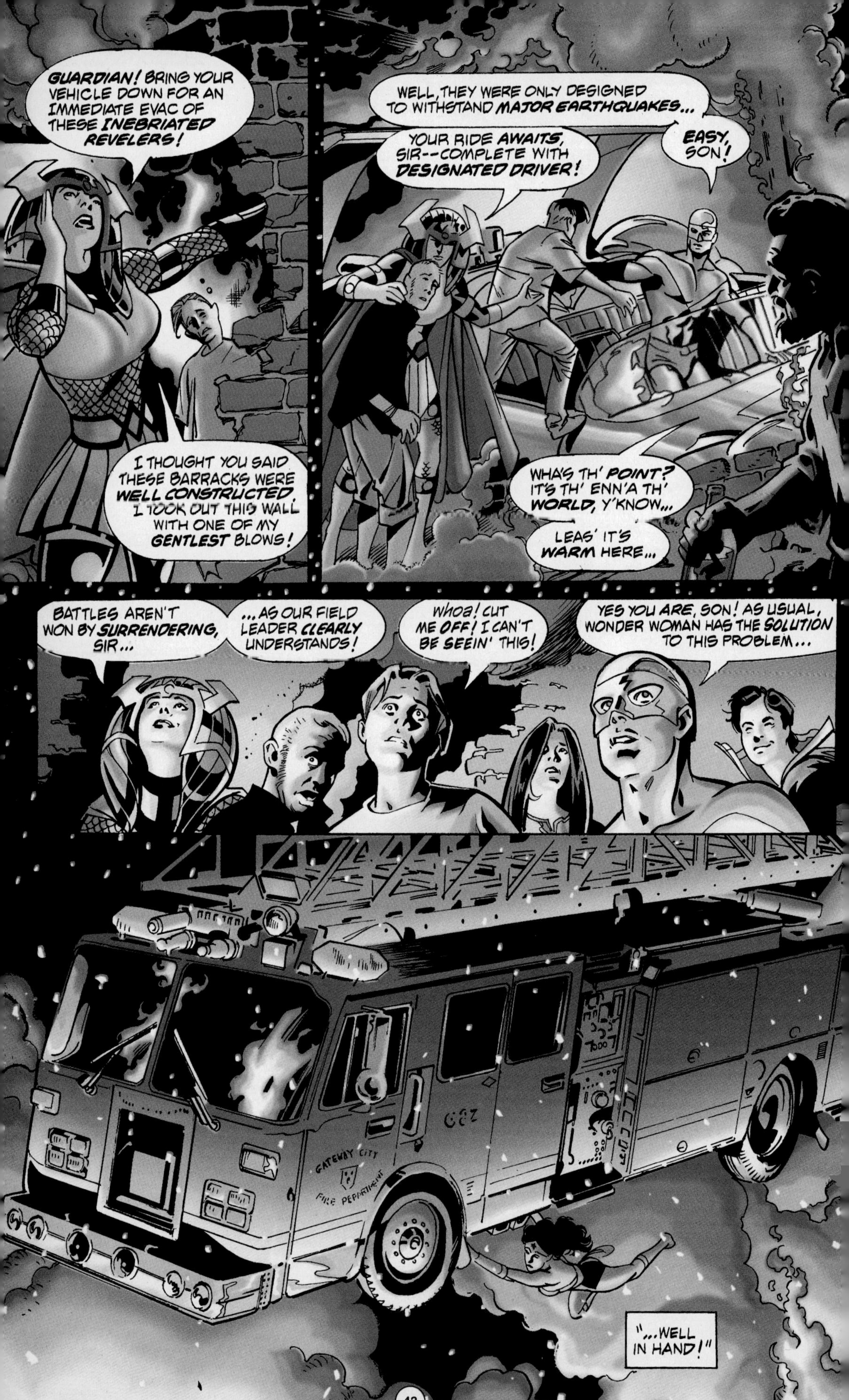
GUARDIAN! BRING YOUR VEHICLE DOWN FOR AN IMMEDIATE EVAC OF THESE INEBRIATED REVELERS!
I THOUGHT YOU SAID THESE BARRACKS WERE WELL CONSTRUCTED. I TOOK OUT THIS WALL WITH ONE OF MY GENTLEST BLOWS!
WELL, THEY WERE ONLY DESIGNED TO WITHSTAND MAJOR EARTHQUAKES...
YOUR RIDE AWAITS, SIR--COMPLETE WITH DESIGNATED DRIVER!
EASY, SON!
WHA'S TH' POINT? IT'S TH' ENN'A TH' WORLD, Y'KNOW...
LEAS' IT'S WARM HERE...
BATTLES AREN'T WON BY SURRENDERING, SIR...
...AS OUR FIELD LEADER CLEARLY UNDERSTANDS!
WHOA! CUT ME OFF! I CAN'T BE SEEIN' THIS!
YES YOU ARE, SON! AS USUAL, WONDER WOMAN HAS THE SOLUTION TO THIS PROBLEM...
GATEWAY CITY FIRE DEPARTMENT
"...WELL IN HAND!"

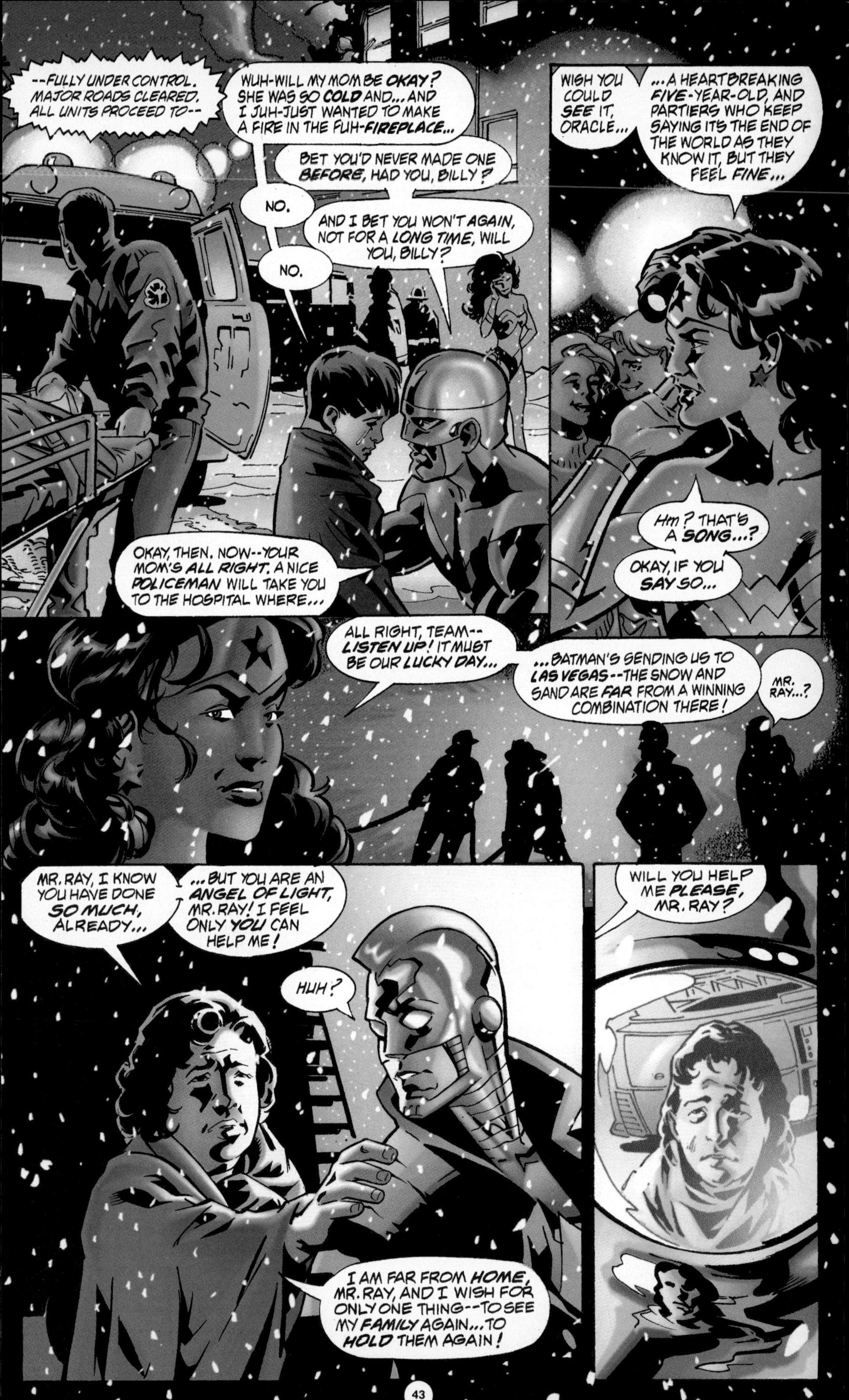
--FULLY UNDER CONTROL. MAJOR ROADS CLEARED. ALL UNITS PROCEED TO--
WUH-WILL MY MOM BE OKAY? SHE WAS SO COLD AND... AND I JUH-JUST WANTED TO MAKE A FIRE IN THE FUH-FIREPLACE...
BET YOU'D NEVER MADE ONE BEFORE, HAD YOU, BILLY?
NO.
AND I BET YOU WON'T AGAIN, NOT FOR A LONG TIME, WILL YOU, BILLY?
NO.
OKAY, THEN. NOW--YOUR MOM'S ALL RIGHT. A NICE POLICEMAN WILL TAKE YOU TO THE HOSPITAL WHERE...
WISH YOU COULD SEE IT, ORACLE...
...A HEARTBREAKING FIVE-YEAR-OLD, AND PARTIERS WHO KEEP SAYING IT'S THE END OF THE WORLD AS THEY KNOW IT, BUT THEY FEEL FINE...
Hm? THAT'S A SONG...?
OKAY, IF YOU SAY SO...
ALL RIGHT, TEAM--LISTEN UP! IT MUST BE OUR LUCKY DAY...
...BATMAN'S SENDING US TO LAS VEGAS--THE SNOW AND SAND ARE FAR FROM A WINNING COMBINATION THERE!
MR. RAY...?
MR. RAY, I KNOW YOU HAVE DONE SO MUCH, ALREADY...
...BUT YOU ARE AN ANGEL OF LIGHT, MR. RAY! I FEEL ONLY YOU CAN HELP ME!
HUH?
I AM FAR FROM HOME, MR. RAY, AND I WISH FOR ONLY ONE THING--TO SEE MY FAMILY AGAIN... TO HOLD THEM AGAIN!
WILL YOU HELP ME PLEASE, MR. RAY?

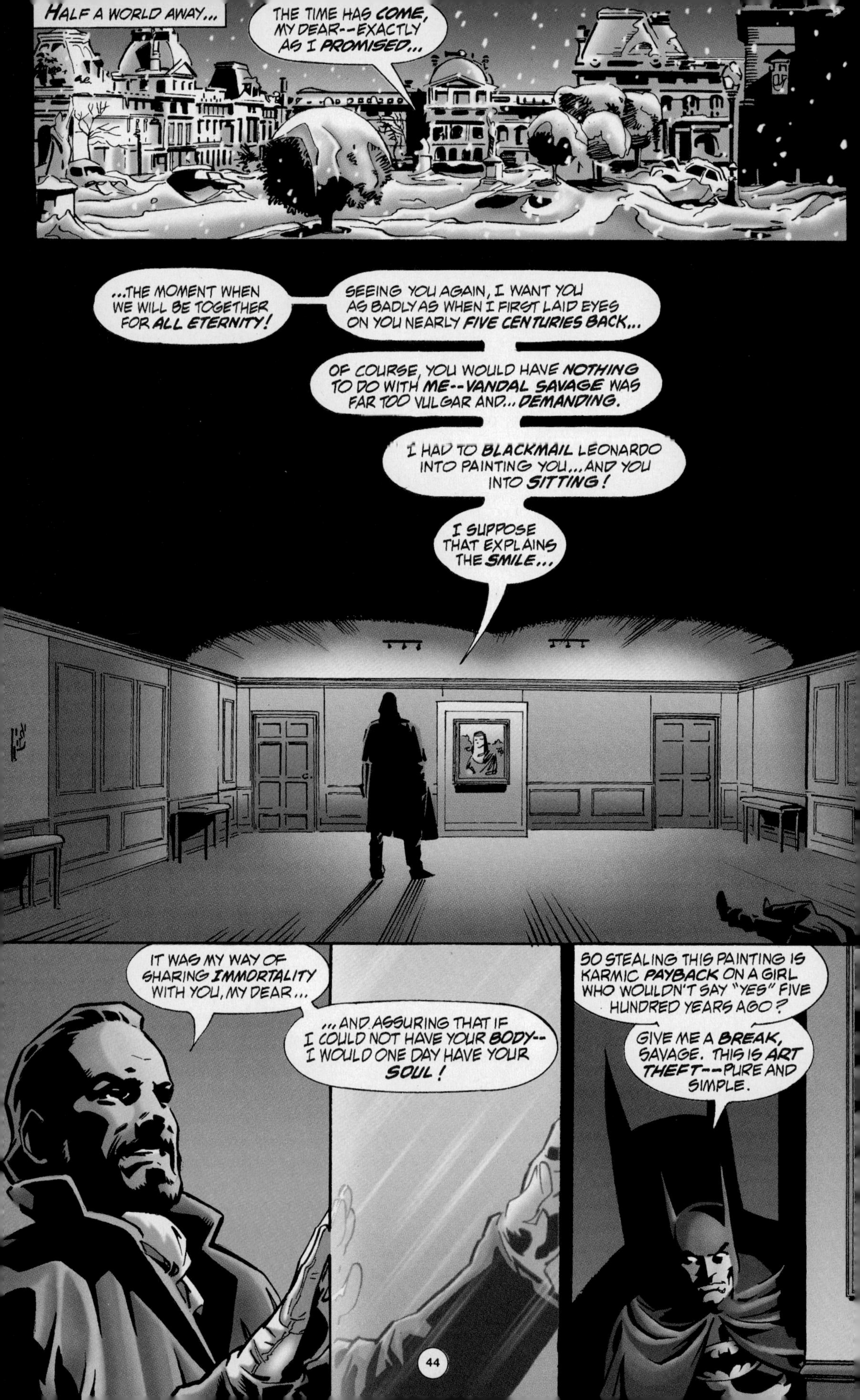
HALF A WORLD AWAY...
THE TIME HAS COME, MY DEAR--EXACTLY AS I PROMISED...
...THE MOMENT WHEN WE WILL BE TOGETHER FOR ALL ETERNITY!
SEEING YOU AGAIN, I WANT YOU AS BADLY AS WHEN I FIRST LAID EYES ON YOU NEARLY FIVE CENTURIES BACK...
OF COURSE, YOU WOULD HAVE NOTHING TO DO WITH ME--VANDAL SAVAGE WAS FAR TOO VULGAR AND... DEMANDING.
I HAD TO BLACKMAIL LEONARDO INTO PAINTING YOU... AND YOU INTO SITTING!
I SUPPOSE THAT EXPLAINS THE SMILE...
IT WAS MY WAY OF SHARING IMMORTALITY WITH YOU, MY DEAR...
...AND ASSURING THAT IF I COULD NOT HAVE YOUR BODY--I WOULD ONE DAY HAVE YOUR SOUL!
SO STEALING THIS PAINTING IS KARMIC PAYBACK ON A GIRL WHO WOULDN'T SAY "YES" FIVE HUNDRED YEARS AGO?
GIVE ME A BREAK, SAVAGE. THIS IS ART THEFT--PURE AND SIMPLE.

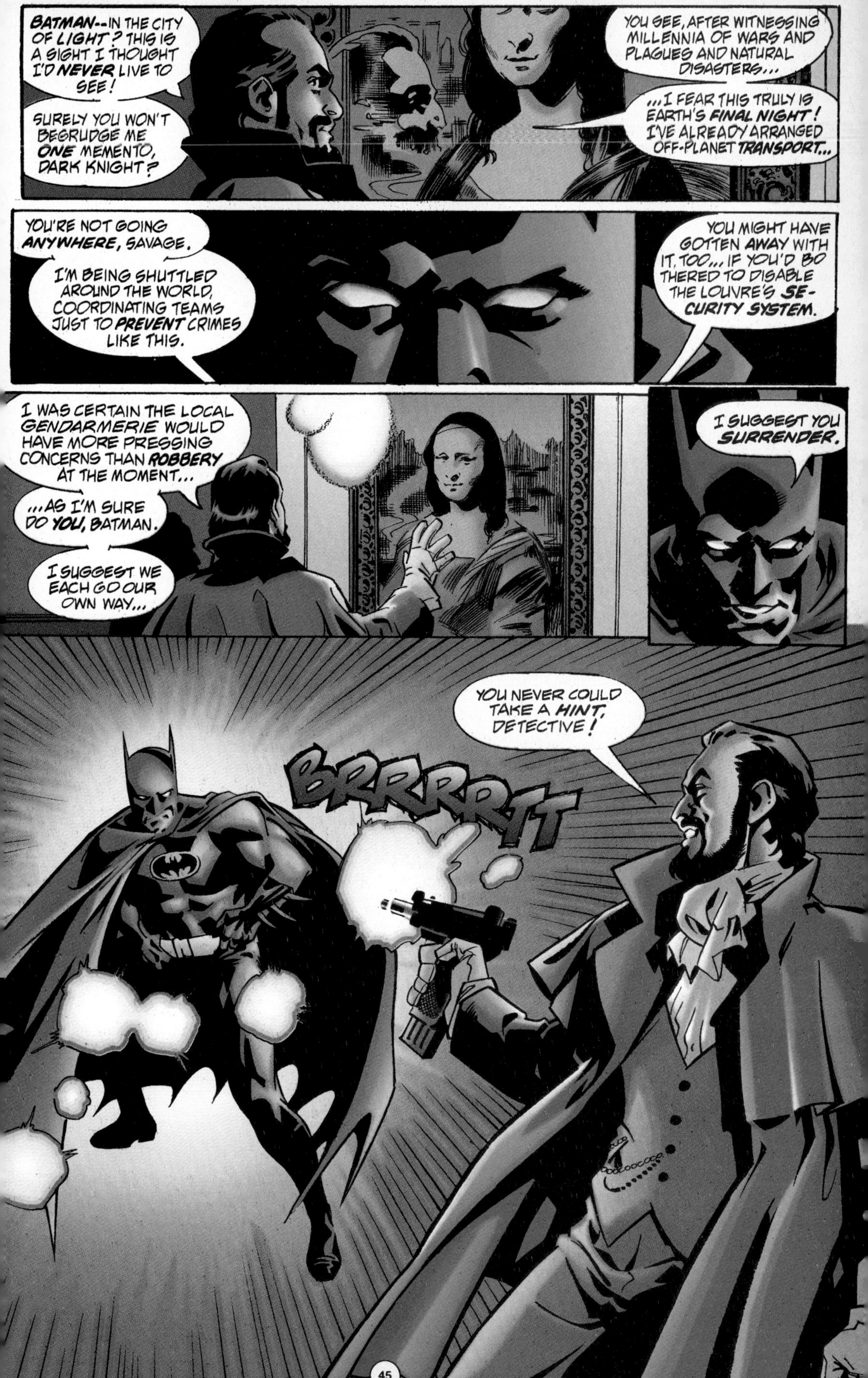
BATMAN--IN THE CITY OF LIGHT? THIS IS A SIGHT I THOUGHT I'D NEVER LIVE TO SEE!
SURELY YOU WON'T BEGRUDGE ME ONE MEMENTO, DARK KNIGHT?
YOU SEE, AFTER WITNESSING MILLENNIA OF WARS AND PLAGUES AND NATURAL DISASTERS...
...I FEAR THIS TRULY IS EARTH'S FINAL NIGHT! I'VE ALREADY ARRANGED OFF-PLANET TRANSPORT...
YOU'RE NOT GOING ANYWHERE, SAVAGE.
I'M BEING SHUTTLED AROUND THE WORLD, COORDINATING TEAMS JUST TO PREVENT CRIMES LIKE THIS.
YOU MIGHT HAVE GOTTEN AWAY WITH IT, TOO... IF YOU'D BOTHERED TO DISABLE THE LOUVRE'S SECURITY SYSTEM.
I WAS CERTAIN THE LOCAL GENDARMERIE WOULD HAVE MORE PRESSING CONCERNS THAN ROBBERY AT THE MOMENT...
...AS I'M SURE DO YOU, BATMAN.
I SUGGEST WE EACH GO OUR OWN WAY...
I SUGGEST YOU SURRENDER.
YOU NEVER COULD TAKE A HINT, DETECTIVE!
BRRRRRT

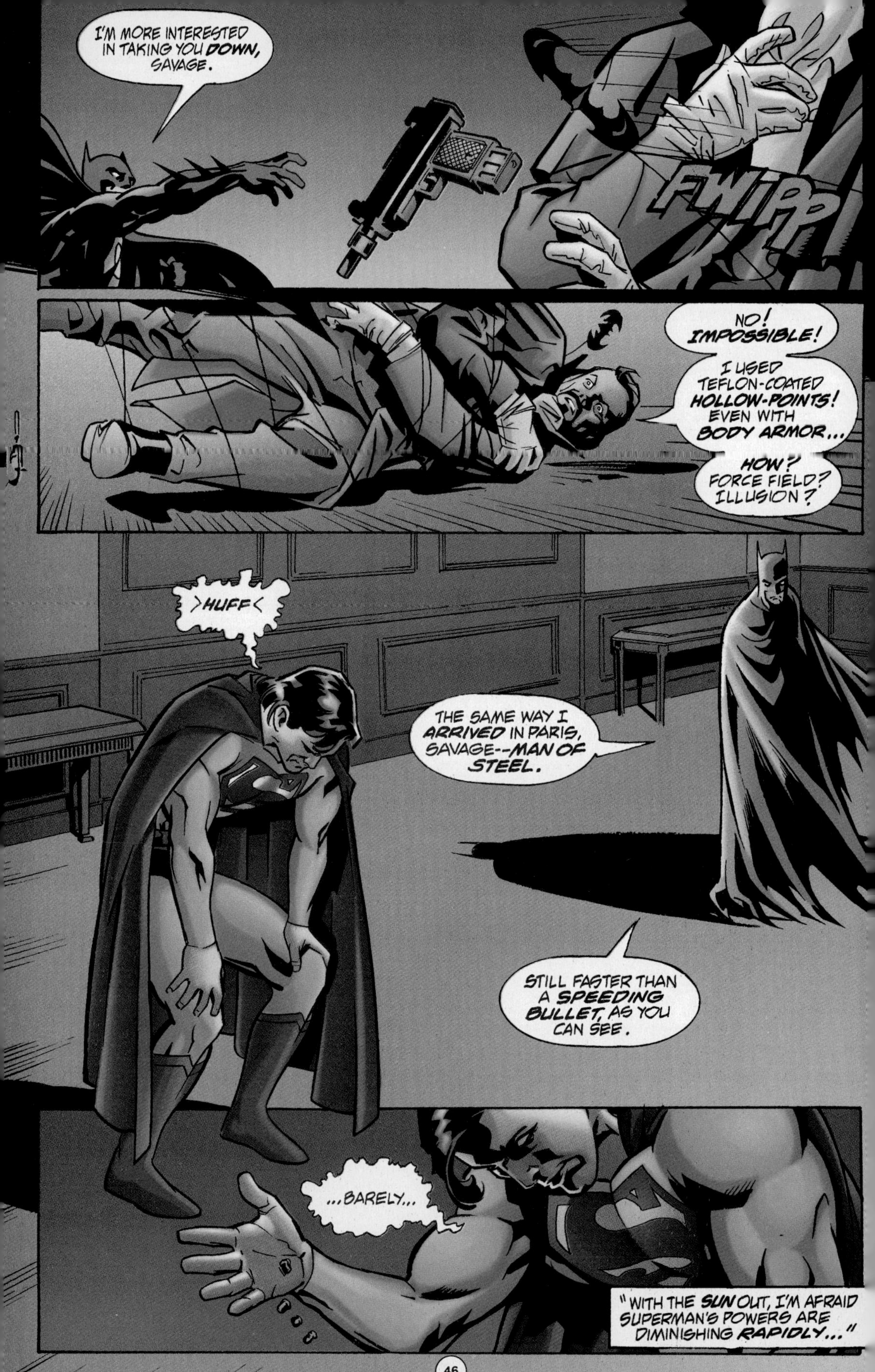

I'M MORE INTERESTED IN TAKING YOU DOWN, SAVAGE.
FWIPP
NO! IMPOSSIBLE!
I USED TEFLON-COATED HOLLOW-POINTS! EVEN WITH BODY ARMOR...
HOW? FORCE FIELD? ILLUSION?
>HUFF<
THE SAME WAY I ARRIVED IN PARIS, SAVAGE--MAN OF STEEL.
STILL FASTER THAN A SPEEDING BULLET, AS YOU CAN SEE.
...BARELY...
"WITH THE SUN OUT, I'M AFRAID SUPERMAN'S POWERS ARE DIMINISHING RAPIDLY..."

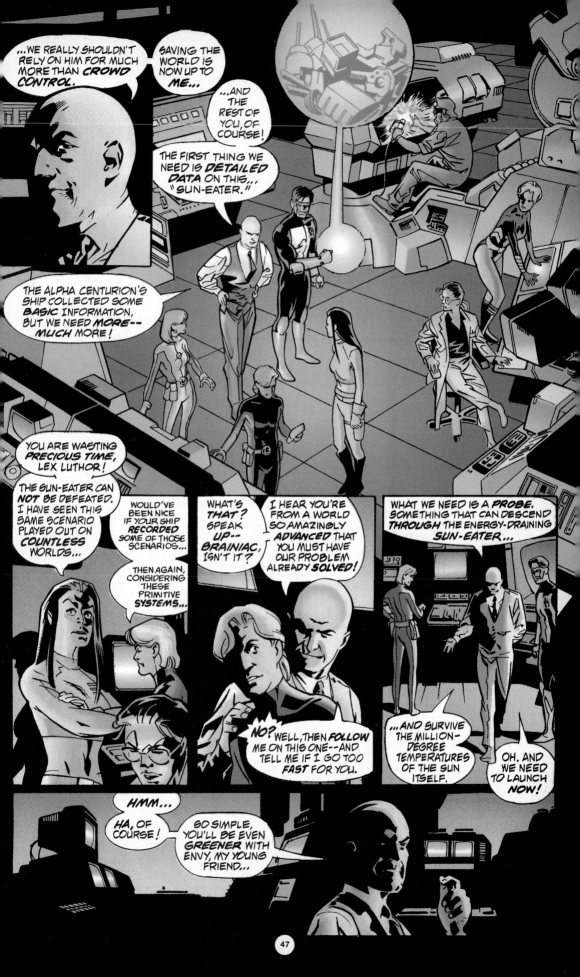

...WE REALLY SHOULDN'T RELY ON HIM FOR MUCH MORE THAN *CROWD CONTROL*.

SAVING THE WORLD IS NOW UP TO *ME*...

...AND THE REST OF YOU, OF COURSE!

THE FIRST THING WE NEED IS *DETAILED DATA* ON THIS... "SUN-EATER."

THE ALPHA CENTURION'S SHIP COLLECTED SOME *BASIC* INFORMATION, BUT WE NEED *MORE-- MUCH* MORE!

YOU ARE WASTING *PRECIOUS TIME*, LEX LUTHOR!

THE SUN-EATER CAN *NOT* BE DEFEATED. I HAVE SEEN THIS SAME SCENARIO PLAYED OUT ON *COUNTLESS WORLDS*...

WOULD'VE BEEN NICE IF YOUR SHIP *RECORDED* SOME OF THOSE SCENARIOS...

THEN AGAIN, CONSIDERING THESE PRIMITIVE *SYSTEMS*...

WHAT'S *THAT*? SPEAK *UP--* BRAINIAC, ISN'T IT?

I HEAR YOU'RE FROM A WORLD SO AMAZINGLY *ADVANCED* THAT YOU MUST HAVE OUR PROBLEM ALREADY *SOLVED*!

WHAT WE NEED IS A *PROBE*. SOMETHING THAT CAN DESCEND *THROUGH* THE ENERGY-DRAINING *SUN-EATER*...

NO? WELL, THEN *FOLLOW* ME ON THIS ONE-- AND TELL ME IF I GO TOO *FAST* FOR YOU.

...AND SURVIVE THE MILLION- DEGREE TEMPERATURES OF THE SUN ITSELF.

OH. AND WE NEED TO LAUNCH *NOW*!

HMM...

HA, OF COURSE!

SO SIMPLE, YOU'LL BE EVEN *GREENER* WITH ENVY, MY YOUNG FRIEND...

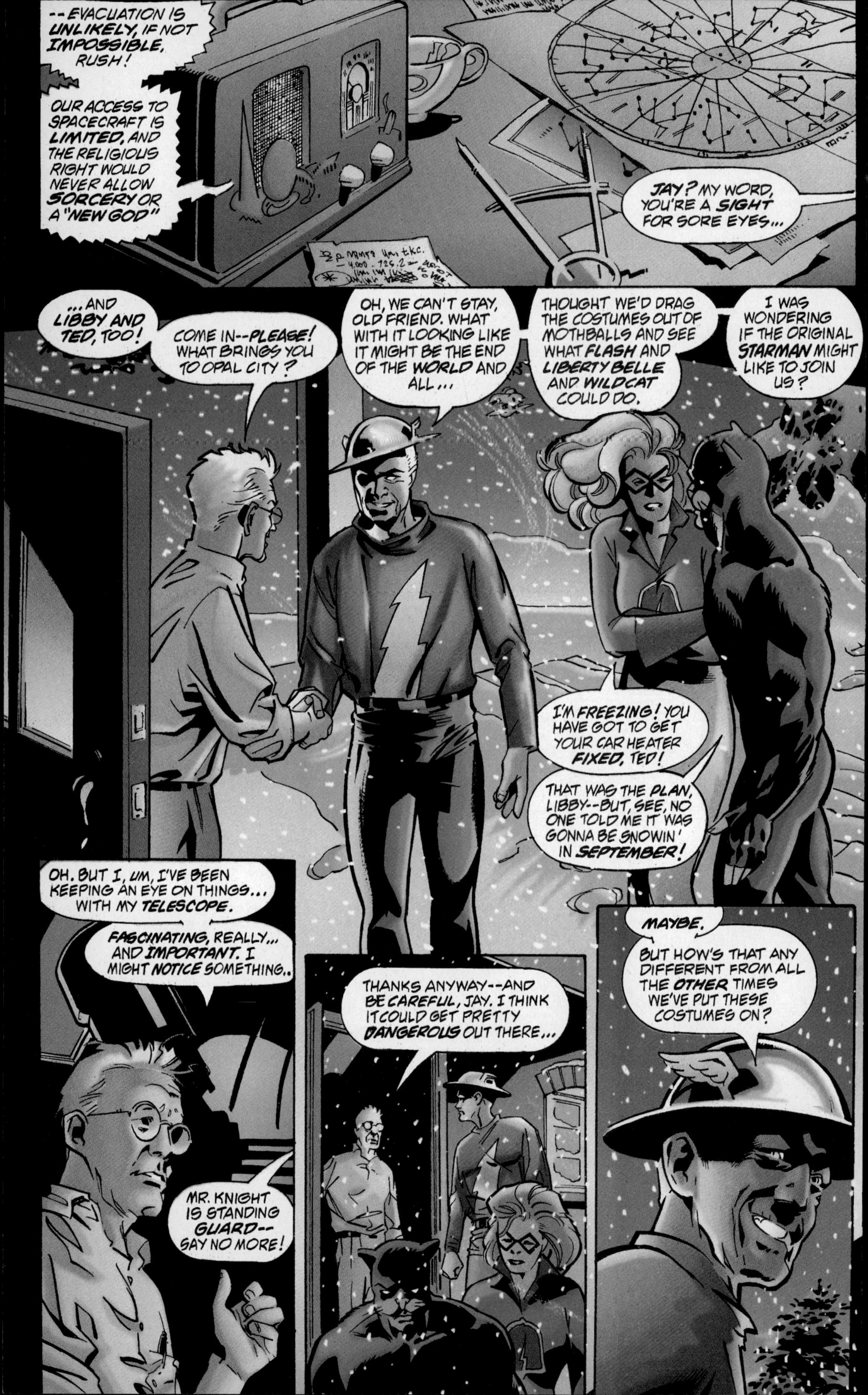
-- EVACUATION IS UNLIKELY, IF NOT IMPOSSIBLE, RUSH!
OUR ACCESS TO SPACECRAFT IS LIMITED, AND THE RELIGIOUS RIGHT WOULD NEVER ALLOW SORCERY OR A "NEW GOD"
JAY? MY WORD, YOU'RE A SIGHT FOR SORE EYES...
...AND LIBBY AND TED, TOO!
COME IN--PLEASE! WHAT BRINGS YOU TO OPAL CITY?
OH, WE CAN'T STAY, OLD FRIEND. WHAT WITH IT LOOKING LIKE IT MIGHT BE THE END OF THE WORLD AND ALL...
THOUGHT WE'D DRAG THE COSTUMES OUT OF MOTHBALLS AND SEE WHAT FLASH AND LIBERTY BELLE AND WILDCAT COULD DO.
I WAS WONDERING IF THE ORIGINAL STARMAN MIGHT LIKE TO JOIN US?
I'M FREEZING! YOU HAVE GOT TO GET YOUR CAR HEATER FIXED, TED!
THAT WAS THE PLAN, LIBBY--BUT, SEE, NO ONE TOLD ME IT WAS GONNA BE SNOWIN' IN SEPTEMBER!
OH. BUT I, UM, I'VE BEEN KEEPING AN EYE ON THINGS... WITH MY TELESCOPE.
FASCINATING, REALLY... AND IMPORTANT. I MIGHT NOTICE SOMETHING..
MR. KNIGHT IS STANDING GUARD-- SAY NO MORE!
THANKS ANYWAY--AND BE CAREFUL, JAY. I THINK IT COULD GET PRETTY DANGEROUS OUT THERE...
MAYBE.
BUT HOW'S THAT ANY DIFFERENT FROM ALL THE OTHER TIMES WE'VE PUT THESE COSTUMES ON?

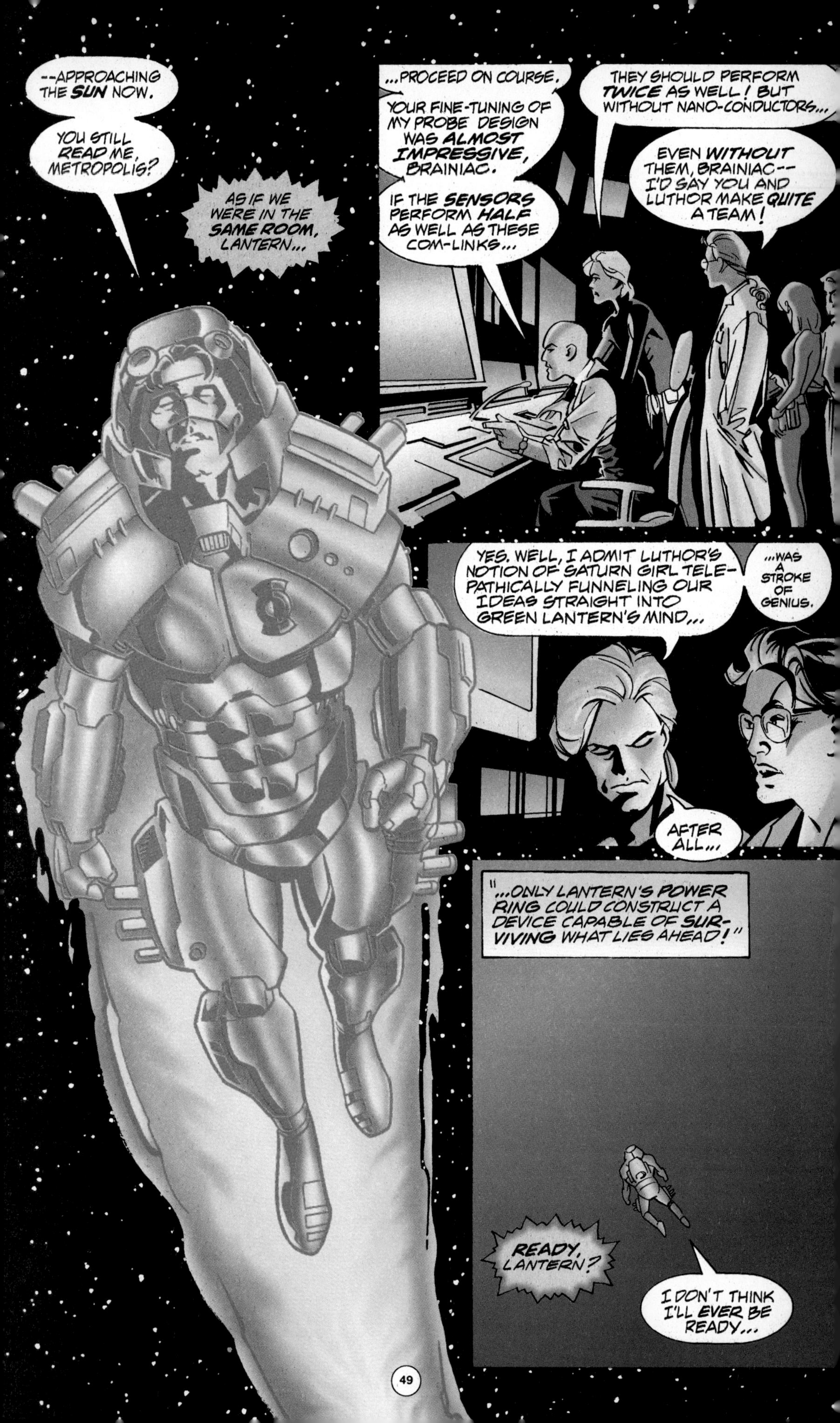
--APPROACHING THE SUN NOW.
YOU STILL READ ME, METROPOLIS?
AS IF WE WERE IN THE SAME ROOM, LANTERN...
...PROCEED ON COURSE.
YOUR FINE-TUNING OF MY PROBE DESIGN WAS ALMOST IMPRESSIVE, BRAINIAC.
IF THE SENSORS PERFORM HALF AS WELL AS THESE COM-LINKS...
THEY SHOULD PERFORM TWICE AS WELL! BUT WITHOUT NANO-CONDUCTORS...
EVEN WITHOUT THEM, BRAINIAC-- I'D SAY YOU AND LUTHOR MAKE QUITE A TEAM!
YES. WELL, I ADMIT LUTHOR'S NOTION OF SATURN GIRL TELEPATHICALLY FUNNELING OUR IDEAS STRAIGHT INTO GREEN LANTERN'S MIND...
...WAS A STROKE OF GENIUS.
AFTER ALL...
"...ONLY LANTERN'S POWER RING COULD CONSTRUCT A DEVICE CAPABLE OF SURVIVING WHAT LIES AHEAD!"
READY, LANTERN?
I DON'T THINK I'LL EVER BE READY...

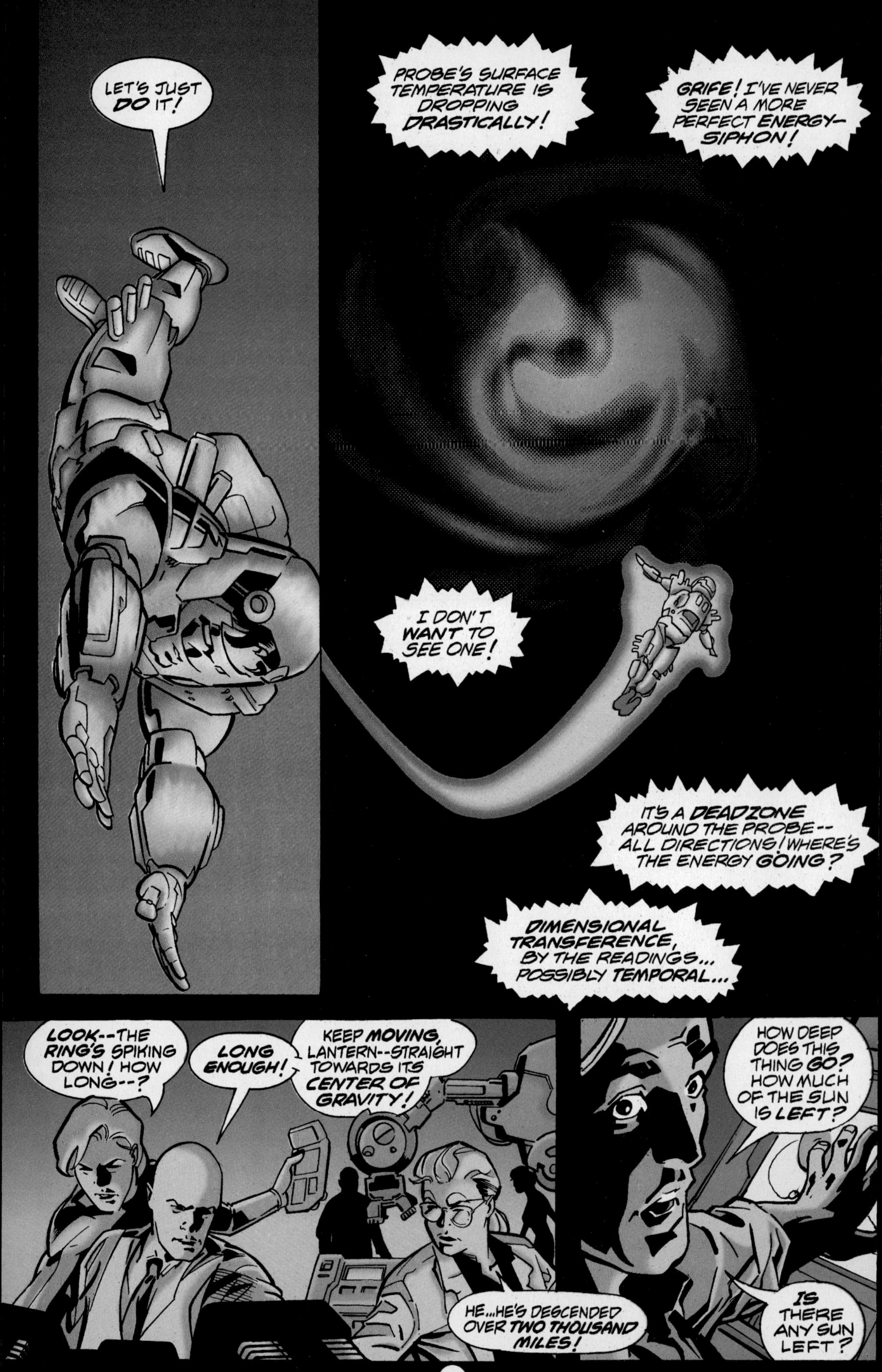
LET'S JUST DO IT!
PROBE'S SURFACE TEMPERATURE IS DROPPING DRASTICALLY!
GRIFE! I'VE NEVER SEEN A MORE PERFECT ENERGY-SIPHON!
I DON'T WANT TO SEE ONE!
IT'S A DEADZONE AROUND THE PROBE-- ALL DIRECTIONS! WHERE'S THE ENERGY GOING?
DIMENSIONAL TRANSFERENCE, BY THE READINGS... POSSIBLY TEMPORAL...
LOOK--THE RING'S SPIKING DOWN! HOW LONG--?
LONG ENOUGH!
KEEP MOVING, LANTERN--STRAIGHT TOWARDS ITS CENTER OF GRAVITY!
HE...HE'S DESCENDED OVER TWO THOUSAND MILES!
HOW DEEP DOES THIS THING GO? HOW MUCH OF THE SUN IS LEFT?
IS THERE ANY SUN LEFT?

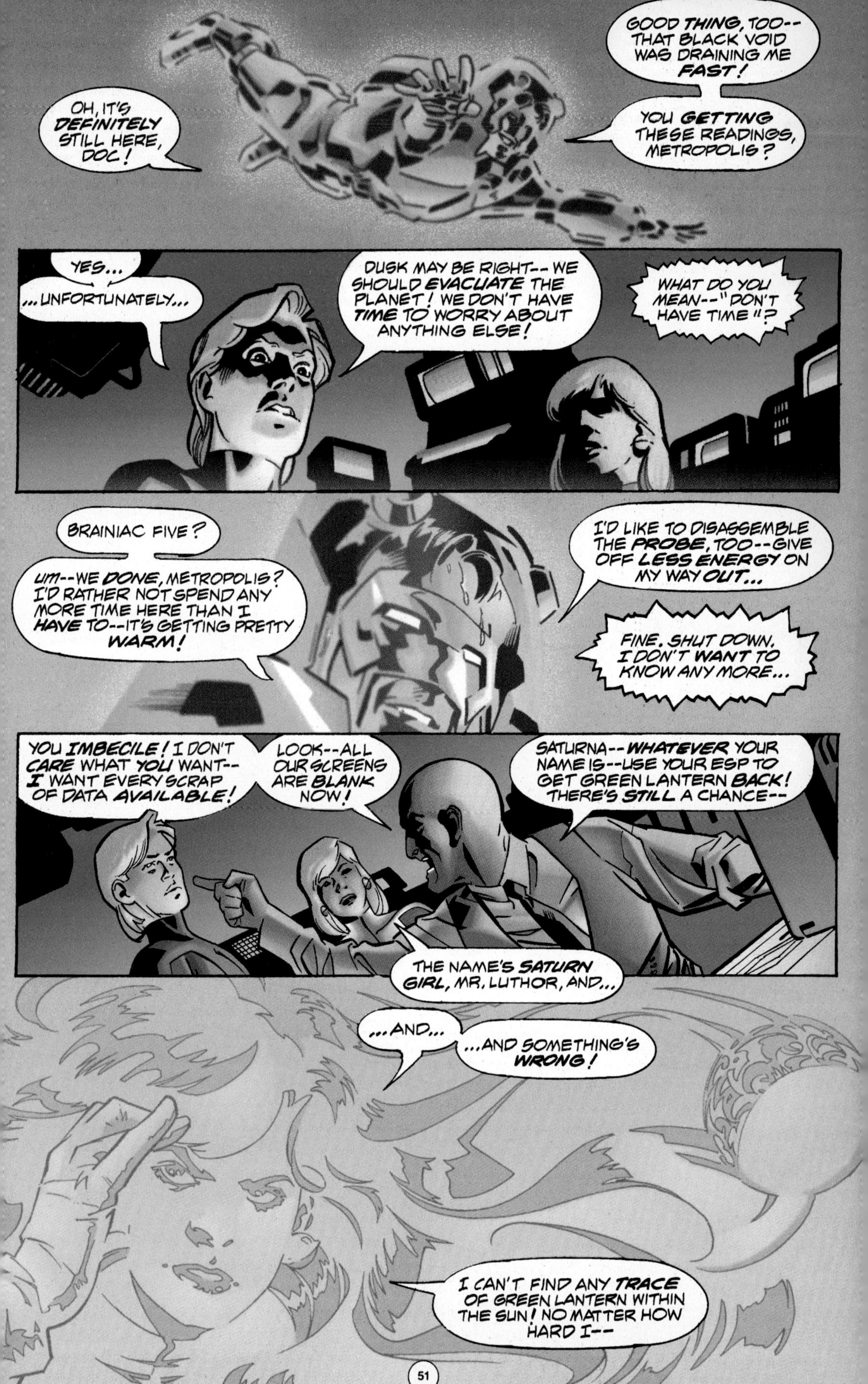
GOOD THING, TOO--THAT BLACK VOID WAS DRAINING ME FAST!
OH, IT'S DEFINITELY STILL HERE, DOC!
YOU GETTING THESE READINGS, METROPOLIS?
YES...
...UNFORTUNATELY...
DUSK MAY BE RIGHT-- WE SHOULD EVACUATE THE PLANET! WE DON'T HAVE TIME TO WORRY ABOUT ANYTHING ELSE!
WHAT DO YOU MEAN--"DON'T HAVE TIME"?
BRAINIAC FIVE?
UM--WE DONE, METROPOLIS? I'D RATHER NOT SPEND ANY MORE TIME HERE THAN I HAVE TO--IT'S GETTING PRETTY WARM!
I'D LIKE TO DISASSEMBLE THE PROBE, TOO--GIVE OFF LESS ENERGY ON MY WAY OUT...
FINE. SHUT DOWN. I DON'T WANT TO KNOW ANY MORE...
YOU IMBECILE! I DON'T CARE WHAT YOU WANT--I WANT EVERY SCRAP OF DATA AVAILABLE!
LOOK--ALL OUR SCREENS ARE BLANK NOW!
SATURNA--WHATEVER YOUR NAME IS--USE YOUR ESP TO GET GREEN LANTERN BACK! THERE'S STILL A CHANCE--
THE NAME'S SATURN GIRL, MR. LUTHOR, AND...
...AND...
...AND SOMETHING'S WRONG!
I CAN'T FIND ANY TRACE OF GREEN LANTERN WITHIN THE SUN! NO MATTER HOW HARD I--

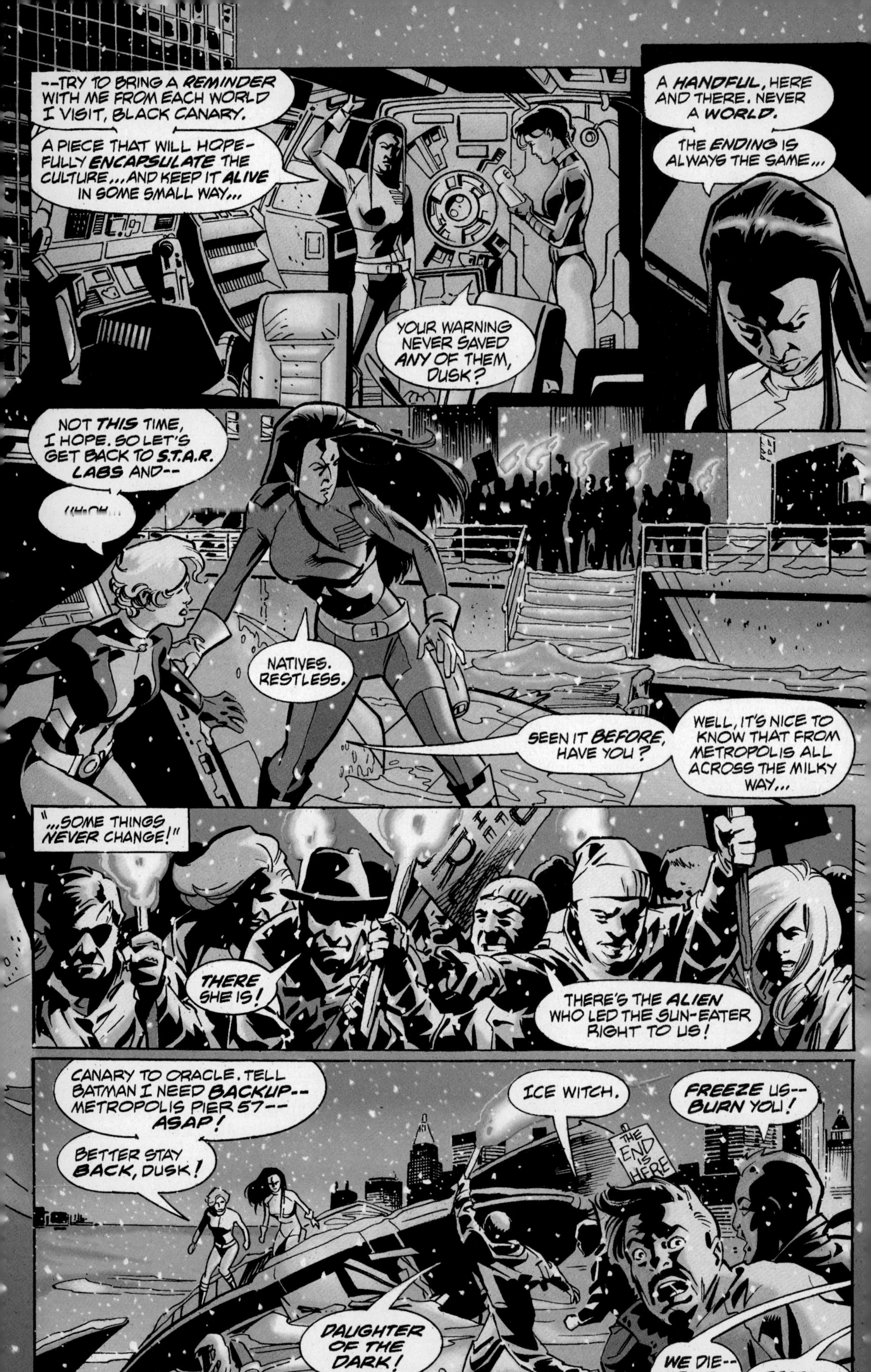
--TRY TO BRING A REMINDER WITH ME FROM EACH WORLD I VISIT, BLACK CANARY.
A PIECE THAT WILL HOPEFULLY ENCAPSULATE THE CULTURE... AND KEEP IT ALIVE IN SOME SMALL WAY...
YOUR WARNING NEVER SAVED ANY OF THEM, DUSK?
A HANDFUL, HERE AND THERE. NEVER A WORLD.
THE ENDING IS ALWAYS THE SAME...
NOT THIS TIME, I HOPE. SO LET'S GET BACK TO S.T.A.R. LABS AND--
NATIVES. RESTLESS.
SEEN IT BEFORE, HAVE YOU?
WELL, IT'S NICE TO KNOW THAT FROM METROPOLIS ALL ACROSS THE MILKY WAY...
"...SOME THINGS NEVER CHANGE!"
THERE SHE IS!
THERE'S THE ALIEN WHO LED THE SUN-EATER RIGHT TO US!
CANARY TO ORACLE. TELL BATMAN I NEED BACKUP-- METROPOLIS PIER 57-- ASAP!
BETTER STAY BACK, DUSK!
ICE WITCH.
FREEZE US-- BURN YOU!
THE END IS HERE
DAUGHTER OF THE DARK!
WE DIE-- SHE DIES!
DESTROY HER SHIP!

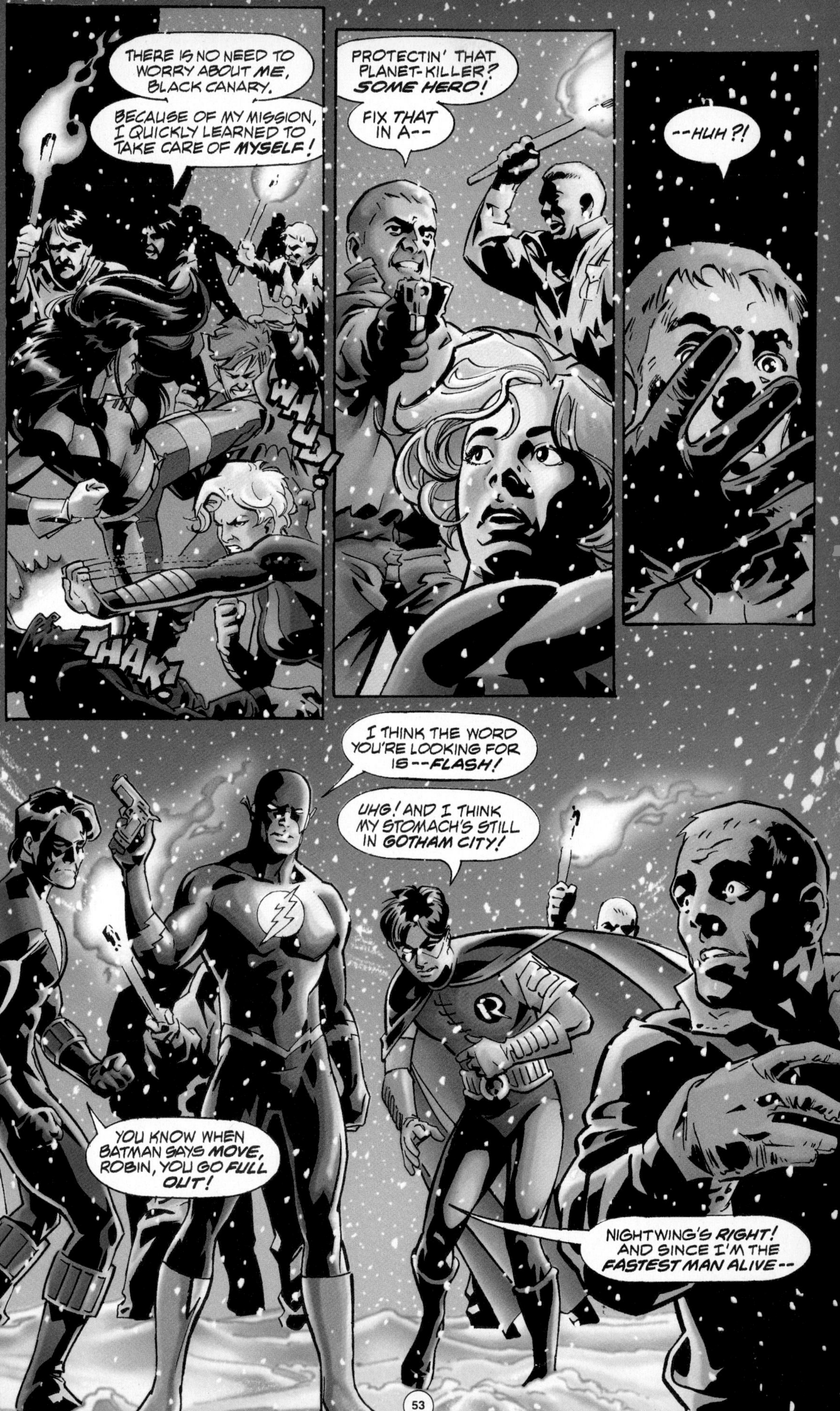
THERE IS NO NEED TO WORRY ABOUT ME, BLACK CANARY.
BECAUSE OF MY MISSION, I QUICKLY LEARNED TO TAKE CARE OF MYSELF!
WHUD!
THAK!
PROTECTIN' THAT PLANET-KILLER? SOME HERO!
FIX THAT IN A--
--HUH?!
I THINK THE WORD YOU'RE LOOKING FOR IS--FLASH!
UHG! AND I THINK MY STOMACH'S STILL IN GOTHAM CITY!
YOU KNOW WHEN BATMAN SAYS MOVE, ROBIN, YOU GO FULL OUT!
NIGHTWING'S RIGHT! AND SINCE I'M THE FASTEST MAN ALIVE--

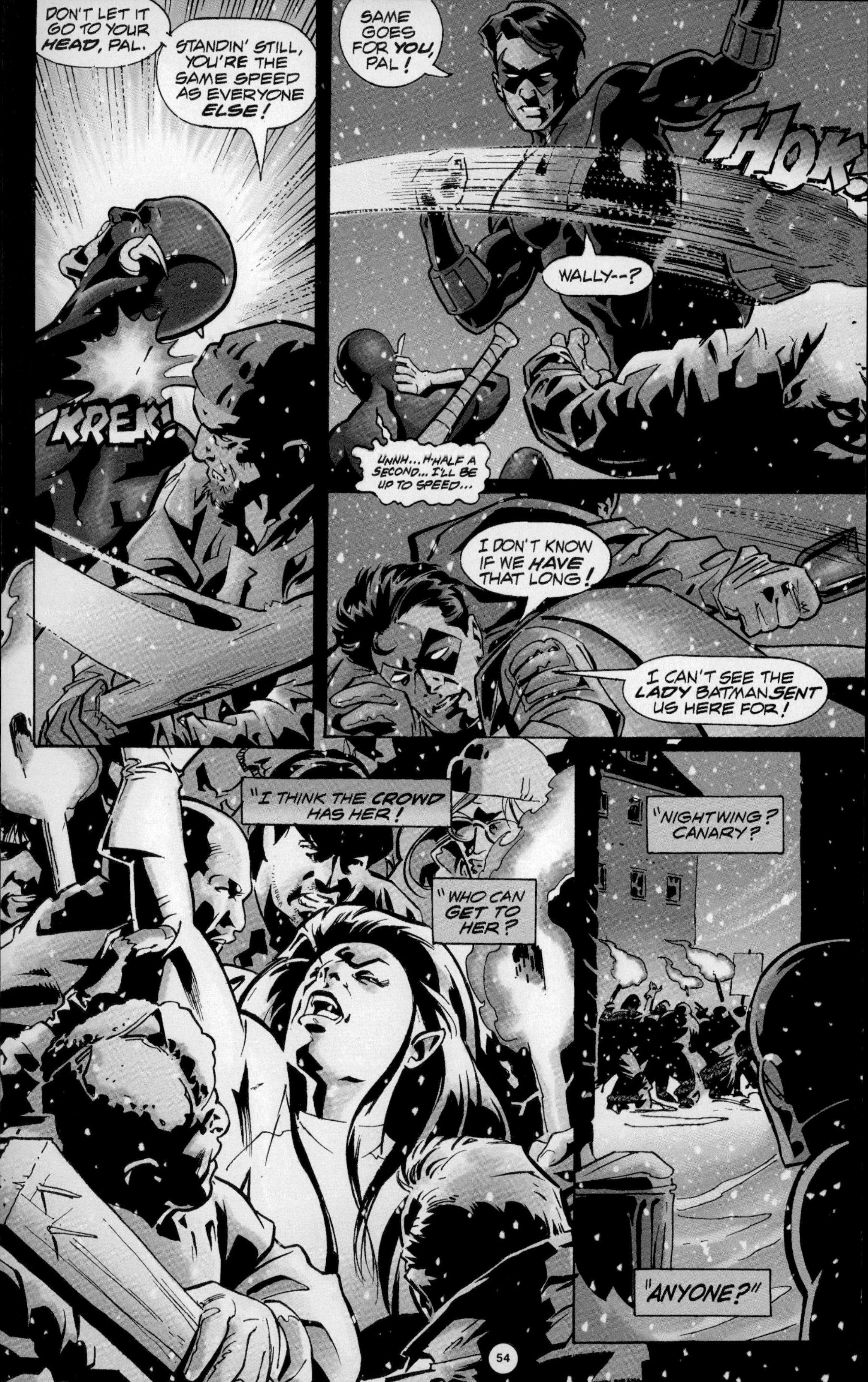
DON'T LET IT GO TO YOUR HEAD, PAL.
STANDIN' STILL, YOU'RE THE SAME SPEED AS EVERYONE ELSE!
KREK!
SAME GOES FOR YOU, PAL!
THOK!
WALLY--?
UNNH... H-HALF A SECOND... I'LL BE UP TO SPEED...
I DON'T KNOW IF WE HAVE THAT LONG!
I CAN'T SEE THE LADY BATMAN SENT US HERE FOR!
"I THINK THE CROWD HAS HER!
"WHO CAN GET TO HER?
"NIGHTWING? CANARY?
"ANYONE?"

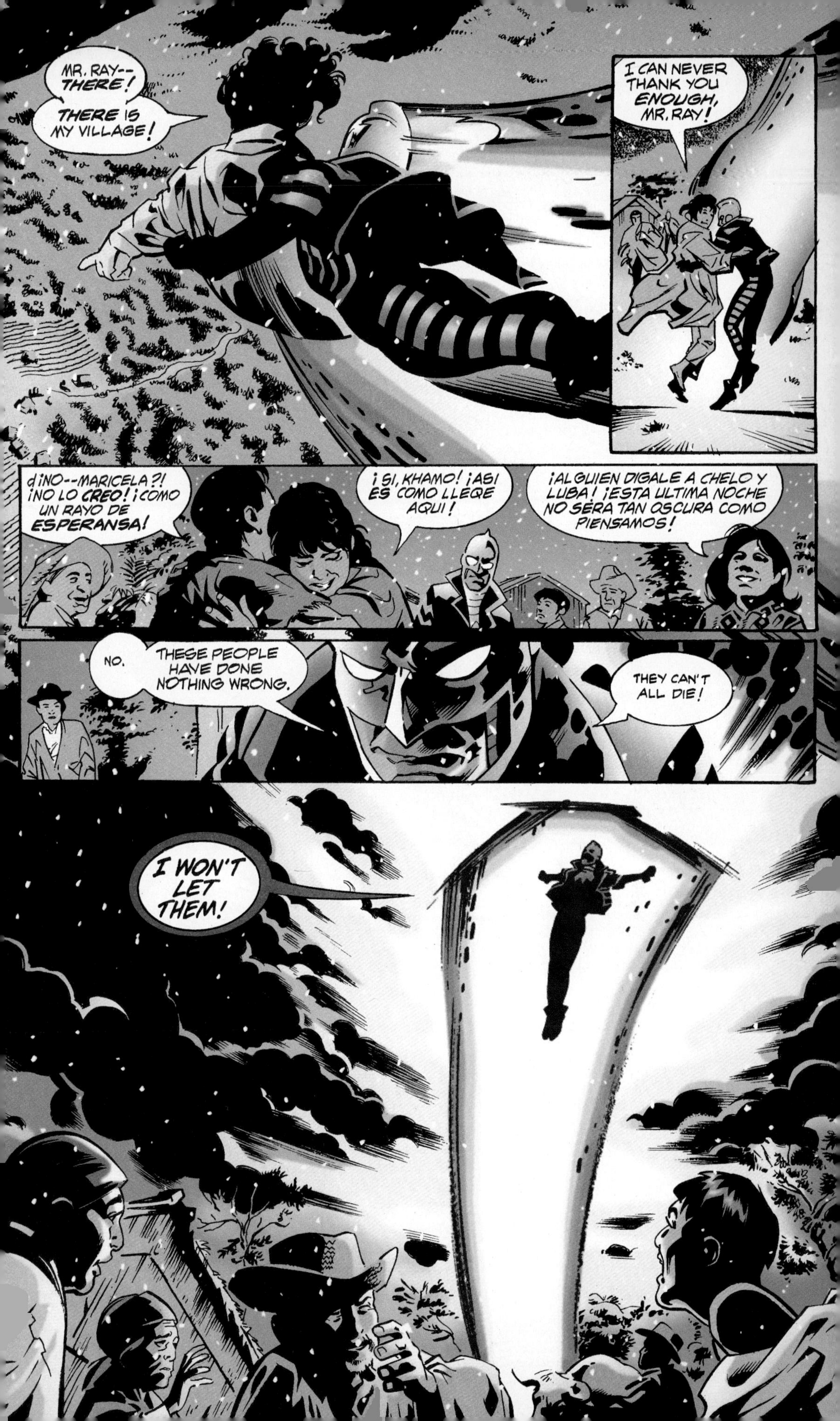
MR. RAY-- THERE! THERE IS MY VILLAGE!
I CAN NEVER THANK YOU ENOUGH, MR. RAY!
¿¡NO--MARICELA?! ¡NO LO CREO! ¡COMO UN RAYO DE ESPERANSA!
¡SI, KHAMO! ¡ASI ES COMO LLEGE AQUI!
¡ALGUIEN DIGALE A CHELO Y LUBA! ¡ESTA ULTIMA NOCHE NO SERA TAN OSCURA COMO PIENSAMOS!
NO.
THESE PEOPLE HAVE DONE NOTHING WRONG.
THEY CAN'T ALL DIE!
I WON'T LET THEM!

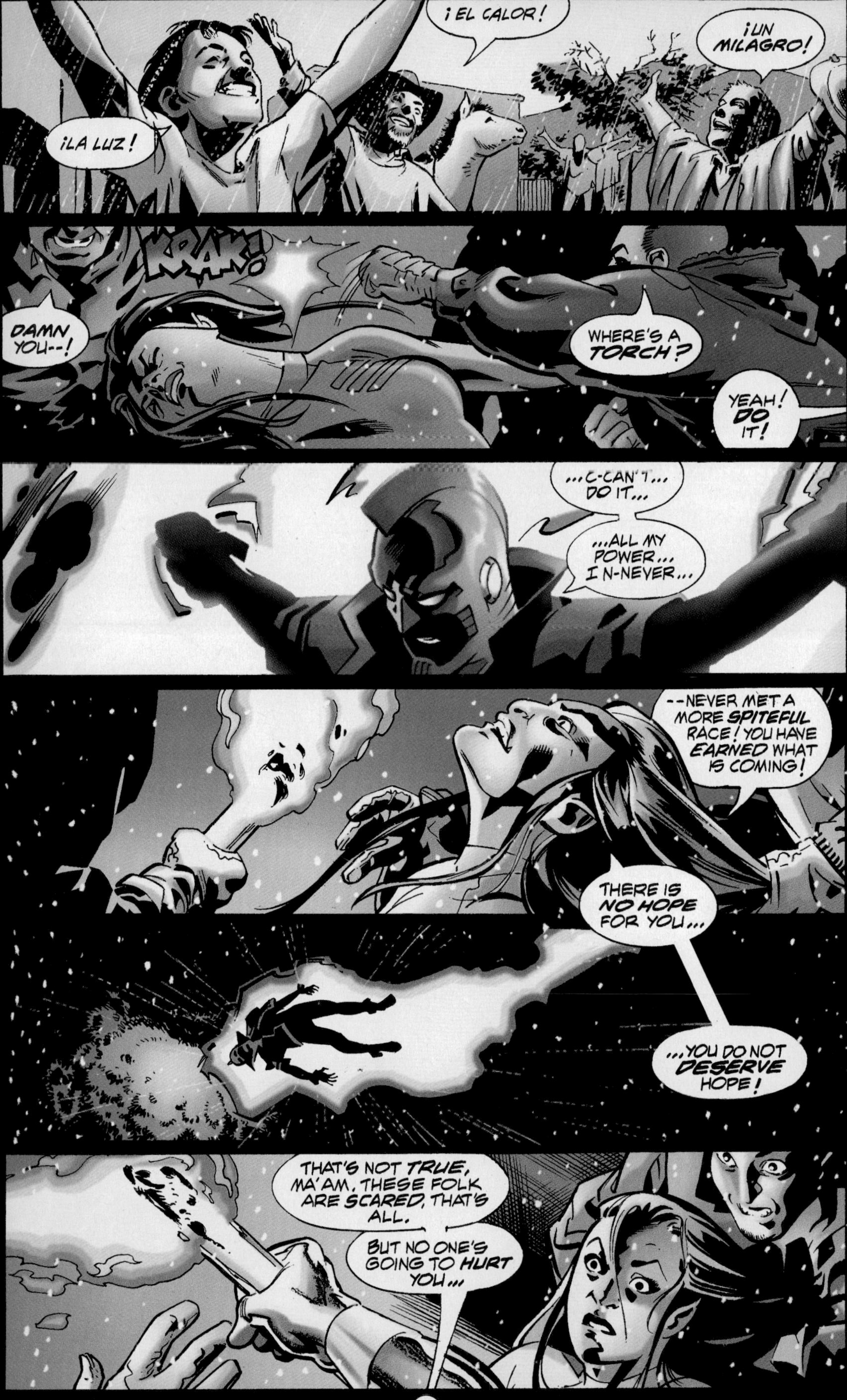

¡EL CALOR!
¡UN MILAGRO!
¡LA LUZ!
KRAK!
DAMN YOU--!
WHERE'S A TORCH?
YEAH! DO IT!
...C-CAN'T... DO IT...
...ALL MY POWER... I N-NEVER...
--NEVER MET A MORE SPITEFUL RACE! YOU HAVE EARNED WHAT IS COMING!
THERE IS NO HOPE FOR YOU...
...YOU DO NOT DESERVE HOPE!
THAT'S NOT TRUE, MA'AM, THESE FOLK ARE SCARED, THAT'S ALL.
BUT NO ONE'S GOING TO HURT YOU...

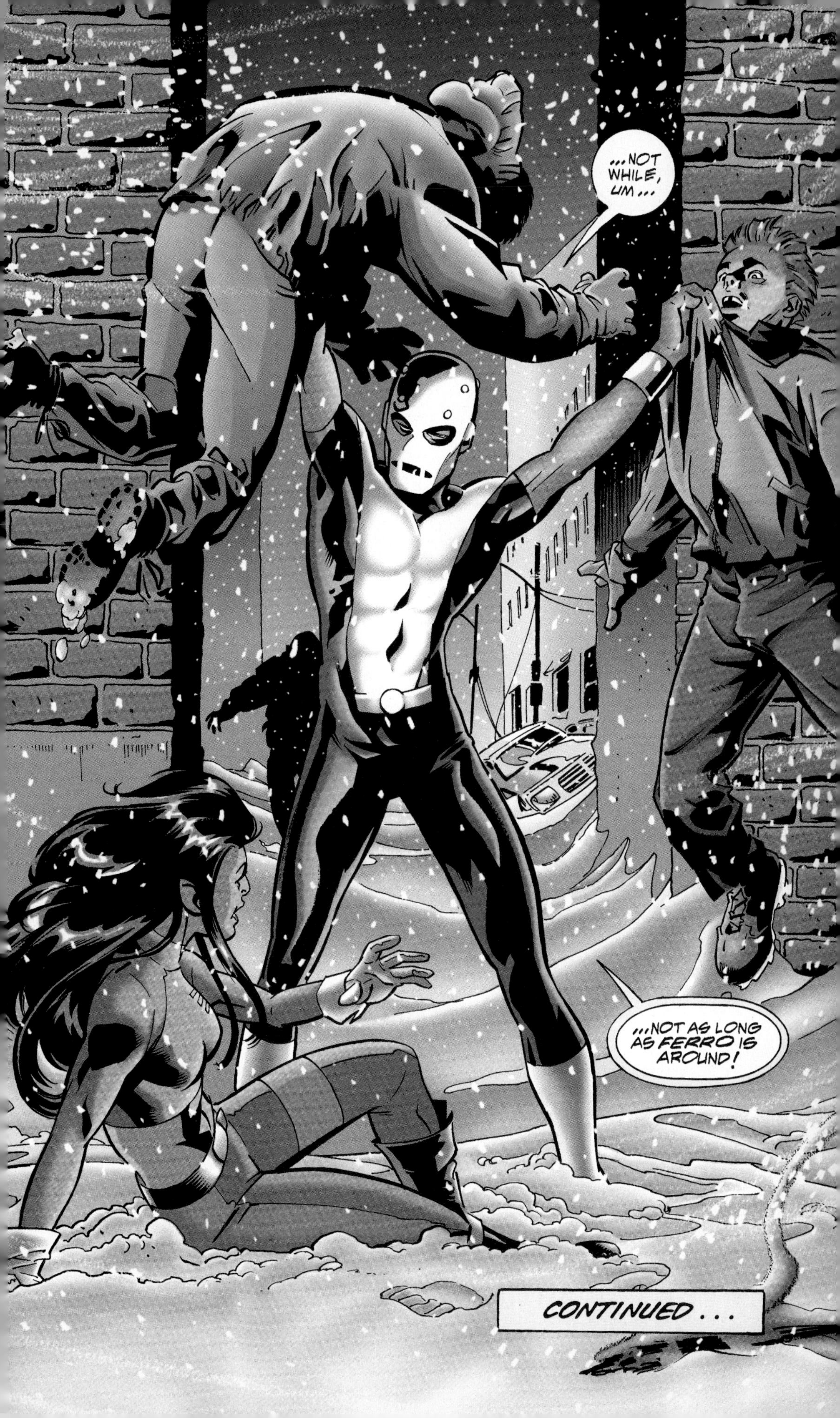
...NOT WHILE, UM...
...NOT AS LONG AS FERRO IS AROUND!
CONTINUED...

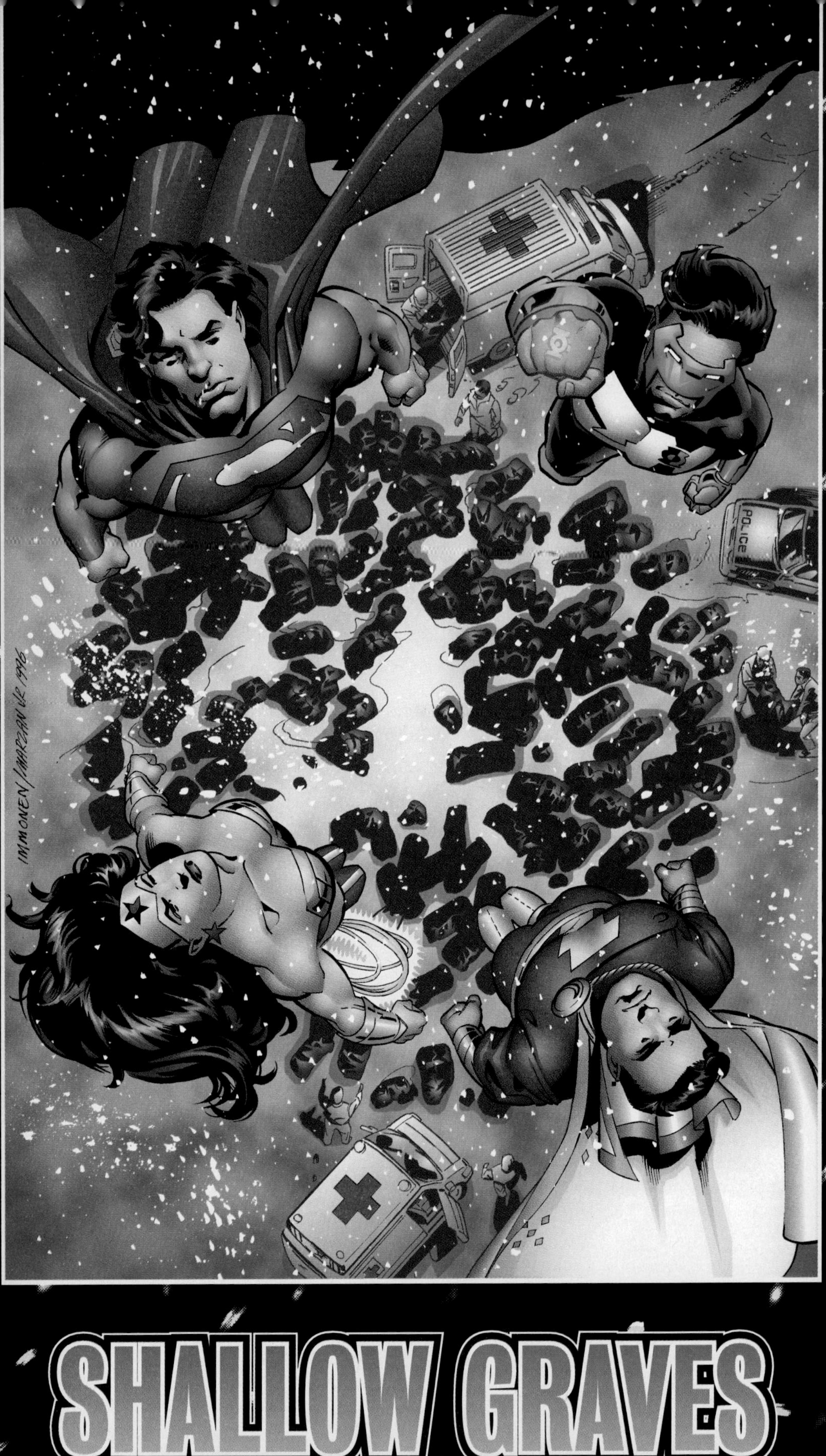
POLICE
IMMONEN/MARZAN JR 1996

SHALLOW GRAVES

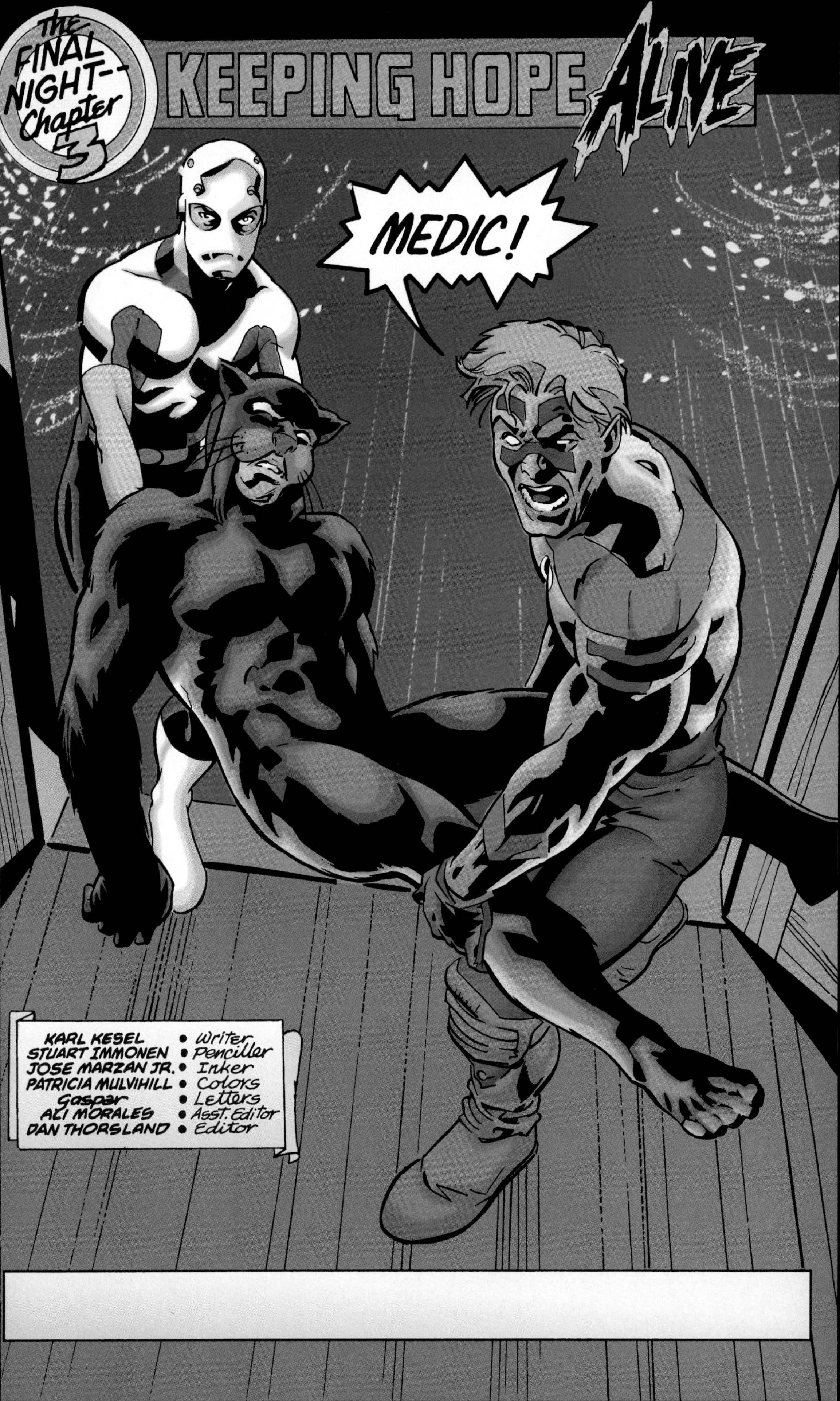
The Final Night-- Chapter 3
KEEPING HOPE ALIVE
MEDIC!
KARL KESEL • Writer
STUART IMMONEN • Penciller
JOSE MARZAN JR. • Inker
PATRICIA MULVIHILL • Colors
Gaspar • Letters
ALI MORALES • Asst. Editor
DAN THORSLAND • Editor

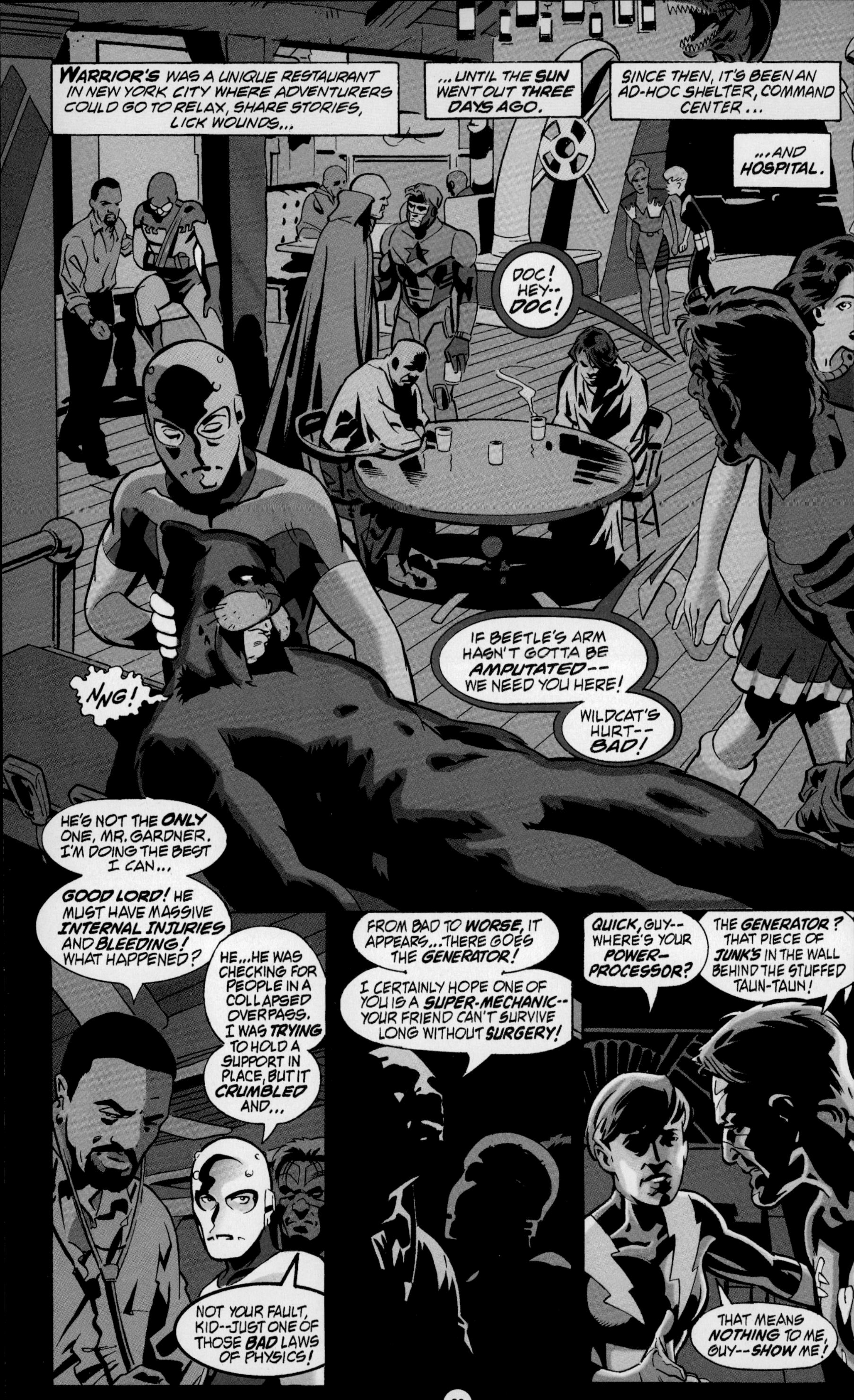
WARRIOR'S WAS A UNIQUE RESTAURANT IN NEW YORK CITY WHERE ADVENTURERS COULD GO TO RELAX, SHARE STORIES, LICK WOUNDS...
...UNTIL THE SUN WENT OUT THREE DAYS AGO.
SINCE THEN, IT'S BEEN AN AD-HOC SHELTER, COMMAND CENTER...
...AND HOSPITAL.
DOC! HEY-- DOC!
IF BEETLE'S ARM HASN'T GOTTA BE AMPUTATED-- WE NEED YOU HERE!
WILDCAT'S HURT-- BAD!
NNG!
HE'S NOT THE ONLY ONE, MR. GARDNER. I'M DOING THE BEST I CAN...
GOOD LORD! HE MUST HAVE MASSIVE INTERNAL INJURIES AND BLEEDING! WHAT HAPPENED?
HE...HE WAS CHECKING FOR PEOPLE IN A COLLAPSED OVERPASS. I WAS TRYING TO HOLD A SUPPORT IN PLACE, BUT IT CRUMBLED AND...
NOT YOUR FAULT, KID--JUST ONE OF THOSE BAD LAWS OF PHYSICS!
FROM BAD TO WORSE, IT APPEARS...THERE GOES THE GENERATOR!
I CERTAINLY HOPE ONE OF YOU IS A SUPER-MECHANIC-- YOUR FRIEND CAN'T SURVIVE LONG WITHOUT SURGERY!
QUICK, GUY-- WHERE'S YOUR POWER-PROCESSOR?
THE GENERATOR? THAT PIECE OF JUNK'S IN THE WALL BEHIND THE STUFFED TAUN-TAUN!
THAT MEANS NOTHING TO ME, GUY-- SHOW ME!

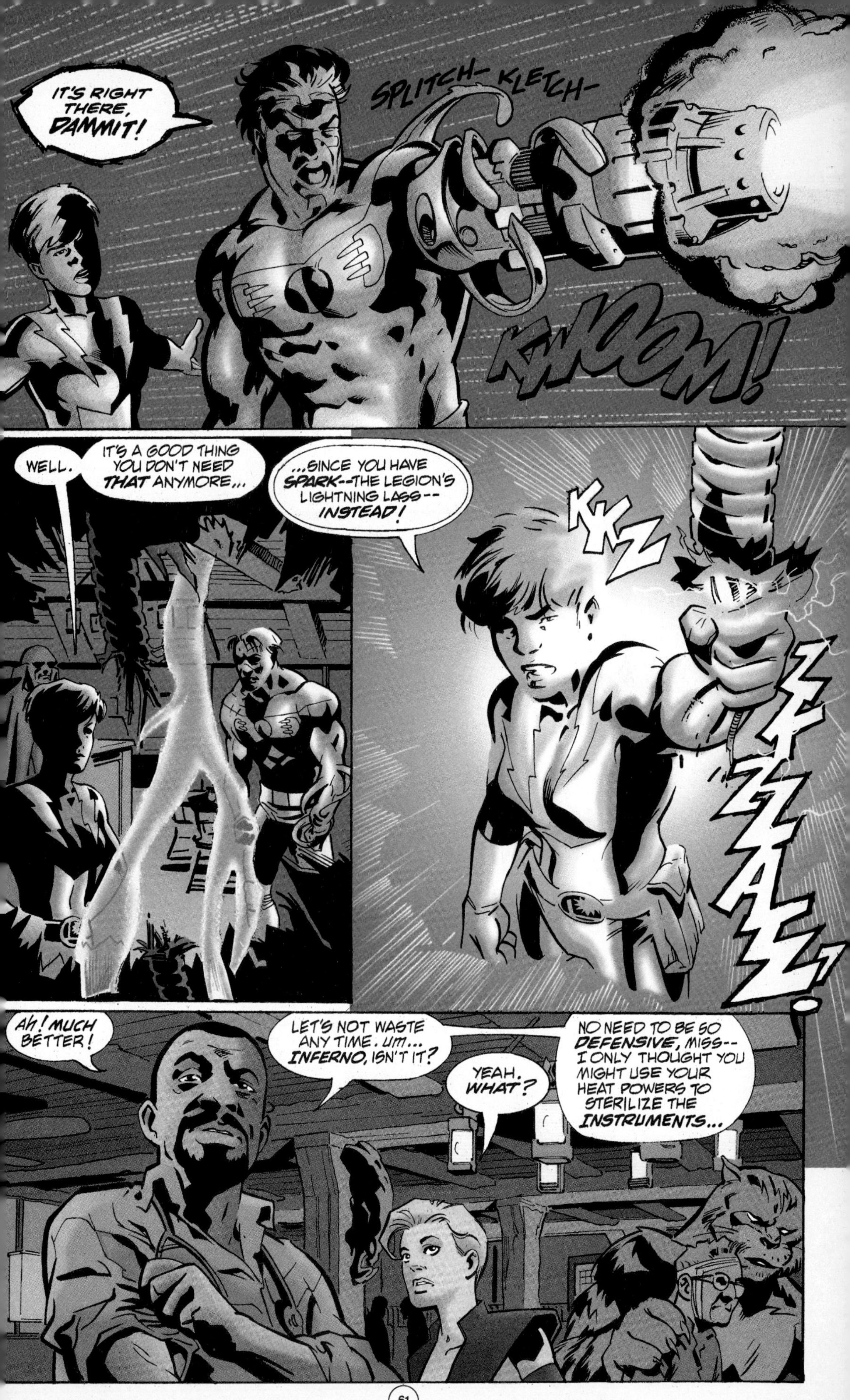

IT'S RIGHT THERE, DAMMIT!
SPLITCH- KLETCH-
KWOOM!
WELL.
IT'S A GOOD THING YOU DON'T NEED THAT ANYMORE...
...SINCE YOU HAVE SPARK--THE LEGION'S LIGHTNING LASS--INSTEAD!
KKZ
ZZZAAZZ!
AH! MUCH BETTER!
LET'S NOT WASTE ANY TIME. UM... INFERNO, ISN'T IT?
YEAH. WHAT?
NO NEED TO BE SO DEFENSIVE, MISS-- I ONLY THOUGHT YOU MIGHT USE YOUR HEAT POWERS TO STERILIZE THE INSTRUMENTS...

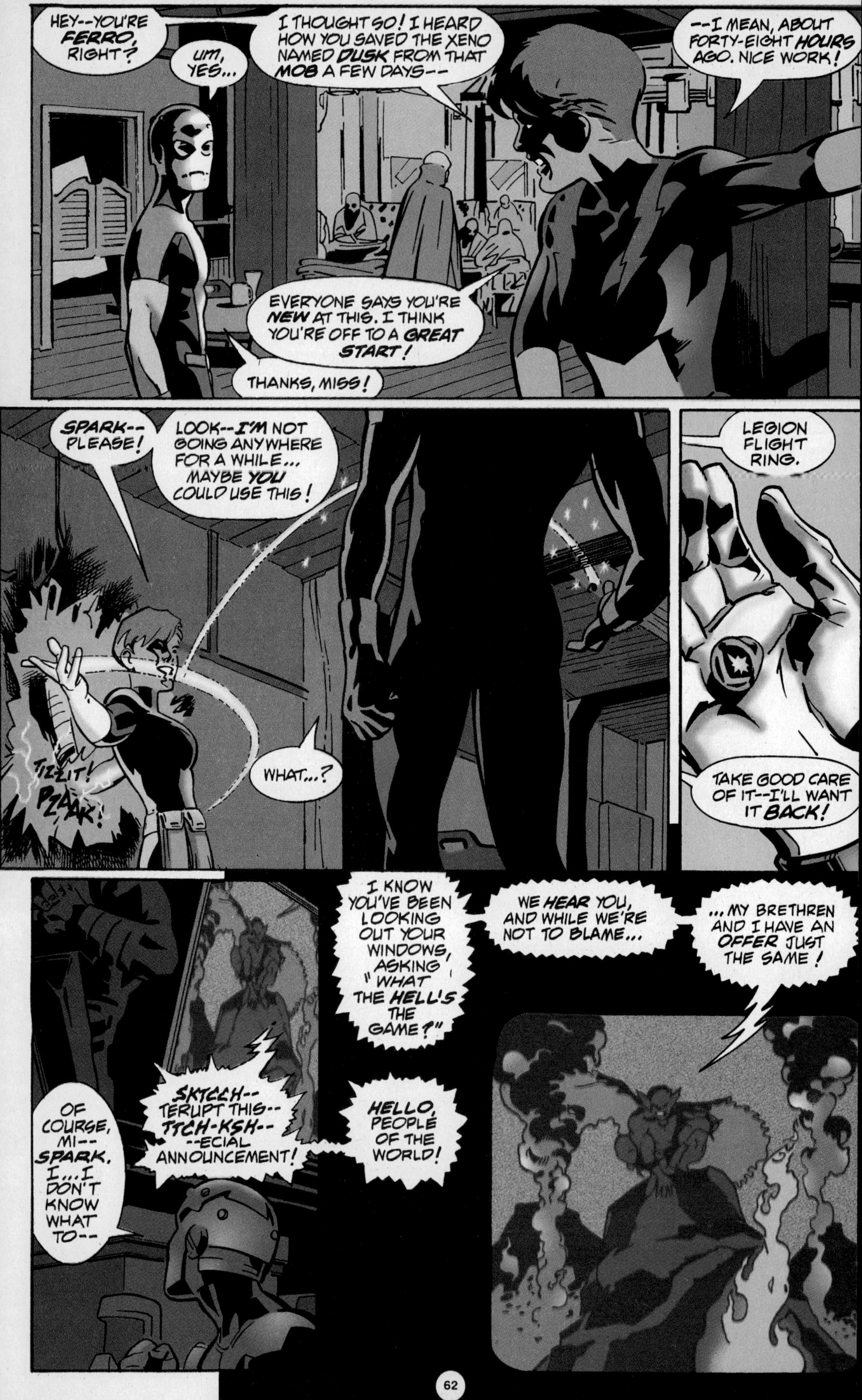

HEY--YOU'RE FERRO, RIGHT?
UM, YES...
I THOUGHT SO! I HEARD HOW YOU SAVED THE XENO NAMED DUSK FROM THAT MOB A FEW DAYS--
--I MEAN, ABOUT FORTY-EIGHT HOURS AGO. NICE WORK!
EVERYONE SAYS YOU'RE NEW AT THIS. I THINK YOU'RE OFF TO A GREAT START!
THANKS, MISS!
SPARK--PLEASE!
LOOK--I'M NOT GOING ANYWHERE FOR A WHILE... MAYBE YOU COULD USE THIS!
TIZZIT!
PZAAK!
WHAT...?
LEGION FLIGHT RING.
TAKE GOOD CARE OF IT--I'LL WANT IT BACK!
OF COURSE, MI--SPARK. I...I DON'T KNOW WHAT TO--
SKTCCH--TERUPT THIS--TTCH-KSH----ECIAL ANNOUNCEMENT!
HELLO, PEOPLE OF THE WORLD!
I KNOW YOU'VE BEEN LOOKING OUT YOUR WINDOWS, ASKING "WHAT THE HELL'S THE GAME?"
WE HEAR YOU, AND WHILE WE'RE NOT TO BLAME...
...MY BRETHREN AND I HAVE AN OFFER JUST THE SAME!

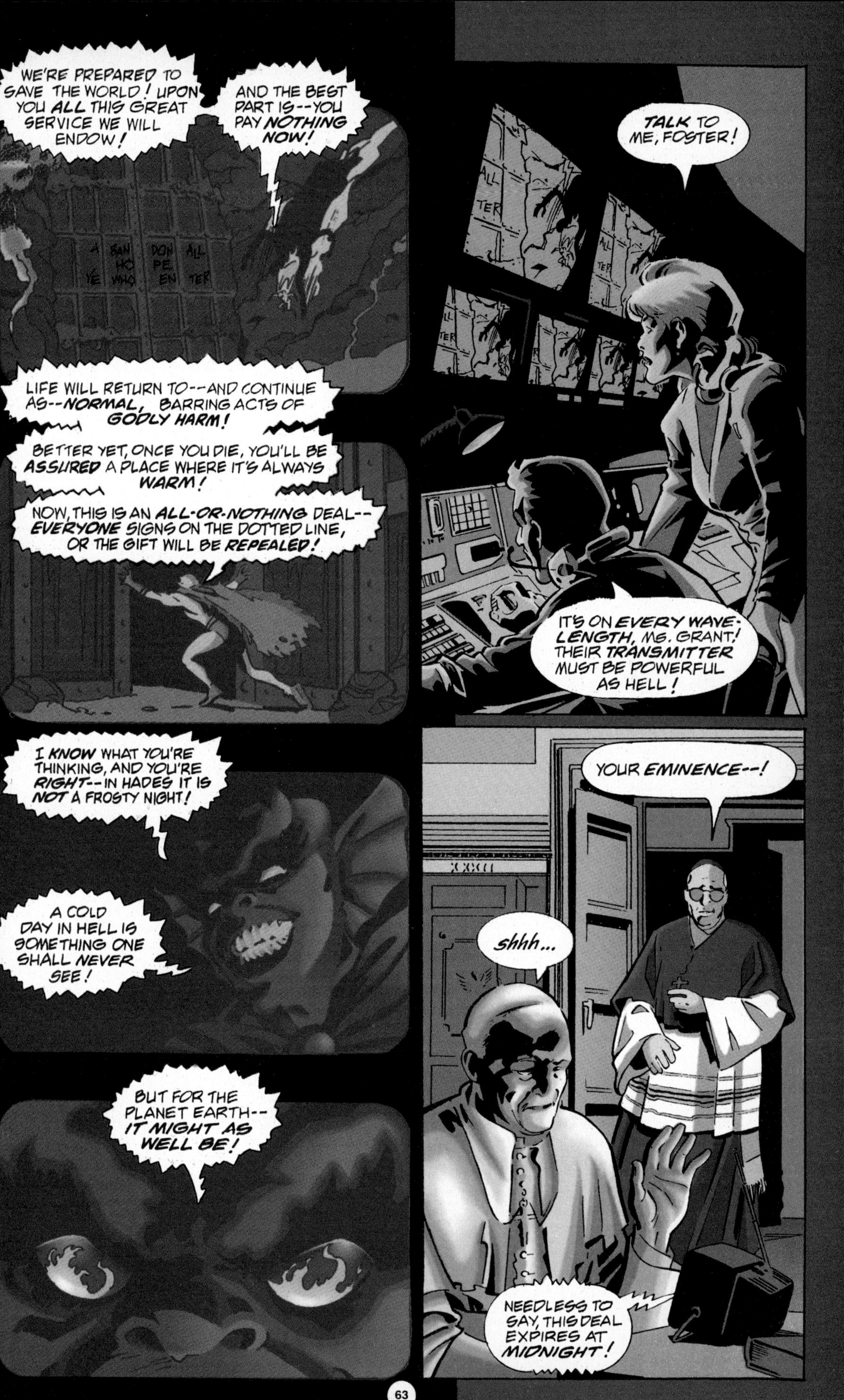
WE'RE PREPARED TO SAVE THE WORLD! UPON YOU ALL THIS GREAT SERVICE WE WILL ENDOW!
AND THE BEST PART IS--YOU PAY NOTHING NOW!
TALK TO ME, FOSTER!
LIFE WILL RETURN TO--AND CONTINUE AS--NORMAL, BARRING ACTS OF GODLY HARM!
BETTER YET, ONCE YOU DIE, YOU'LL BE ASSURED A PLACE WHERE IT'S ALWAYS WARM!
NOW, THIS IS AN ALL-OR-NOTHING DEAL--EVERYONE SIGNS ON THE DOTTED LINE, OR THE GIFT WILL BE REPEALED!
IT'S ON EVERY WAVE-LENGTH, MS. GRANT! THEIR TRANSMITTER MUST BE POWERFUL AS HELL!
I KNOW WHAT YOU'RE THINKING, AND YOU'RE RIGHT--IN HADES IT IS NOT A FROSTY NIGHT!
YOUR EMINENCE--!
A COLD DAY IN HELL IS SOMETHING ONE SHALL NEVER SEE!
shhh...
BUT FOR THE PLANET EARTH--IT MIGHT AS WELL BE!
NEEDLESS TO SAY, THIS DEAL EXPIRES AT MIDNIGHT!

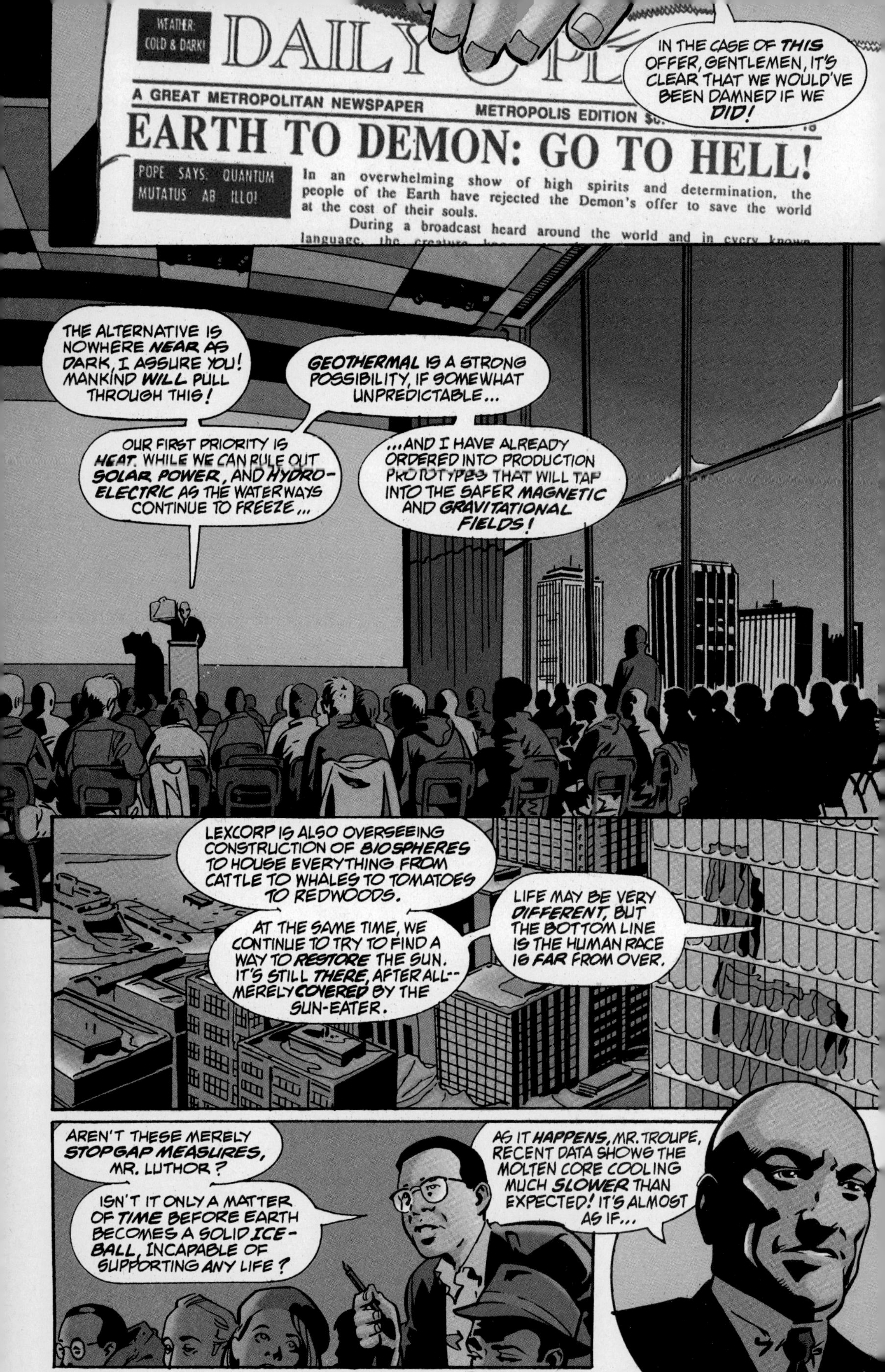
WEATHER: COLD & DARK!
DAILY
A GREAT METROPOLITAN NEWSPAPER
METROPOLIS EDITION
EARTH TO DEMON: GO TO HELL!
POPE SAYS: QUANTUM MUTATUS AB ILLO!
In an overwhelming show of high spirits and determination, the people of the Earth have rejected the Demon's offer to save the world at the cost of their souls.
During a broadcast heard around the world and in every known
IN THE CASE OF THIS OFFER, GENTLEMEN, IT'S CLEAR THAT WE WOULD'VE BEEN DAMNED IF WE DID!
THE ALTERNATIVE IS NOWHERE NEAR AS DARK, I ASSURE YOU! MANKIND WILL PULL THROUGH THIS!
OUR FIRST PRIORITY IS HEAT. WHILE WE CAN RULE OUT SOLAR POWER, AND HYDRO-ELECTRIC AS THE WATERWAYS CONTINUE TO FREEZE...
GEOTHERMAL IS A STRONG POSSIBILITY, IF SOMEWHAT UNPREDICTABLE...
...AND I HAVE ALREADY ORDERED INTO PRODUCTION PROTOTYPES THAT WILL TAP INTO THE SAFER MAGNETIC AND GRAVITATIONAL FIELDS!
LEXCORP IS ALSO OVERSEEING CONSTRUCTION OF BIOSPHERES TO HOUSE EVERYTHING FROM CATTLE TO WHALES TO TOMATOES TO REDWOODS.
AT THE SAME TIME, WE CONTINUE TO TRY TO FIND A WAY TO RESTORE THE SUN. IT'S STILL THERE, AFTER ALL-- MERELY COVERED BY THE SUN-EATER.
LIFE MAY BE VERY DIFFERENT, BUT THE BOTTOM LINE IS THE HUMAN RACE IS FAR FROM OVER.
AREN'T THESE MERELY STOPGAP MEASURES, MR. LUTHOR?
ISN'T IT ONLY A MATTER OF TIME BEFORE EARTH BECOMES A SOLID ICE-BALL, INCAPABLE OF SUPPORTING ANY LIFE?
AS IT HAPPENS, MR. TROUPE, RECENT DATA SHOWS THE MOLTEN CORE COOLING MUCH SLOWER THAN EXPECTED! IT'S ALMOST AS IF...

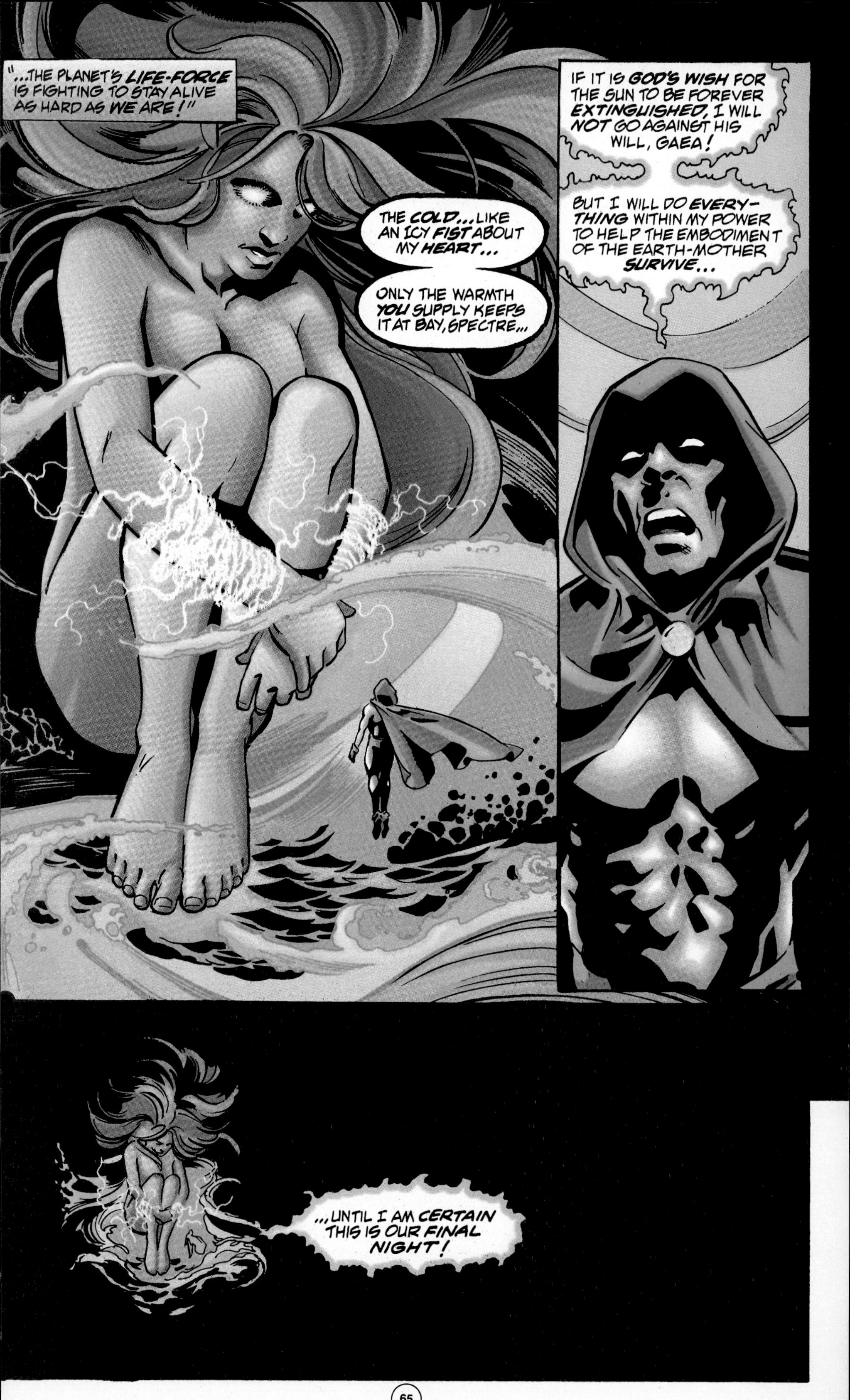
"...THE PLANET'S LIFE-FORCE IS FIGHTING TO STAY ALIVE AS HARD AS WE ARE!"
THE COLD... LIKE AN ICY FIST ABOUT MY HEART...
ONLY THE WARMTH YOU SUPPLY KEEPS IT AT BAY, SPECTRE...
IF IT IS GOD'S WISH FOR THE SUN TO BE FOREVER EXTINGUISHED, I WILL NOT GO AGAINST HIS WILL, GAEA!
BUT I WILL DO EVERYTHING WITHIN MY POWER TO HELP THE EMBODIMENT OF THE EARTH-MOTHER SURVIVE...
...UNTIL I AM CERTAIN THIS IS OUR FINAL NIGHT!

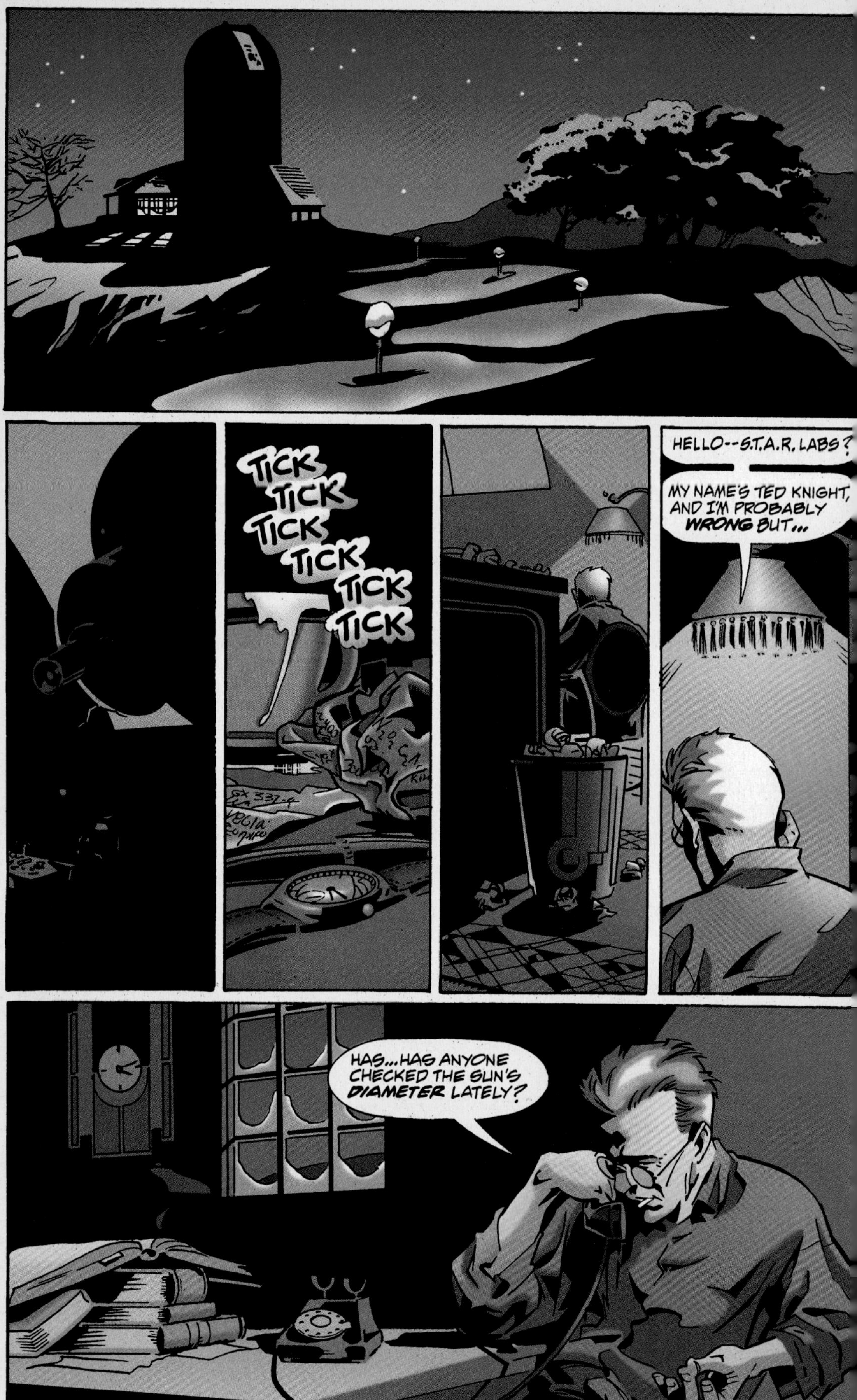
TICK TICK TICK TICK TICK TICK
HELLO--S.T.A.R. LABS?
MY NAME'S TED KNIGHT, AND I'M PROBABLY WRONG BUT...
HAS...HAS ANYONE CHECKED THE SUN'S DIAMETER LATELY?

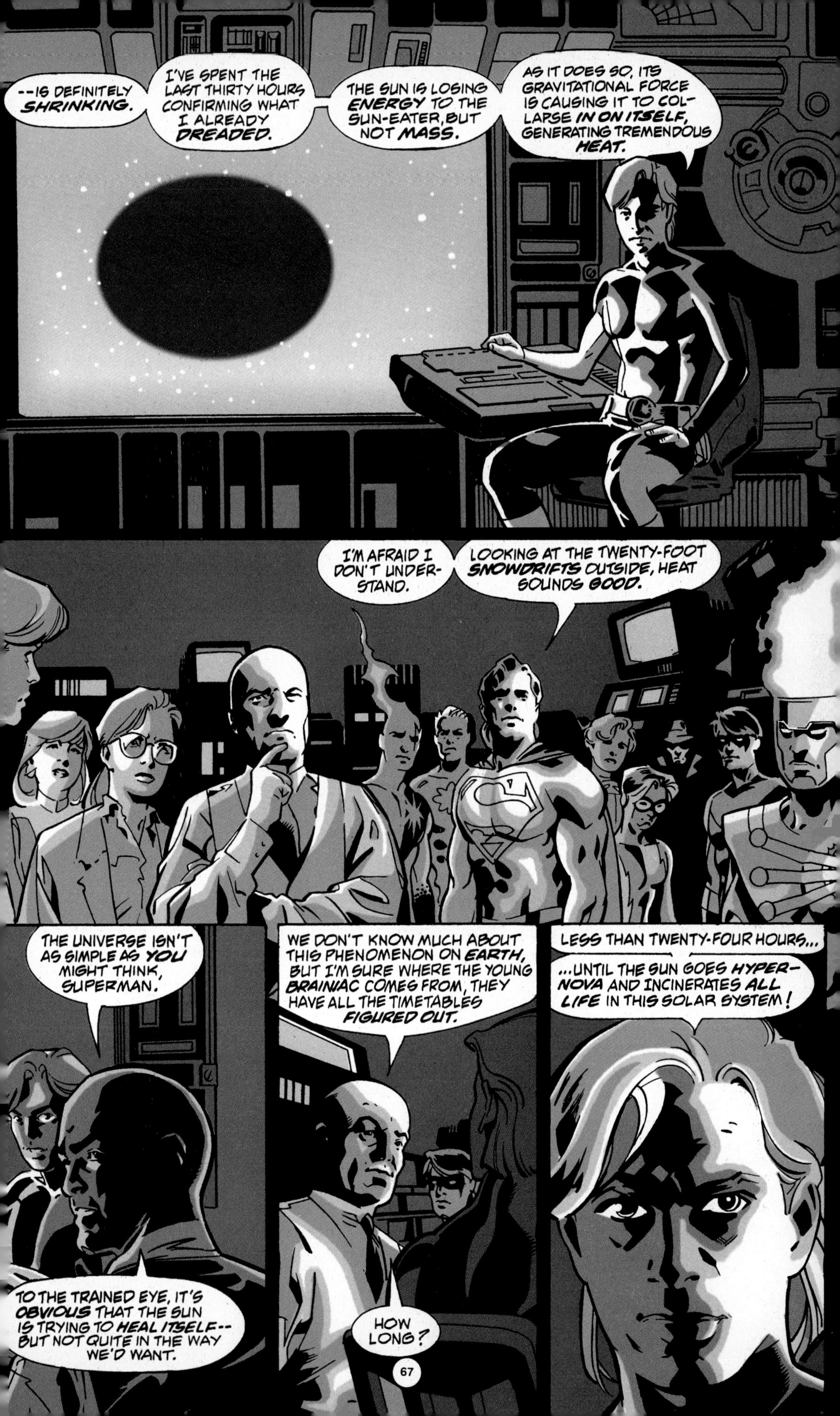
--IS DEFINITELY SHRINKING.
I'VE SPENT THE LAST THIRTY HOURS CONFIRMING WHAT I ALREADY DREADED.
THE SUN IS LOSING ENERGY TO THE SUN-EATER, BUT NOT MASS.
AS IT DOES SO, ITS GRAVITATIONAL FORCE IS CAUSING IT TO COLLAPSE IN ON ITSELF, GENERATING TREMENDOUS HEAT.
I'M AFRAID I DON'T UNDERSTAND.
LOOKING AT THE TWENTY-FOOT SNOWDRIFTS OUTSIDE, HEAT SOUNDS GOOD.
THE UNIVERSE ISN'T AS SIMPLE AS YOU MIGHT THINK, SUPERMAN.
TO THE TRAINED EYE, IT'S OBVIOUS THAT THE SUN IS TRYING TO HEAL ITSELF--BUT NOT QUITE IN THE WAY WE'D WANT.
WE DON'T KNOW MUCH ABOUT THIS PHENOMENON ON EARTH, BUT I'M SURE WHERE THE YOUNG BRAINIAC COMES FROM, THEY HAVE ALL THE TIMETABLES FIGURED OUT.
HOW LONG?
LESS THAN TWENTY-FOUR HOURS...
...UNTIL THE SUN GOES HYPERNOVA AND INCINERATES ALL LIFE IN THIS SOLAR SYSTEM!

HOW CAN YOU JUST *STAND* THERE, LUTHOR? WE MUST BE ABLE TO DO *SOMETHING!*

THE *GOOD* NEWS IS WE CERTAINLY WON'T NEED TO WORRY ABOUT *FREEZING.*

HM. I SUSPECT THE *NOVA* IS WHAT HURTLES THE SUN-EATER BACK THROUGH SPACE TOWARD ITS *NEXT* ENERGY SOURCE...

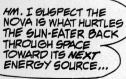

"WE," KEMO SABE?

WITHOUT THE SUN YOUR POWERS ARE NEARLY *GONE.*

I REALLY THINK YOU SHOULD LEAVE THIS TO THE *BIG BOYS...*

DR. FAULKNER, BRAINIAC, TAKION, COSMIC BOY--IF YOU AND THOSE *LIKE* YOU WOULD FOLLOW *ME* ? THE CLOCK IS *TICKING* ...

AND WITH ANY LUCK IT'S A *TIME BOMB* AND IT'LL GO OFF RIGHT *UNDER* THAT EGOTISTICAL--

NO, BLACK CANARY--LUTHOR'S *RIGHT.* WE ALL HAVE TO DO WHAT'S WITHIN OUR *POWER* TO DO.

AND WE ALL HAVE TO MAKE *CHOICES*-- THESE NEXT FEW HOURS COULD BE EARTH'S *LAST.*

ORACLE ? SUPERMAN.

THERE'S SOMETHING ALL THE *FIELD TEAMS* NEED TO KNOW.

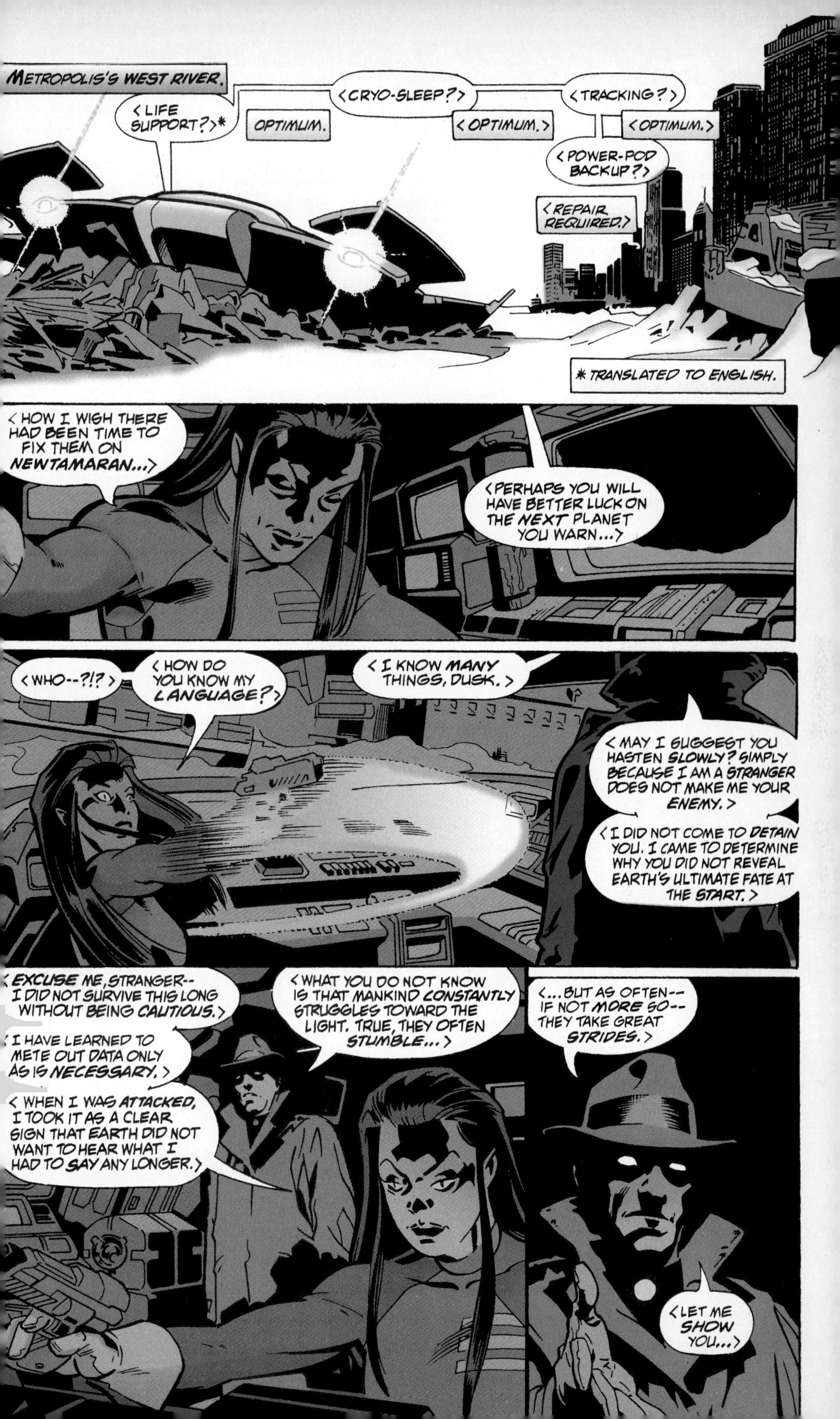
METROPOLIS'S WEST RIVER.
< LIFE SUPPORT? >*
OPTIMUM.
< CRYO-SLEEP? >
< OPTIMUM. >
< TRACKING? >
< OPTIMUM. >
< POWER-POD BACKUP? >
< REPAIR REQUIRED. >
* TRANSLATED TO ENGLISH.
< HOW I WISH THERE HAD BEEN TIME TO FIX THEM ON NEWTAMARAN... >
< PERHAPS YOU WILL HAVE BETTER LUCK ON THE NEXT PLANET YOU WARN... >
< WHO--?!? >
< HOW DO YOU KNOW MY LANGUAGE? >
< I KNOW MANY THINGS, DUSK. >
< MAY I SUGGEST YOU HASTEN SLOWLY? SIMPLY BECAUSE I AM A STRANGER DOES NOT MAKE ME YOUR ENEMY. >
< I DID NOT COME TO DETAIN YOU. I CAME TO DETERMINE WHY YOU DID NOT REVEAL EARTH'S ULTIMATE FATE AT THE START. >
< EXCUSE ME, STRANGER-- I DID NOT SURVIVE THIS LONG WITHOUT BEING CAUTIOUS. >
< I HAVE LEARNED TO METE OUT DATA ONLY AS IS NECESSARY. >
< WHEN I WAS ATTACKED, I TOOK IT AS A CLEAR SIGN THAT EARTH DID NOT WANT TO HEAR WHAT I HAD TO SAY ANY LONGER. >
< WHAT YOU DO NOT KNOW IS THAT MANKIND CONSTANTLY STRUGGLES TOWARD THE LIGHT. TRUE, THEY OFTEN STUMBLE... >
< ...BUT AS OFTEN-- IF NOT MORE SO-- THEY TAKE GREAT STRIDES. >
< LET ME SHOW YOU... >

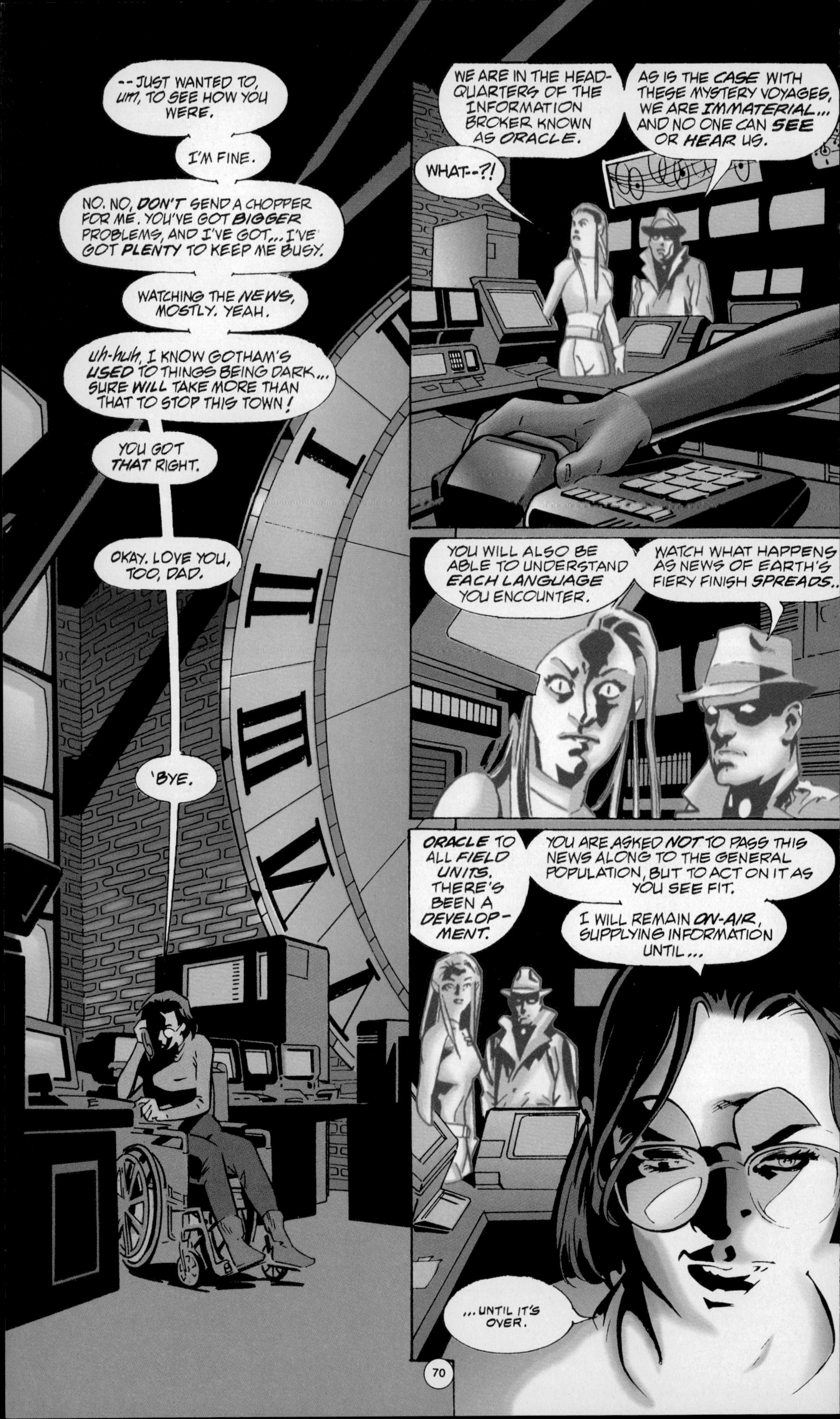
--JUST WANTED TO, UM, TO SEE HOW YOU WERE.
I'M FINE.
NO. NO, DON'T SEND A CHOPPER FOR ME. YOU'VE GOT BIGGER PROBLEMS, AND I'VE GOT... I'VE GOT PLENTY TO KEEP ME BUSY.
WATCHING THE NEWS, MOSTLY. YEAH.
UH-HUH, I KNOW GOTHAM'S USED TO THINGS BEING DARK... SURE WILL TAKE MORE THAN THAT TO STOP THIS TOWN!
YOU GOT THAT RIGHT.
OKAY. LOVE YOU, TOO, DAD.
'BYE.
WE ARE IN THE HEAD-QUARTERS OF THE INFORMATION BROKER KNOWN AS ORACLE.
AS IS THE CASE WITH THESE MYSTERY VOYAGES, WE ARE IMMATERIAL... AND NO ONE CAN SEE OR HEAR US.
WHAT--?!
YOU WILL ALSO BE ABLE TO UNDERSTAND EACH LANGUAGE YOU ENCOUNTER.
WATCH WHAT HAPPENS AS NEWS OF EARTH'S FIERY FINISH SPREADS...
ORACLE TO ALL FIELD UNITS. THERE'S BEEN A DEVELOPMENT.
YOU ARE ASKED NOT TO PASS THIS NEWS ALONG TO THE GENERAL POPULATION, BUT TO ACT ON IT AS YOU SEE FIT.
I WILL REMAIN ON-AIR, SUPPLYING INFORMATION UNTIL...
...UNTIL IT'S OVER.

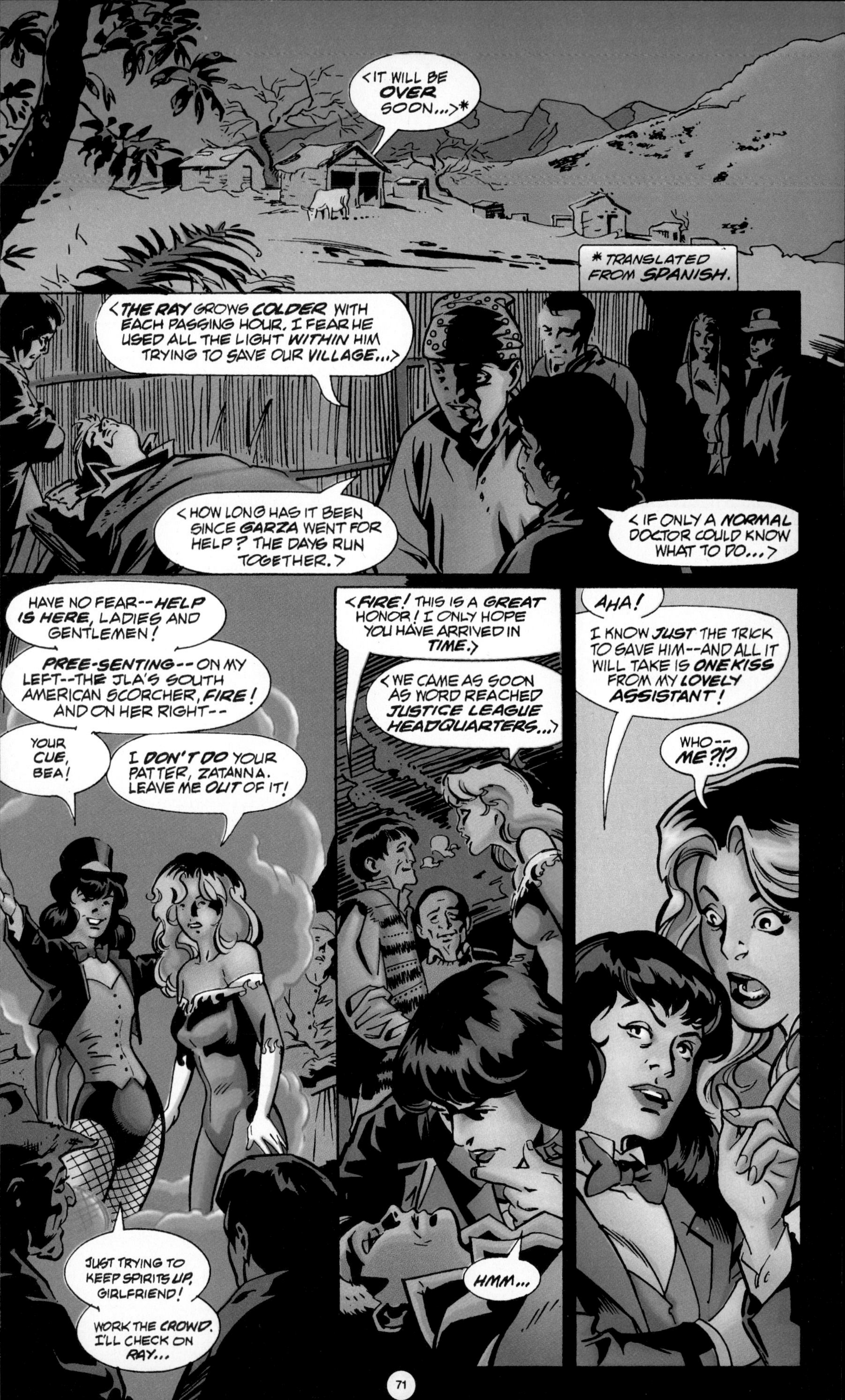

<IT WILL BE OVER SOON...>*
* TRANSLATED FROM SPANISH.
<THE RAY GROWS COLDER WITH EACH PASSING HOUR. I FEAR HE USED ALL THE LIGHT WITHIN HIM TRYING TO SAVE OUR VILLAGE...>
<HOW LONG HAS IT BEEN SINCE GARZA WENT FOR HELP? THE DAYS RUN TOGETHER.>
<IF ONLY A NORMAL DOCTOR COULD KNOW WHAT TO DO...>
HAVE NO FEAR--HELP IS HERE, LADIES AND GENTLEMEN!
PREE-SENTING--ON MY LEFT--THE JLA'S SOUTH AMERICAN SCORCHER, FIRE! AND ON HER RIGHT--
YOUR CUE, BEA!
I DON'T DO YOUR PATTER, ZATANNA. LEAVE ME OUT OF IT!
JUST TRYING TO KEEP SPIRITS UP, GIRLFRIEND!
WORK THE CROWD. I'LL CHECK ON RAY...
<FIRE! THIS IS A GREAT HONOR! I ONLY HOPE YOU HAVE ARRIVED IN TIME.>
<WE CAME AS SOON AS WORD REACHED JUSTICE LEAGUE HEADQUARTERS...>
HMM...
AHA!
I KNOW JUST THE TRICK TO SAVE HIM--AND ALL IT WILL TAKE IS ONE KISS FROM MY LOVELY ASSISTANT!
WHO--ME?!?

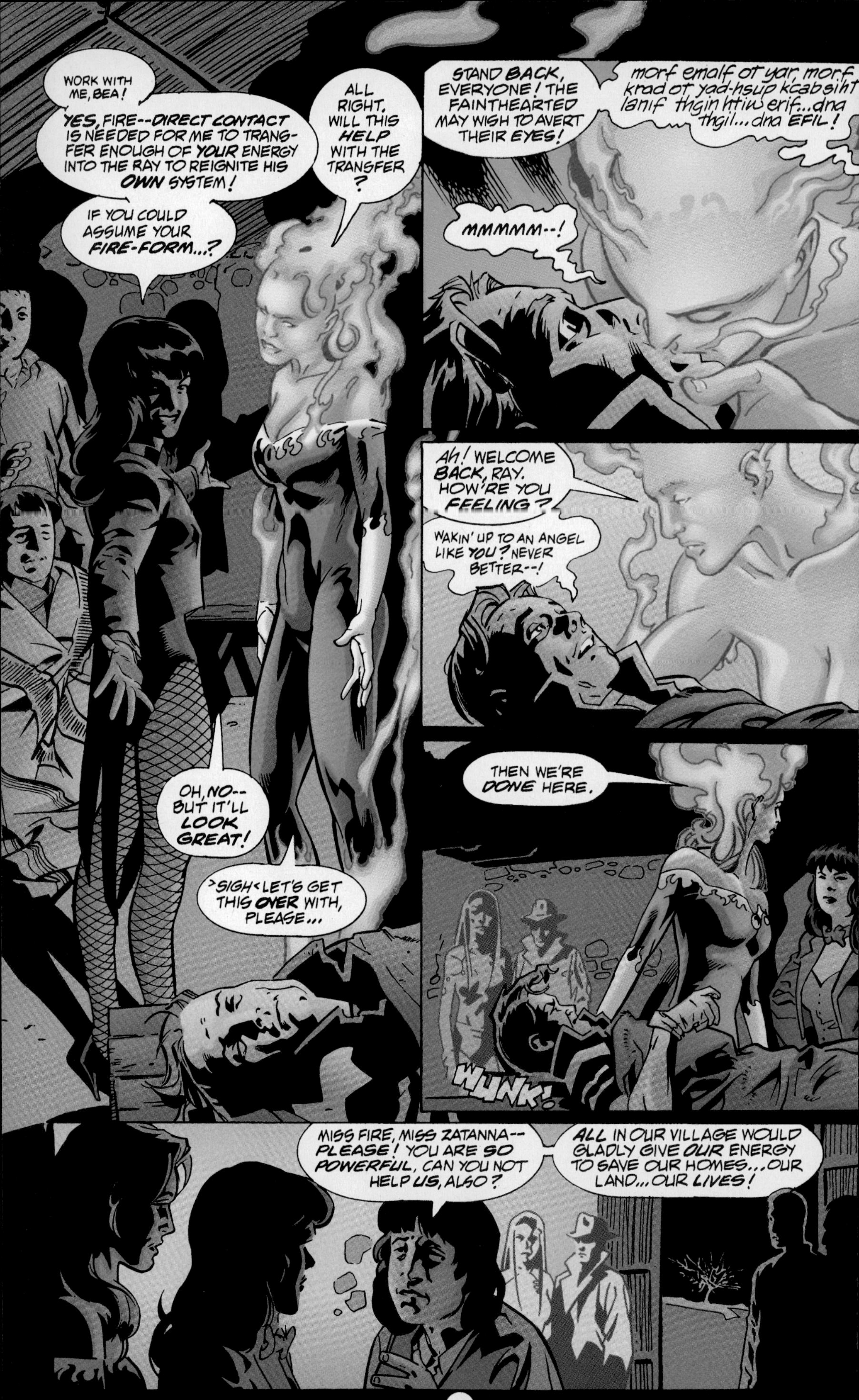
WORK WITH ME, BEA!
YES, FIRE--DIRECT CONTACT IS NEEDED FOR ME TO TRANS-FER ENOUGH OF YOUR ENERGY INTO THE RAY TO REIGNITE HIS OWN SYSTEM!
IF YOU COULD ASSUME YOUR FIRE-FORM...?
ALL RIGHT. WILL THIS HELP WITH THE TRANSFER?
OH, NO-- BUT IT'LL LOOK GREAT!
>SIGH< LET'S GET THIS OVER WITH, PLEASE...
STAND BACK, EVERYONE! THE FAINTHEARTED MAY WISH TO AVERT THEIR EYES!
morf emalf ot yar, morf krad ot yad-hsup kcabsiht lanif thgin htiw erif...dna thgil...dna EFIL!
MMMMM--!
Ah! WELCOME BACK, RAY. HOW'RE YOU FEELING?
WAKIN' UP TO AN ANGEL LIKE YOU? NEVER BETTER--!
THEN WE'RE DONE HERE.
WUNK!
MISS FIRE, MISS ZATANNA-- PLEASE! YOU ARE SO POWERFUL, CAN YOU NOT HELP US, ALSO?
ALL IN OUR VILLAGE WOULD GLADLY GIVE OUR ENERGY TO SAVE OUR HOMES...OUR LAND...OUR LIVES!

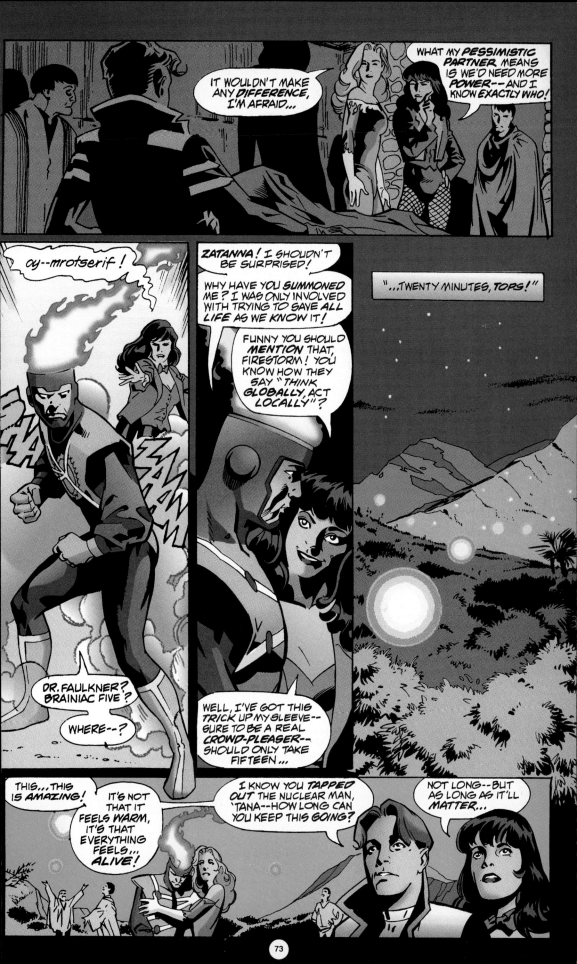

IT WOULDN'T MAKE ANY *DIFFERENCE*, I'M AFRAID...

WHAT MY *PESSIMISTIC PARTNER* MEANS IS WE'D NEED MORE *POWER*-- AND I KNOW *EXACTLY* WHO!

oy--mrotserif!

ZATANNA! I SHOULDN'T BE SURPRISED!

WHY HAVE YOU *SUMMONED* ME? I WAS ONLY INVOLVED WITH TRYING TO SAVE *ALL LIFE* AS WE KNOW IT!

FUNNY YOU SHOULD *MENTION* THAT, FIRESTORM! YOU KNOW HOW THEY SAY "*THINK GLOBALLY, ACT LOCALLY*"?

"...TWENTY MINUTES, *TOPS!*"

DR. FAULKNER? BRAINIAC FIVE?

WHERE--?

WELL, I'VE GOT THIS *TRICK* UP MY SLEEVE-- SURE TO BE A REAL *CROWD-PLEASER*-- SHOULD ONLY TAKE *FIFTEEN*...

THIS...THIS IS *AMAZING!*

IT'S NOT THAT IT FEELS WARM, IT'S THAT EVERYTHING FEELS... *ALIVE!*

I KNOW YOU *TAPPED OUT* THE NUCLEAR MAN, 'TANA--HOW LONG CAN YOU KEEP THIS GOING?

NOT LONG--BUT AS LONG AS IT'LL *MATTER*...

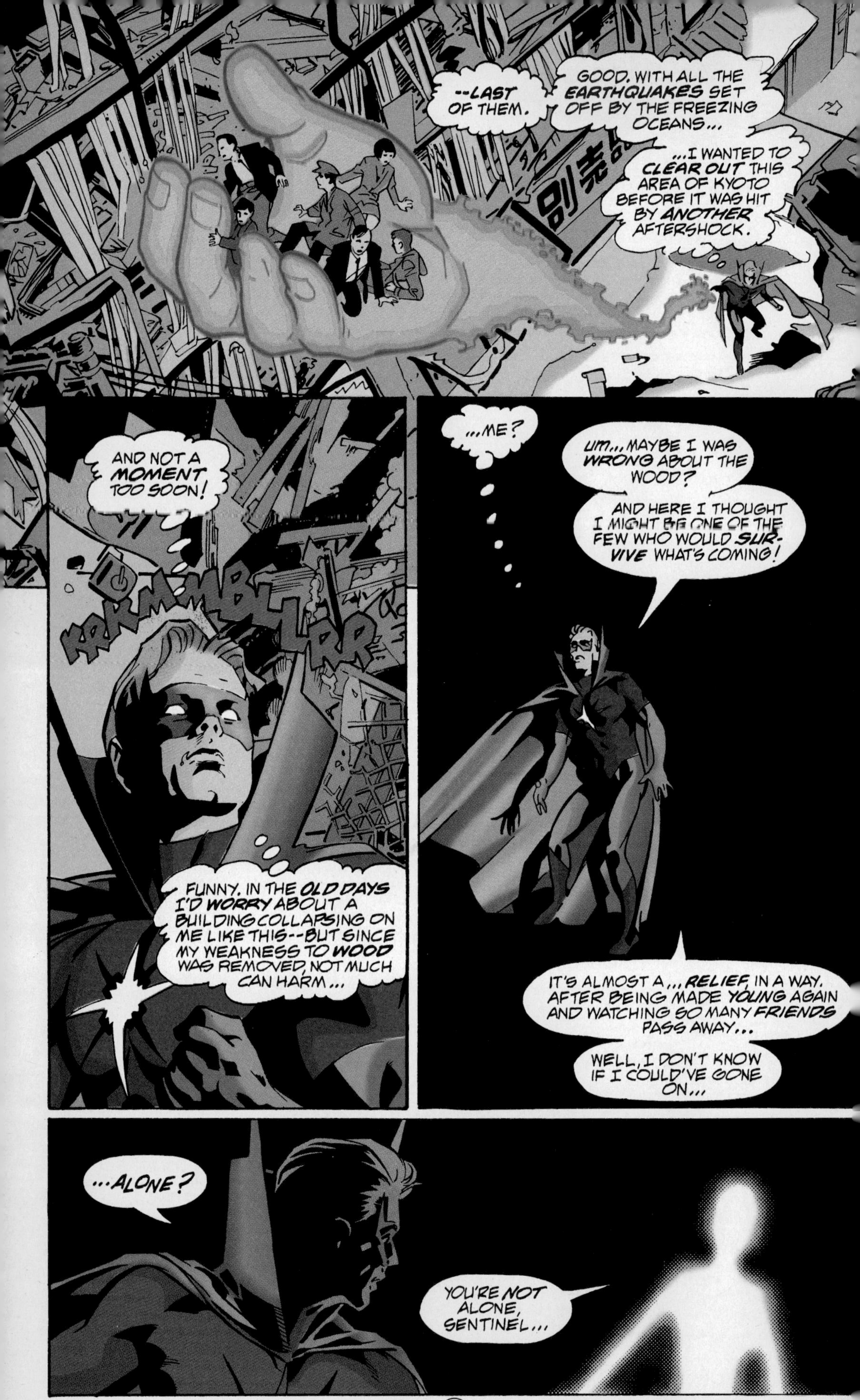
--LAST OF THEM.
GOOD. WITH ALL THE EARTHQUAKES SET OFF BY THE FREEZING OCEANS...
...I WANTED TO CLEAR OUT THIS AREA OF KYOTO BEFORE IT WAS HIT BY ANOTHER AFTERSHOCK.
AND NOT A MOMENT TOO SOON!
KRKMMBLLRR
FUNNY. IN THE OLD DAYS I'D WORRY ABOUT A BUILDING COLLAPSING ON ME LIKE THIS--BUT SINCE MY WEAKNESS TO WOOD WAS REMOVED, NOT MUCH CAN HARM...
...ME?
UM... MAYBE I WAS WRONG ABOUT THE WOOD?
AND HERE I THOUGHT I MIGHT BE ONE OF THE FEW WHO WOULD SURVIVE WHAT'S COMING!
IT'S ALMOST A... RELIEF, IN A WAY. AFTER BEING MADE YOUNG AGAIN AND WATCHING SO MANY FRIENDS PASS AWAY...
WELL, I DON'T KNOW IF I COULD'VE GONE ON...
...ALONE?
YOU'RE NOT ALONE, SENTINEL...

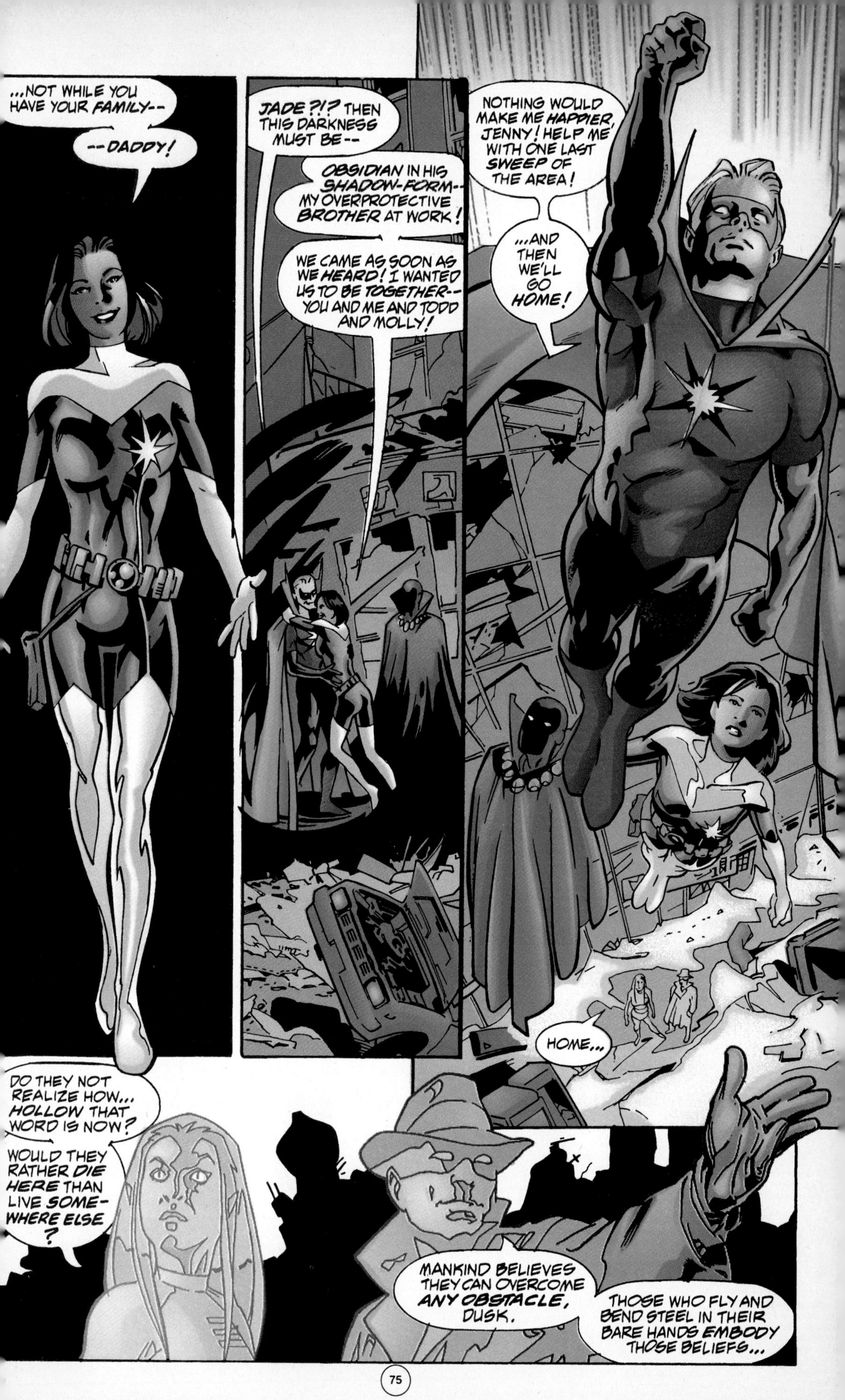

...NOT WHILE YOU HAVE YOUR FAMILY--
--DADDY!
JADE?!? THEN THIS DARKNESS MUST BE--
OBSIDIAN IN HIS SHADOW-FORM-- MY OVERPROTECTIVE BROTHER AT WORK!
WE CAME AS SOON AS WE HEARD! I WANTED US TO BE TOGETHER-- YOU AND ME AND TODD AND MOLLY!
NOTHING WOULD MAKE ME HAPPIER, JENNY! HELP ME WITH ONE LAST SWEEP OF THE AREA!
...AND THEN WE'LL GO HOME!
HOME...
DO THEY NOT REALIZE HOW... HOLLOW THAT WORD IS NOW?
WOULD THEY RATHER DIE HERE THAN LIVE SOMEWHERE ELSE?
MANKIND BELIEVES THEY CAN OVERCOME ANY OBSTACLE, DUSK.
THOSE WHO FLY AND BEND STEEL IN THEIR BARE HANDS EMBODY THOSE BELIEFS...

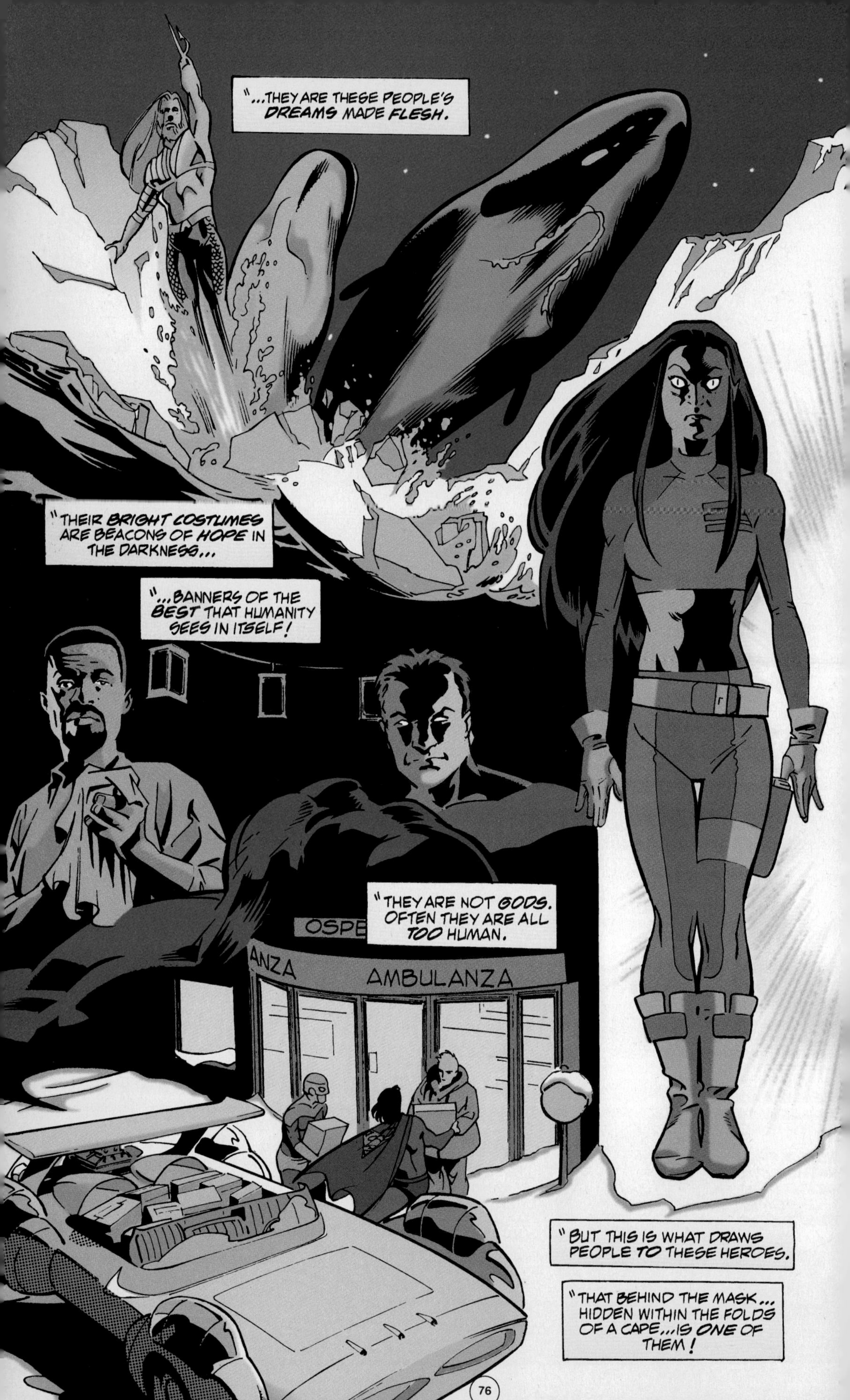
"...THEY ARE THESE PEOPLE'S DREAMS MADE FLESH.
"THEIR BRIGHT COSTUMES ARE BEACONS OF HOPE IN THE DARKNESS...
"...BANNERS OF THE BEST THAT HUMANITY SEES IN ITSELF!
"THEY ARE NOT GODS. OFTEN THEY ARE ALL TOO HUMAN.
OSPE
ANZA
AMBULANZA
"BUT THIS IS WHAT DRAWS PEOPLE TO THESE HEROES.
"THAT BEHIND THE MASK... HIDDEN WITHIN THE FOLDS OF A CAPE...IS ONE OF THEM!

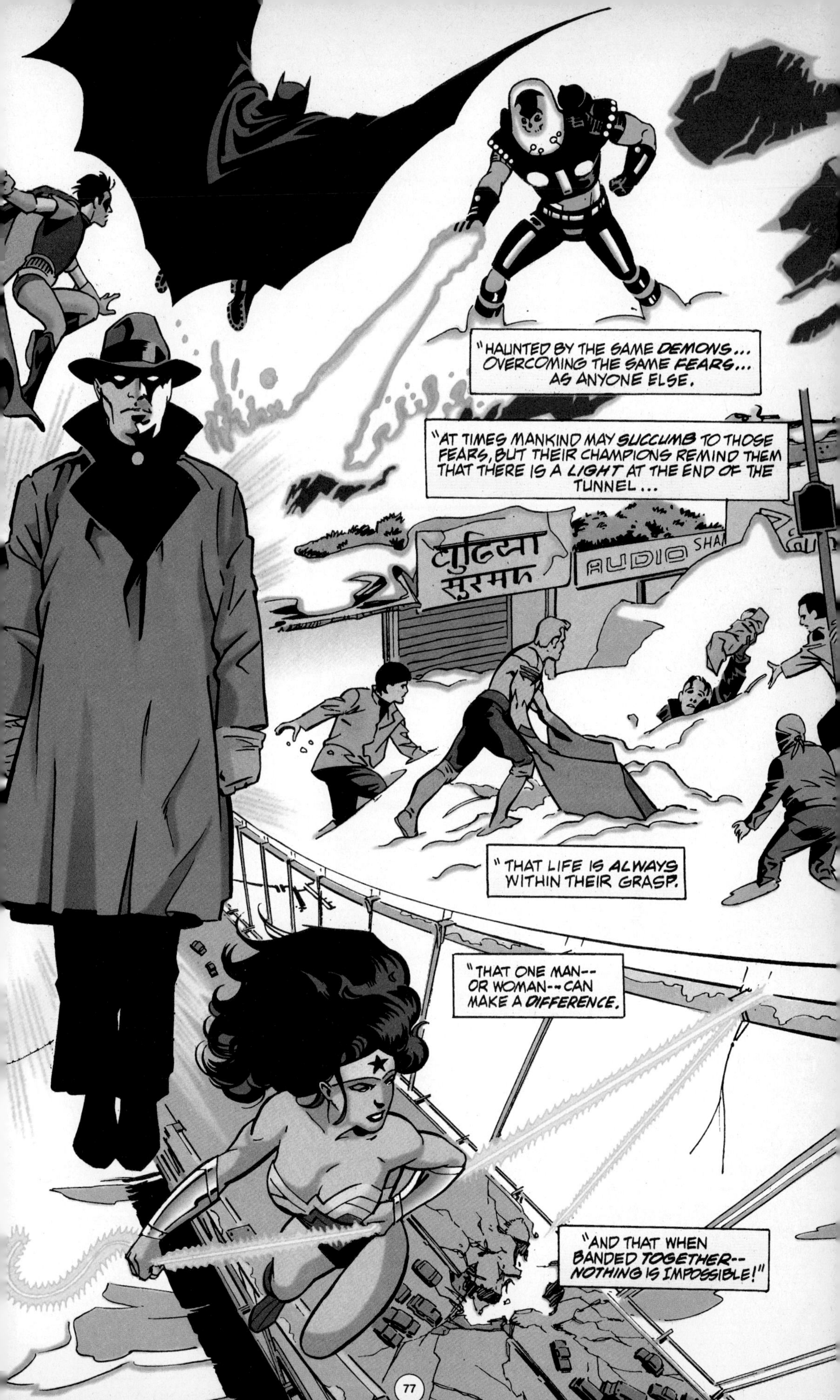
"HAUNTED BY THE SAME DEMONS... OVERCOMING THE SAME FEARS... AS ANYONE ELSE.
"AT TIMES MANKIND MAY SUCCUMB TO THOSE FEARS, BUT THEIR CHAMPIONS REMIND THEM THAT THERE IS A LIGHT AT THE END OF THE TUNNEL...
AUDIO
"THAT LIFE IS ALWAYS WITHIN THEIR GRASP.
"THAT ONE MAN-- OR WOMAN-- CAN MAKE A DIFFERENCE.
"AND THAT WHEN BANDED TOGETHER-- NOTHING IS IMPOSSIBLE!"

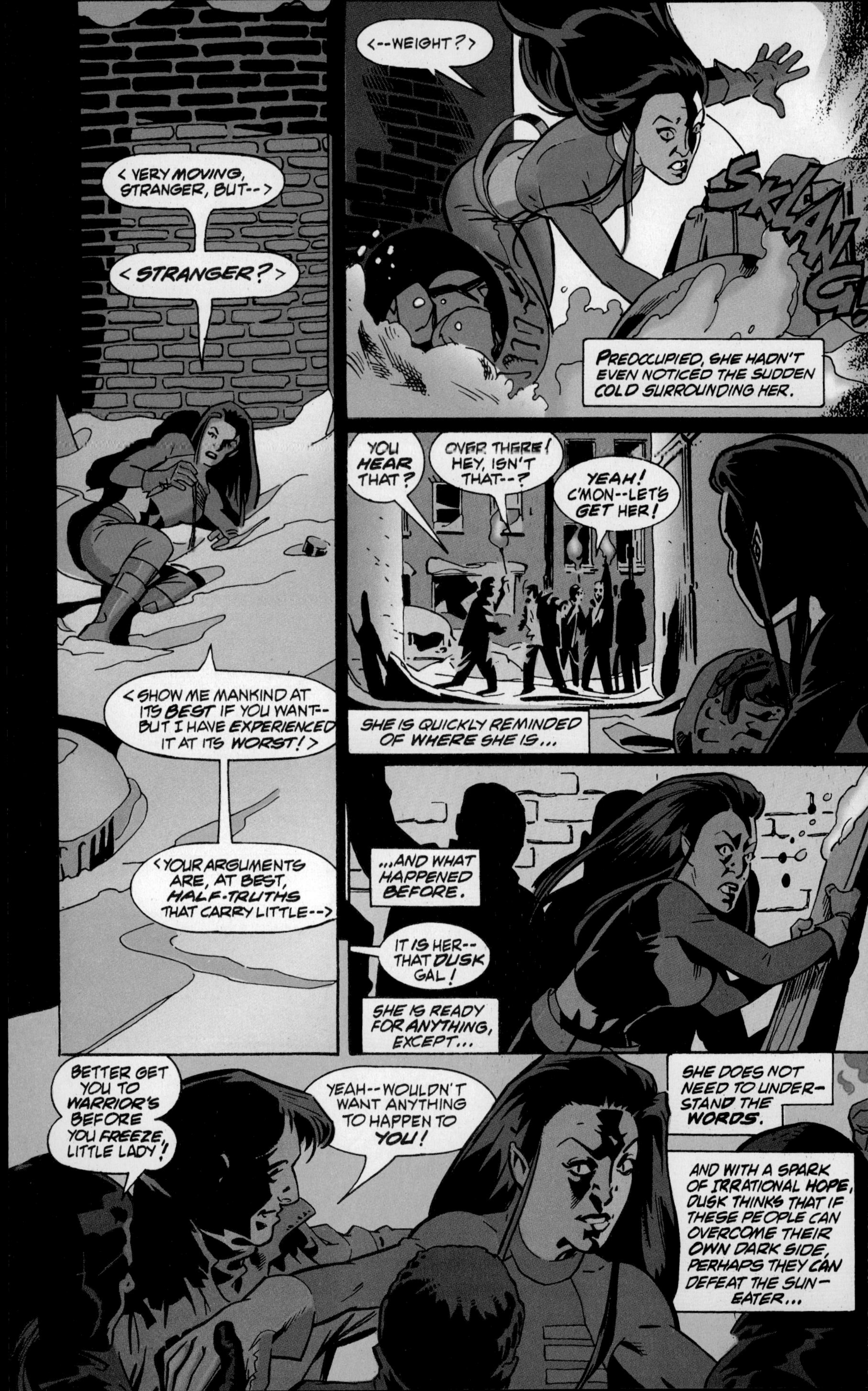
<--WEIGHT?>
SKLANG!
PREOCCUPIED, SHE HADN'T EVEN NOTICED THE SUDDEN COLD SURROUNDING HER.
< VERY MOVING, STRANGER, BUT-->
< STRANGER? >
YOU HEAR THAT?
OVER THERE! HEY, ISN'T THAT--?
YEAH! C'MON--LET'S GET HER!
SHE IS QUICKLY REMINDED OF WHERE SHE IS...
< SHOW ME MANKIND AT ITS BEST IF YOU WANT-- BUT I HAVE EXPERIENCED IT AT ITS WORST! >
< YOUR ARGUMENTS ARE, AT BEST, HALF-TRUTHS THAT CARRY LITTLE-->
...AND WHAT HAPPENED BEFORE.
IT IS HER-- THAT DUSK GAL!
SHE IS READY FOR ANYTHING, EXCEPT...
BETTER GET YOU TO WARRIOR'S BEFORE YOU FREEZE, LITTLE LADY!
YEAH--WOULDN'T WANT ANYTHING TO HAPPEN TO YOU!
SHE DOES NOT NEED TO UNDERSTAND THE WORDS.
AND WITH A SPARK OF IRRATIONAL HOPE, DUSK THINKS THAT IF THESE PEOPLE CAN OVERCOME THEIR OWN DARK SIDE, PERHAPS THEY CAN DEFEAT THE SUN-EATER...

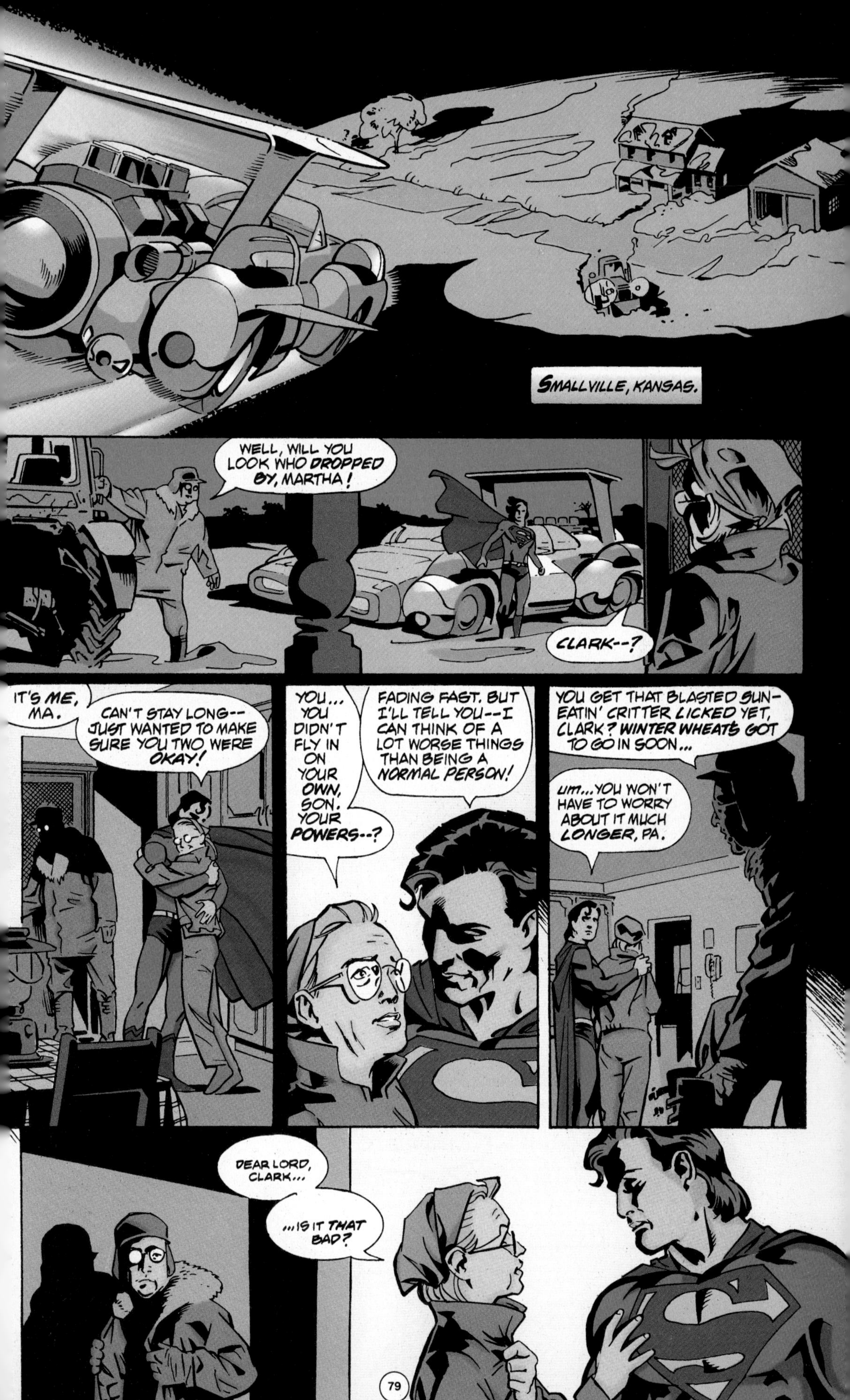

SMALLVILLE, KANSAS.
WELL, WILL YOU LOOK WHO DROPPED BY, MARTHA!
CLARK--?
IT'S ME, MA.
CAN'T STAY LONG-- JUST WANTED TO MAKE SURE YOU TWO WERE OKAY!
YOU... YOU DIDN'T FLY IN ON YOUR OWN, SON. YOUR POWERS--?
FADING FAST. BUT I'LL TELL YOU--I CAN THINK OF A LOT WORSE THINGS THAN BEING A NORMAL PERSON!
YOU GET THAT BLASTED SUN-EATIN' CRITTER LICKED YET, CLARK? WINTER WHEAT'S GOT TO GO IN SOON...
UM...YOU WON'T HAVE TO WORRY ABOUT IT MUCH LONGER, PA.
DEAR LORD, CLARK...
...IS IT THAT BAD?

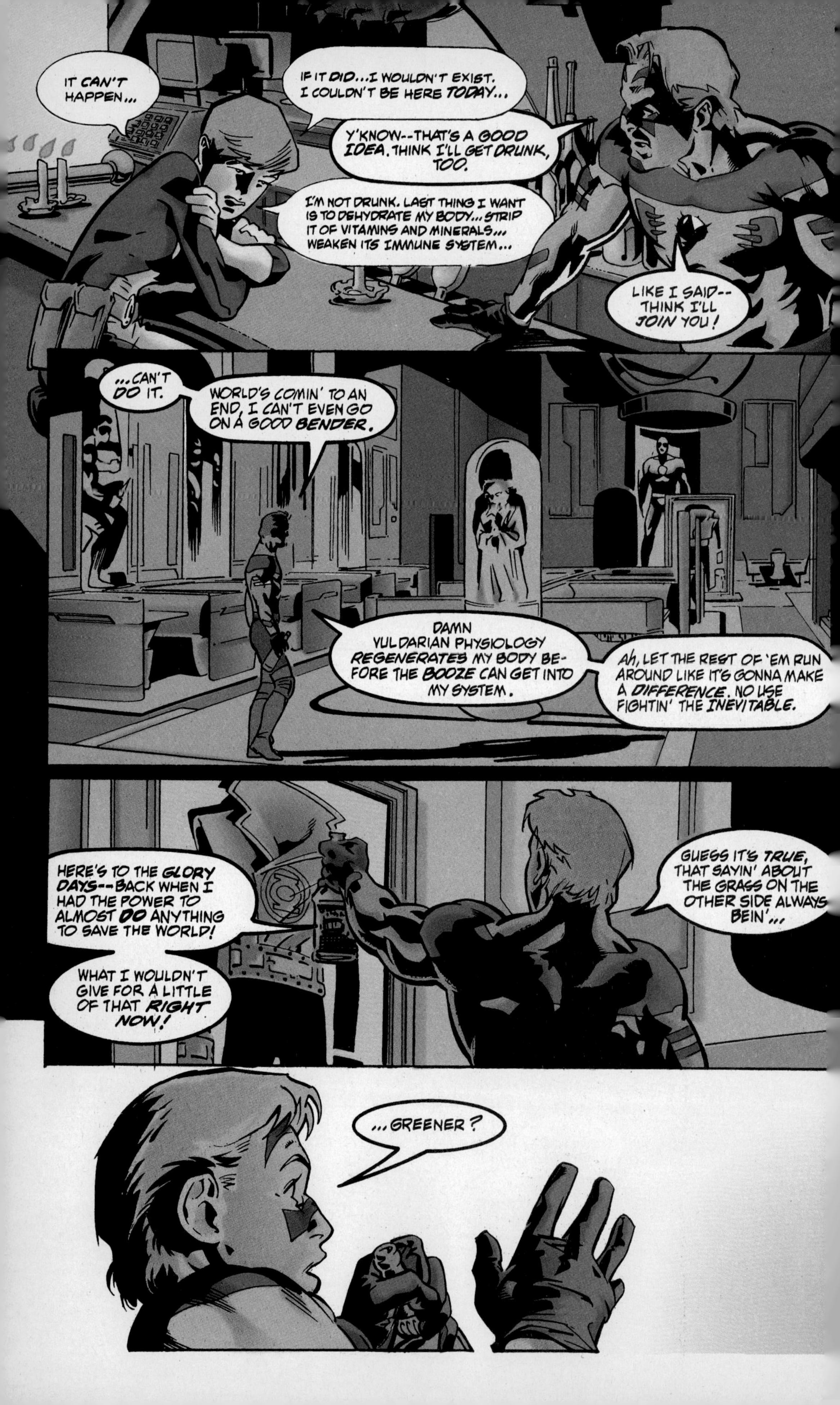
IT CAN'T HAPPEN...
IF IT DID...I WOULDN'T EXIST. I COULDN'T BE HERE TODAY...
Y'KNOW--THAT'S A GOOD IDEA. THINK I'LL GET DRUNK, TOO.
I'M NOT DRUNK. LAST THING I WANT IS TO DEHYDRATE MY BODY...STRIP IT OF VITAMINS AND MINERALS... WEAKEN ITS IMMUNE SYSTEM...
LIKE I SAID-- THINK I'LL JOIN YOU!
...CAN'T DO IT.
WORLD'S COMIN' TO AN END, I CAN'T EVEN GO ON A GOOD BENDER.
DAMN VULDARIAN PHYSIOLOGY REGENERATES MY BODY BEFORE THE BOOZE CAN GET INTO MY SYSTEM.
AH, LET THE REST OF 'EM RUN AROUND LIKE IT'S GONNA MAKE A DIFFERENCE. NO USE FIGHTIN' THE INEVITABLE.
HERE'S TO THE GLORY DAYS--BACK WHEN I HAD THE POWER TO ALMOST DO ANYTHING TO SAVE THE WORLD!
WHAT I WOULDN'T GIVE FOR A LITTLE OF THAT RIGHT NOW!
GUESS IT'S TRUE, THAT SAYIN' ABOUT THE GRASS ON THE OTHER SIDE ALWAYS BEIN'...
...GREENER?

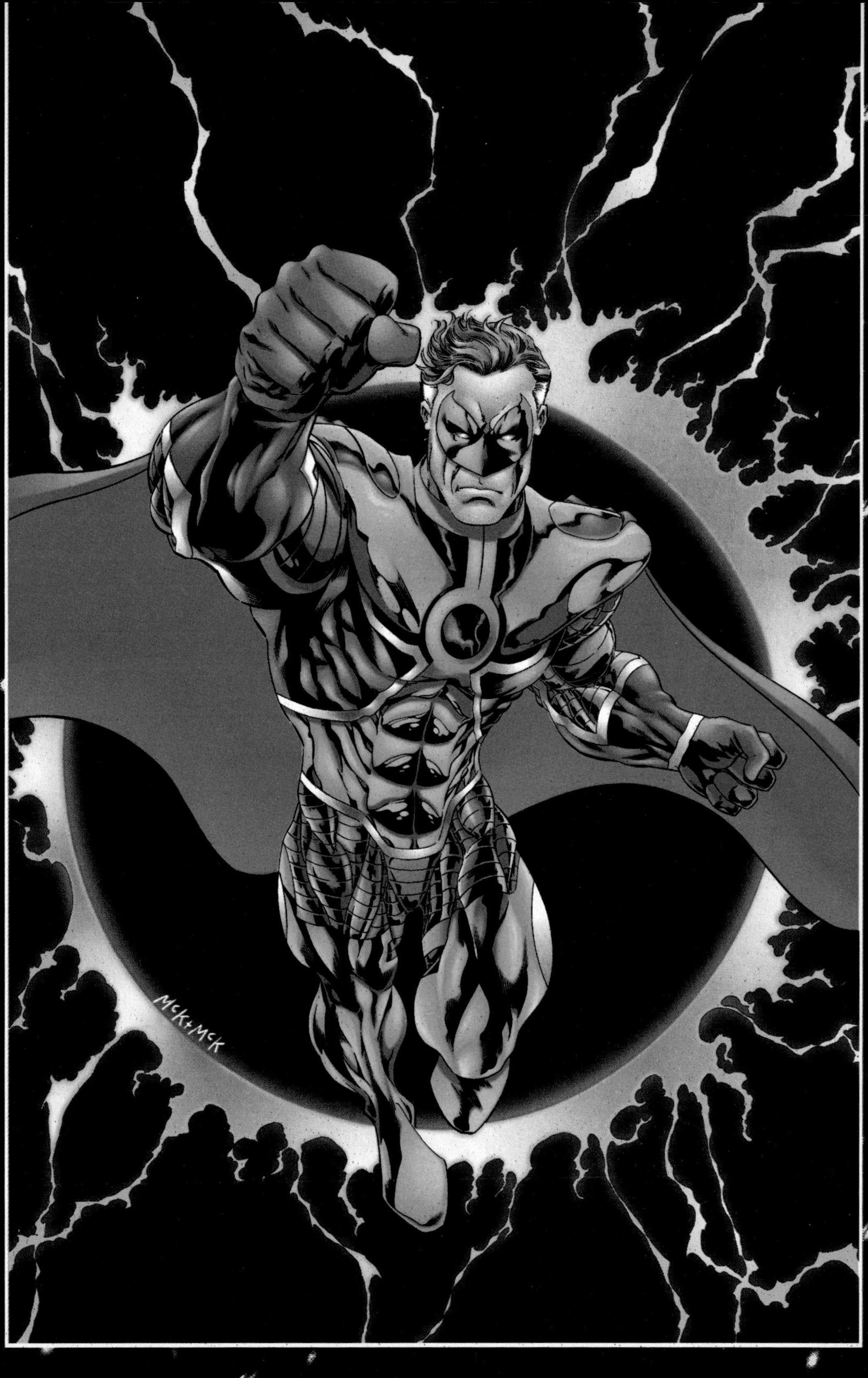
McK+McK

EMERALD NIGHT

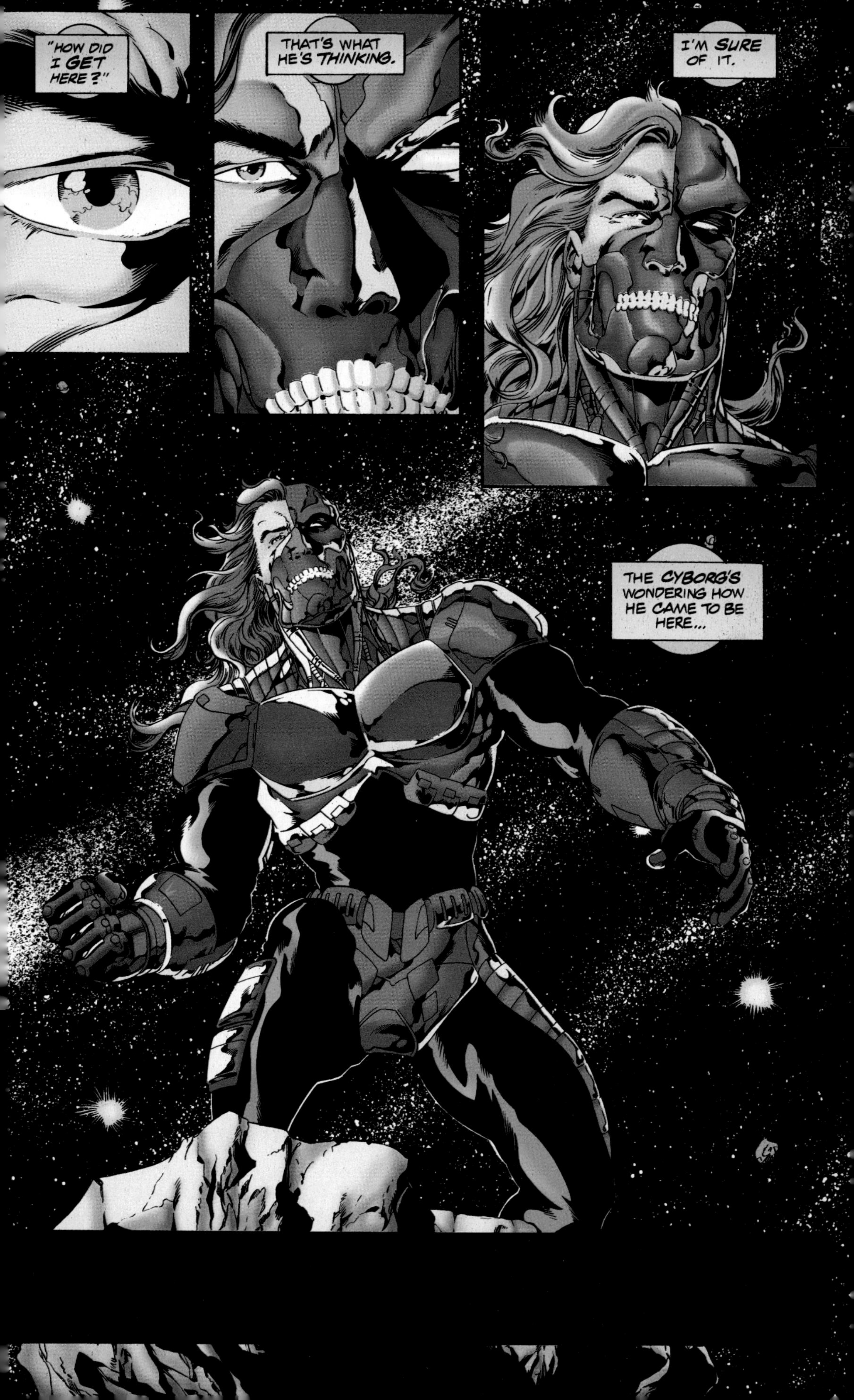
"HOW DID I GET HERE?"
THAT'S WHAT HE'S THINKING.
I'M SURE OF IT.
THE CYBORG'S WONDERING HOW HE CAME TO BE HERE...

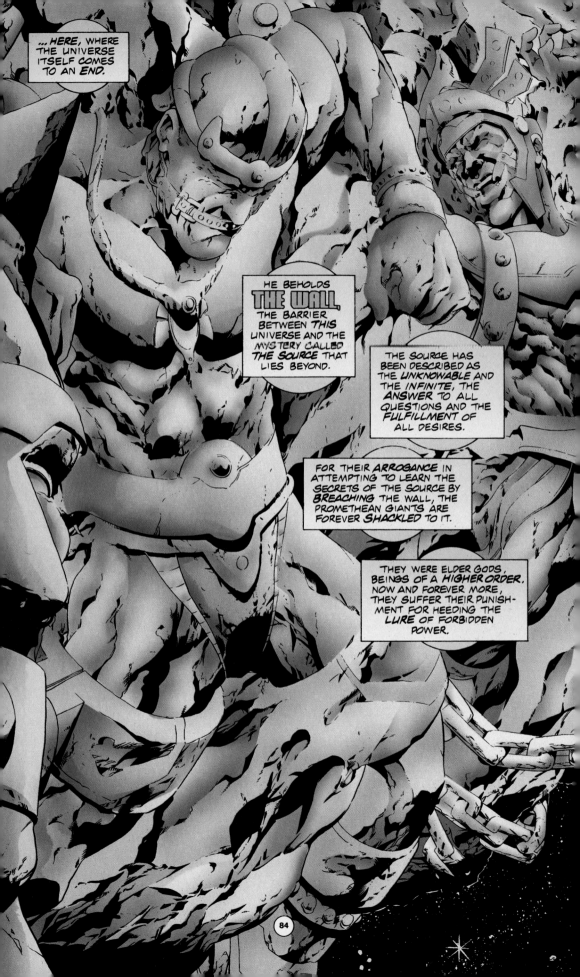

...HERE, WHERE THE UNIVERSE ITSELF COMES TO AN END.

HE BEHOLDS **THE WALL**, THE BARRIER BETWEEN *THIS* UNIVERSE AND THE MYSTERY CALLED *THE SOURCE* THAT LIES BEYOND.

THE SOURCE HAS BEEN DESCRIBED AS THE *UNKNOWABLE* AND THE *INFINITE*, THE *ANSWER* TO ALL QUESTIONS AND THE *FULFILLMENT* OF ALL DESIRES.

FOR THEIR *ARROGANCE* IN ATTEMPTING TO LEARN THE SECRETS OF THE SOURCE BY *BREACHING* THE WALL, THE PROMETHEAN GIANTS ARE FOREVER *SHACKLED* TO IT.

THEY WERE ELDER GODS, BEINGS OF A *HIGHER ORDER*, NOW AND FOREVER MORE, THEY SUFFER THEIR PUNISHMENT FOR HEEDING THE *LURE* OF FORBIDDEN POWER.

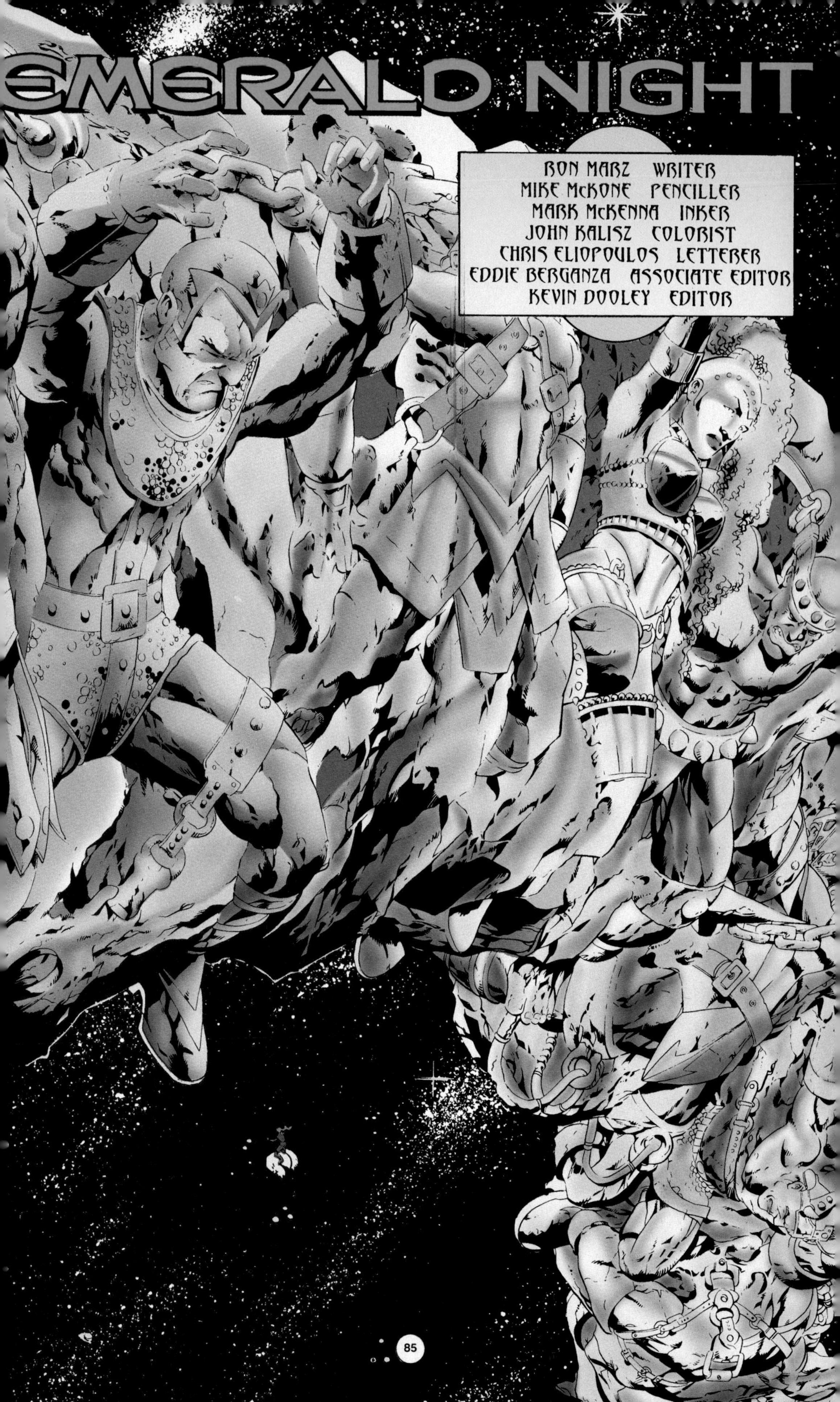
EMERALD NIGHT
RON MARZ WRITER
MIKE McKONE PENCILLER
MARK McKENNA INKER
JOHN KALISZ COLORIST
CHRIS ELIOPOULOS LETTERER
EDDIE BERGANZA ASSOCIATE EDITOR
KEVIN DOOLEY EDITOR

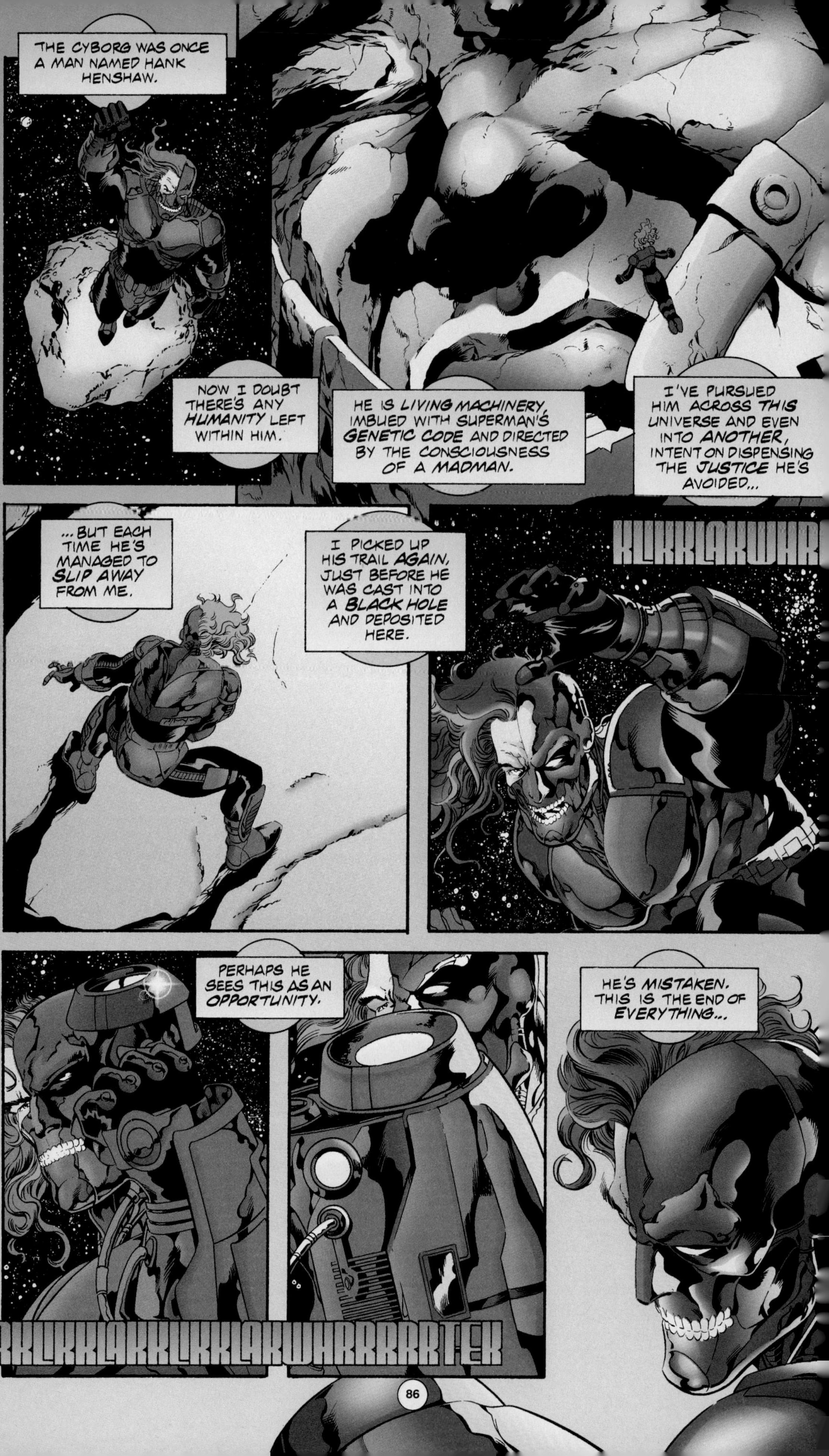
THE CYBORG WAS ONCE A MAN NAMED HANK HENSHAW.
NOW I DOUBT THERE'S ANY HUMANITY LEFT WITHIN HIM.
HE IS LIVING MACHINERY, IMBUED WITH SUPERMAN'S GENETIC CODE AND DIRECTED BY THE CONSCIOUSNESS OF A MADMAN.
I'VE PURSUED HIM ACROSS THIS UNIVERSE AND EVEN INTO ANOTHER, INTENT ON DISPENSING THE JUSTICE HE'S AVOIDED...
...BUT EACH TIME HE'S MANAGED TO SLIP AWAY FROM ME.
I PICKED UP HIS TRAIL AGAIN, JUST BEFORE HE WAS CAST INTO A BLACK HOLE AND DEPOSITED HERE.
KLKKLAKWHR
PERHAPS HE SEES THIS AS AN OPPORTUNITY.
HE'S MISTAKEN. THIS IS THE END OF EVERYTHING...
RRKLKKLAKKLKKLAKWHRRRRRRTEK

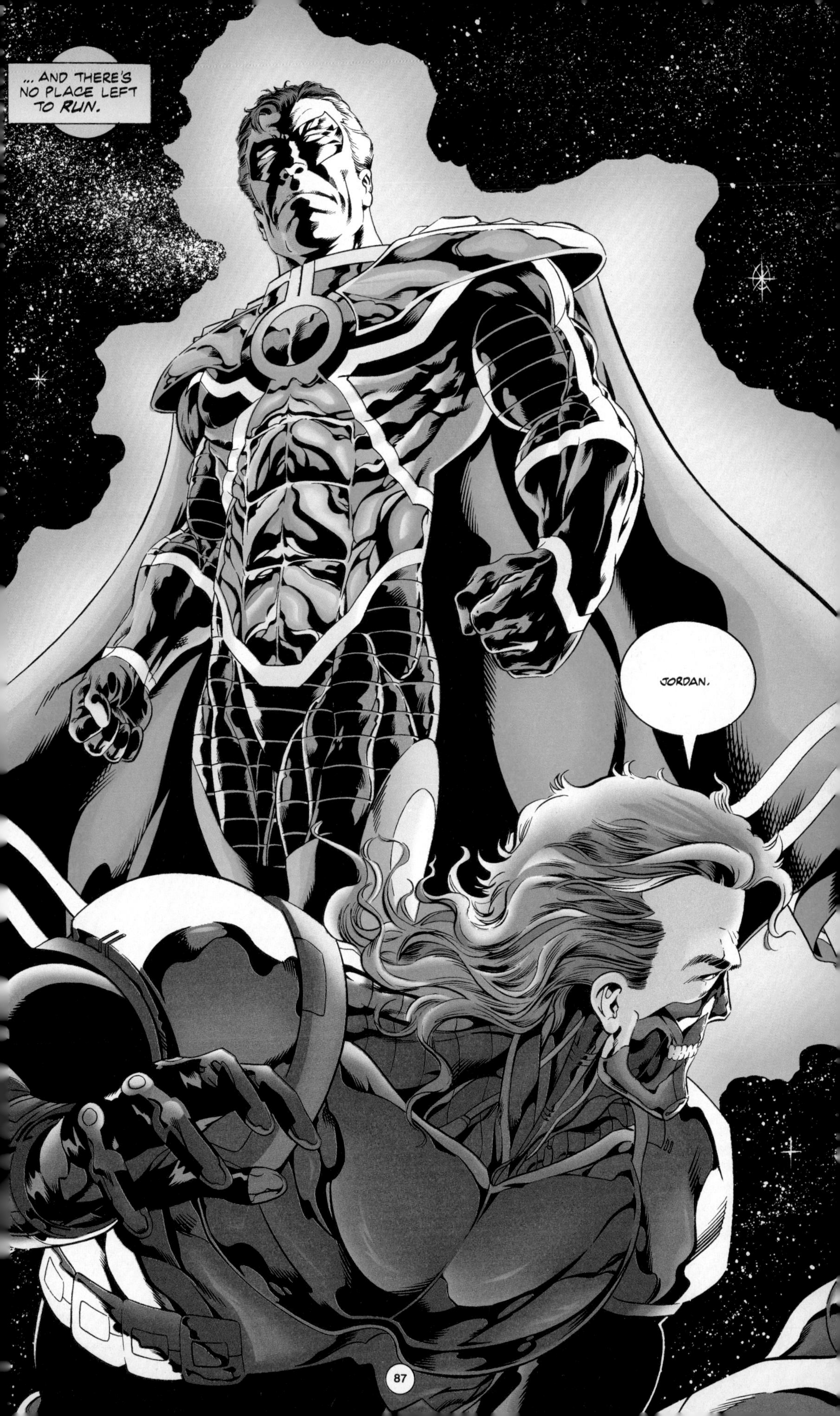
...AND THERE'S NO PLACE LEFT TO RUN.
JORDAN.

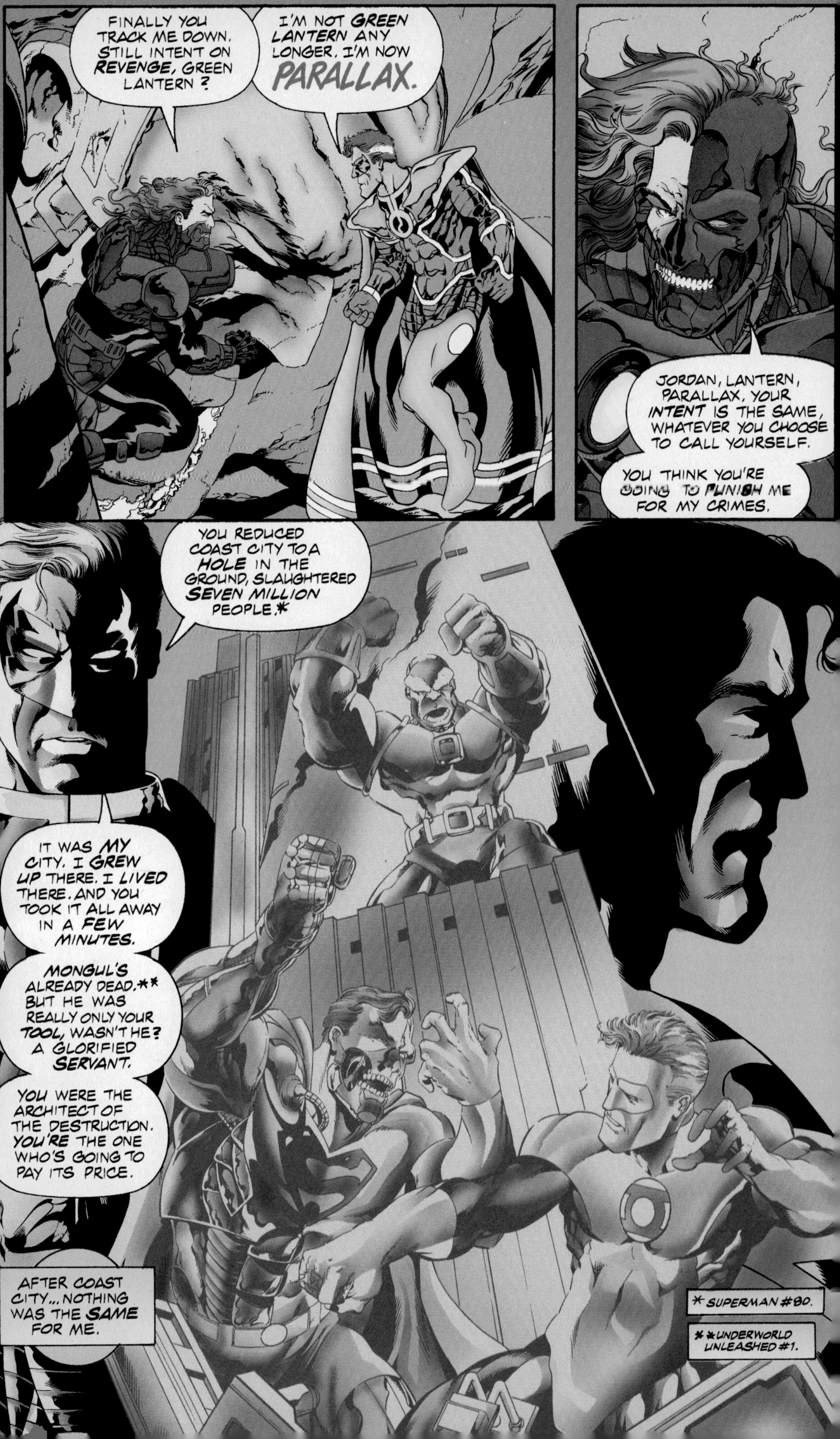
FINALLY YOU TRACK ME DOWN. STILL INTENT ON REVENGE, GREEN LANTERN?
I'M NOT GREEN LANTERN ANY LONGER. I'M NOW PARALLAX.
JORDAN, LANTERN, PARALLAX, YOUR INTENT IS THE SAME, WHATEVER YOU CHOOSE TO CALL YOURSELF.
YOU THINK YOU'RE GOING TO PUNISH ME FOR MY CRIMES.
YOU REDUCED COAST CITY TO A HOLE IN THE GROUND, SLAUGHTERED SEVEN MILLION PEOPLE.*
IT WAS MY CITY. I GREW UP THERE. I LIVED THERE. AND YOU TOOK IT ALL AWAY IN A FEW MINUTES.
MONGUL'S ALREADY DEAD.** BUT HE WAS REALLY ONLY YOUR TOOL, WASN'T HE? A GLORIFIED SERVANT.
YOU WERE THE ARCHITECT OF THE DESTRUCTION. YOU'RE THE ONE WHO'S GOING TO PAY ITS PRICE.
AFTER COAST CITY... NOTHING WAS THE SAME FOR ME.
*SUPERMAN #80.
**UNDERWORLD UNLEASHED #1.

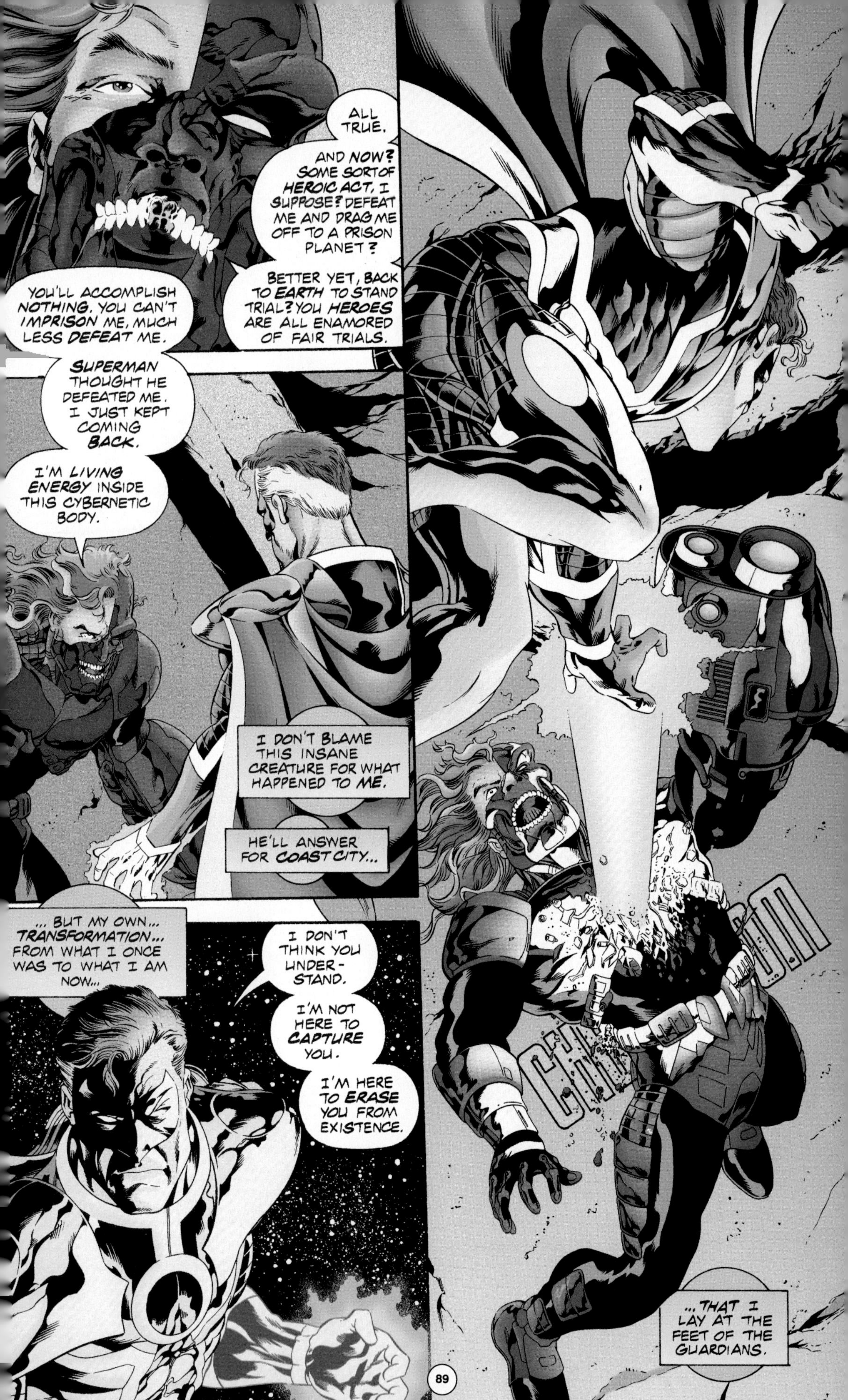
ALL TRUE.
AND NOW? SOME SORT OF HEROIC ACT, I SUPPOSE? DEFEAT ME AND DRAG ME OFF TO A PRISON PLANET?
BETTER YET, BACK TO EARTH TO STAND TRIAL? YOU HEROES ARE ALL ENAMORED OF FAIR TRIALS.
YOU'LL ACCOMPLISH NOTHING. YOU CAN'T IMPRISON ME, MUCH LESS DEFEAT ME.
SUPERMAN THOUGHT HE DEFEATED ME. I JUST KEPT COMING BACK.
I'M LIVING ENERGY INSIDE THIS CYBERNETIC BODY.
I DON'T BLAME THIS INSANE CREATURE FOR WHAT HAPPENED TO ME.
HE'LL ANSWER FOR COAST CITY...
... BUT MY OWN... TRANSFORMATION... FROM WHAT I ONCE WAS TO WHAT I AM NOW...
I DON'T THINK YOU UNDER-STAND.
I'M NOT HERE TO CAPTURE YOU.
I'M HERE TO ERASE YOU FROM EXISTENCE.
... THAT I LAY AT THE FEET OF THE GUARDIANS.

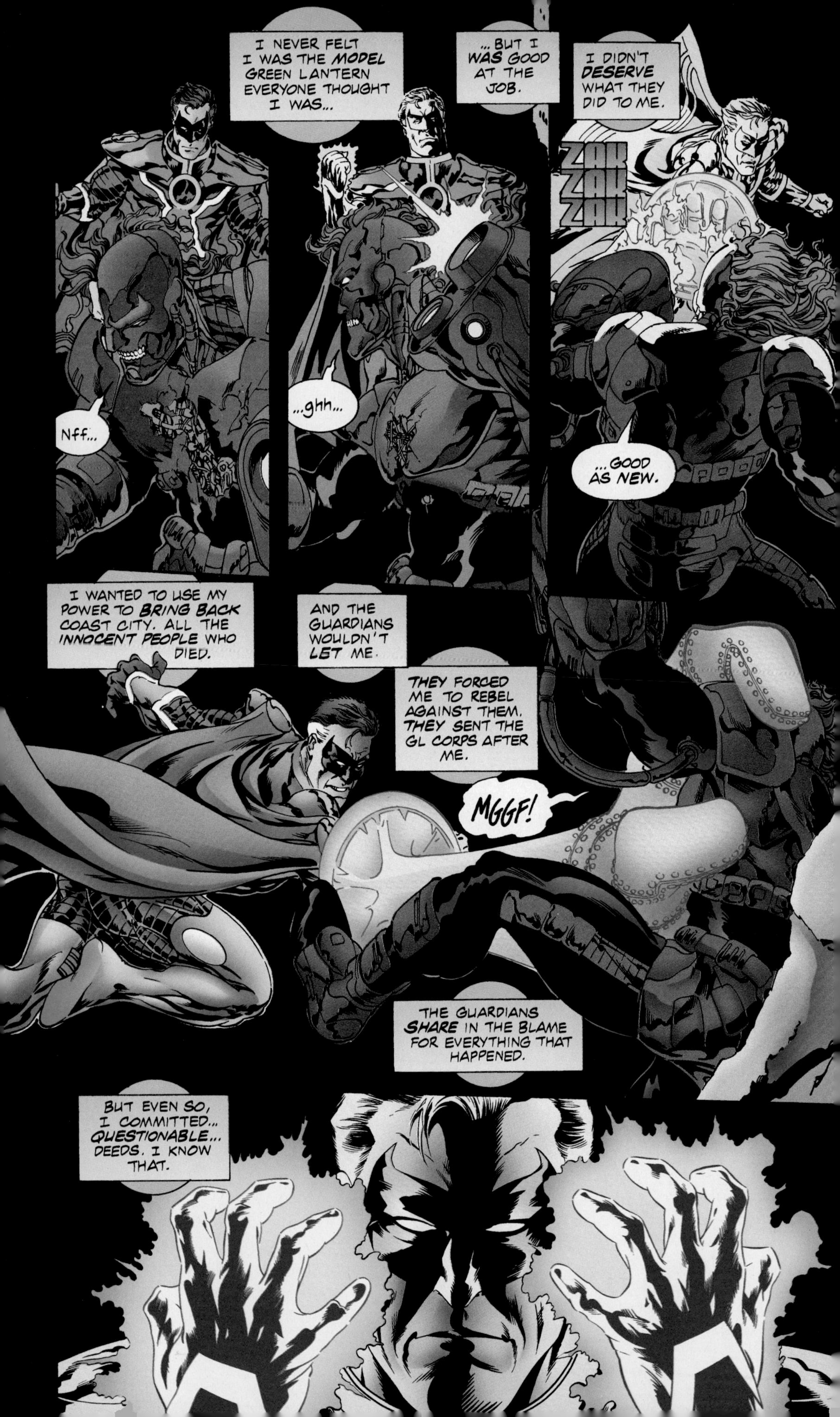

I NEVER FELT I WAS THE MODEL GREEN LANTERN EVERYONE THOUGHT I WAS...
Nff...
...BUT I WAS GOOD AT THE JOB.
...ghh...
I DIDN'T DESERVE WHAT THEY DID TO ME.
ZAK ZAK ZAK
...GOOD AS NEW.
I WANTED TO USE MY POWER TO BRING BACK COAST CITY. ALL THE INNOCENT PEOPLE WHO DIED.
AND THE GUARDIANS WOULDN'T LET ME.
THEY FORCED ME TO REBEL AGAINST THEM. THEY SENT THE GL CORPS AFTER ME.
MGGF!
THE GUARDIANS SHARE IN THE BLAME FOR EVERYTHING THAT HAPPENED.
BUT EVEN SO, I COMMITTED... QUESTIONABLE... DEEDS. I KNOW THAT.

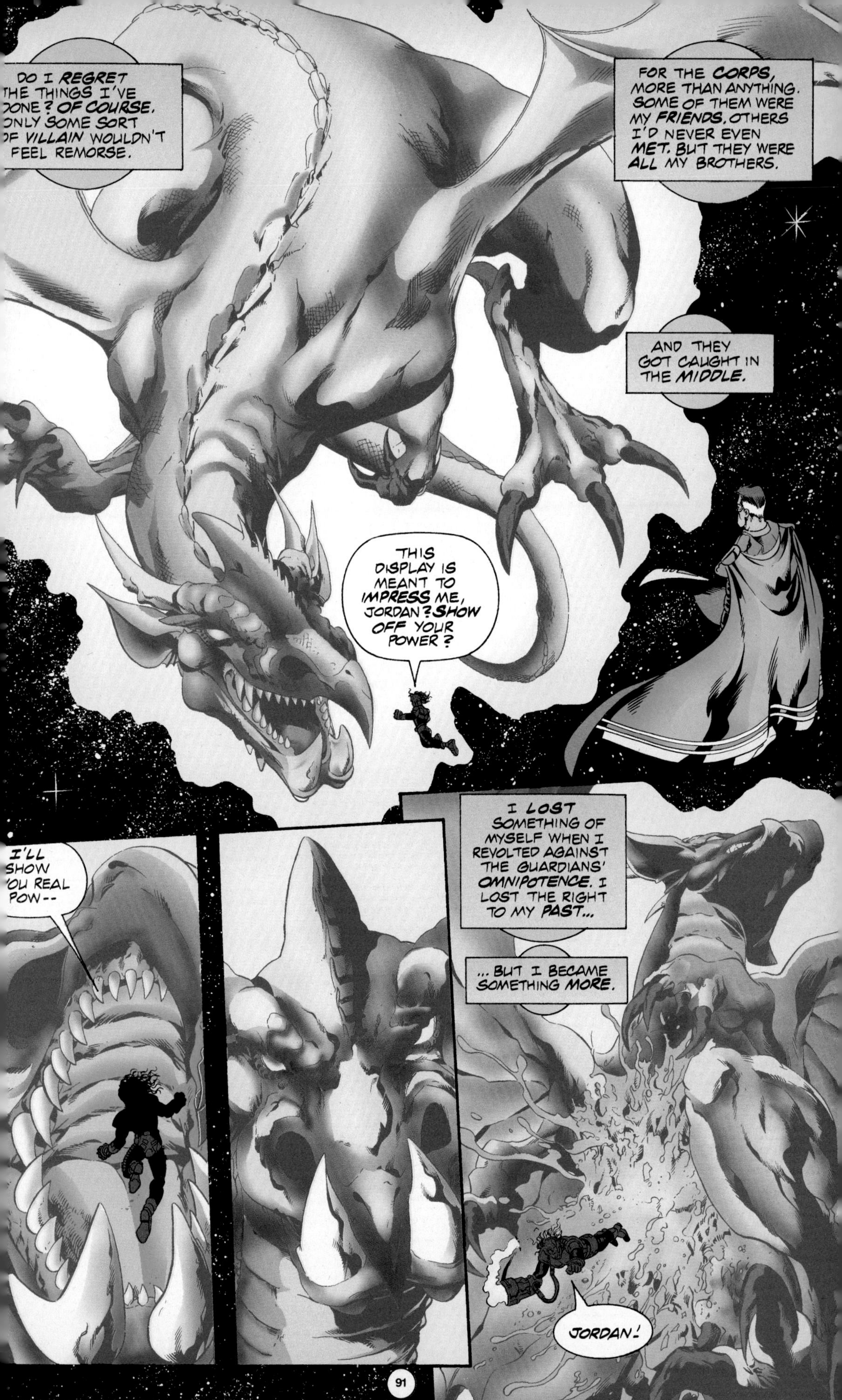

DO I REGRET THE THINGS I'VE DONE? OF COURSE. ONLY SOME SORT OF VILLAIN WOULDN'T FEEL REMORSE.
FOR THE CORPS, MORE THAN ANYTHING. SOME OF THEM WERE MY FRIENDS. OTHERS I'D NEVER EVEN MET. BUT THEY WERE ALL MY BROTHERS.
AND THEY GOT CAUGHT IN THE MIDDLE.
THIS DISPLAY IS MEANT TO IMPRESS ME, JORDAN? SHOW OFF YOUR POWER?
I'LL SHOW YOU REAL POW--
I LOST SOMETHING OF MYSELF WHEN I REVOLTED AGAINST THE GUARDIANS' OMNIPOTENCE. I LOST THE RIGHT TO MY PAST...
...BUT I BECAME SOMETHING MORE.
JORDAN!

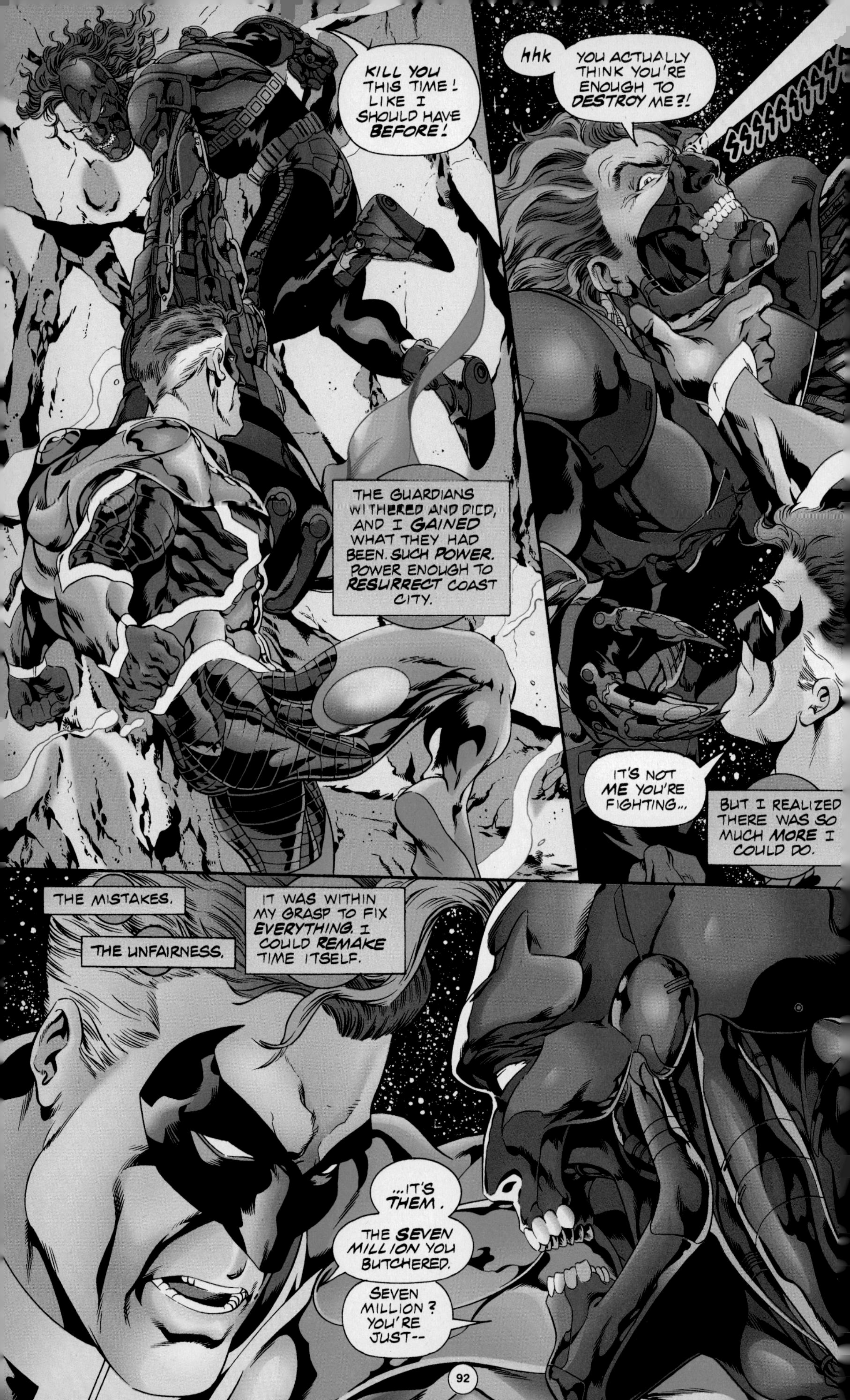
KILL YOU THIS TIME! LIKE I SHOULD HAVE BEFORE!
THE GUARDIANS WITHERED AND DIED, AND I GAINED WHAT THEY HAD BEEN. SUCH POWER. POWER ENOUGH TO RESURRECT COAST CITY.
hhk
YOU ACTUALLY THINK YOU'RE ENOUGH TO DESTROY ME?!
SSSSSSSSS
IT'S NOT ME YOU'RE FIGHTING...
BUT I REALIZED THERE WAS SO MUCH MORE I COULD DO.
THE MISTAKES.
THE UNFAIRNESS.
IT WAS WITHIN MY GRASP TO FIX EVERYTHING. I COULD REMAKE TIME ITSELF.
...IT'S THEM.
THE SEVEN MILLION YOU BUTCHERED.
SEVEN MILLION? YOU'RE JUST--

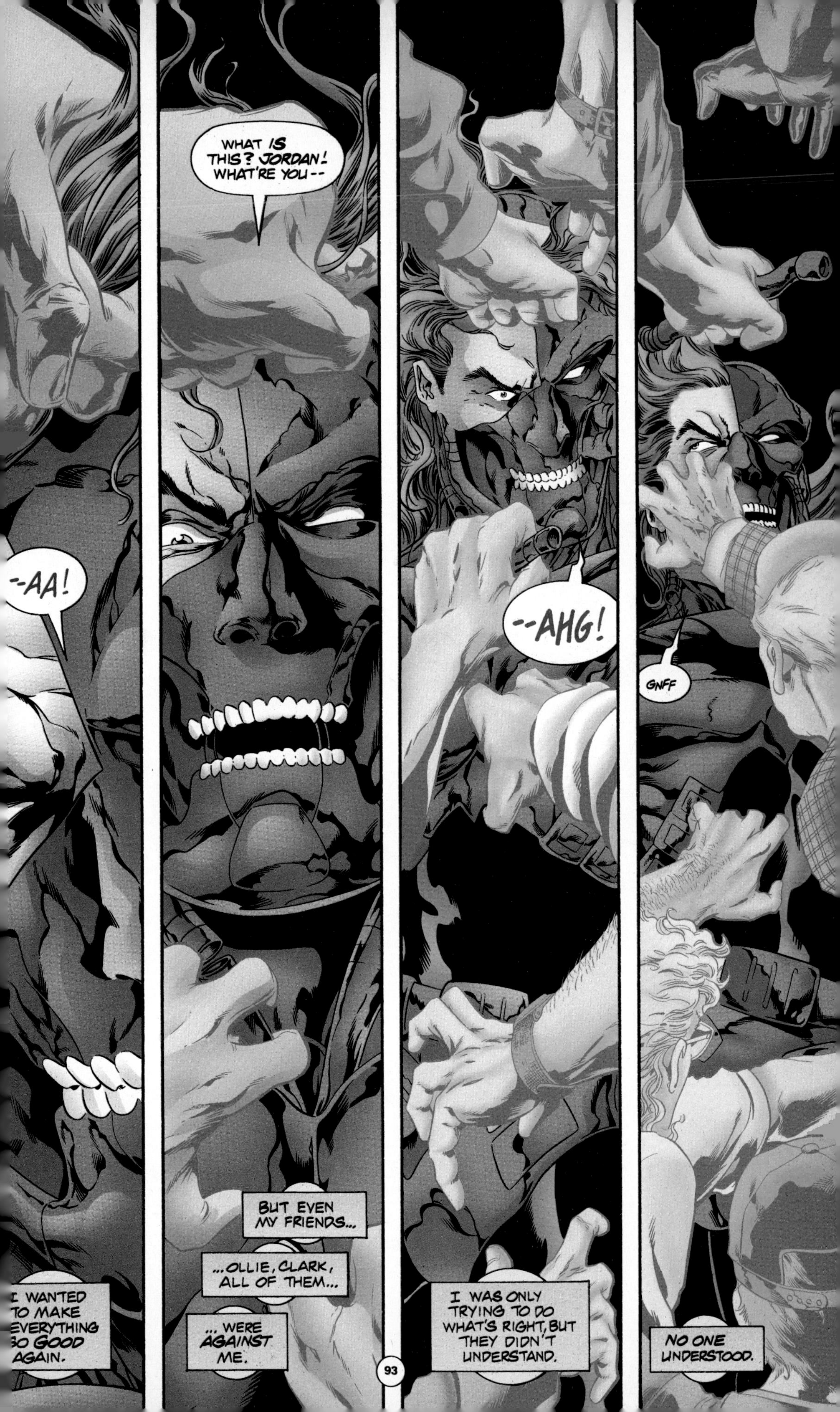
--AA!
I WANTED TO MAKE EVERYTHING SO GOOD AGAIN.
WHAT IS THIS? JORDAN! WHAT'RE YOU--
BUT EVEN MY FRIENDS...
...OLLIE, CLARK, ALL OF THEM...
...WERE AGAINST ME.
--AHG!
I WAS ONLY TRYING TO DO WHAT'S RIGHT, BUT THEY DIDN'T UNDERSTAND.
GNFF
NO ONE UNDERSTOOD.

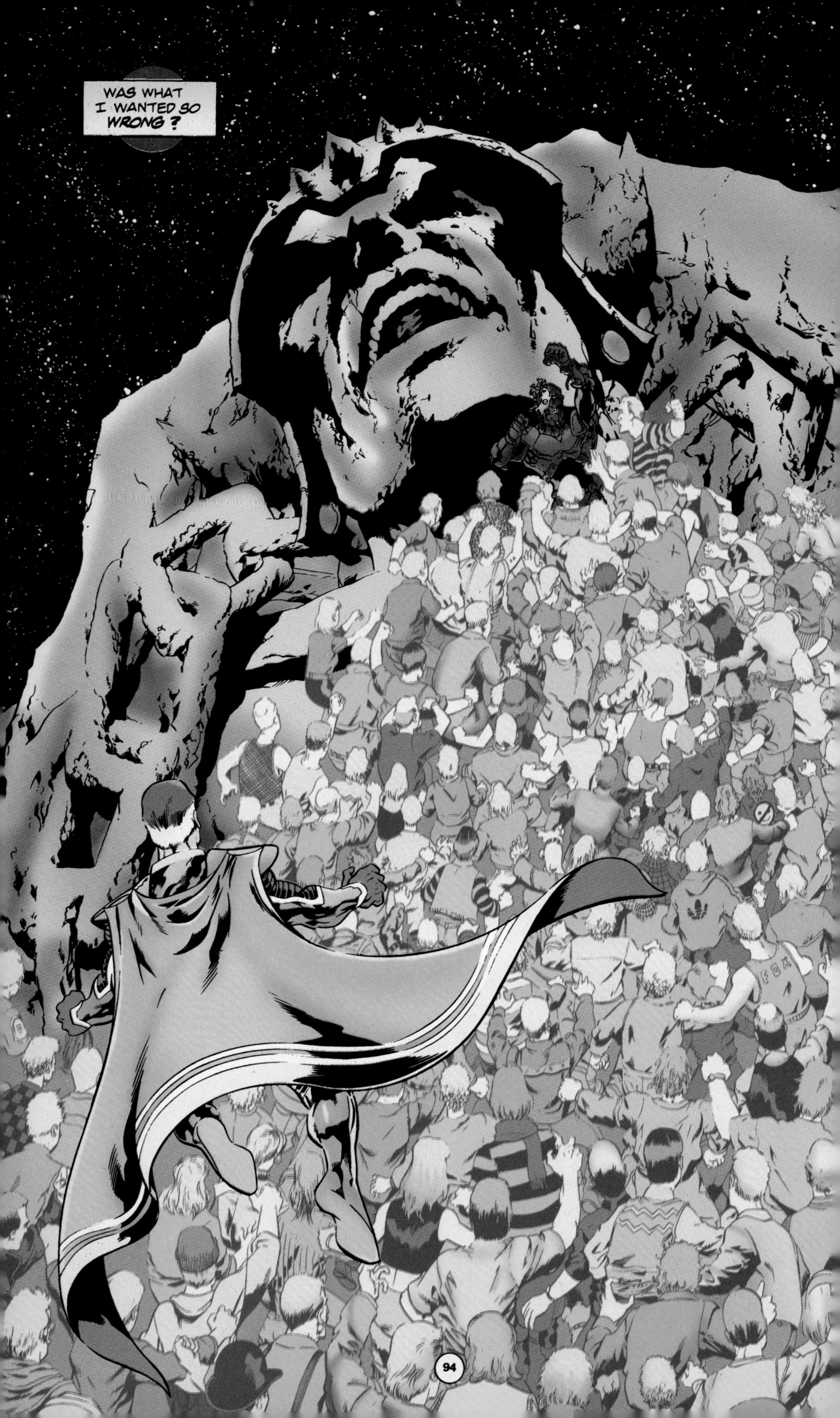
WAS WHAT I WANTED SO WRONG?

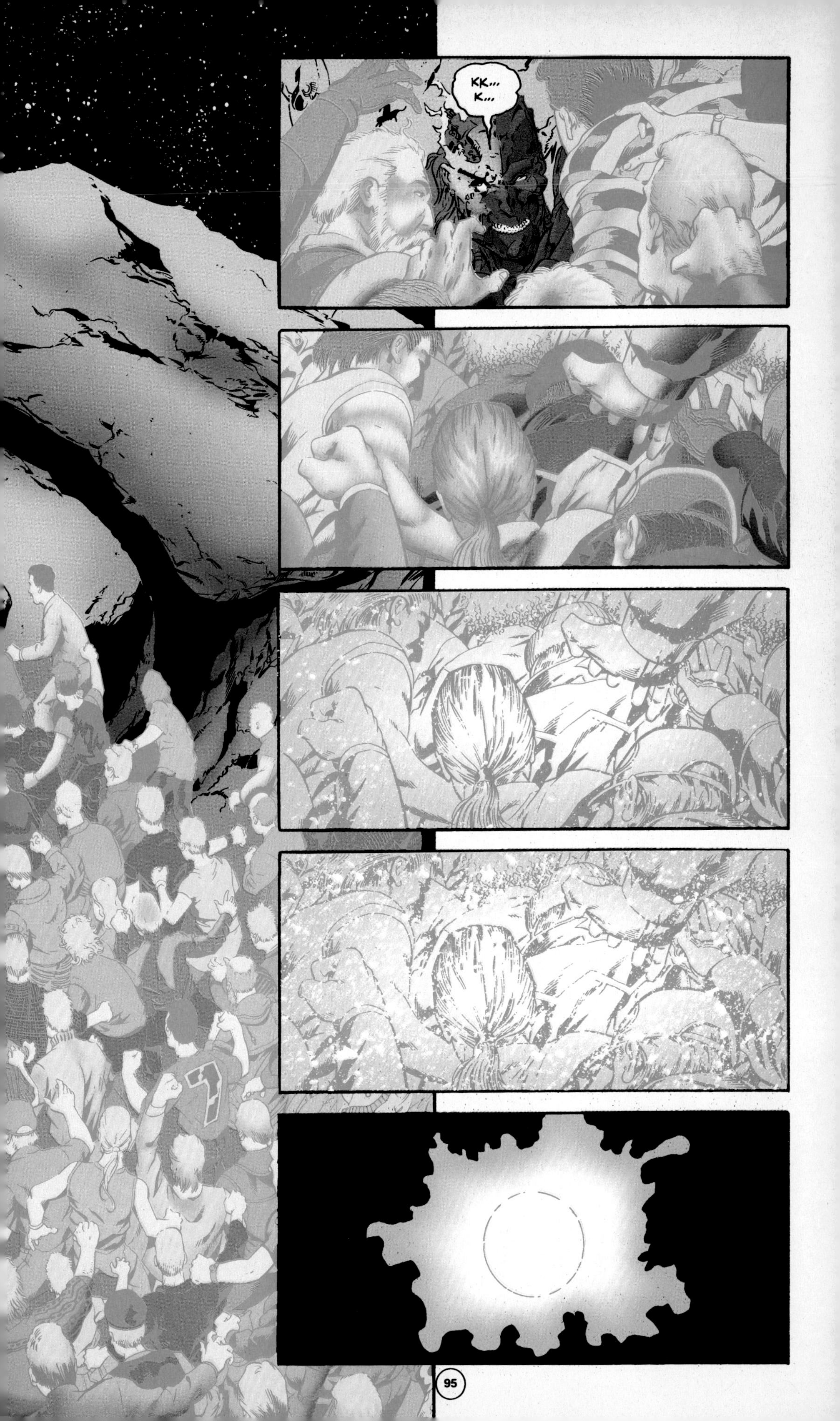
KK...
K...

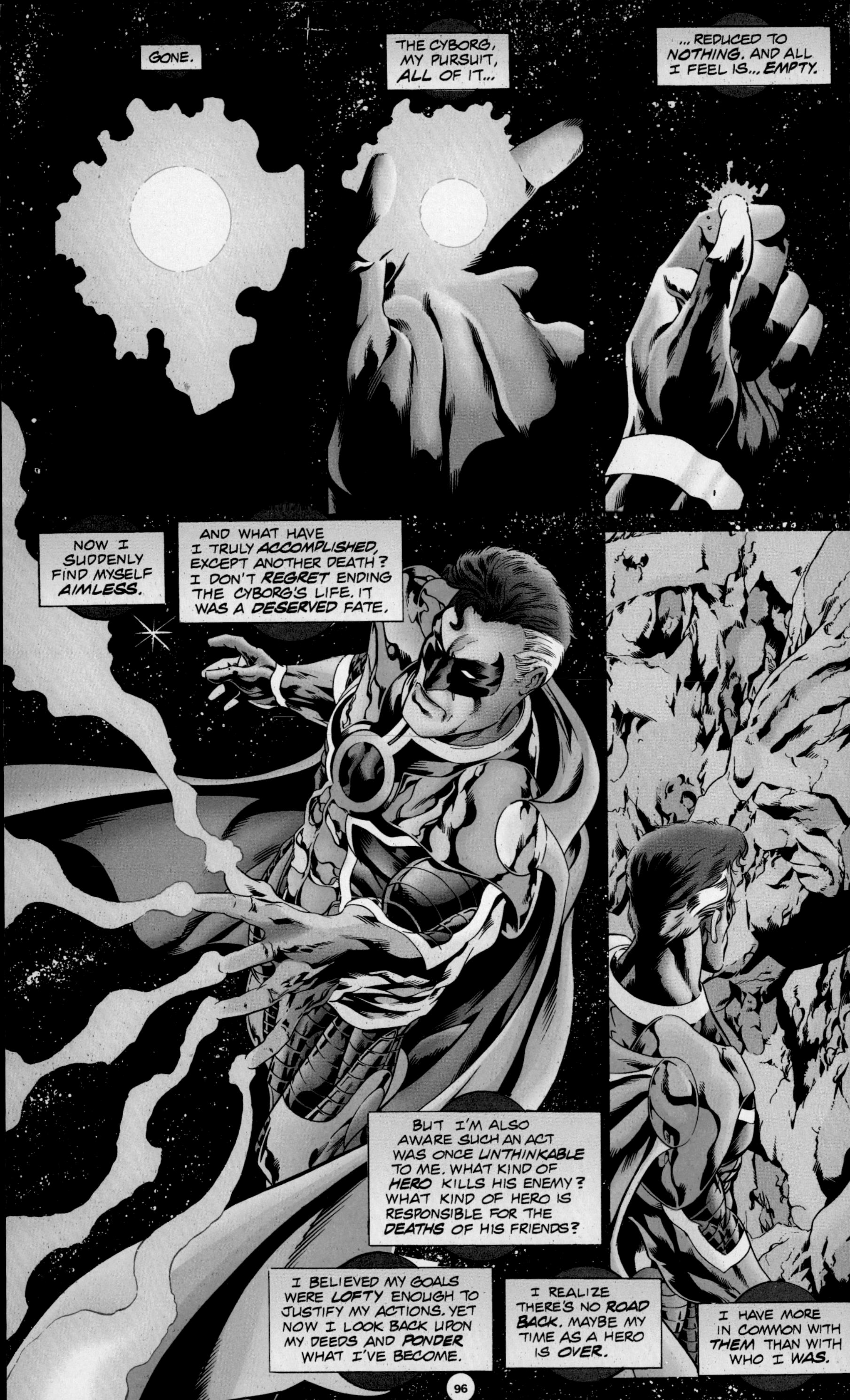
GONE.
THE CYBORG, MY PURSUIT, ALL OF IT...
...REDUCED TO NOTHING. AND ALL I FEEL IS... EMPTY.
NOW I SUDDENLY FIND MYSELF AIMLESS.
AND WHAT HAVE I TRULY ACCOMPLISHED, EXCEPT ANOTHER DEATH? I DON'T REGRET ENDING THE CYBORG'S LIFE. IT WAS A DESERVED FATE.
BUT I'M ALSO AWARE SUCH AN ACT WAS ONCE UNTHINKABLE TO ME. WHAT KIND OF HERO KILLS HIS ENEMY? WHAT KIND OF HERO IS RESPONSIBLE FOR THE DEATHS OF HIS FRIENDS?
I BELIEVED MY GOALS WERE LOFTY ENOUGH TO JUSTIFY MY ACTIONS. YET NOW I LOOK BACK UPON MY DEEDS AND PONDER WHAT I'VE BECOME.
I REALIZE THERE'S NO ROAD BACK. MAYBE MY TIME AS A HERO IS OVER.
I HAVE MORE IN COMMON WITH THEM THAN WITH WHO I WAS.

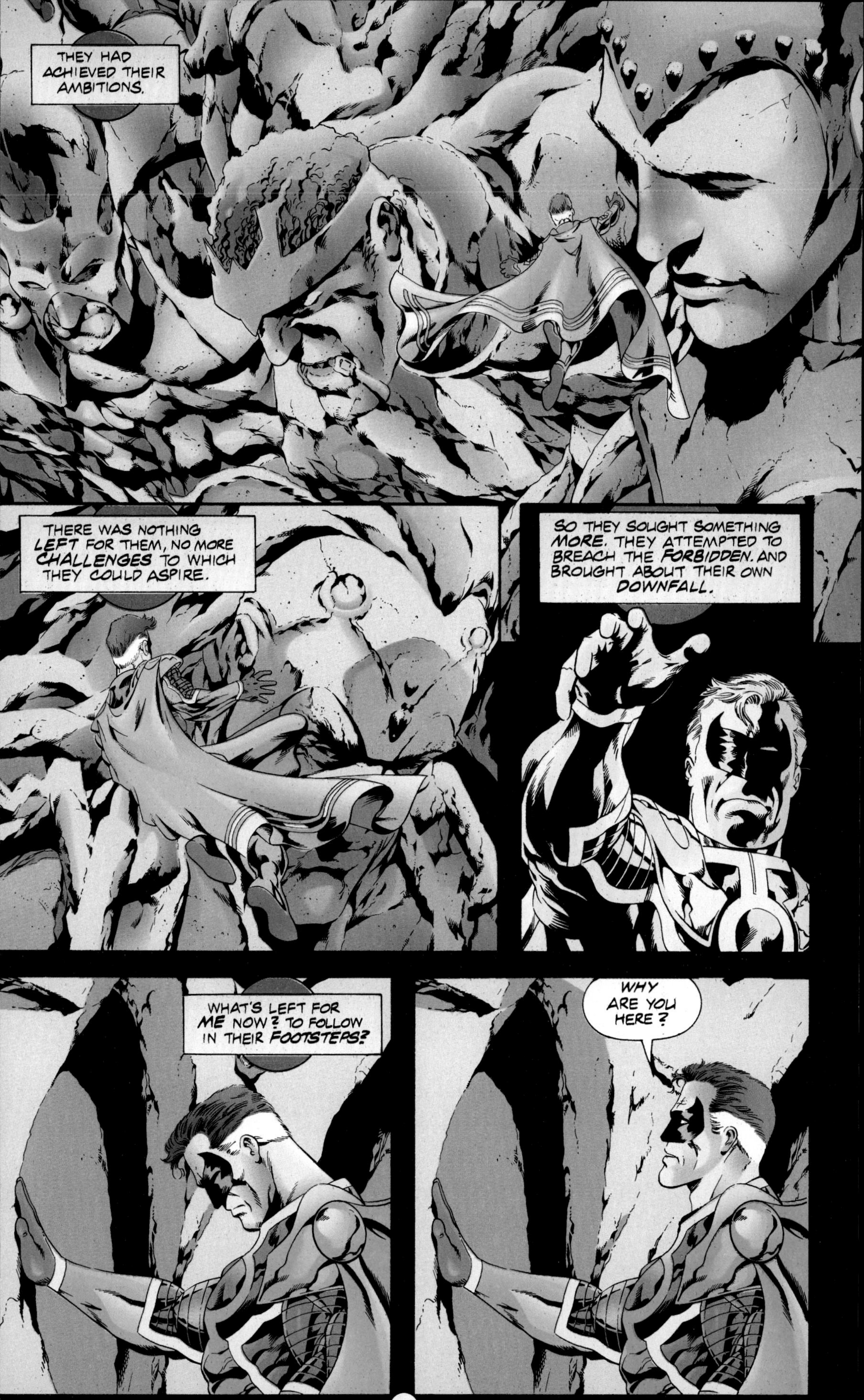

THEY HAD ACHIEVED THEIR AMBITIONS.
THERE WAS NOTHING LEFT FOR THEM, NO MORE CHALLENGES TO WHICH THEY COULD ASPIRE.
SO THEY SOUGHT SOMETHING MORE. THEY ATTEMPTED TO BREACH THE FORBIDDEN. AND BROUGHT ABOUT THEIR OWN DOWNFALL.
WHAT'S LEFT FOR ME NOW? TO FOLLOW IN THEIR FOOTSTEPS?
WHY ARE YOU HERE?

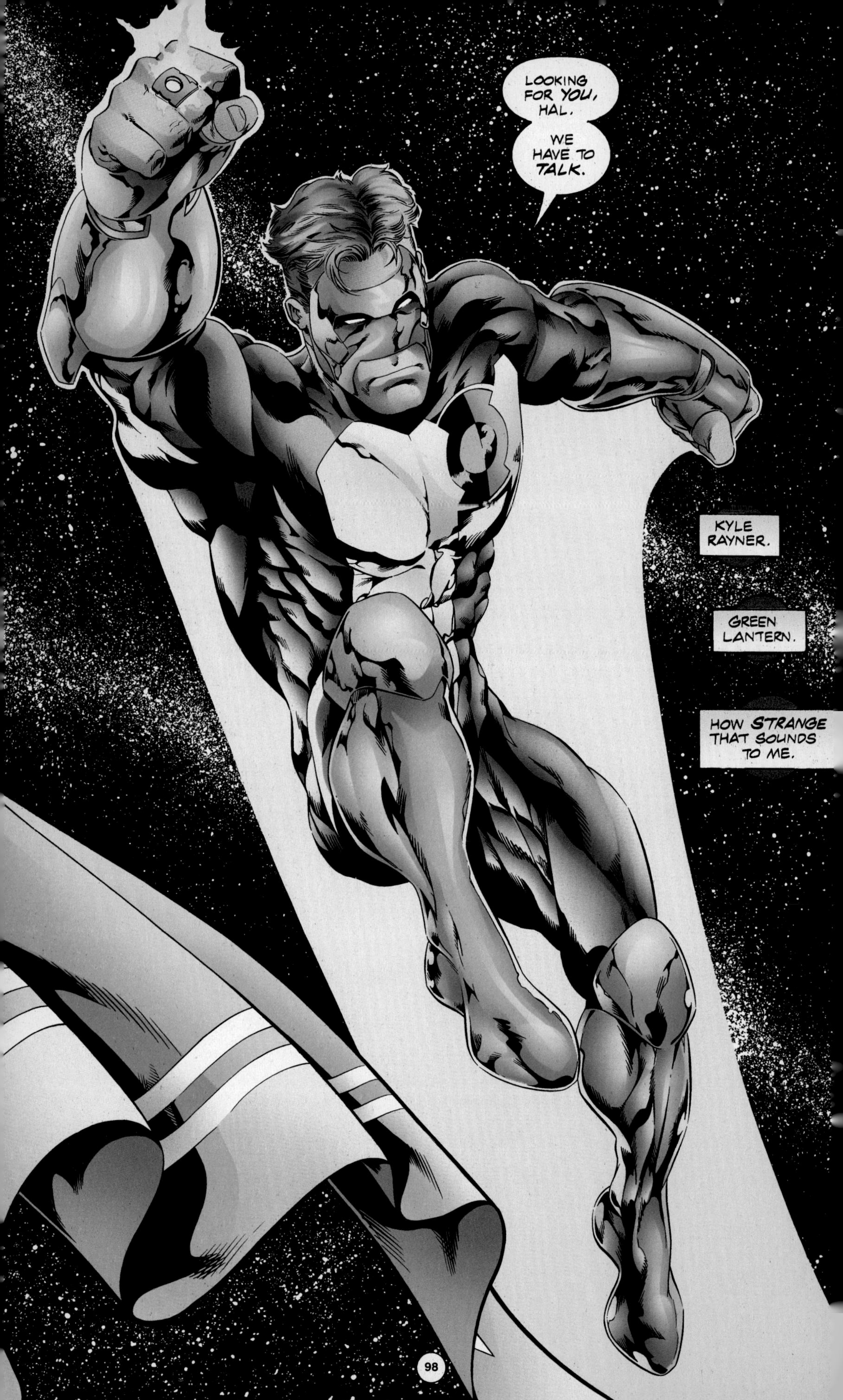

LOOKING FOR YOU, HAL.
WE HAVE TO TALK.
KYLE RAYNER.
GREEN LANTERN.
HOW STRANGE THAT SOUNDS TO ME.

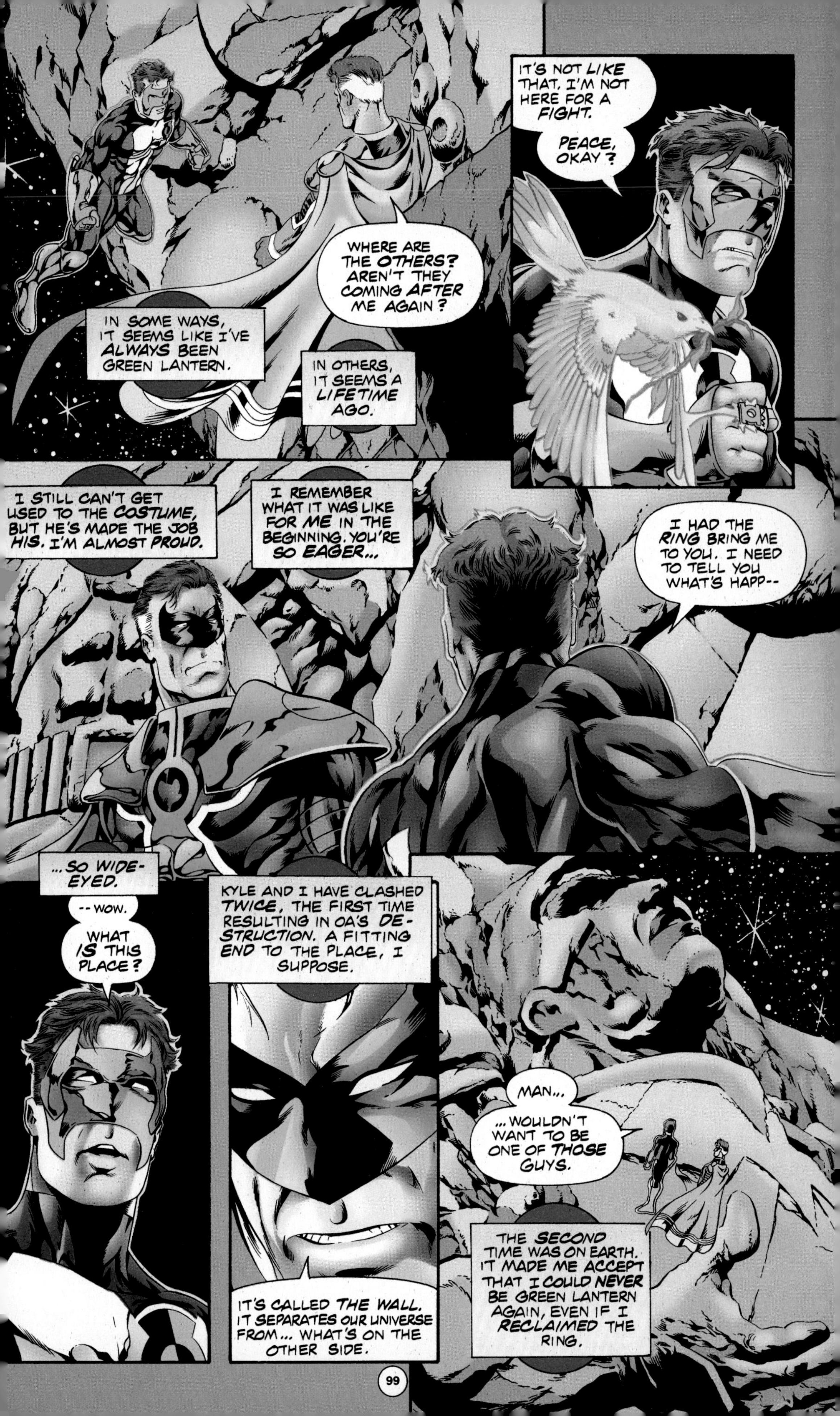

IN SOME WAYS, IT SEEMS LIKE I'VE ALWAYS BEEN GREEN LANTERN.
WHERE ARE THE OTHERS? AREN'T THEY COMING AFTER ME AGAIN?
IN OTHERS, IT SEEMS A LIFETIME AGO.
IT'S NOT LIKE THAT. I'M NOT HERE FOR A FIGHT.
PEACE, OKAY?
I STILL CAN'T GET USED TO THE COSTUME, BUT HE'S MADE THE JOB HIS. I'M ALMOST PROUD.
I REMEMBER WHAT IT WAS LIKE FOR ME IN THE BEGINNING. YOU'RE SO EAGER...
I HAD THE RING BRING ME TO YOU. I NEED TO TELL YOU WHAT'S HAPP--
...SO WIDE-EYED.
--WOW.
WHAT IS THIS PLACE?
KYLE AND I HAVE CLASHED TWICE, THE FIRST TIME RESULTING IN OA'S DESTRUCTION. A FITTING END TO THE PLACE, I SUPPOSE.
IT'S CALLED THE WALL. IT SEPARATES OUR UNIVERSE FROM... WHAT'S ON THE OTHER SIDE.
MAN...
...WOULDN'T WANT TO BE ONE OF THOSE GUYS.
THE SECOND TIME WAS ON EARTH. IT MADE ME ACCEPT THAT I COULD NEVER BE GREEN LANTERN AGAIN, EVEN IF I RECLAIMED THE RING.

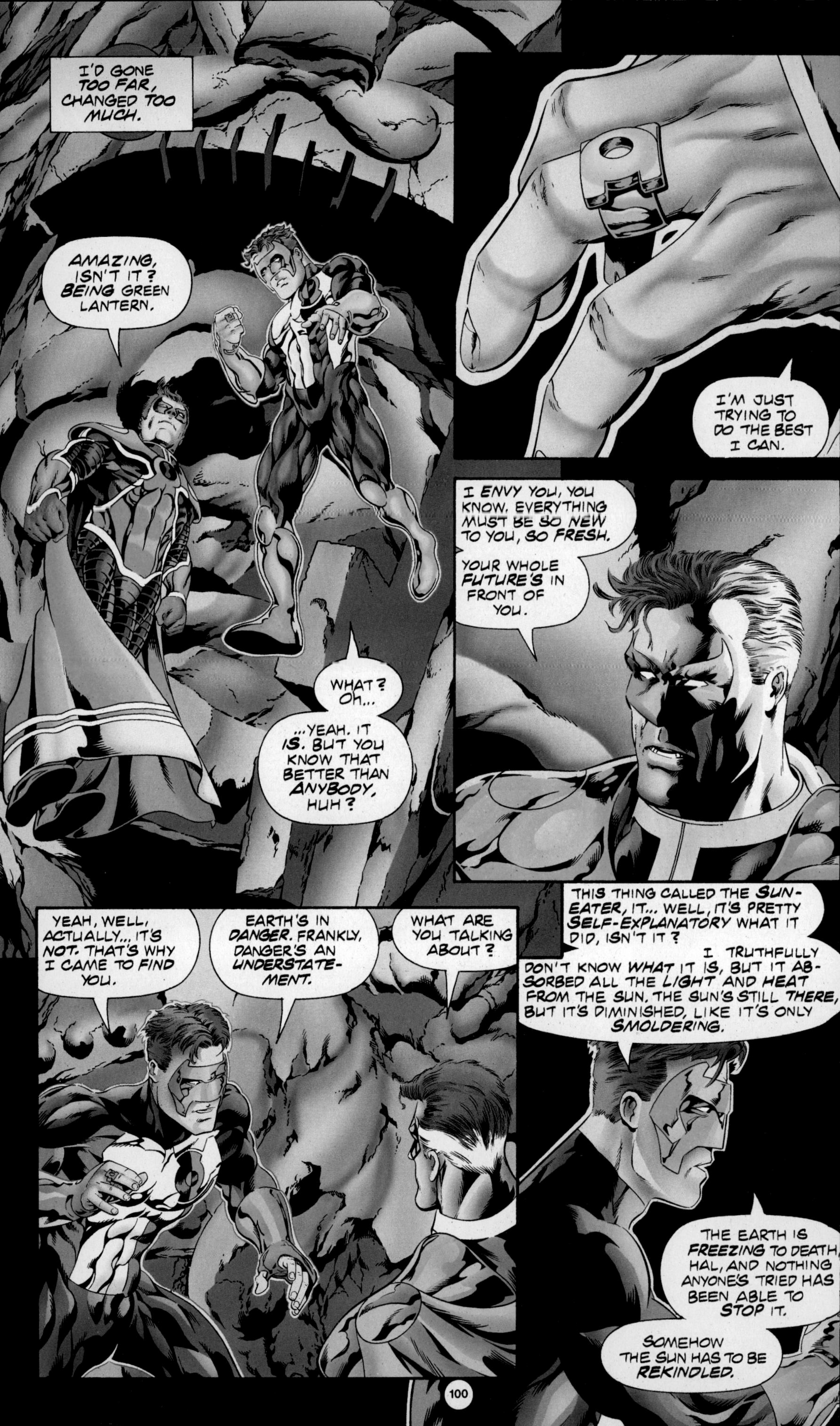

I'D GONE TOO FAR, CHANGED TOO MUCH.
AMAZING, ISN'T IT? BEING GREEN LANTERN.
I'M JUST TRYING TO DO THE BEST I CAN.
I ENVY YOU, YOU KNOW. EVERYTHING MUST BE SO NEW TO YOU, SO FRESH.
YOUR WHOLE FUTURE'S IN FRONT OF YOU.
WHAT? OH...
...YEAH. IT IS. BUT YOU KNOW THAT BETTER THAN ANYBODY, HUH?
YEAH, WELL, ACTUALLY... IT'S NOT. THAT'S WHY I CAME TO FIND YOU.
EARTH'S IN DANGER. FRANKLY, DANGER'S AN UNDERSTATEMENT.
WHAT ARE YOU TALKING ABOUT?
THIS THING CALLED THE SUN-EATER, IT... WELL, IT'S PRETTY SELF-EXPLANATORY WHAT IT DID, ISN'T IT?
I TRUTHFULLY DON'T KNOW WHAT IT IS, BUT IT ABSORBED ALL THE LIGHT AND HEAT FROM THE SUN. THE SUN'S STILL THERE, BUT IT'S DIMINISHED, LIKE IT'S ONLY SMOLDERING.
THE EARTH IS FREEZING TO DEATH, HAL, AND NOTHING ANYONE'S TRIED HAS BEEN ABLE TO STOP IT.
SOMEHOW THE SUN HAS TO BE REKINDLED.

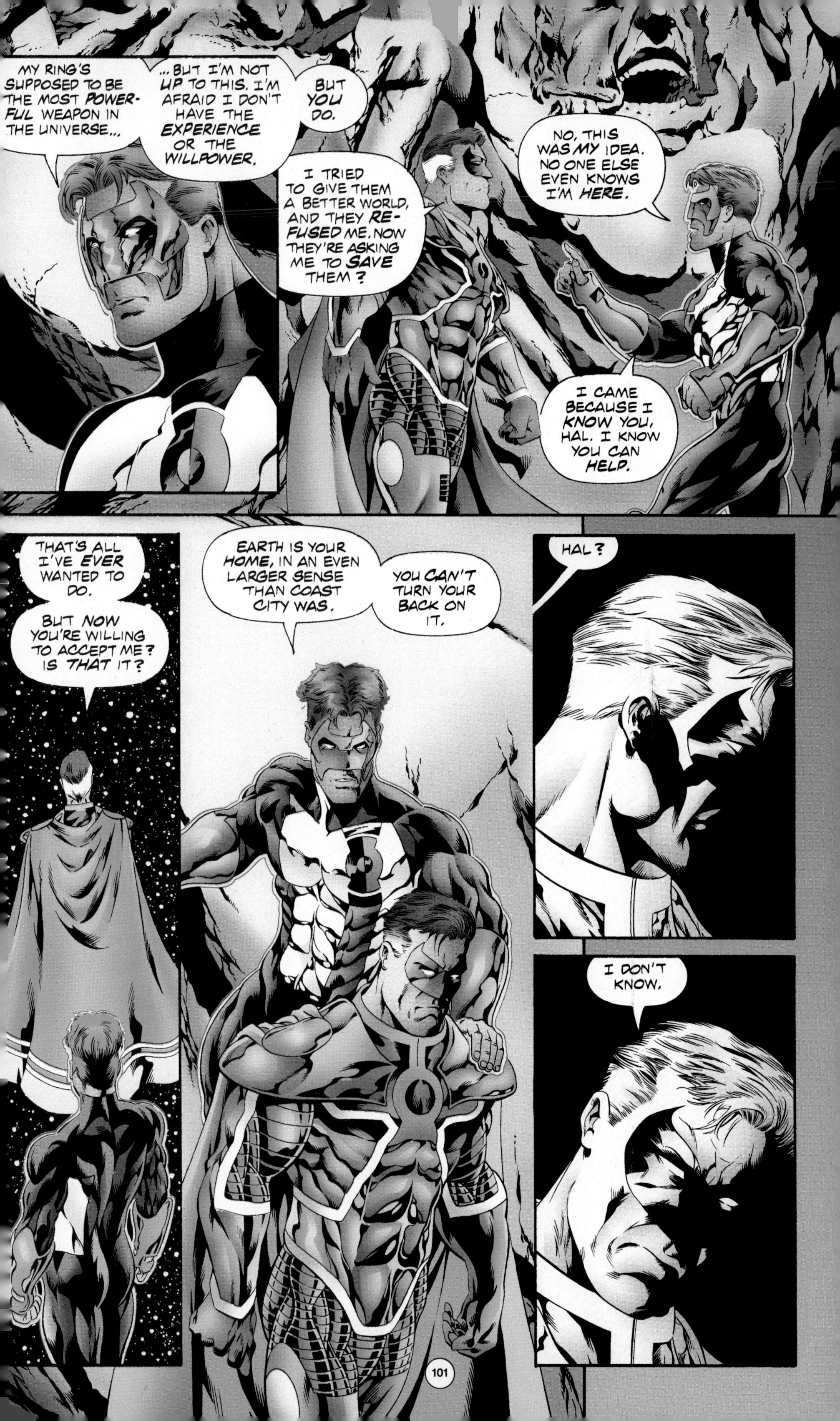
MY RING'S SUPPOSED TO BE THE MOST POWERFUL WEAPON IN THE UNIVERSE...
...BUT I'M NOT UP TO THIS. I'M AFRAID I DON'T HAVE THE EXPERIENCE OR THE WILLPOWER.
BUT YOU DO.
I TRIED TO GIVE THEM A BETTER WORLD, AND THEY REFUSED ME. NOW THEY'RE ASKING ME TO SAVE THEM?
NO, THIS WAS MY IDEA. NO ONE ELSE EVEN KNOWS I'M HERE.
I CAME BECAUSE I KNOW YOU, HAL. I KNOW YOU CAN HELP.
THAT'S ALL I'VE EVER WANTED TO DO.
BUT NOW YOU'RE WILLING TO ACCEPT ME? IS THAT IT?
EARTH IS YOUR HOME, IN AN EVEN LARGER SENSE THAN COAST CITY WAS.
YOU CAN'T TURN YOUR BACK ON IT.
HAL?
I DON'T KNOW.

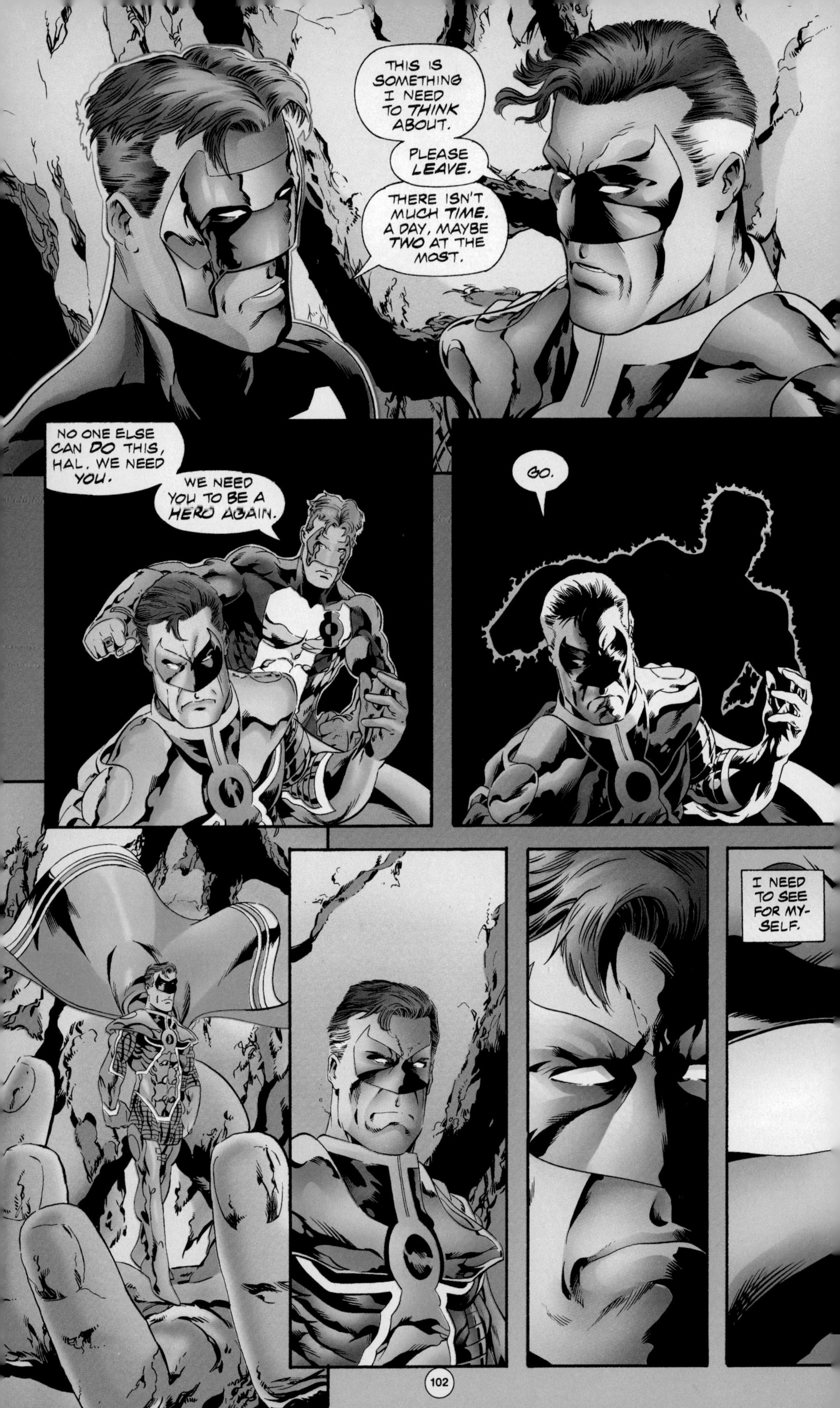
THIS IS SOMETHING I NEED TO THINK ABOUT.
PLEASE LEAVE.
THERE ISN'T MUCH TIME. A DAY, MAYBE TWO AT THE MOST.
NO ONE ELSE CAN DO THIS, HAL. WE NEED YOU.
WE NEED YOU TO BE A HERO AGAIN.
GO.
I NEED TO SEE FOR MY-SELF.

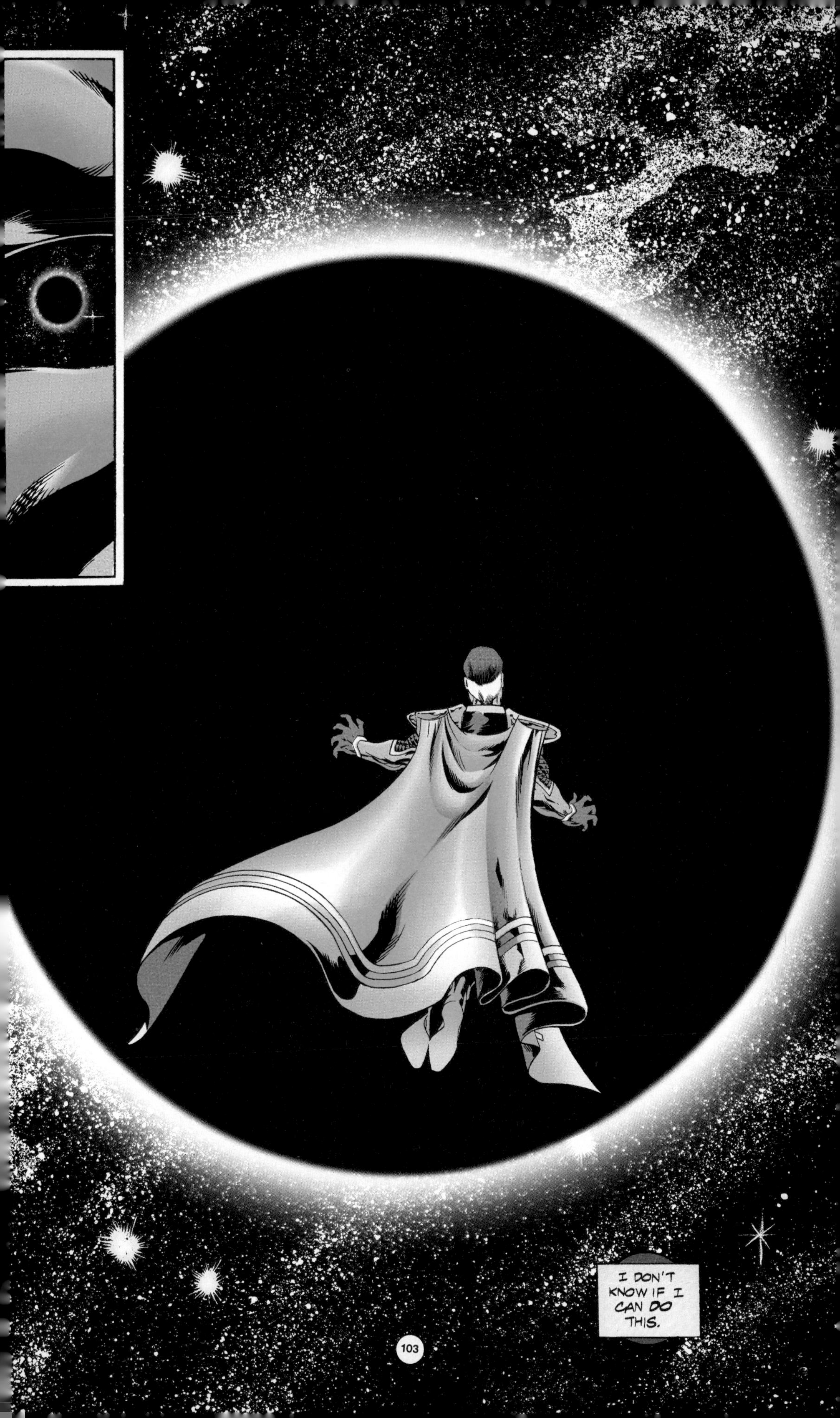
I DON'T KNOW IF I CAN DO THIS.

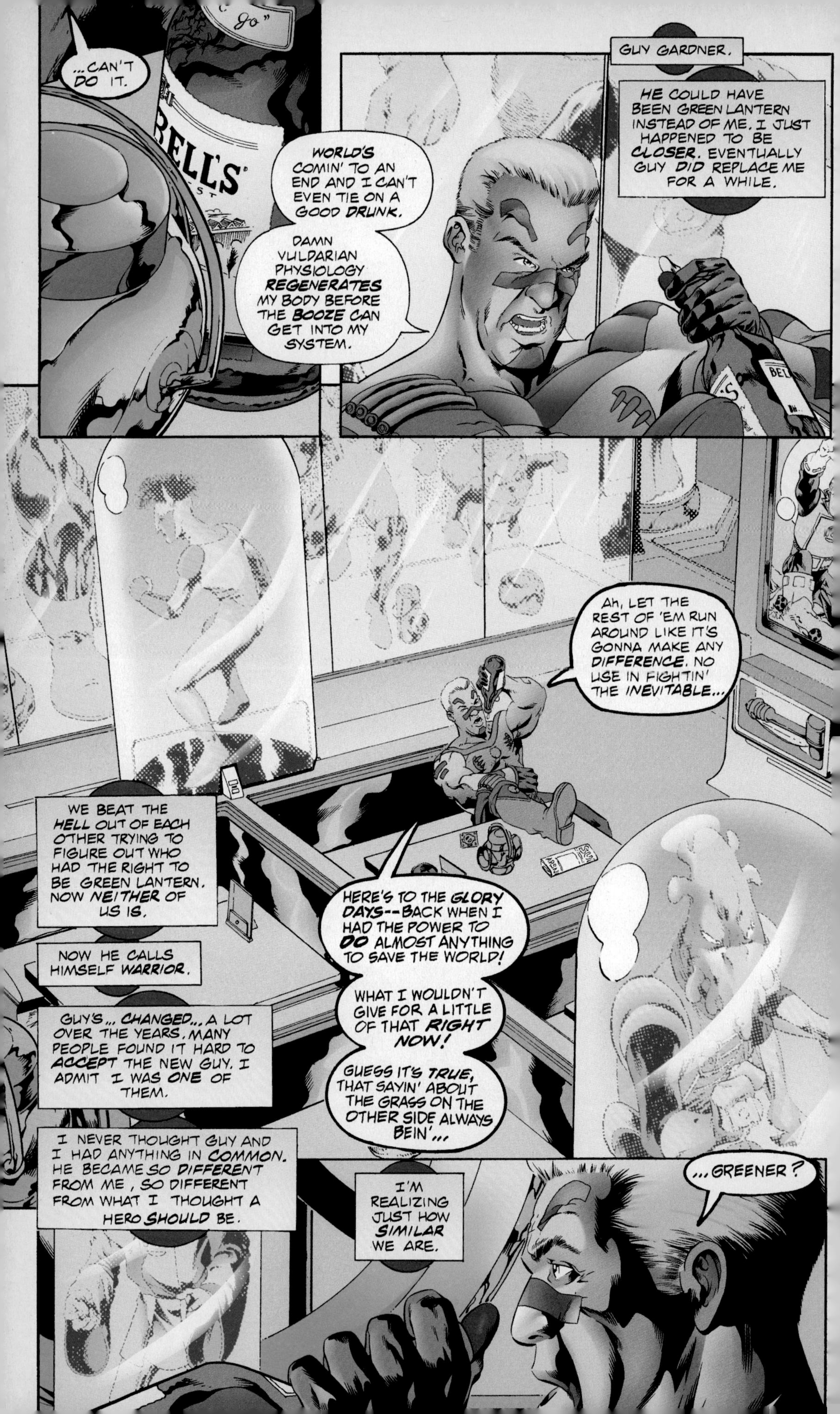
"go"
...CAN'T DO IT.
BELL'S
GUY GARDNER.
HE COULD HAVE BEEN GREEN LANTERN INSTEAD OF ME. I JUST HAPPENED TO BE CLOSER. EVENTUALLY GUY DID REPLACE ME FOR A WHILE.
WORLD'S COMIN' TO AN END AND I CAN'T EVEN TIE ON A GOOD DRUNK.
DAMN VULDARIAN PHYSIOLOGY REGENERATES MY BODY BEFORE THE BOOZE CAN GET INTO MY SYSTEM.
AH, LET THE REST OF 'EM RUN AROUND LIKE IT'S GONNA MAKE ANY DIFFERENCE. NO USE IN FIGHTIN' THE INEVITABLE...
WE BEAT THE HELL OUT OF EACH OTHER TRYING TO FIGURE OUT WHO HAD THE RIGHT TO BE GREEN LANTERN. NOW NEITHER OF US IS.
NOW HE CALLS HIMSELF WARRIOR.
GUY'S... CHANGED... A LOT OVER THE YEARS. MANY PEOPLE FOUND IT HARD TO ACCEPT THE NEW GUY. I ADMIT I WAS ONE OF THEM.
HERE'S TO THE GLORY DAYS--BACK WHEN I HAD THE POWER TO DO ALMOST ANYTHING TO SAVE THE WORLD!
WHAT I WOULDN'T GIVE FOR A LITTLE OF THAT RIGHT NOW!
GUESS IT'S TRUE, THAT SAYIN' ABOUT THE GRASS ON THE OTHER SIDE ALWAYS BEIN'...
I NEVER THOUGHT GUY AND I HAD ANYTHING IN COMMON. HE BECAME SO DIFFERENT FROM ME, SO DIFFERENT FROM WHAT I THOUGHT A HERO SHOULD BE.
I'M REALIZING JUST HOW SIMILAR WE ARE.
...GREENER?

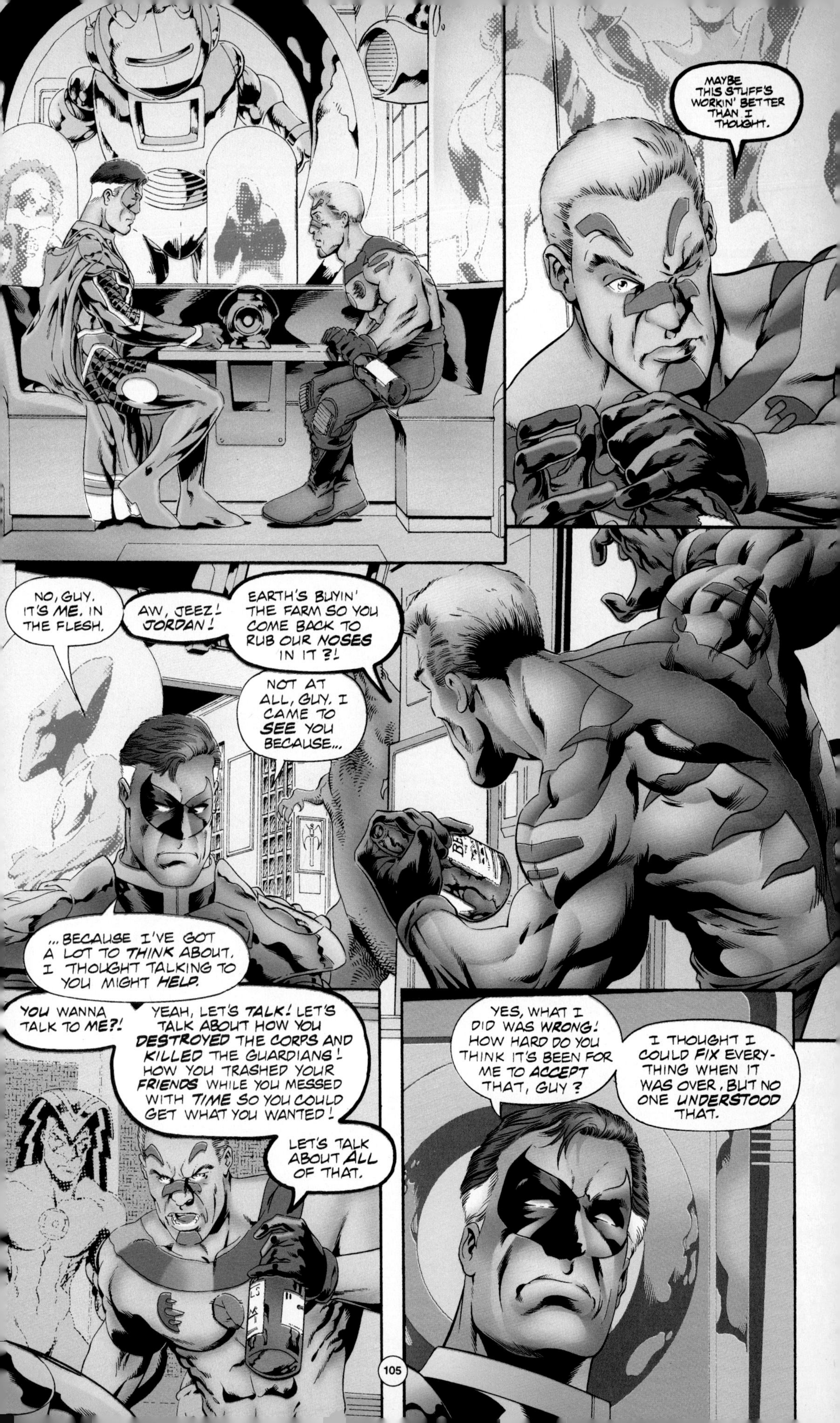

MAYBE THIS STUFF'S WORKIN' BETTER THAN I THOUGHT.
NO, GUY. IT'S ME. IN THE FLESH.
AW, JEEZ! JORDAN!
EARTH'S BUYIN' THE FARM SO YOU COME BACK TO RUB OUR NOSES IN IT?!
NOT AT ALL, GUY. I CAME TO SEE YOU BECAUSE...
...BECAUSE I'VE GOT A LOT TO THINK ABOUT. I THOUGHT TALKING TO YOU MIGHT HELP.
YOU WANNA TALK TO ME?!
YEAH, LET'S TALK! LET'S TALK ABOUT HOW YOU DESTROYED THE CORPS AND KILLED THE GUARDIANS! HOW YOU TRASHED YOUR FRIENDS WHILE YOU MESSED WITH TIME SO YOU COULD GET WHAT YOU WANTED!
LET'S TALK ABOUT ALL OF THAT.
YES, WHAT I DID WAS WRONG! HOW HARD DO YOU THINK IT'S BEEN FOR ME TO ACCEPT THAT, GUY?
I THOUGHT I COULD FIX EVERYTHING WHEN IT WAS OVER, BUT NO ONE UNDERSTOOD THAT.

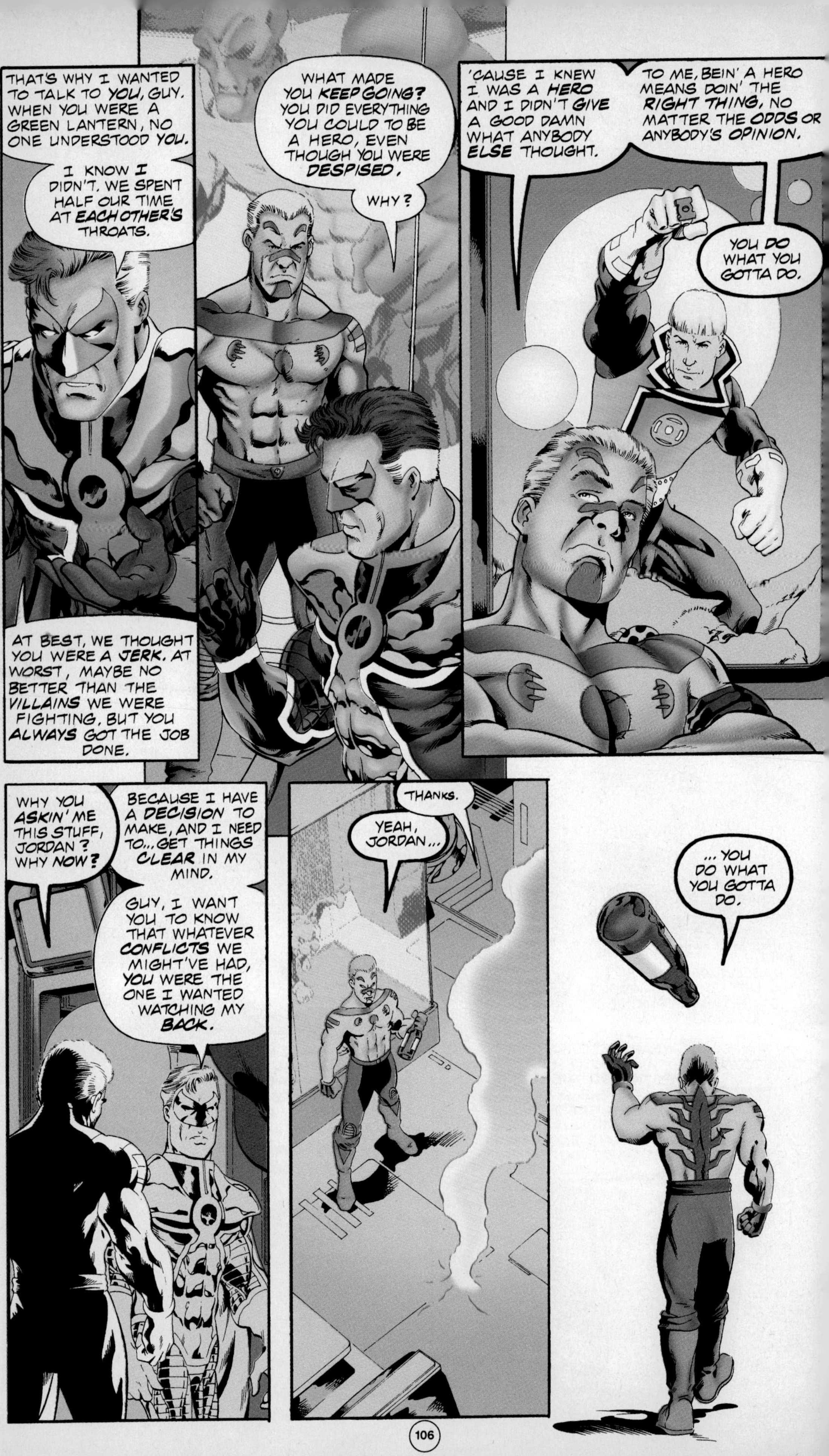

THAT'S WHY I WANTED TO TALK TO YOU, GUY. WHEN YOU WERE A GREEN LANTERN, NO ONE UNDERSTOOD YOU.
I KNOW I DIDN'T. WE SPENT HALF OUR TIME AT EACH OTHER'S THROATS.
WHAT MADE YOU KEEP GOING? YOU DID EVERYTHING YOU COULD TO BE A HERO, EVEN THOUGH YOU WERE DESPISED.
WHY?
AT BEST, WE THOUGHT YOU WERE A JERK. AT WORST, MAYBE NO BETTER THAN THE VILLAINS WE WERE FIGHTING, BUT YOU ALWAYS GOT THE JOB DONE.
'CAUSE I KNEW I WAS A HERO AND I DIDN'T GIVE A GOOD DAMN WHAT ANYBODY ELSE THOUGHT.
TO ME, BEIN' A HERO MEANS DOIN' THE RIGHT THING, NO MATTER THE ODDS OR ANYBODY'S OPINION.
YOU DO WHAT YOU GOTTA DO.
WHY YOU ASKIN' ME THIS STUFF, JORDAN? WHY NOW?
BECAUSE I HAVE A DECISION TO MAKE, AND I NEED TO... GET THINGS CLEAR IN MY MIND.
GUY, I WANT YOU TO KNOW THAT WHATEVER CONFLICTS WE MIGHT'VE HAD, YOU WERE THE ONE I WANTED WATCHING MY BACK.
THANKS.
YEAH, JORDAN...
...YOU DO WHAT YOU GOTTA DO.

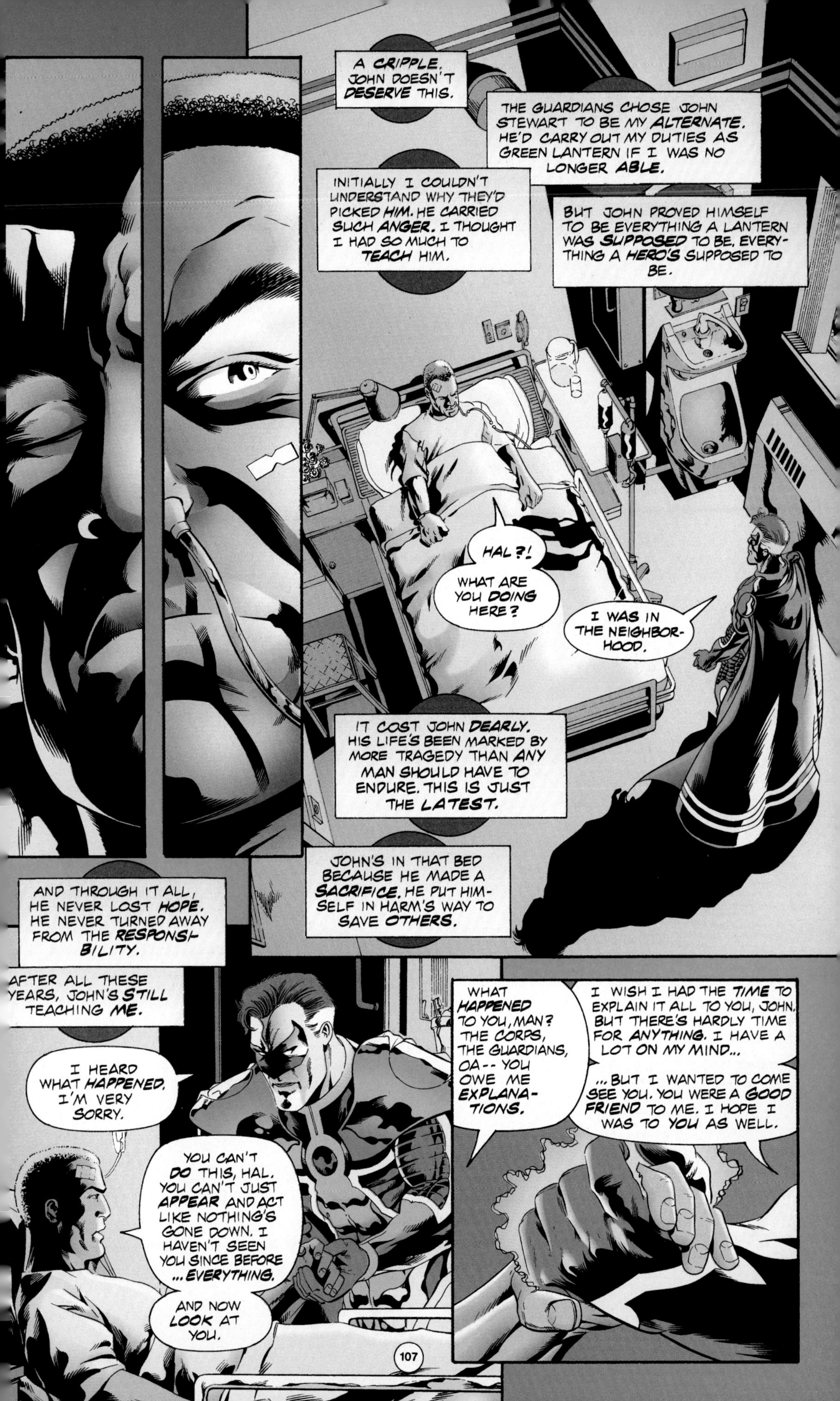

A CRIPPLE. JOHN DOESN'T DESERVE THIS.
THE GUARDIANS CHOSE JOHN STEWART TO BE MY ALTERNATE. HE'D CARRY OUT MY DUTIES AS GREEN LANTERN IF I WAS NO LONGER ABLE.
INITIALLY I COULDN'T UNDERSTAND WHY THEY'D PICKED HIM. HE CARRIED SUCH ANGER. I THOUGHT I HAD SO MUCH TO TEACH HIM.
BUT JOHN PROVED HIMSELF TO BE EVERYTHING A LANTERN WAS SUPPOSED TO BE. EVERYTHING A HERO'S SUPPOSED TO BE.
HAL?!
WHAT ARE YOU DOING HERE?
I WAS IN THE NEIGHBORHOOD.
IT COST JOHN DEARLY. HIS LIFE'S BEEN MARKED BY MORE TRAGEDY THAN ANY MAN SHOULD HAVE TO ENDURE. THIS IS JUST THE LATEST.
JOHN'S IN THAT BED BECAUSE HE MADE A SACRIFICE. HE PUT HIMSELF IN HARM'S WAY TO SAVE OTHERS.
AND THROUGH IT ALL, HE NEVER LOST HOPE. HE NEVER TURNED AWAY FROM THE RESPONSIBILITY.
AFTER ALL THESE YEARS, JOHN'S STILL TEACHING ME.
I HEARD WHAT HAPPENED. I'M VERY SORRY.
YOU CAN'T DO THIS, HAL. YOU CAN'T JUST APPEAR AND ACT LIKE NOTHING'S GONE DOWN. I HAVEN'T SEEN YOU SINCE BEFORE ...EVERYTHING.
AND NOW LOOK AT YOU.
WHAT HAPPENED TO YOU, MAN? THE CORPS, THE GUARDIANS, OA-- YOU OWE ME EXPLANATIONS.
I WISH I HAD THE TIME TO EXPLAIN IT ALL TO YOU, JOHN, BUT THERE'S HARDLY TIME FOR ANYTHING. I HAVE A LOT ON MY MIND...
...BUT I WANTED TO COME SEE YOU. YOU WERE A GOOD FRIEND TO ME. I HOPE I WAS TO YOU AS WELL.

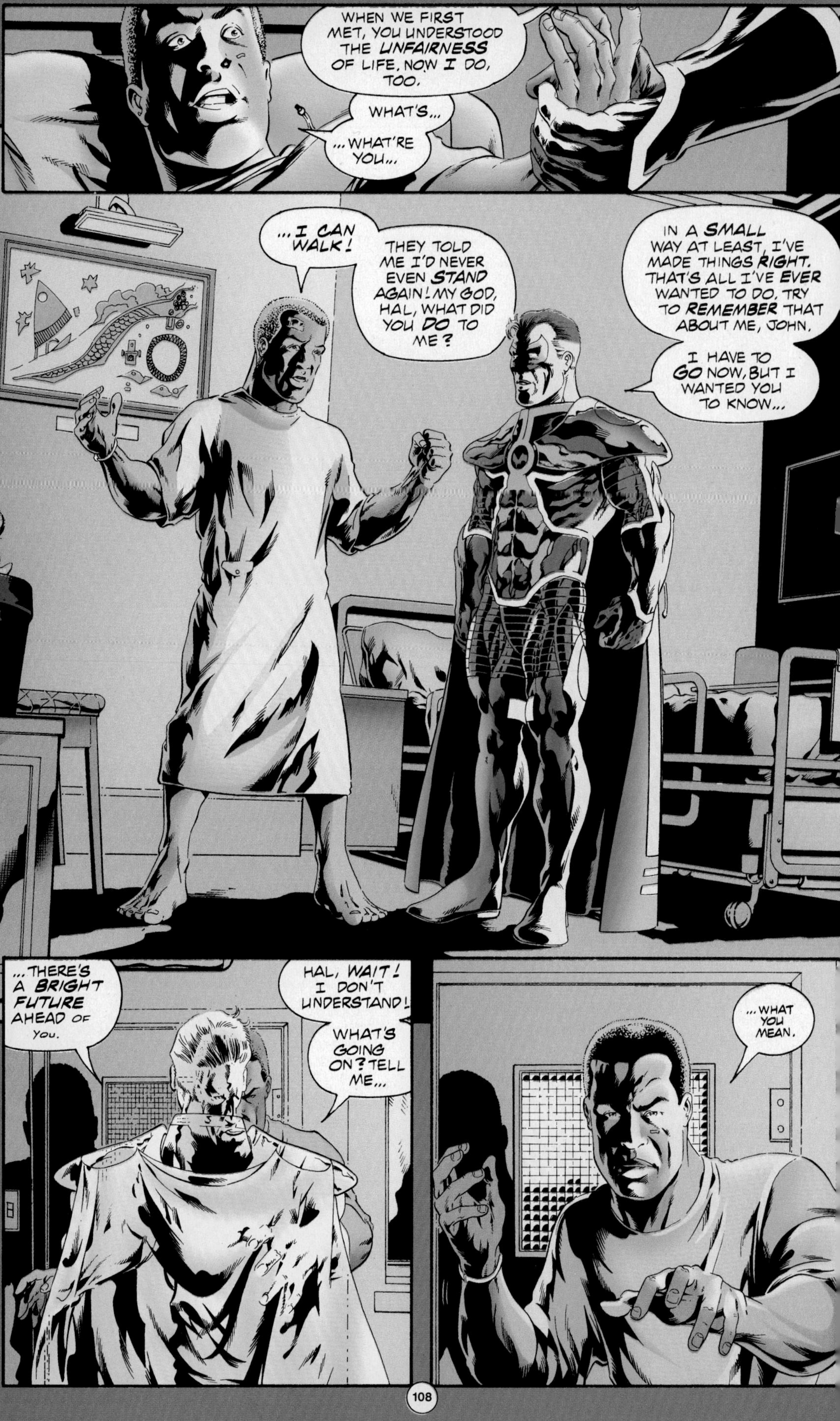
WHEN WE FIRST MET, YOU UNDERSTOOD THE UNFAIRNESS OF LIFE. NOW I DO, TOO.
WHAT'S...
...WHAT'RE YOU...
...I CAN WALK!
THEY TOLD ME I'D NEVER EVEN STAND AGAIN! MY GOD, HAL, WHAT DID YOU DO TO ME?
IN A SMALL WAY AT LEAST, I'VE MADE THINGS RIGHT. THAT'S ALL I'VE EVER WANTED TO DO. TRY TO REMEMBER THAT ABOUT ME, JOHN.
I HAVE TO GO NOW, BUT I WANTED YOU TO KNOW...
...THERE'S A BRIGHT FUTURE AHEAD OF YOU.
HAL, WAIT! I DON'T UNDERSTAND!
WHAT'S GOING ON? TELL ME...
...WHAT YOU MEAN.

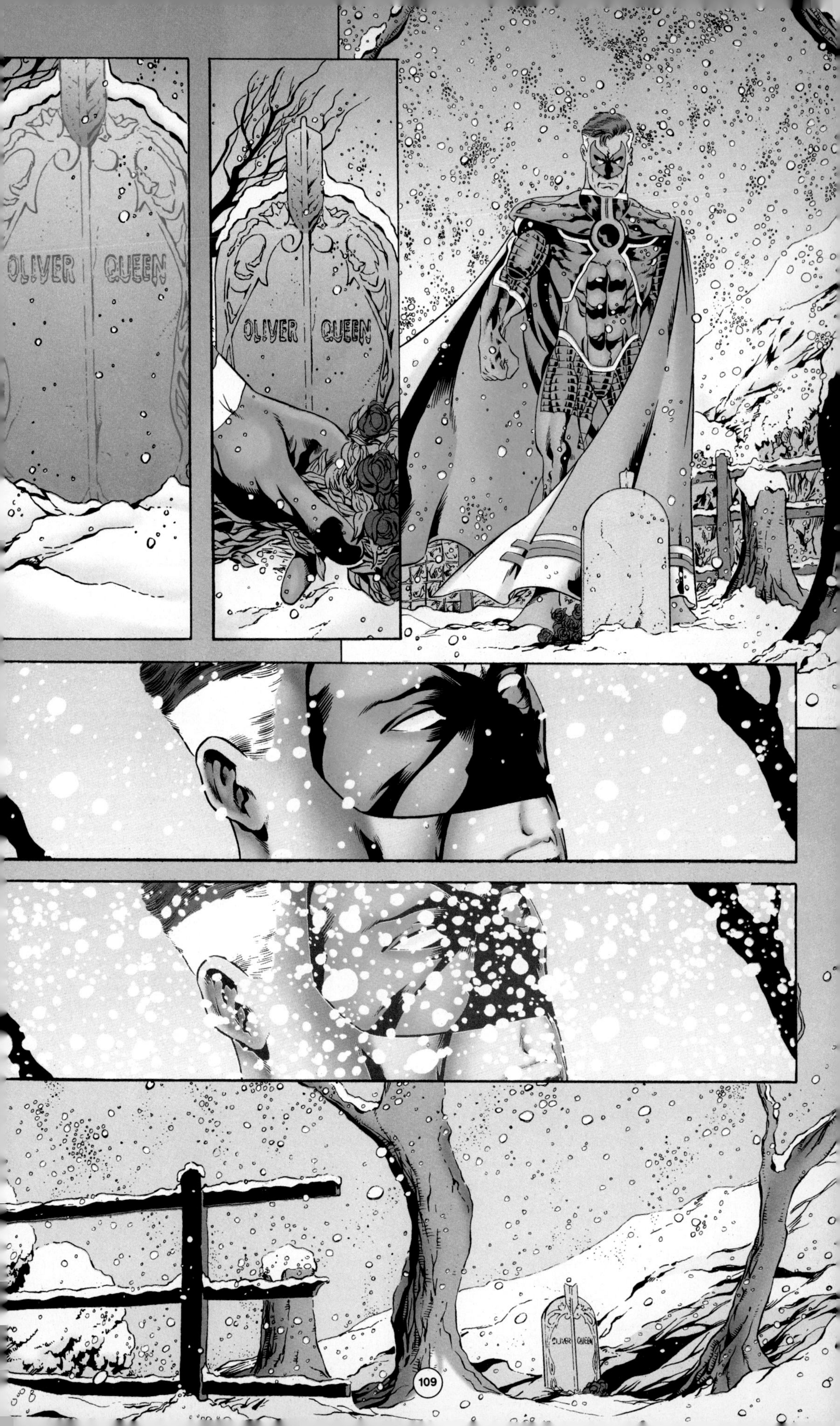
OLIVER QUEEN
OLIVER QUEEN
OLIVER QUEEN

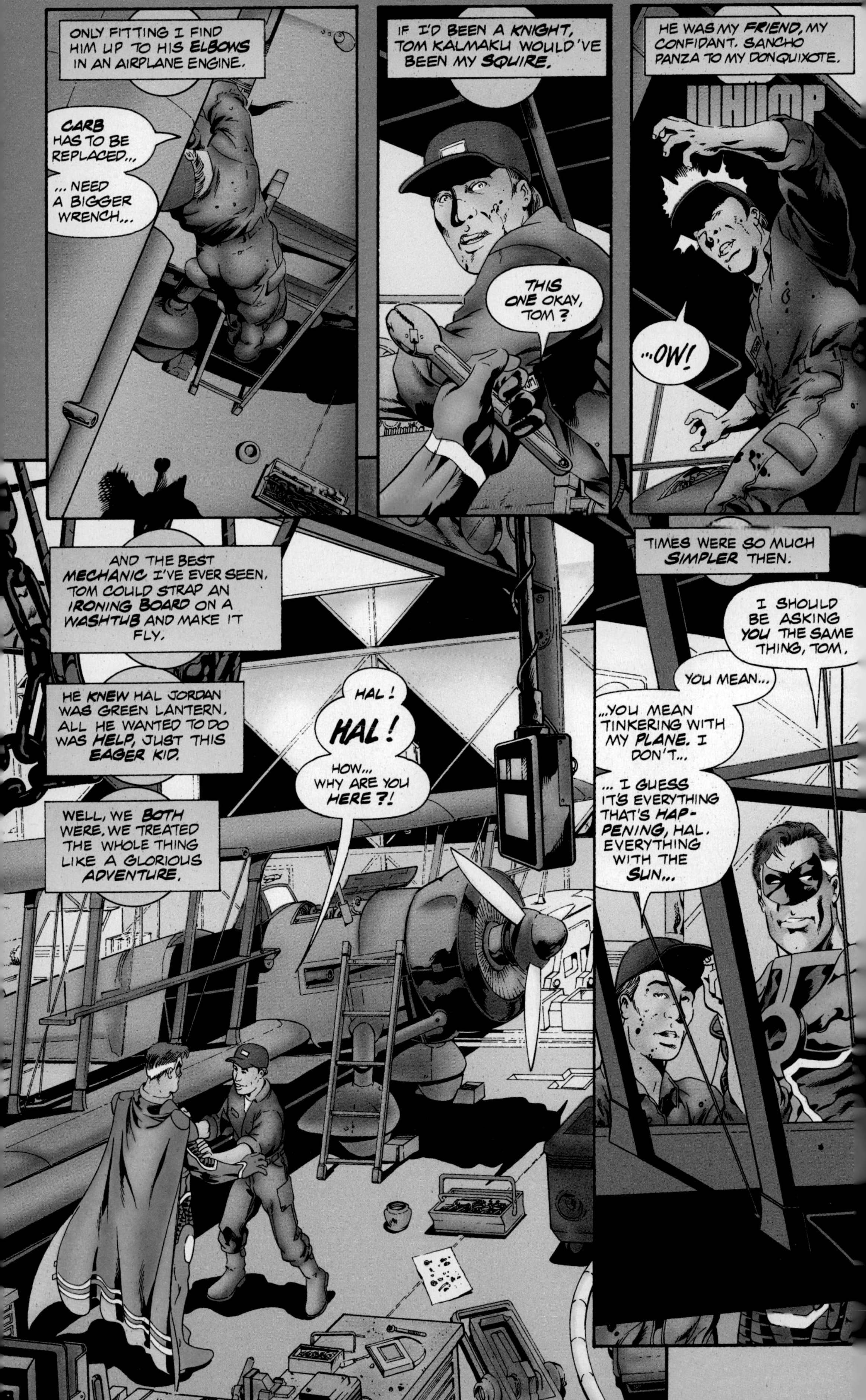
ONLY FITTING I FIND HIM UP TO HIS ELBOWS IN AN AIRPLANE ENGINE.
CARB HAS TO BE REPLACED...
... NEED A BIGGER WRENCH...
IF I'D BEEN A KNIGHT, TOM KALMAKU WOULD'VE BEEN MY SQUIRE.
THIS ONE OKAY, TOM?
HE WAS MY FRIEND, MY CONFIDANT. SANCHO PANZA TO MY DON QUIXOTE.
WHUMP
...OW!
AND THE BEST MECHANIC I'VE EVER SEEN. TOM COULD STRAP AN IRONING BOARD ON A WASHTUB AND MAKE IT FLY.
HE KNEW HAL JORDAN WAS GREEN LANTERN. ALL HE WANTED TO DO WAS HELP, JUST THIS EAGER KID.
WELL, WE BOTH WERE. WE TREATED THE WHOLE THING LIKE A GLORIOUS ADVENTURE.
HAL!
HAL!
HOW... WHY ARE YOU HERE?!
TIMES WERE SO MUCH SIMPLER THEN.
I SHOULD BE ASKING YOU THE SAME THING, TOM.
YOU MEAN...
...YOU MEAN TINKERING WITH MY PLANE. I DON'T...
... I GUESS IT'S EVERYTHING THAT'S HAP-PENING, HAL. EVERYTHING WITH THE SUN...

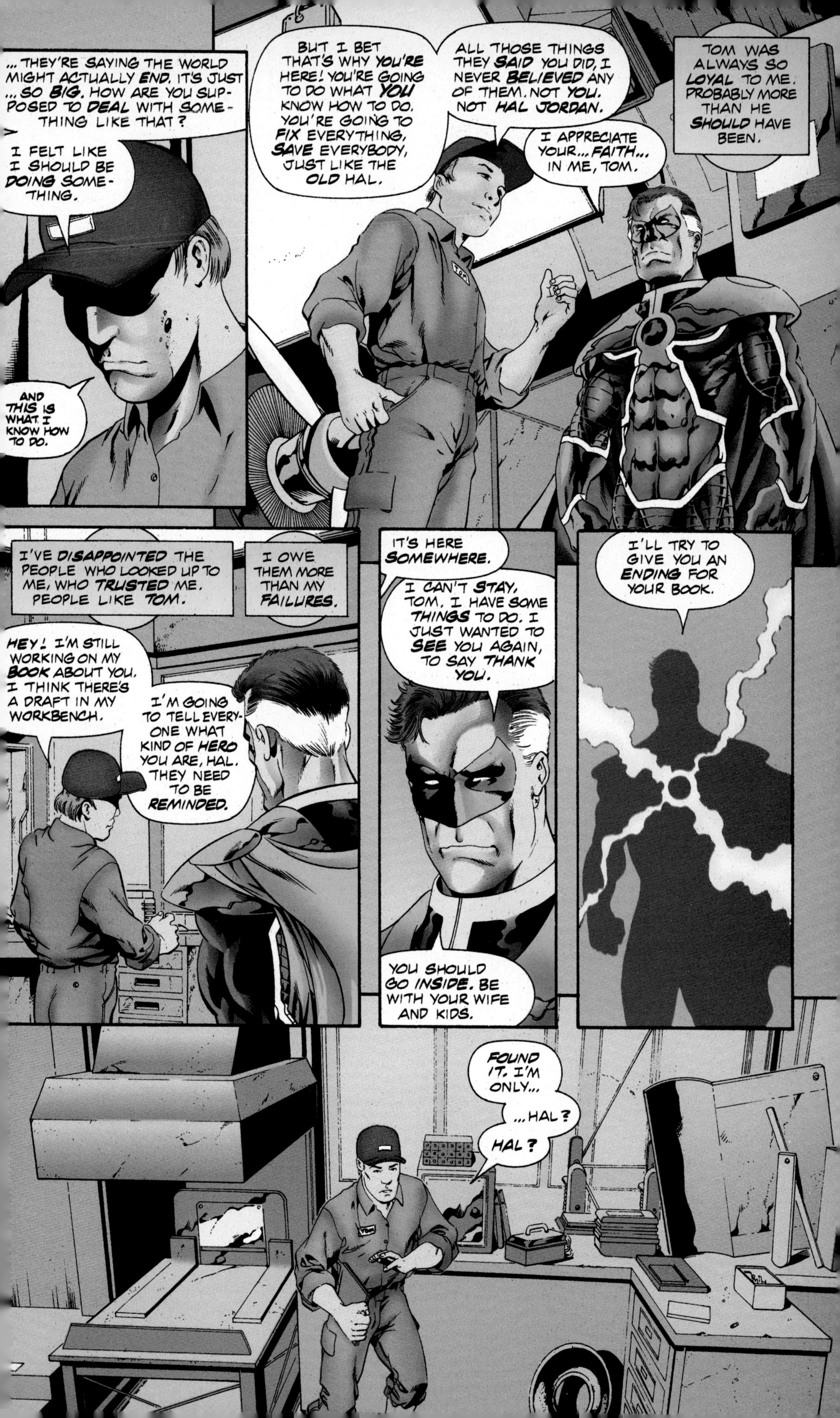
...THEY'RE SAYING THE WORLD MIGHT ACTUALLY END. IT'S JUST ...SO BIG. HOW ARE YOU SUPPOSED TO DEAL WITH SOMETHING LIKE THAT?
I FELT LIKE I SHOULD BE DOING SOMETHING.
AND THIS IS WHAT I KNOW HOW TO DO.
BUT I BET THAT'S WHY YOU'RE HERE! YOU'RE GOING TO DO WHAT YOU KNOW HOW TO DO. YOU'RE GOING TO FIX EVERYTHING, SAVE EVERYBODY, JUST LIKE THE OLD HAL.
ALL THOSE THINGS THEY SAID YOU DID, I NEVER BELIEVED ANY OF THEM. NOT YOU. NOT HAL JORDAN.
I APPRECIATE YOUR... FAITH... IN ME, TOM.
TOM WAS ALWAYS SO LOYAL TO ME. PROBABLY MORE THAN HE SHOULD HAVE BEEN.
I'VE DISAPPOINTED THE PEOPLE WHO LOOKED UP TO ME, WHO TRUSTED ME. PEOPLE LIKE TOM.
I OWE THEM MORE THAN MY FAILURES.
HEY! I'M STILL WORKING ON MY BOOK ABOUT YOU. I THINK THERE'S A DRAFT IN MY WORKBENCH.
I'M GOING TO TELL EVERYONE WHAT KIND OF HERO YOU ARE, HAL. THEY NEED TO BE REMINDED.
IT'S HERE SOMEWHERE.
I CAN'T STAY, TOM. I HAVE SOME THINGS TO DO. I JUST WANTED TO SEE YOU AGAIN, TO SAY THANK YOU.
YOU SHOULD GO INSIDE. BE WITH YOUR WIFE AND KIDS.
I'LL TRY TO GIVE YOU AN ENDING FOR YOUR BOOK.
FOUND IT. I'M ONLY...
...HAL?
HAL?

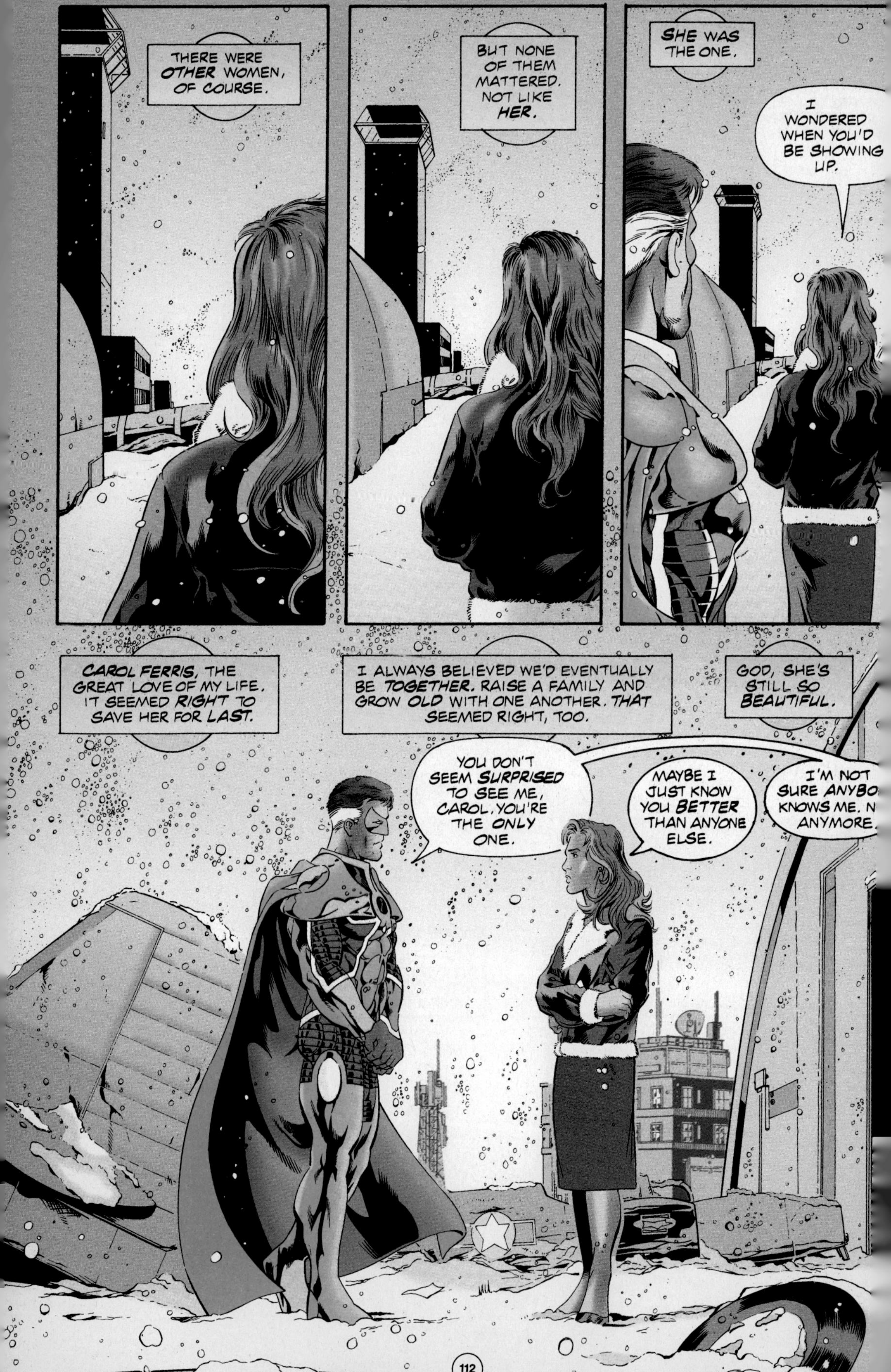
THERE WERE OTHER WOMEN, OF COURSE.
BUT NONE OF THEM MATTERED. NOT LIKE HER.
SHE WAS THE ONE.
I WONDERED WHEN YOU'D BE SHOWING UP.
CAROL FERRIS, THE GREAT LOVE OF MY LIFE. IT SEEMED RIGHT TO SAVE HER FOR LAST.
I ALWAYS BELIEVED WE'D EVENTUALLY BE TOGETHER. RAISE A FAMILY AND GROW OLD WITH ONE ANOTHER. THAT SEEMED RIGHT, TOO.
GOD, SHE'S STILL SO BEAUTIFUL.
YOU DON'T SEEM SURPRISED TO SEE ME, CAROL. YOU'RE THE ONLY ONE.
MAYBE I JUST KNOW YOU BETTER THAN ANYONE ELSE.
I'M NOT SURE ANYBO KNOWS ME. N ANYMORE.

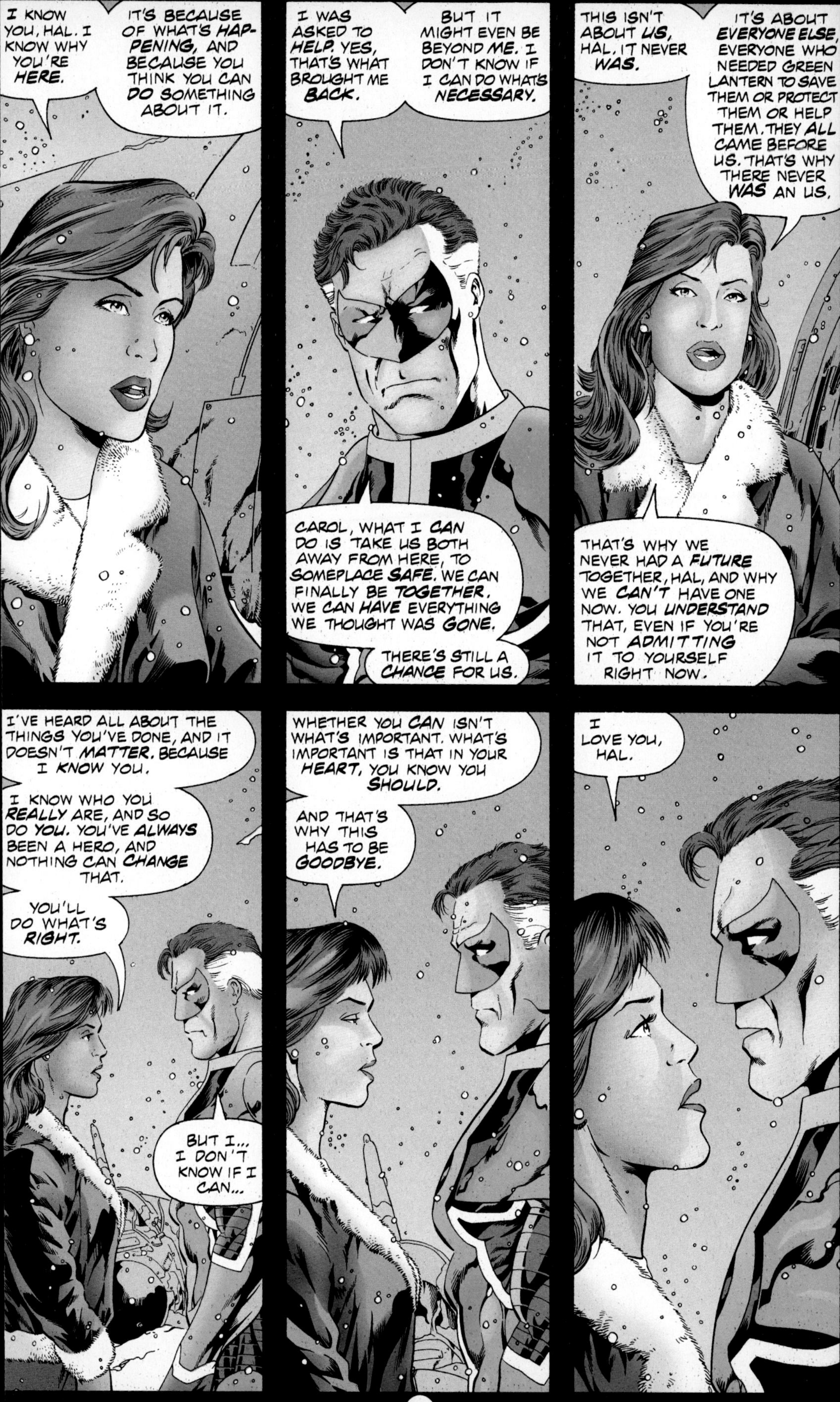
I KNOW YOU, HAL. I KNOW WHY YOU'RE HERE.
IT'S BECAUSE OF WHAT'S HAPPENING, AND BECAUSE YOU THINK YOU CAN DO SOMETHING ABOUT IT.
I WAS ASKED TO HELP. YES, THAT'S WHAT BROUGHT ME BACK.
BUT IT MIGHT EVEN BE BEYOND ME. I DON'T KNOW IF I CAN DO WHAT'S NECESSARY.
CAROL, WHAT I CAN DO IS TAKE US BOTH AWAY FROM HERE, TO SOMEPLACE SAFE. WE CAN FINALLY BE TOGETHER. WE CAN HAVE EVERYTHING WE THOUGHT WAS GONE.
THERE'S STILL A CHANCE FOR US.
THIS ISN'T ABOUT US, HAL. IT NEVER WAS.
IT'S ABOUT EVERYONE ELSE, EVERYONE WHO NEEDED GREEN LANTERN TO SAVE THEM OR PROTECT THEM OR HELP THEM. THEY ALL CAME BEFORE US. THAT'S WHY THERE NEVER WAS AN US.
THAT'S WHY WE NEVER HAD A FUTURE TOGETHER, HAL, AND WHY WE CAN'T HAVE ONE NOW. YOU UNDERSTAND THAT, EVEN IF YOU'RE NOT ADMITTING IT TO YOURSELF RIGHT NOW.
I'VE HEARD ALL ABOUT THE THINGS YOU'VE DONE, AND IT DOESN'T MATTER. BECAUSE I KNOW YOU.
I KNOW WHO YOU REALLY ARE, AND SO DO YOU. YOU'VE ALWAYS BEEN A HERO, AND NOTHING CAN CHANGE THAT.
YOU'LL DO WHAT'S RIGHT.
BUT I... I DON'T KNOW IF I CAN...
WHETHER YOU CAN ISN'T WHAT'S IMPORTANT. WHAT'S IMPORTANT IS THAT IN YOUR HEART, YOU KNOW YOU SHOULD.
AND THAT'S WHY THIS HAS TO BE GOODBYE.
I LOVE YOU, HAL.

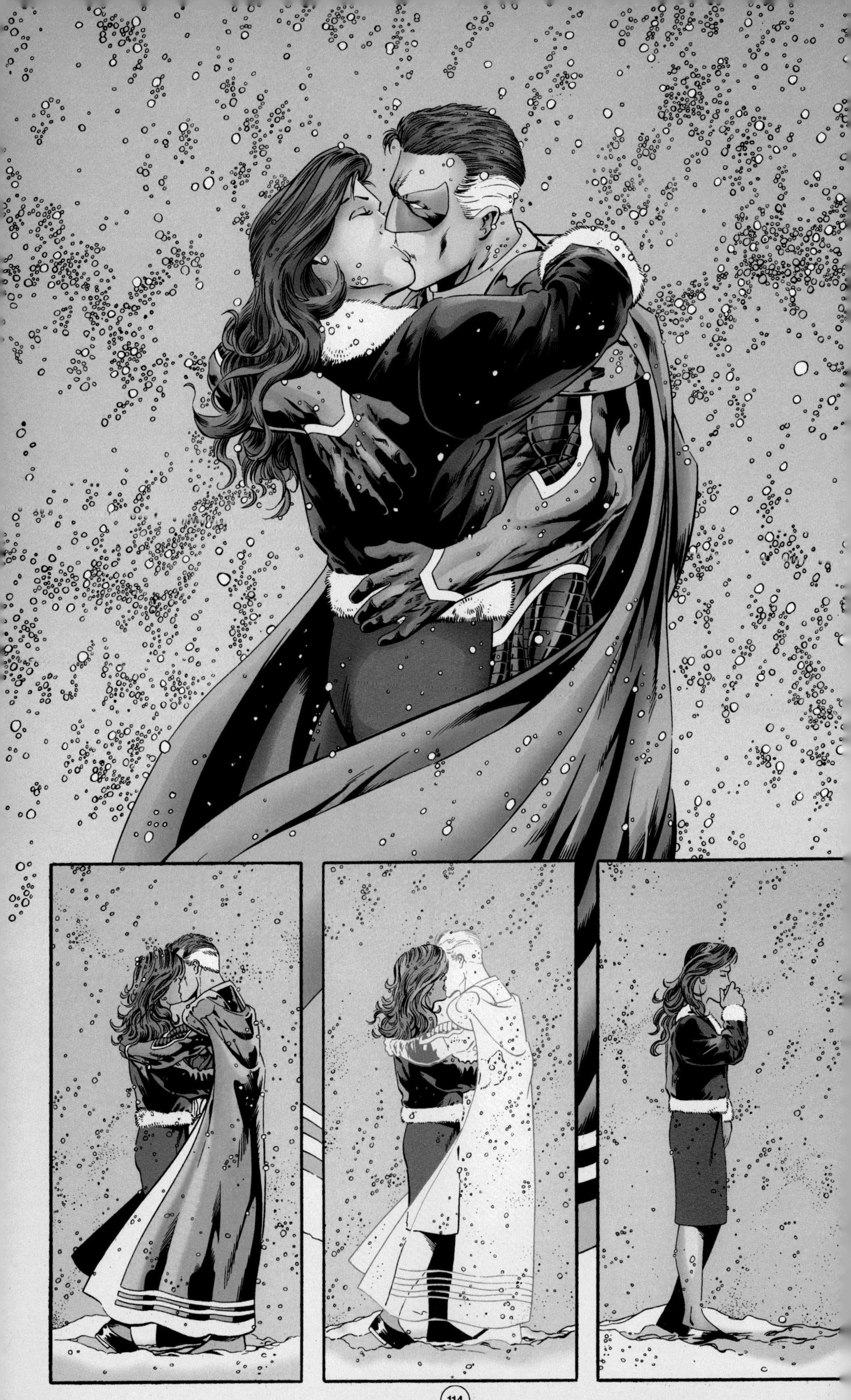

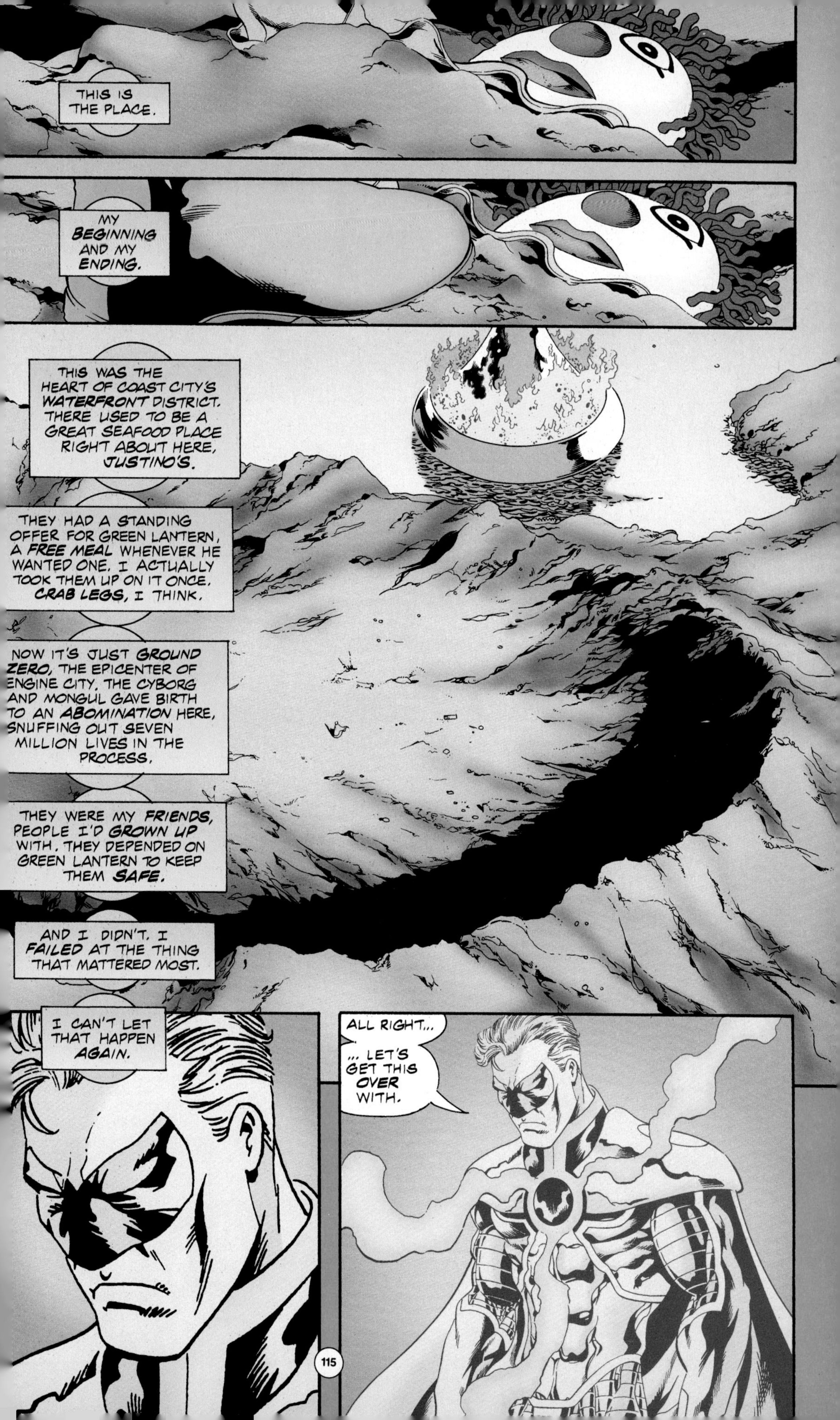

THIS IS THE PLACE.
MY BEGINNING AND MY ENDING.
THIS WAS THE HEART OF COAST CITY'S WATERFRONT DISTRICT. THERE USED TO BE A GREAT SEAFOOD PLACE RIGHT ABOUT HERE, JUSTINO'S.
THEY HAD A STANDING OFFER FOR GREEN LANTERN, A FREE MEAL WHENEVER HE WANTED ONE. I ACTUALLY TOOK THEM UP ON IT ONCE. CRAB LEGS, I THINK.
NOW IT'S JUST GROUND ZERO, THE EPICENTER OF ENGINE CITY. THE CYBORG AND MONGUL GAVE BIRTH TO AN ABOMINATION HERE, SNUFFING OUT SEVEN MILLION LIVES IN THE PROCESS.
THEY WERE MY FRIENDS, PEOPLE I'D GROWN UP WITH. THEY DEPENDED ON GREEN LANTERN TO KEEP THEM SAFE.
AND I DIDN'T. I FAILED AT THE THING THAT MATTERED MOST.
I CAN'T LET THAT HAPPEN AGAIN.
ALL RIGHT...
... LET'S GET THIS OVER WITH.

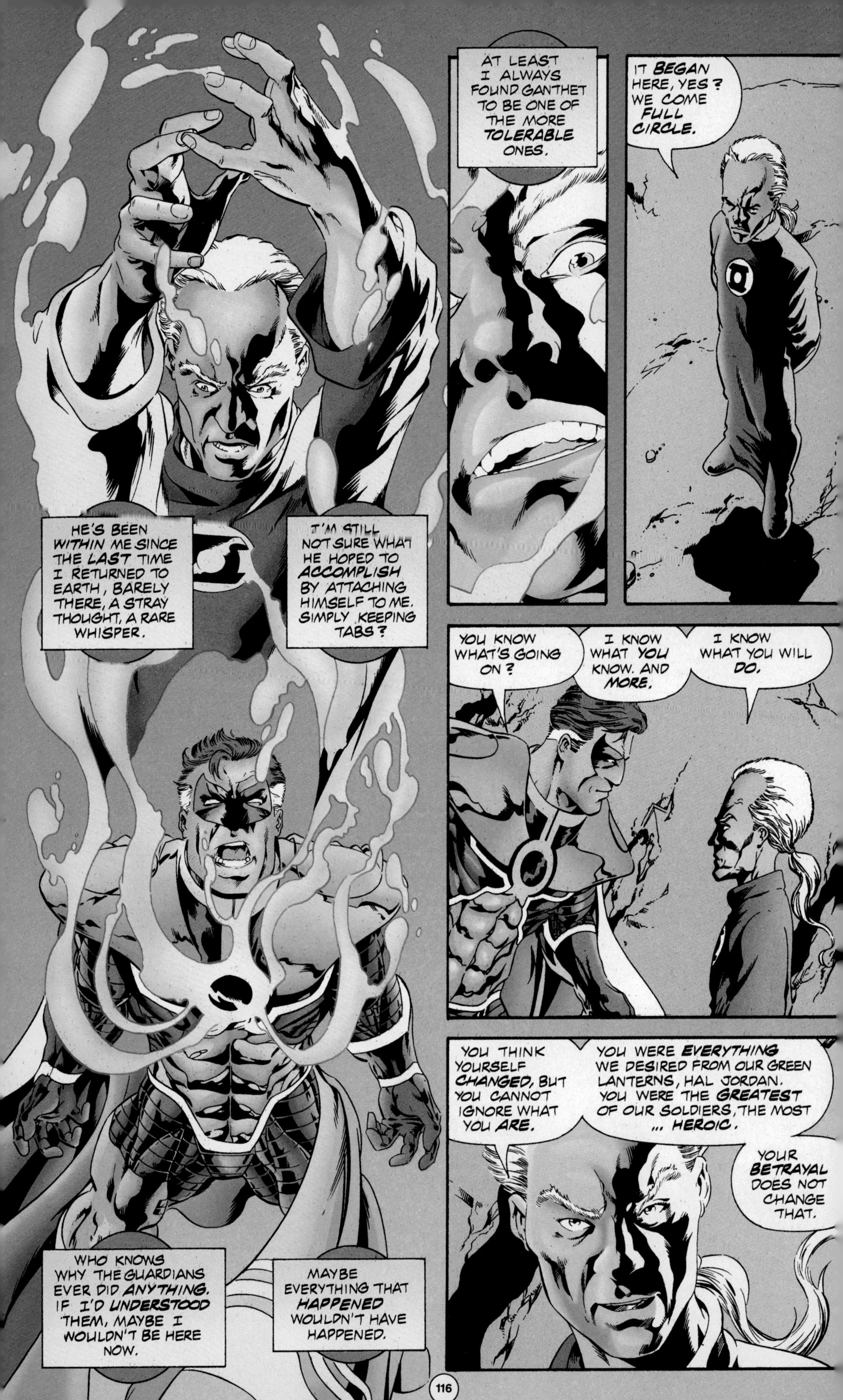
AT LEAST I ALWAYS FOUND GANTHET TO BE ONE OF THE MORE TOLERABLE ONES.
IT BEGAN HERE, YES? WE COME FULL CIRCLE.
HE'S BEEN WITHIN ME SINCE THE LAST TIME I RETURNED TO EARTH, BARELY THERE, A STRAY THOUGHT, A RARE WHISPER.
I'M STILL NOT SURE WHAT HE HOPED TO ACCOMPLISH BY ATTACHING HIMSELF TO ME. SIMPLY KEEPING TABS?
YOU KNOW WHAT'S GOING ON?
I KNOW WHAT YOU KNOW. AND MORE.
I KNOW WHAT YOU WILL DO.
YOU THINK YOURSELF CHANGED, BUT YOU CANNOT IGNORE WHAT YOU ARE.
YOU WERE EVERYTHING WE DESIRED FROM OUR GREEN LANTERNS, HAL JORDAN. YOU WERE THE GREATEST OF OUR SOLDIERS, THE MOST ... HEROIC.
YOUR BETRAYAL DOES NOT CHANGE THAT.
WHO KNOWS WHY THE GUARDIANS EVER DID ANYTHING. IF I'D UNDERSTOOD THEM, MAYBE I WOULDN'T BE HERE NOW.
MAYBE EVERYTHING THAT HAPPENED WOULDN'T HAVE HAPPENED.

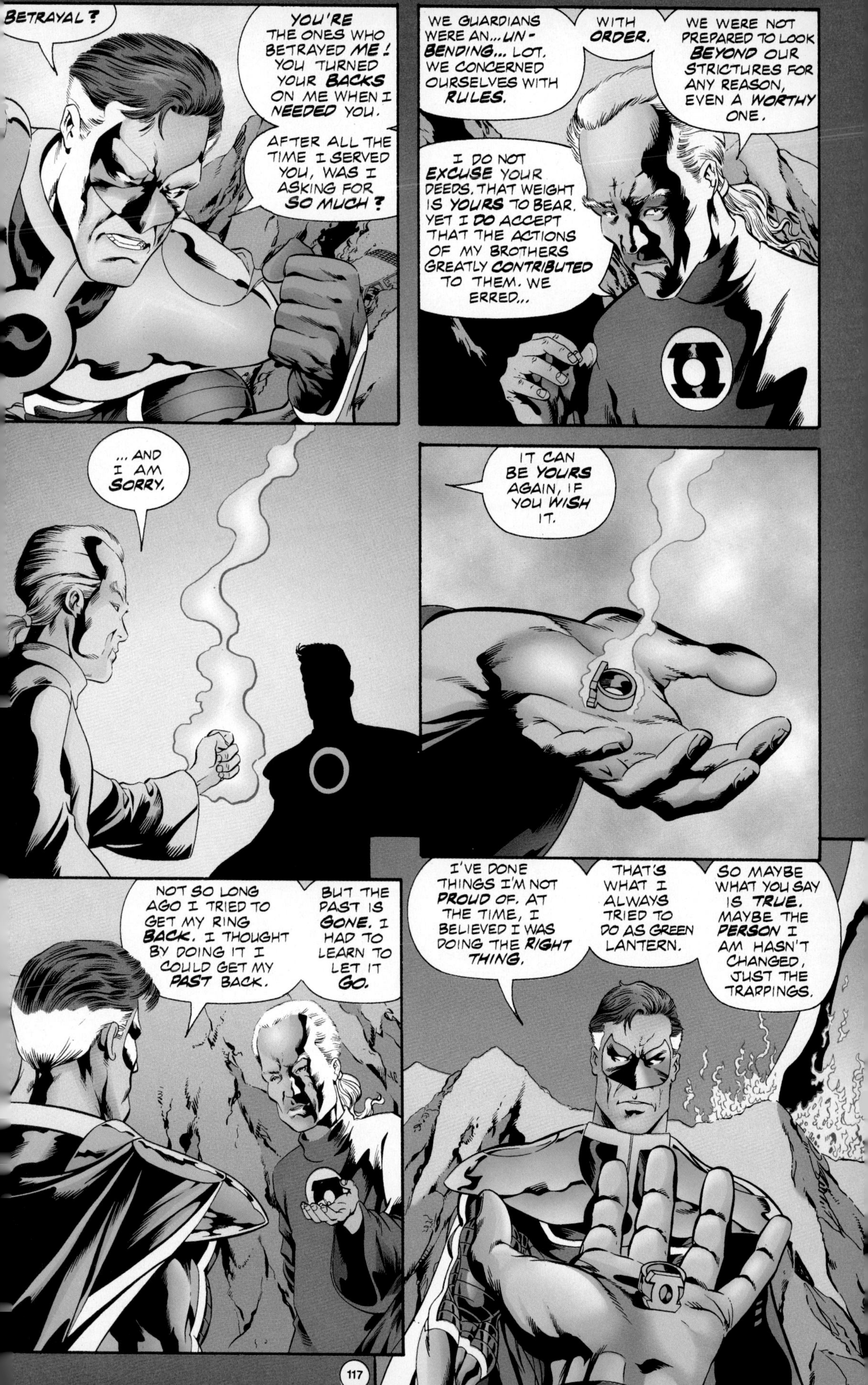
BETRAYAL?
YOU'RE THE ONES WHO BETRAYED ME! YOU TURNED YOUR BACKS ON ME WHEN I NEEDED YOU.
AFTER ALL THE TIME I SERVED YOU, WAS I ASKING FOR SO MUCH?
WE GUARDIANS WERE AN... UN-BENDING... LOT. WE CONCERNED OURSELVES WITH RULES.
WITH ORDER.
WE WERE NOT PREPARED TO LOOK BEYOND OUR STRICTURES FOR ANY REASON, EVEN A WORTHY ONE.
I DO NOT EXCUSE YOUR DEEDS. THAT WEIGHT IS YOURS TO BEAR. YET I DO ACCEPT THAT THE ACTIONS OF MY BROTHERS GREATLY CONTRIBUTED TO THEM. WE ERRED...
... AND I AM SORRY.
IT CAN BE YOURS AGAIN, IF YOU WISH IT.
NOT SO LONG AGO I TRIED TO GET MY RING BACK. I THOUGHT BY DOING IT I COULD GET MY PAST BACK.
BUT THE PAST IS GONE. I HAD TO LEARN TO LET IT GO.
I'VE DONE THINGS I'M NOT PROUD OF. AT THE TIME, I BELIEVED I WAS DOING THE RIGHT THING.
THAT'S WHAT I ALWAYS TRIED TO DO AS GREEN LANTERN.
SO MAYBE WHAT YOU SAY IS TRUE. MAYBE THE PERSON I AM HASN'T CHANGED, JUST THE TRAPPINGS.

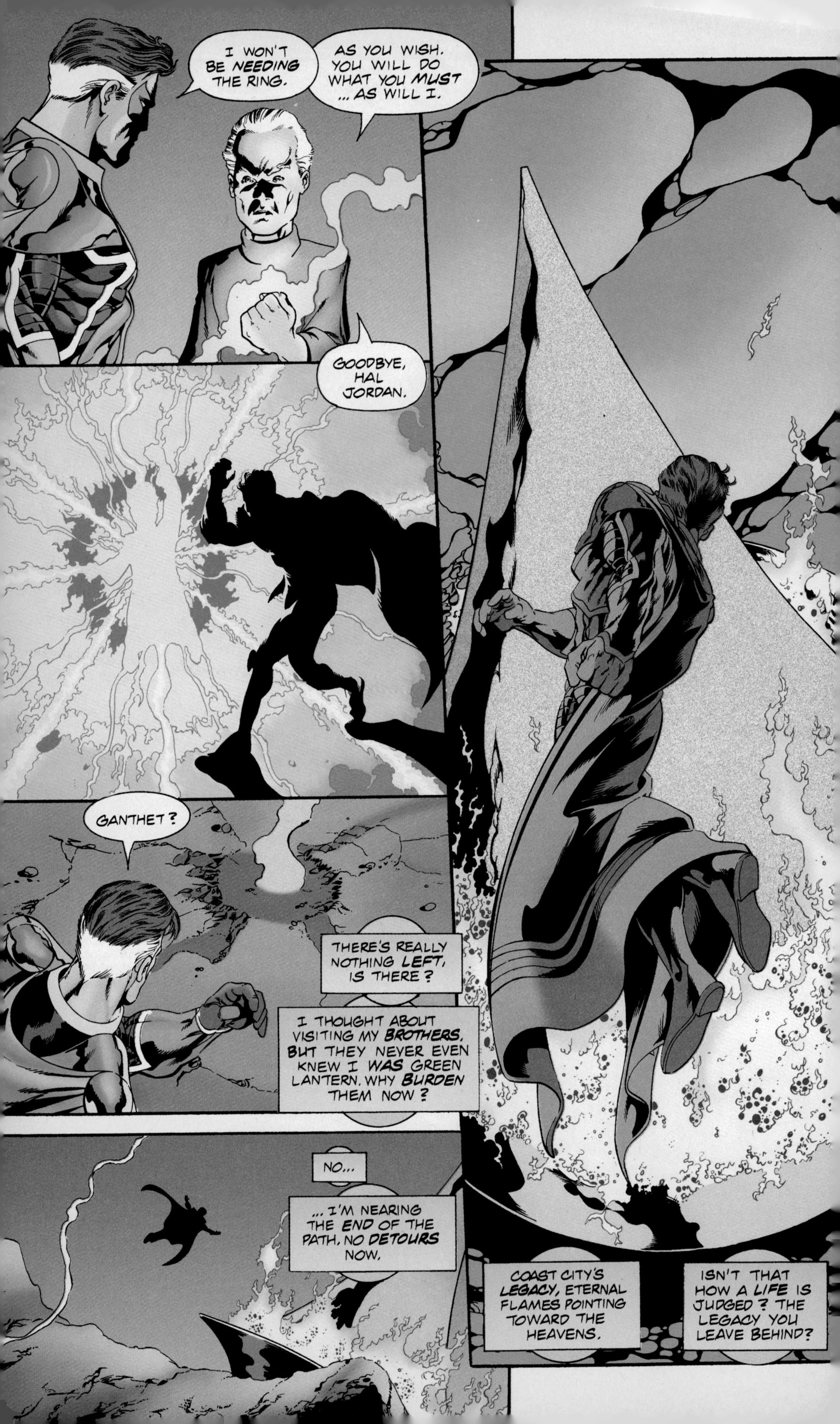

I WON'T BE NEEDING THE RING.
AS YOU WISH. YOU WILL DO WHAT YOU MUST ...AS WILL I.
GOODBYE, HAL JORDAN.
GANTHET?
THERE'S REALLY NOTHING LEFT, IS THERE?
I THOUGHT ABOUT VISITING MY BROTHERS, BUT THEY NEVER EVEN KNEW I WAS GREEN LANTERN. WHY BURDEN THEM NOW?
NO...
...I'M NEARING THE END OF THE PATH. NO DETOURS NOW.
COAST CITY'S LEGACY, ETERNAL FLAMES POINTING TOWARD THE HEAVENS.
ISN'T THAT HOW A LIFE IS JUDGED? THE LEGACY YOU LEAVE BEHIND?

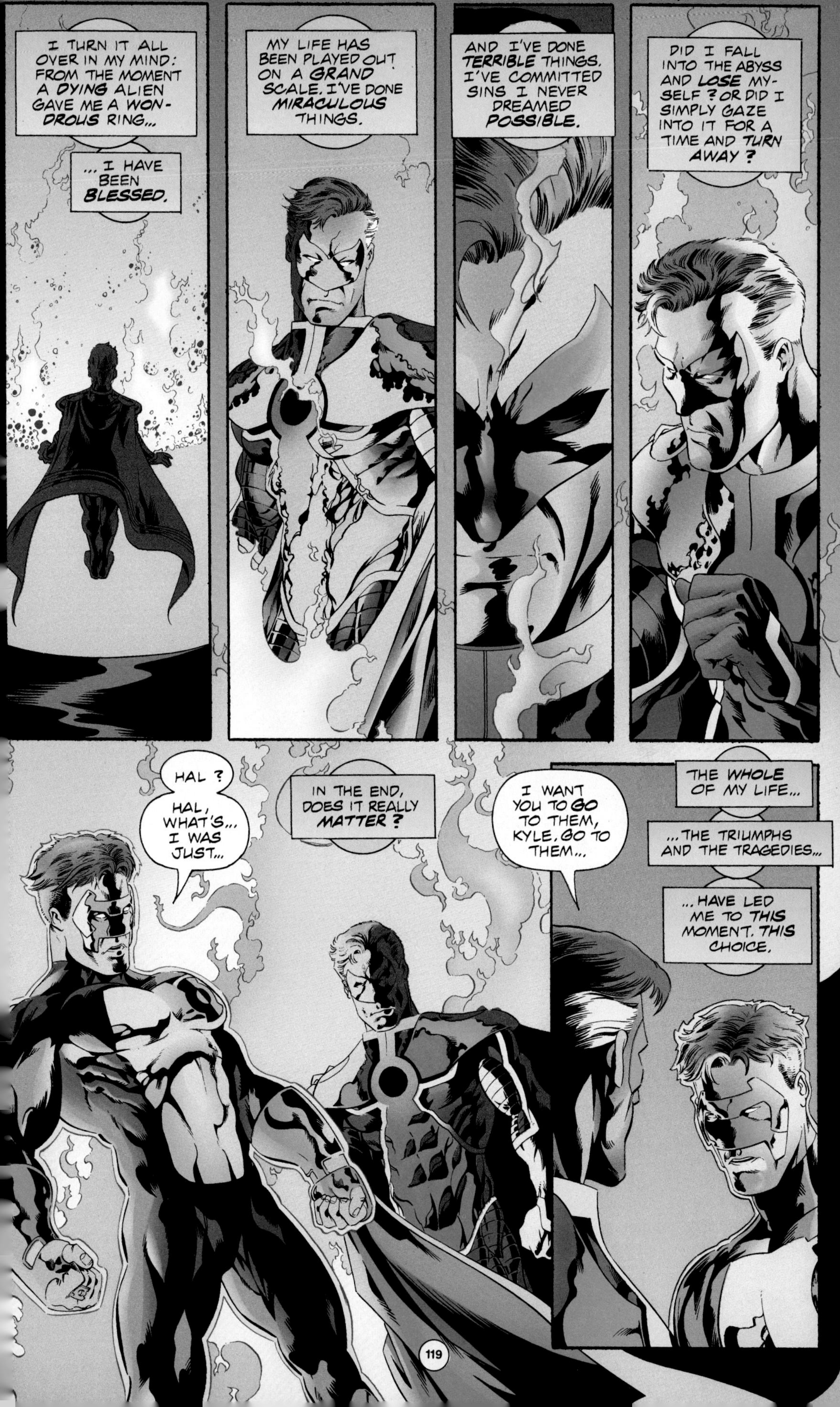

I TURN IT ALL OVER IN MY MIND: FROM THE MOMENT A DYING ALIEN GAVE ME A WONDROUS RING...
... I HAVE BEEN BLESSED.
MY LIFE HAS BEEN PLAYED OUT ON A GRAND SCALE. I'VE DONE MIRACULOUS THINGS.
AND I'VE DONE TERRIBLE THINGS. I'VE COMMITTED SINS I NEVER DREAMED POSSIBLE.
DID I FALL INTO THE ABYSS AND LOSE MYSELF ? OR DID I SIMPLY GAZE INTO IT FOR A TIME AND TURN AWAY ?
HAL ?
HAL, WHAT'S... I WAS JUST...
IN THE END, DOES IT REALLY MATTER ?
I WANT YOU TO GO TO THEM, KYLE. GO TO THEM...
THE WHOLE OF MY LIFE...
...THE TRIUMPHS AND THE TRAGEDIES...
... HAVE LED ME TO THIS MOMENT. THIS CHOICE.

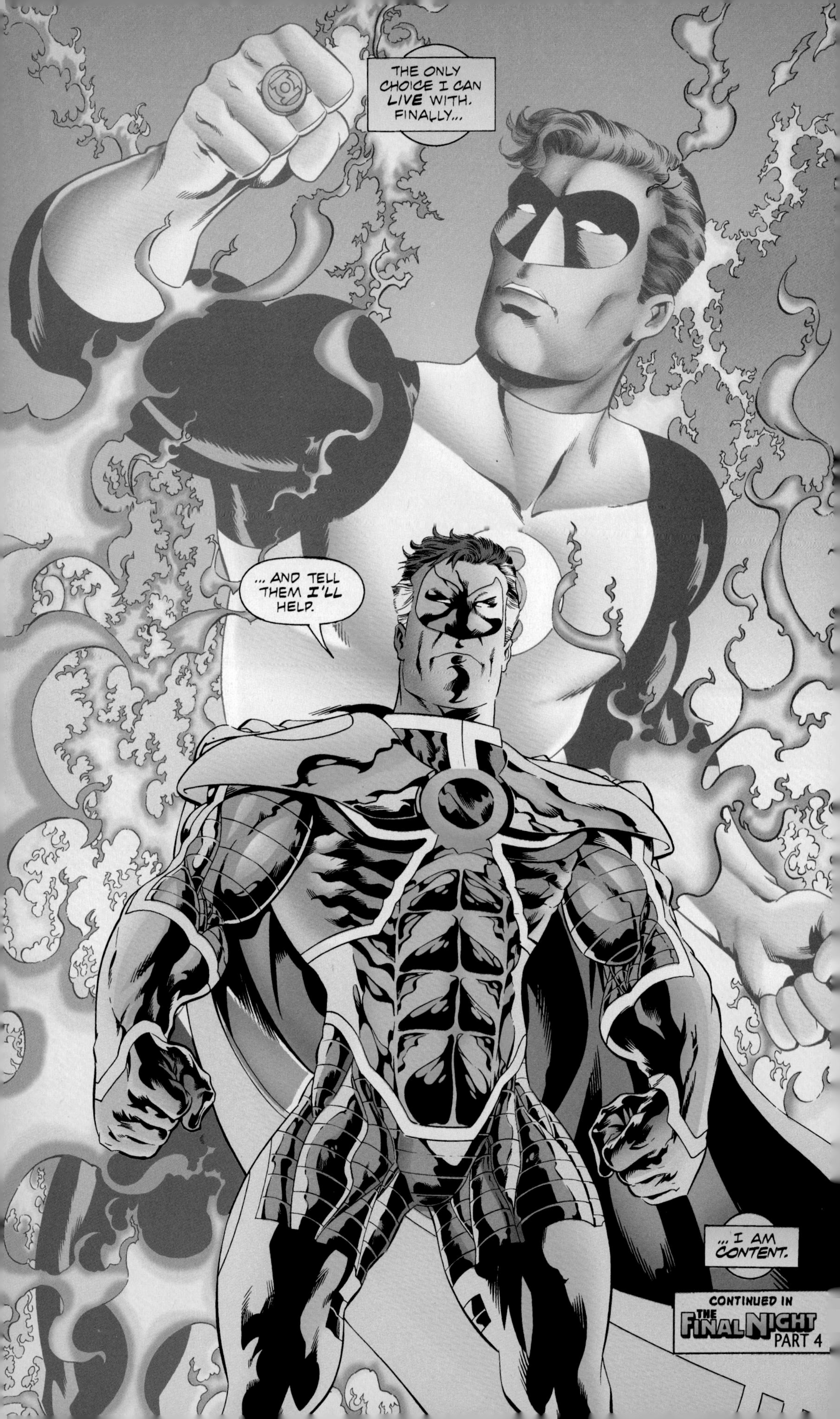
THE ONLY CHOICE I CAN LIVE WITH. FINALLY...
...AND TELL THEM I'LL HELP.
...I AM CONTENT.
CONTINUED IN THE FINAL NIGHT PART 4

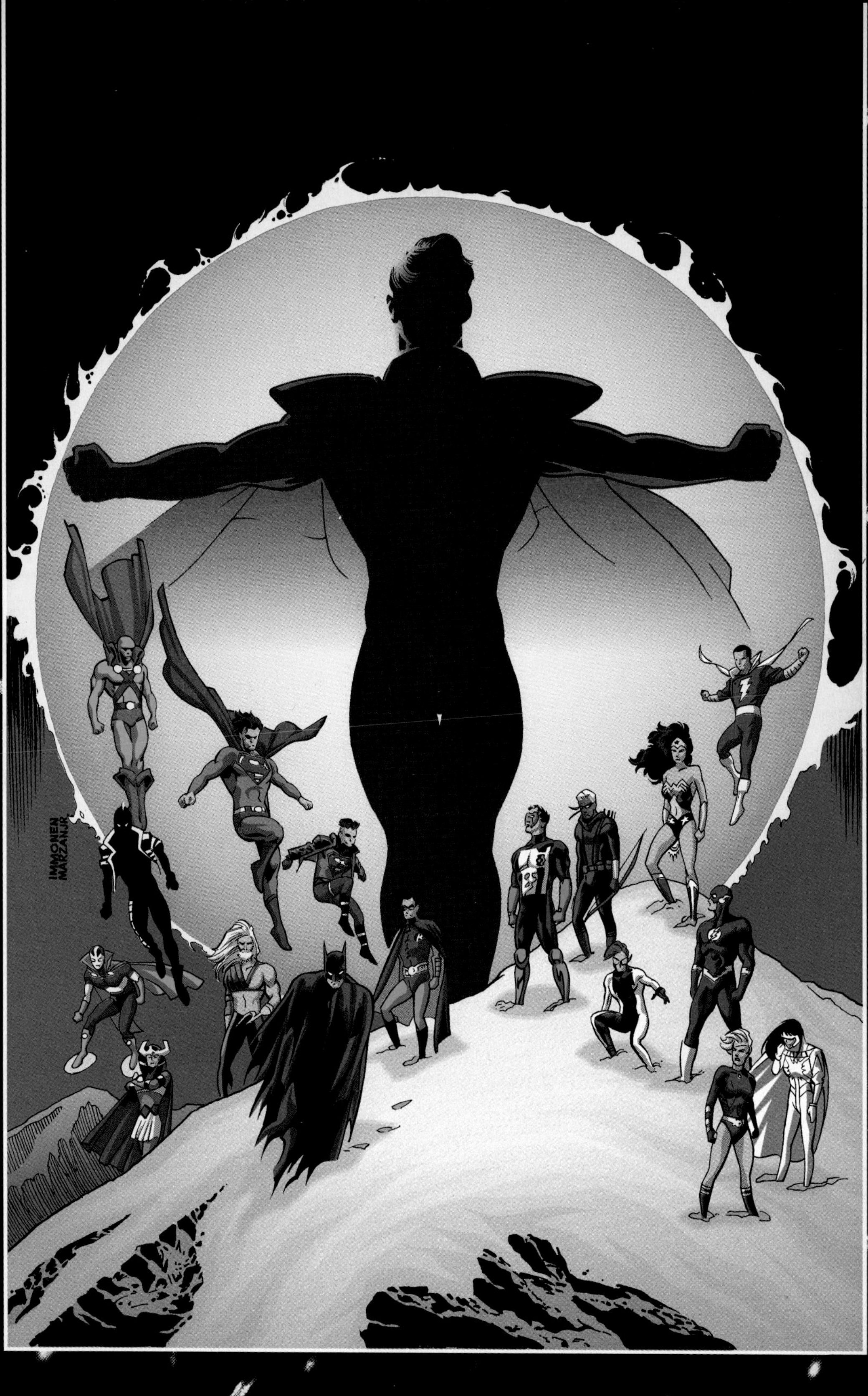
IMMONEN
MARZANJR

EMERALD DAWN

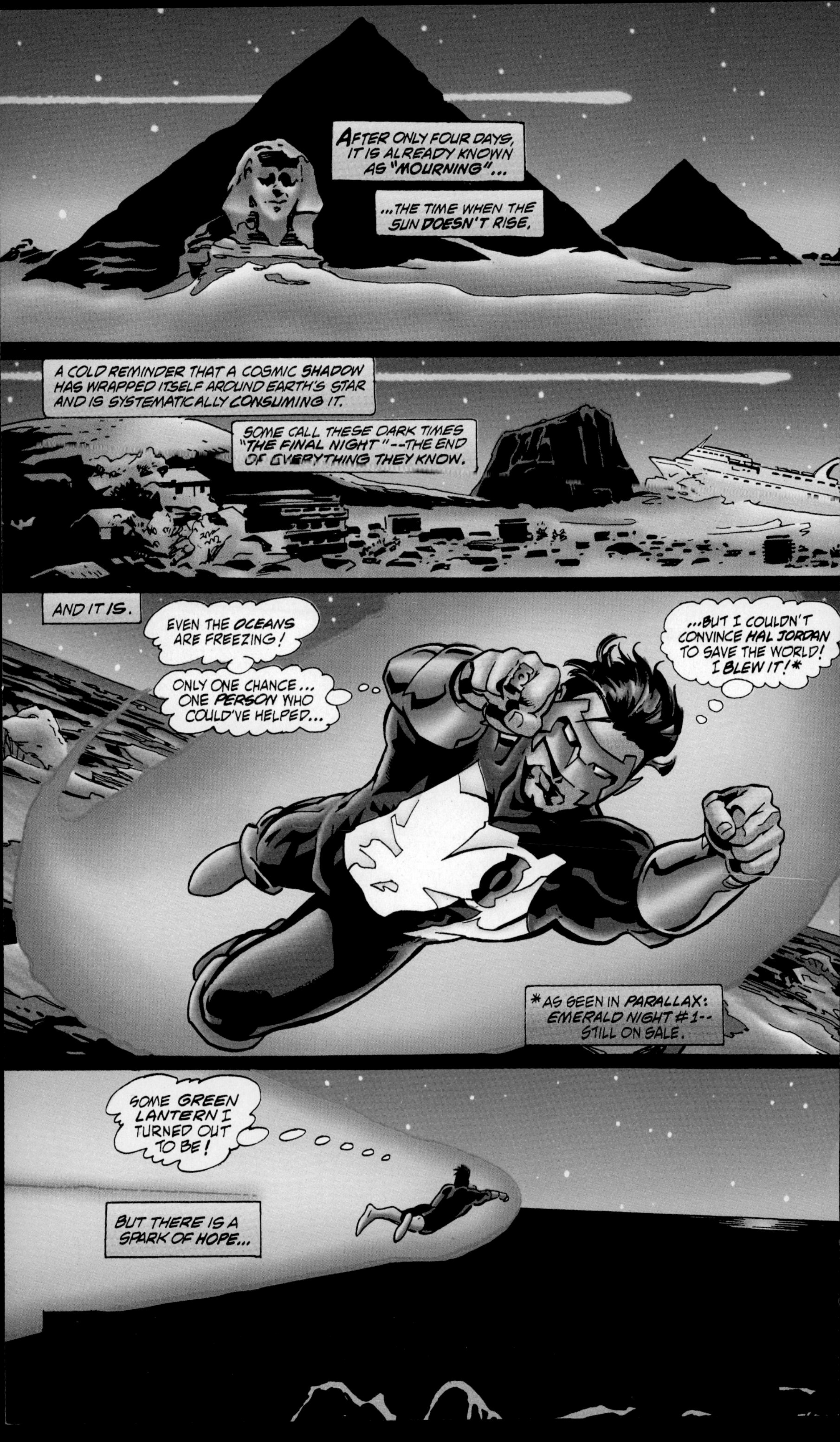
AFTER ONLY FOUR DAYS, IT IS ALREADY KNOWN AS "MOURNING"...
...THE TIME WHEN THE SUN DOESN'T RISE.
A COLD REMINDER THAT A COSMIC SHADOW HAS WRAPPED ITSELF AROUND EARTH'S STAR AND IS SYSTEMATICALLY CONSUMING IT.
SOME CALL THESE DARK TIMES "THE FINAL NIGHT"--THE END OF EVERYTHING THEY KNOW.
AND IT IS.
EVEN THE OCEANS ARE FREEZING!
ONLY ONE CHANCE... ONE PERSON WHO COULD'VE HELPED...
...BUT I COULDN'T CONVINCE HAL JORDAN TO SAVE THE WORLD! I BLEW IT!*
*AS SEEN IN PARALLAX: EMERALD NIGHT #1--STILL ON SALE.
SOME GREEN LANTERN I TURNED OUT TO BE!
BUT THERE IS A SPARK OF HOPE...

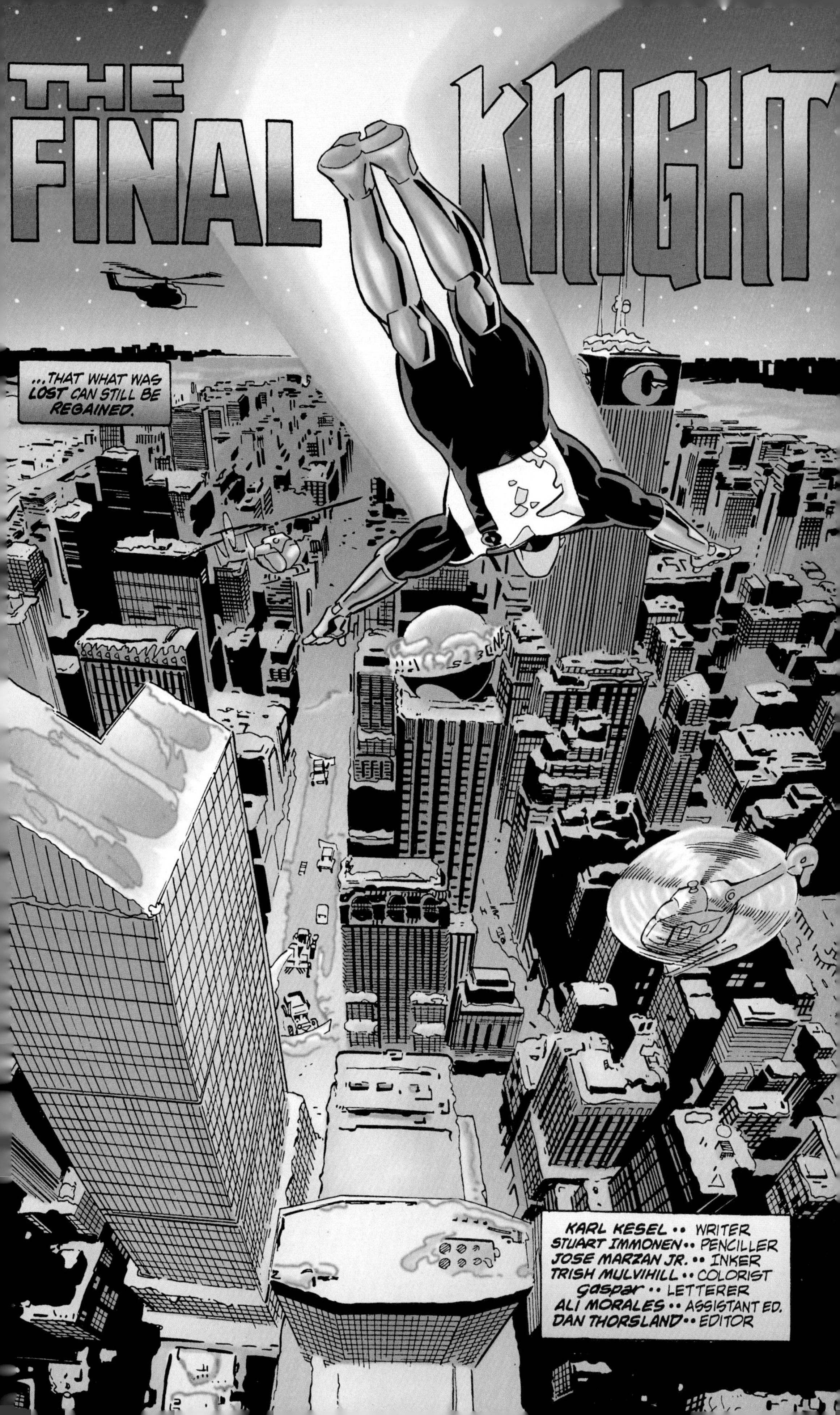
THE FINAL KNIGHT
...THAT WHAT WAS LOST CAN STILL BE REGAINED.
KARL KESEL •• WRITER
STUART IMMONEN •• PENCILLER
JOSE MARZAN JR. •• INKER
TRISH MULVIHILL •• COLORIST
gaspar •• LETTERER
ALI MORALES •• ASSISTANT ED.
DAN THORSLAND •• EDITOR

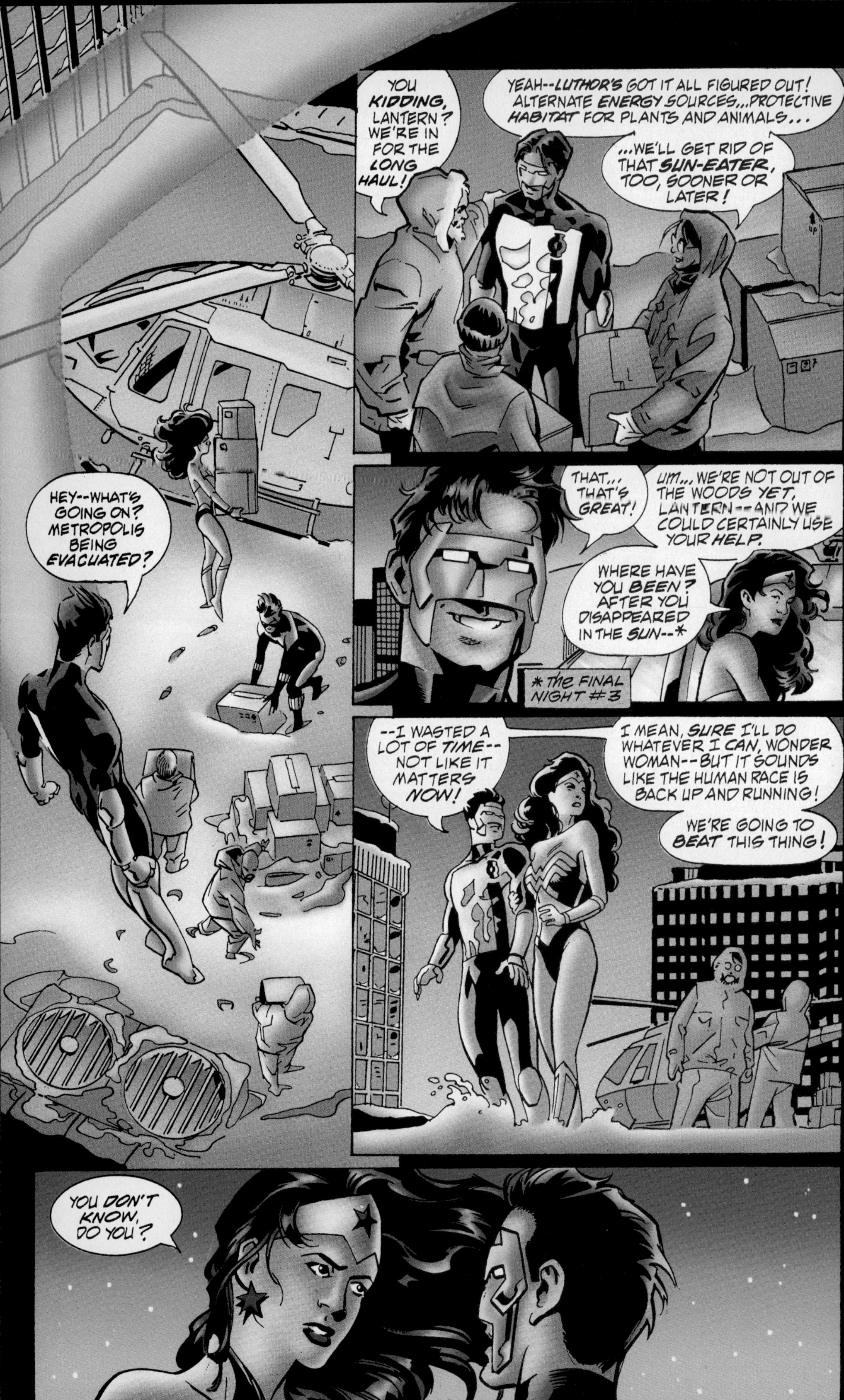
YOU KIDDING, LANTERN? WE'RE IN FOR THE LONG HAUL!
YEAH--LUTHOR'S GOT IT ALL FIGURED OUT! ALTERNATE ENERGY SOURCES... PROTECTIVE HABITAT FOR PLANTS AND ANIMALS...
...WE'LL GET RID OF THAT SUN-EATER, TOO, SOONER OR LATER!
HEY--WHAT'S GOING ON? METROPOLIS BEING EVACUATED?
THAT... THAT'S GREAT!
UM... WE'RE NOT OUT OF THE WOODS YET, LANTERN--AND WE COULD CERTAINLY USE YOUR HELP.
WHERE HAVE YOU BEEN? AFTER YOU DISAPPEARED IN THE SUN--*
* THE FINAL NIGHT #3
--I WASTED A LOT OF TIME--NOT LIKE IT MATTERS NOW!
I MEAN, SURE I'LL DO WHATEVER I CAN, WONDER WOMAN--BUT IT SOUNDS LIKE THE HUMAN RACE IS BACK UP AND RUNNING!
WE'RE GOING TO BEAT THIS THING!
YOU DON'T KNOW, DO YOU?

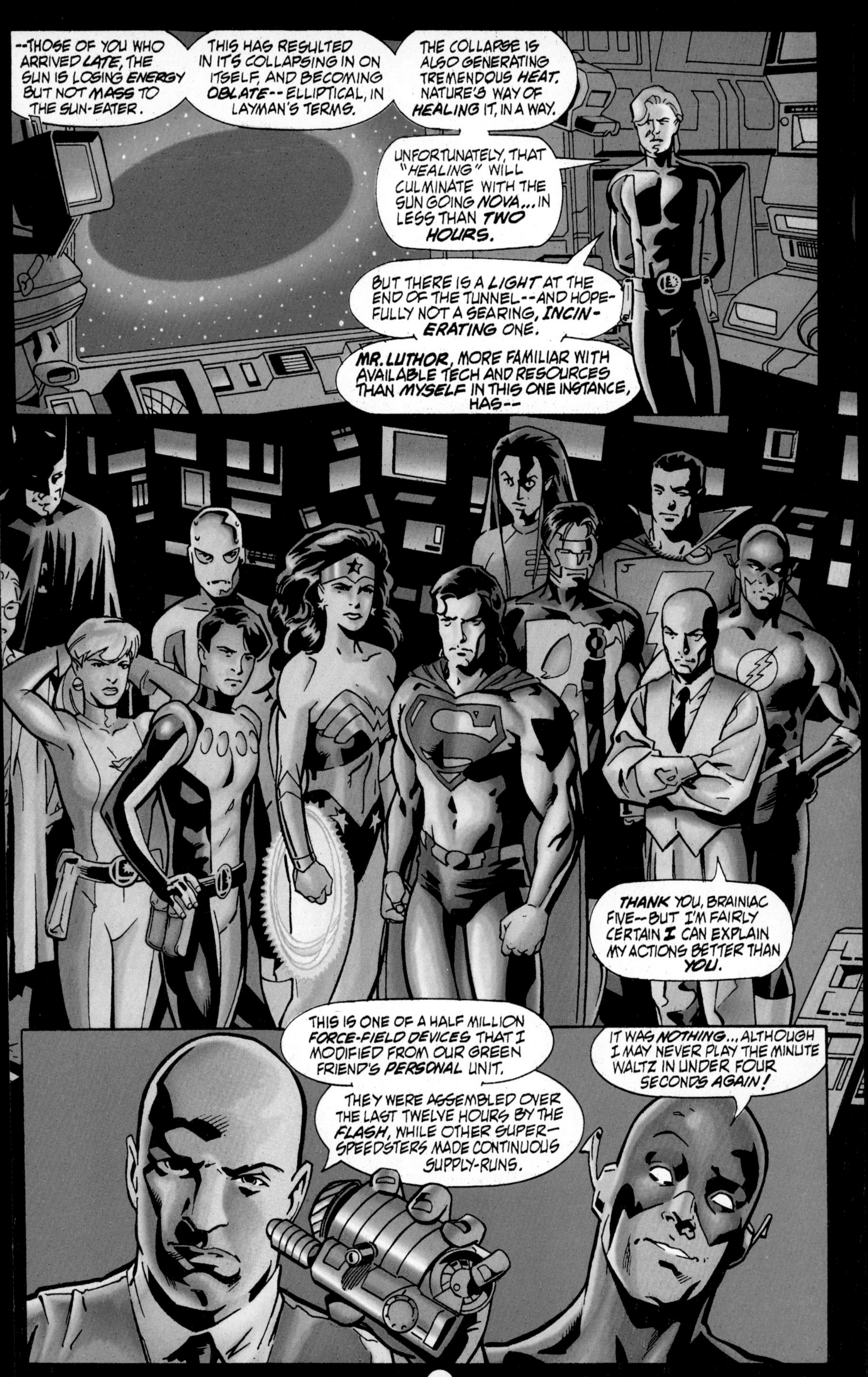
--THOSE OF YOU WHO ARRIVED LATE, THE SUN IS LOSING ENERGY BUT NOT MASS TO THE SUN-EATER.
THIS HAS RESULTED IN IT'S COLLAPSING IN ON ITSELF, AND BECOMING OBLATE--ELLIPTICAL, IN LAYMAN'S TERMS.
THE COLLAPSE IS ALSO GENERATING TREMENDOUS HEAT. NATURE'S WAY OF HEALING IT, IN A WAY.
UNFORTUNATELY, THAT "HEALING" WILL CULMINATE WITH THE SUN GOING NOVA... IN LESS THAN TWO HOURS.
BUT THERE IS A LIGHT AT THE END OF THE TUNNEL--AND HOPEFULLY NOT A SEARING, INCINERATING ONE.
MR. LUTHOR, MORE FAMILIAR WITH AVAILABLE TECH AND RESOURCES THAN MYSELF IN THIS ONE INSTANCE, HAS--
THANK YOU, BRAINIAC FIVE--BUT I'M FAIRLY CERTAIN I CAN EXPLAIN MY ACTIONS BETTER THAN YOU.
THIS IS ONE OF A HALF MILLION FORCE-FIELD DEVICES THAT I MODIFIED FROM OUR GREEN FRIEND'S PERSONAL UNIT.
THEY WERE ASSEMBLED OVER THE LAST TWELVE HOURS BY THE FLASH, WHILE OTHER SUPER-SPEEDSTERS MADE CONTINUOUS SUPPLY-RUNS.
IT WAS NOTHING... ALTHOUGH I MAY NEVER PLAY THE MINUTE WALTZ IN UNDER FOUR SECONDS AGAIN!

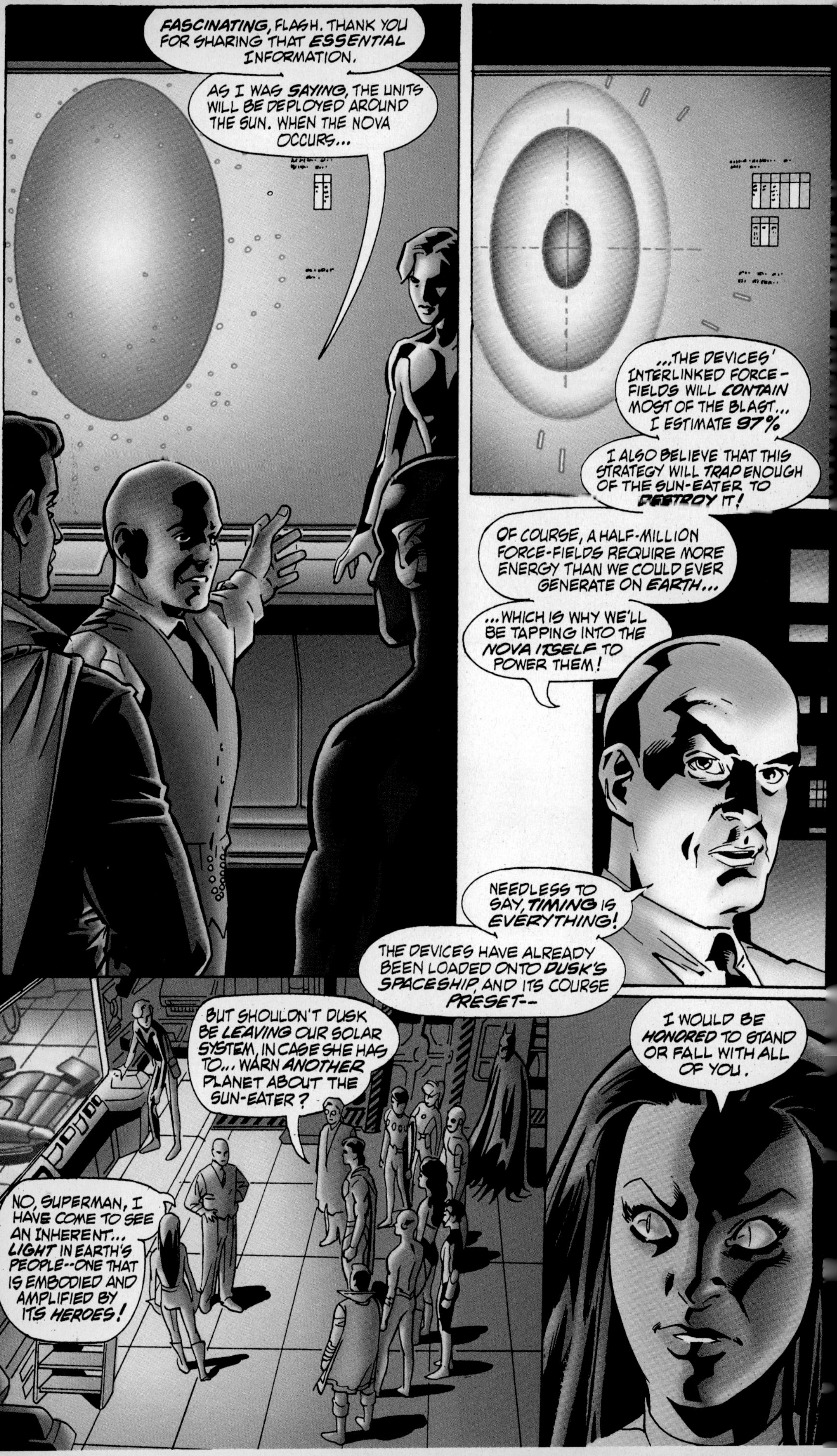
FASCINATING, FLASH. THANK YOU FOR SHARING THAT ESSENTIAL INFORMATION.
AS I WAS SAYING, THE UNITS WILL BE DEPLOYED AROUND THE SUN. WHEN THE NOVA OCCURS...
...THE DEVICES' INTERLINKED FORCE-FIELDS WILL CONTAIN MOST OF THE BLAST... I ESTIMATE 97%
I ALSO BELIEVE THAT THIS STRATEGY WILL TRAP ENOUGH OF THE SUN-EATER TO DESTROY IT!
OF COURSE, A HALF-MILLION FORCE-FIELDS REQUIRE MORE ENERGY THAN WE COULD EVER GENERATE ON EARTH...
...WHICH IS WHY WE'LL BE TAPPING INTO THE NOVA ITSELF TO POWER THEM!
NEEDLESS TO SAY, TIMING IS EVERYTHING!
THE DEVICES HAVE ALREADY BEEN LOADED ONTO DUSK'S SPACESHIP, AND ITS COURSE PRESET--
BUT SHOULDN'T DUSK BE LEAVING OUR SOLAR SYSTEM, IN CASE SHE HAS TO... WARN ANOTHER PLANET ABOUT THE SUN-EATER?
NO, SUPERMAN, I HAVE COME TO SEE AN INHERENT... LIGHT IN EARTH'S PEOPLE--ONE THAT IS EMBODIED AND AMPLIFIED BY ITS HEROES!
I WOULD BE HONORED TO STAND OR FALL WITH ALL OF YOU.

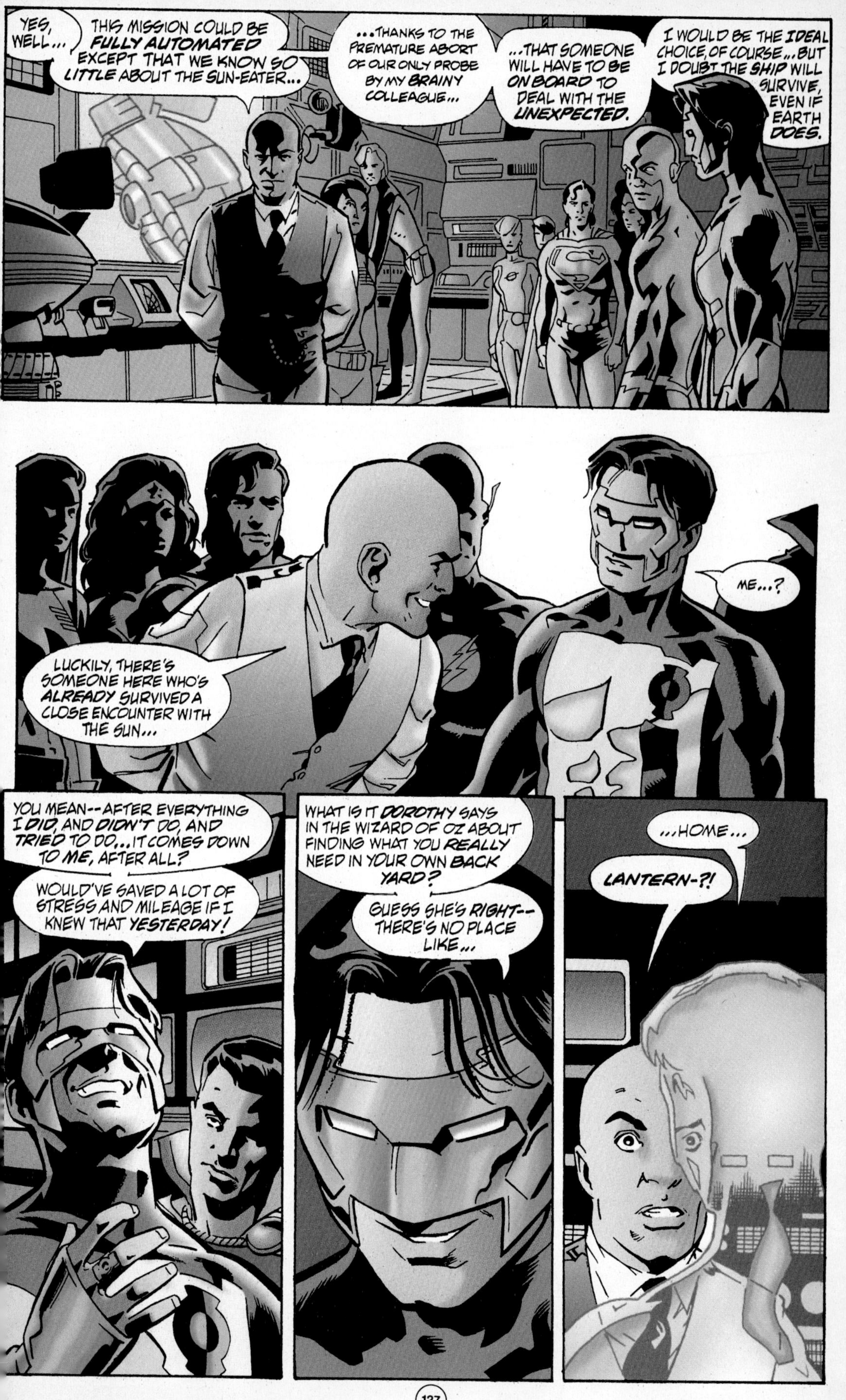
YES, WELL...
THIS MISSION COULD BE FULLY AUTOMATED EXCEPT THAT WE KNOW SO LITTLE ABOUT THE SUN-EATER...
...THANKS TO THE PREMATURE ABORT OF OUR ONLY PROBE BY MY BRAINY COLLEAGUE...
...THAT SOMEONE WILL HAVE TO BE ON BOARD TO DEAL WITH THE UNEXPECTED.
I WOULD BE THE IDEAL CHOICE, OF COURSE... BUT I DOUBT THE SHIP WILL SURVIVE, EVEN IF EARTH DOES.
LUCKILY, THERE'S SOMEONE HERE WHO'S ALREADY SURVIVED A CLOSE ENCOUNTER WITH THE SUN...
ME...?
YOU MEAN--AFTER EVERYTHING I DID, AND DIDN'T DO, AND TRIED TO DO... IT COMES DOWN TO ME, AFTER ALL?
WOULD'VE SAVED A LOT OF STRESS AND MILEAGE IF I KNEW THAT YESTERDAY!
WHAT IS IT DOROTHY SAYS IN THE WIZARD OF OZ ABOUT FINDING WHAT YOU REALLY NEED IN YOUR OWN BACK YARD?
GUESS SHE'S RIGHT--THERE'S NO PLACE LIKE...
...HOME...
LANTERN-?!

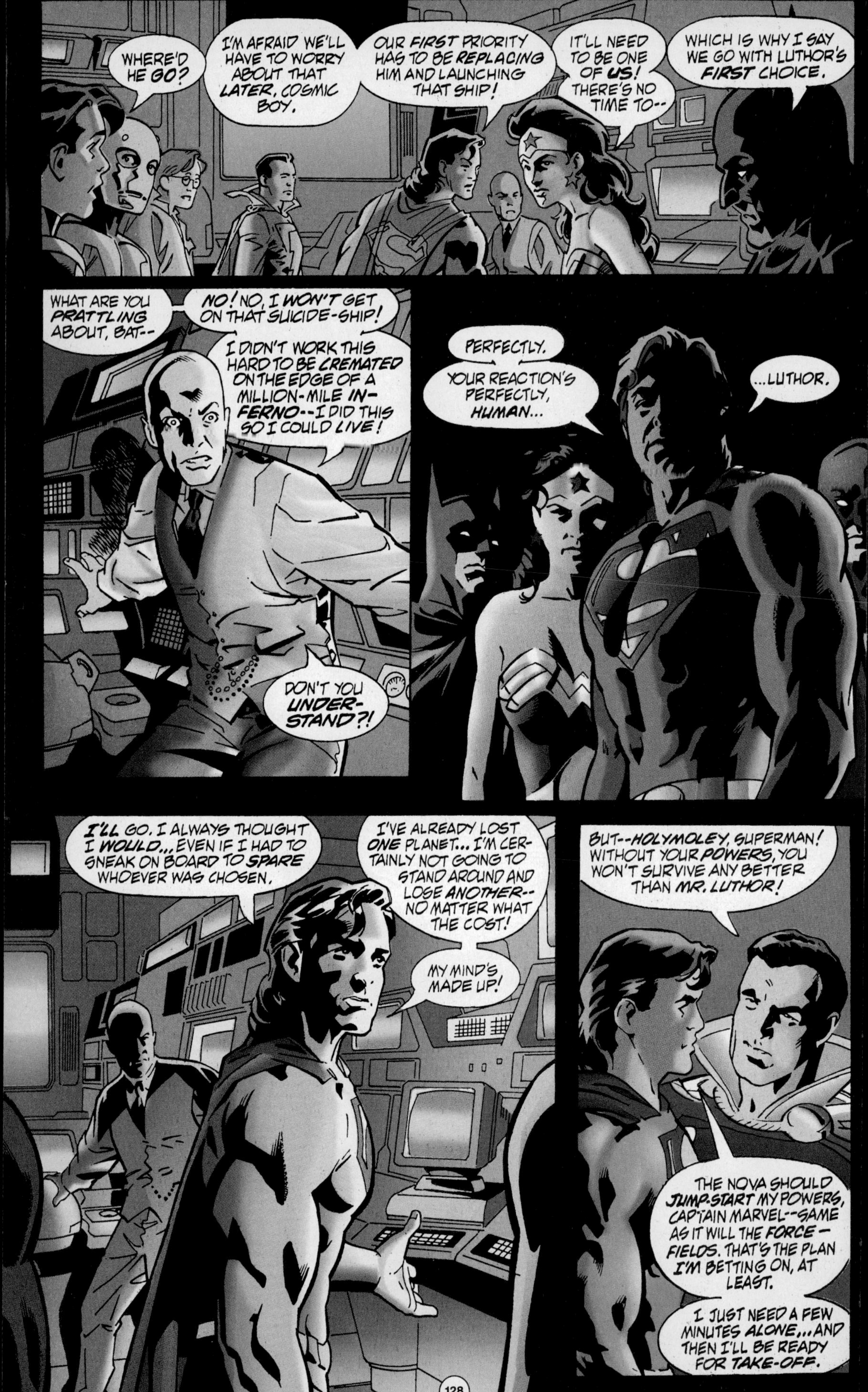
WHERE'D HE GO?
I'M AFRAID WE'LL HAVE TO WORRY ABOUT THAT LATER, COSMIC BOY.
OUR FIRST PRIORITY HAS TO BE REPLACING HIM AND LAUNCHING THAT SHIP!
IT'LL NEED TO BE ONE OF US! THERE'S NO TIME TO--
WHICH IS WHY I SAY WE GO WITH LUTHOR'S FIRST CHOICE.
WHAT ARE YOU PRATTLING ABOUT, BAT--
NO! NO, I WON'T GET ON THAT SUICIDE-SHIP!
I DIDN'T WORK THIS HARD TO BE CREMATED ON THE EDGE OF A MILLION-MILE IN-FERNO--I DID THIS SO I COULD LIVE!
DON'T YOU UNDER-STAND?!
PERFECTLY.
YOUR REACTION'S PERFECTLY, HUMAN...
...LUTHOR.
I'LL GO. I ALWAYS THOUGHT I WOULD... EVEN IF I HAD TO SNEAK ON BOARD TO SPARE WHOEVER WAS CHOSEN.
I'VE ALREADY LOST ONE PLANET... I'M CER-TAINLY NOT GOING TO STAND AROUND AND LOSE ANOTHER-- NO MATTER WHAT THE COST!
MY MIND'S MADE UP!
BUT--HOLYMOLEY, SUPERMAN! WITHOUT YOUR POWERS, YOU WON'T SURVIVE ANY BETTER THAN MR. LUTHOR!
THE NOVA SHOULD JUMP-START MY POWERS, CAPTAIN MARVEL--SAME AS IT WILL THE FORCE-FIELDS. THAT'S THE PLAN I'M BETTING ON, AT LEAST.
I JUST NEED A FEW MINUTES ALONE... AND THEN I'LL BE READY FOR TAKE-OFF.

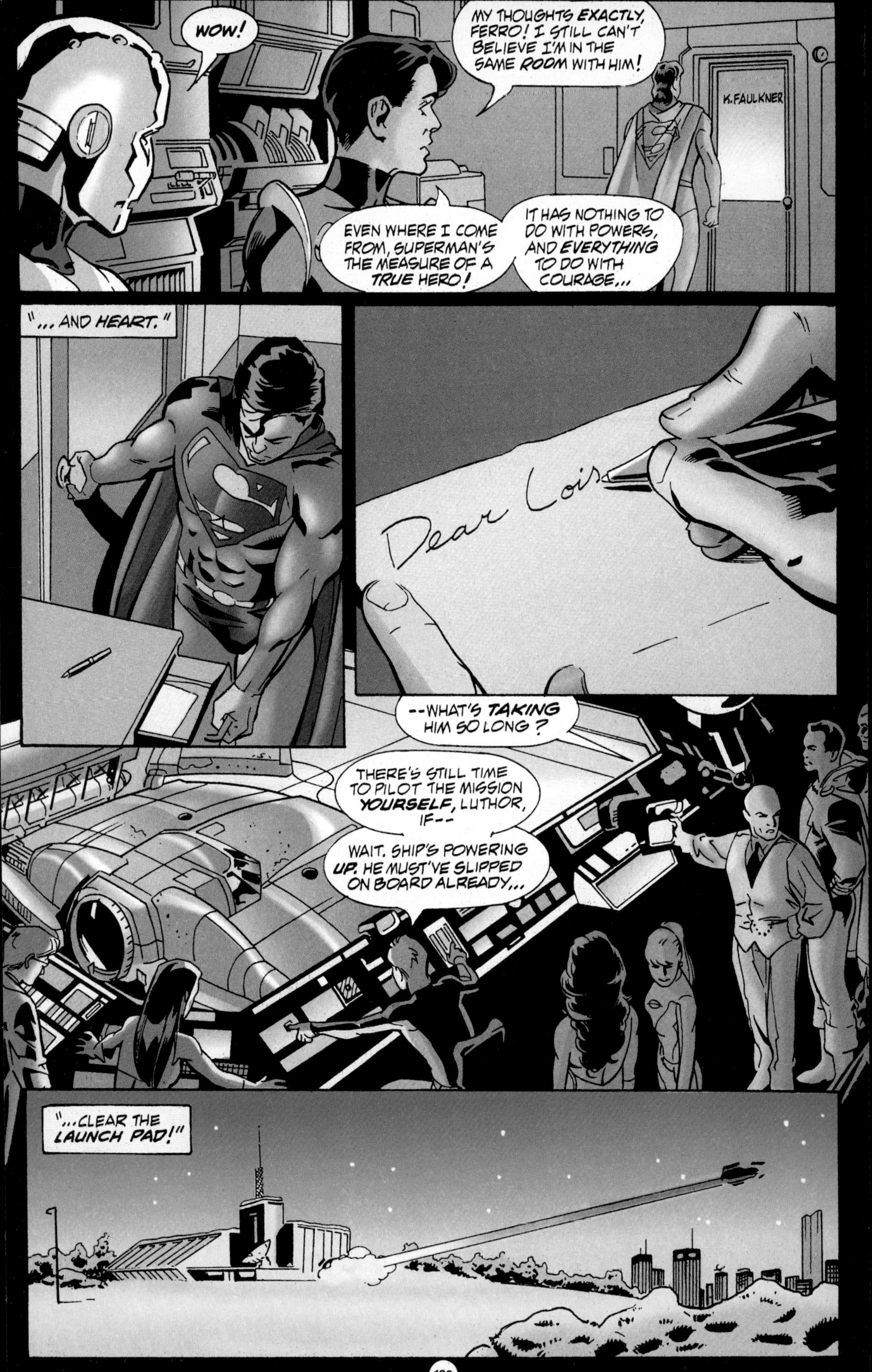
WOW!
MY THOUGHTS EXACTLY, FERRO! I STILL CAN'T BELIEVE I'M IN THE SAME ROOM WITH HIM!
K. FAULKNER
EVEN WHERE I COME FROM, SUPERMAN'S THE MEASURE OF A TRUE HERO!
IT HAS NOTHING TO DO WITH POWERS, AND EVERYTHING TO DO WITH COURAGE...
"...AND HEART."
Dear Lois
--WHAT'S TAKING HIM SO LONG?
THERE'S STILL TIME TO PILOT THE MISSION YOURSELF, LUTHOR, IF--
WAIT. SHIP'S POWERING UP. HE MUST'VE SLIPPED ON BOARD ALREADY...
"...CLEAR THE LAUNCH PAD!"

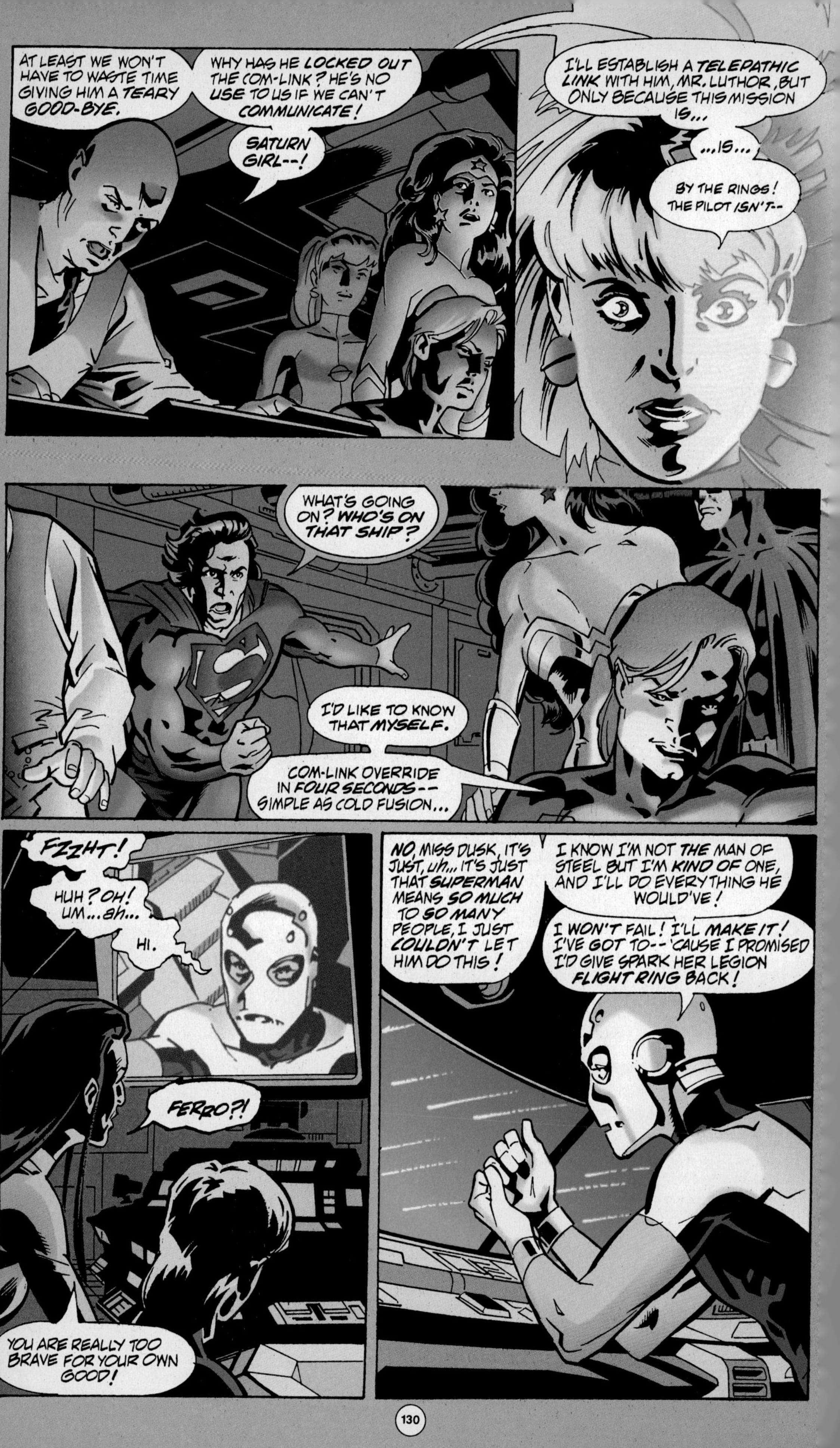
AT LEAST WE WON'T HAVE TO WASTE TIME GIVING HIM A TEARY GOOD-BYE.
WHY HAS HE LOCKED OUT THE COM-LINK? HE'S NO USE TO US IF WE CAN'T COMMUNICATE!
SATURN GIRL--!
I'LL ESTABLISH A TELEPATHIC LINK WITH HIM, MR. LUTHOR, BUT ONLY BECAUSE THIS MISSION IS...
...IS...
BY THE RINGS! THE PILOT ISN'T--
WHAT'S GOING ON? WHO'S ON THAT SHIP?
I'D LIKE TO KNOW THAT MYSELF.
COM-LINK OVERRIDE IN FOUR SECONDS-- SIMPLE AS COLD FUSION...
FZZHT!
HUH? OH! UM...ah...
HI.
FERRO?!
YOU ARE REALLY TOO BRAVE FOR YOUR OWN GOOD!
NO, MISS DUSK, IT'S JUST, uh... IT'S JUST THAT SUPERMAN MEANS SO MUCH TO SO MANY PEOPLE, I JUST COULDN'T LET HIM DO THIS!
I KNOW I'M NOT THE MAN OF STEEL BUT I'M KIND OF ONE, AND I'LL DO EVERYTHING HE WOULD'VE!
I WON'T FAIL! I'LL MAKE IT! I'VE GOT TO-- 'CAUSE I PROMISED I'D GIVE SPARK HER LEGION FLIGHT RING BACK!

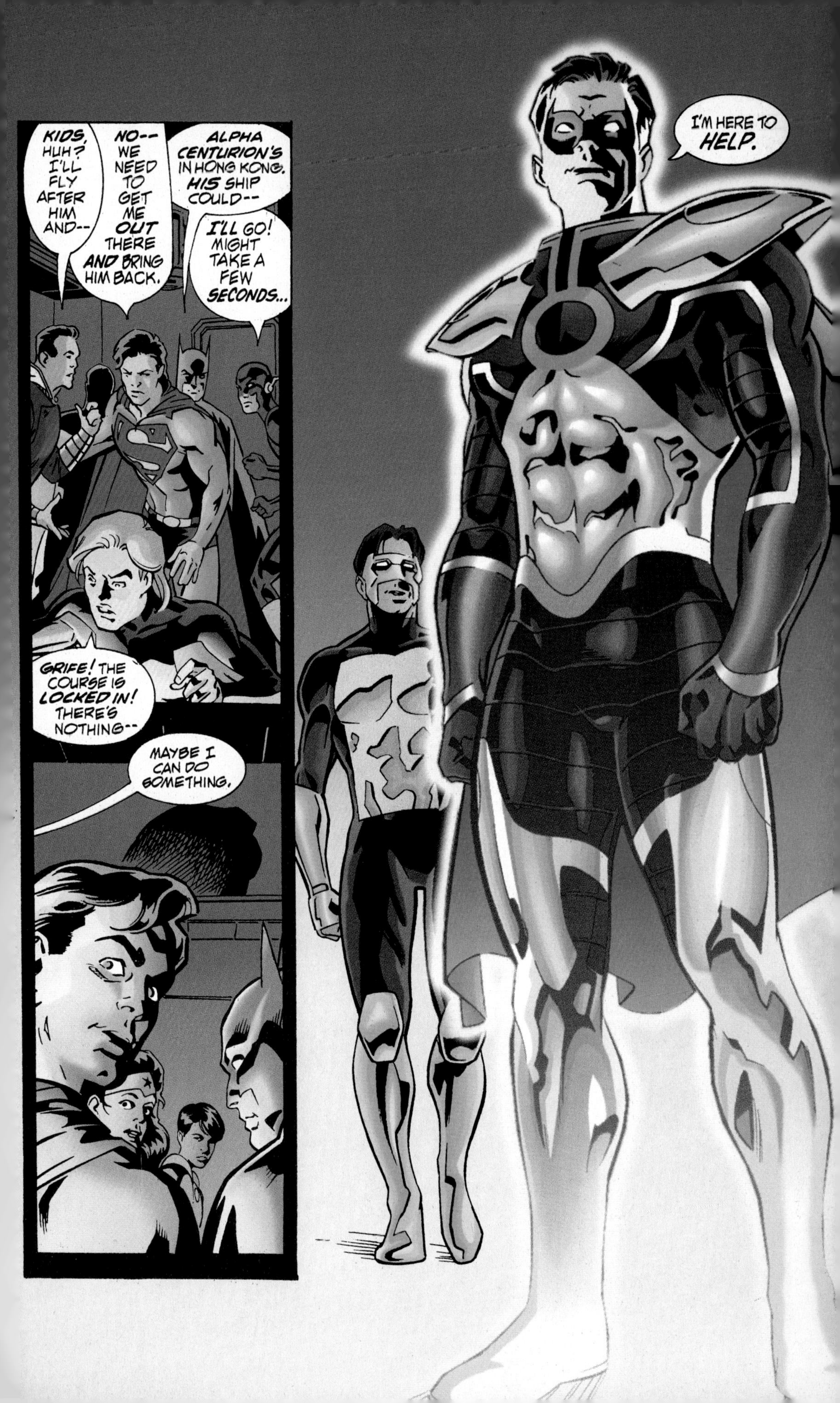

KIDS, HUH? I'LL FLY AFTER HIM AND--
NO-- WE NEED TO GET ME OUT THERE AND BRING HIM BACK.
ALPHA CENTURION'S IN HONG KONG. HIS SHIP COULD--
I'LL GO! MIGHT TAKE A FEW SECONDS...
GRIFE! THE COURSE IS LOCKED IN! THERE'S NOTHING--
MAYBE I CAN DO SOMETHING.
I'M HERE TO HELP.

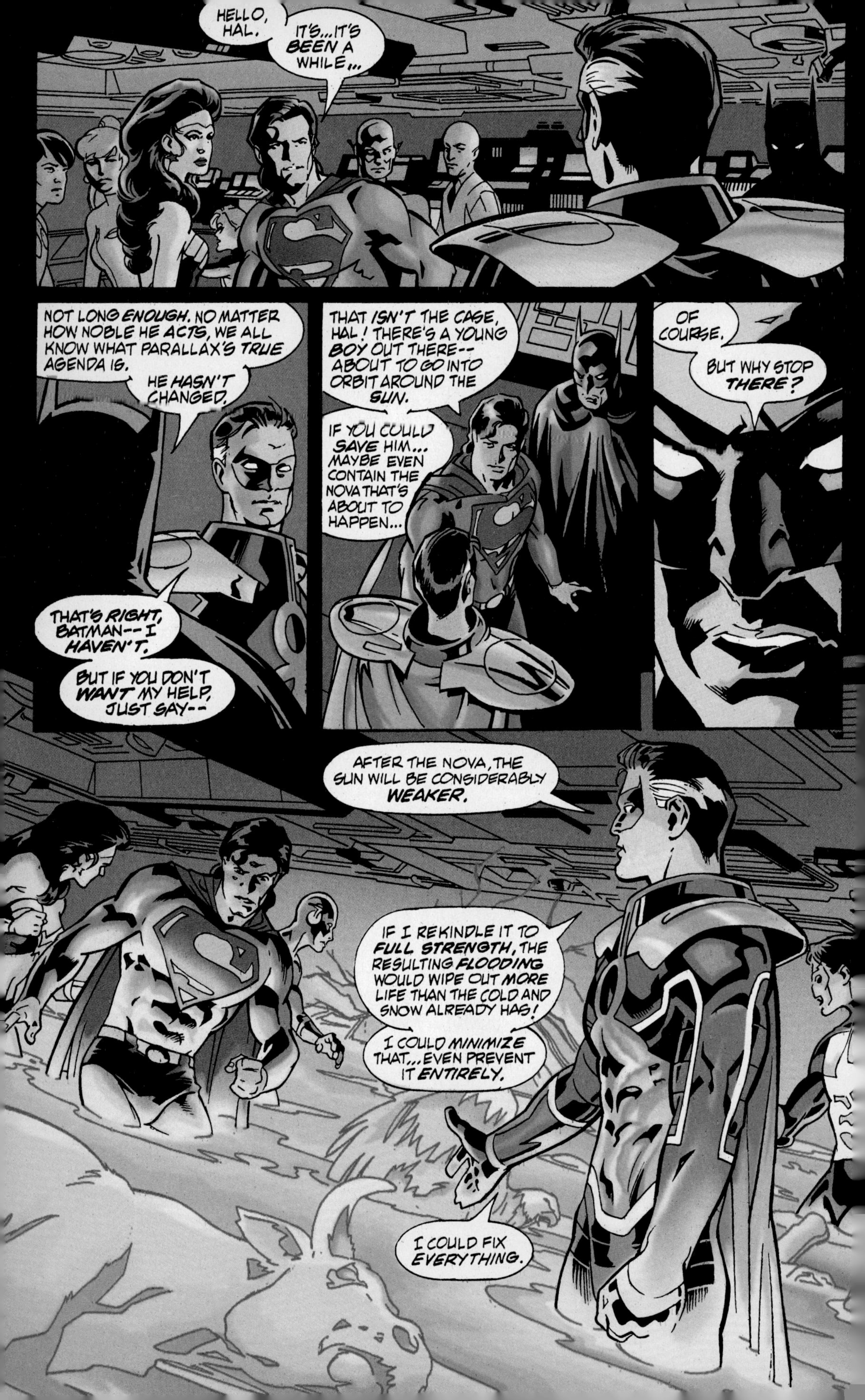
HELLO, HAL.
IT'S...IT'S BEEN A WHILE...
NOT LONG ENOUGH. NO MATTER HOW NOBLE HE ACTS, WE ALL KNOW WHAT PARALLAX'S TRUE AGENDA IS.
HE HASN'T CHANGED.
THAT'S RIGHT, BATMAN-- I HAVEN'T.
BUT IF YOU DON'T WANT MY HELP, JUST SAY--
THAT ISN'T THE CASE, HAL! THERE'S A YOUNG BOY OUT THERE-- ABOUT TO GO INTO ORBIT AROUND THE SUN.
IF YOU COULD SAVE HIM... MAYBE EVEN CONTAIN THE NOVA THAT'S ABOUT TO HAPPEN...
OF COURSE.
BUT WHY STOP THERE?
AFTER THE NOVA, THE SUN WILL BE CONSIDERABLY WEAKER.
IF I REKINDLE IT TO FULL STRENGTH, THE RESULTING FLOODING WOULD WIPE OUT MORE LIFE THAN THE COLD AND SNOW ALREADY HAS!
I COULD MINIMIZE THAT... EVEN PREVENT IT ENTIRELY.
I COULD FIX EVERYTHING.

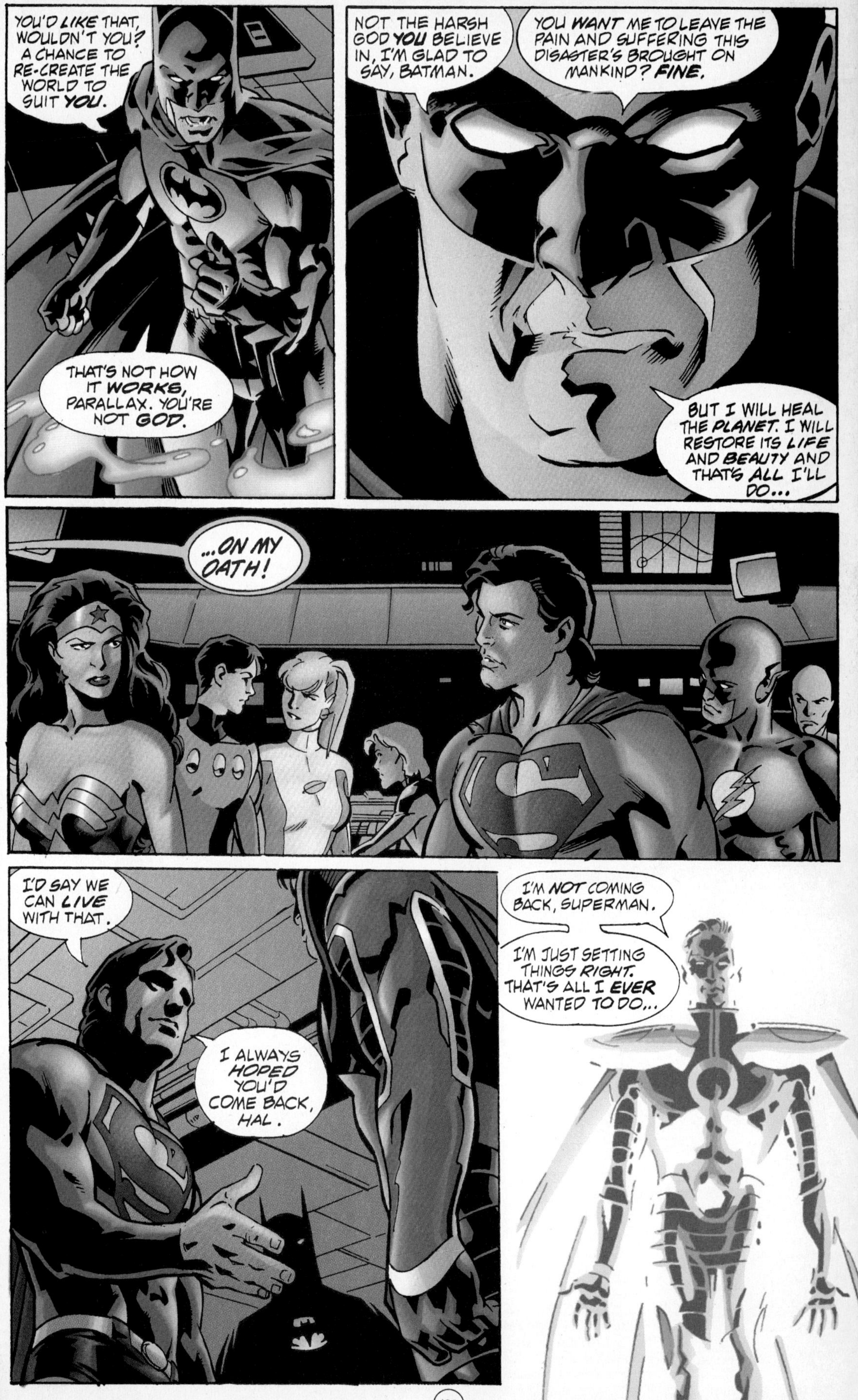

YOU'D LIKE THAT, WOULDN'T YOU? A CHANCE TO RE-CREATE THE WORLD TO SUIT YOU.
THAT'S NOT HOW IT WORKS, PARALLAX. YOU'RE NOT GOD.
NOT THE HARSH GOD YOU BELIEVE IN, I'M GLAD TO SAY, BATMAN.
YOU WANT ME TO LEAVE THE PAIN AND SUFFERING THIS DISASTER'S BROUGHT ON MANKIND? FINE.
BUT I WILL HEAL THE PLANET. I WILL RESTORE ITS LIFE AND BEAUTY AND THAT'S ALL I'LL DO...
...ON MY OATH!
I'D SAY WE CAN LIVE WITH THAT.
I ALWAYS HOPED YOU'D COME BACK, HAL.
I'M NOT COMING BACK, SUPERMAN.
I'M JUST SETTING THINGS RIGHT. THAT'S ALL I EVER WANTED TO DO...

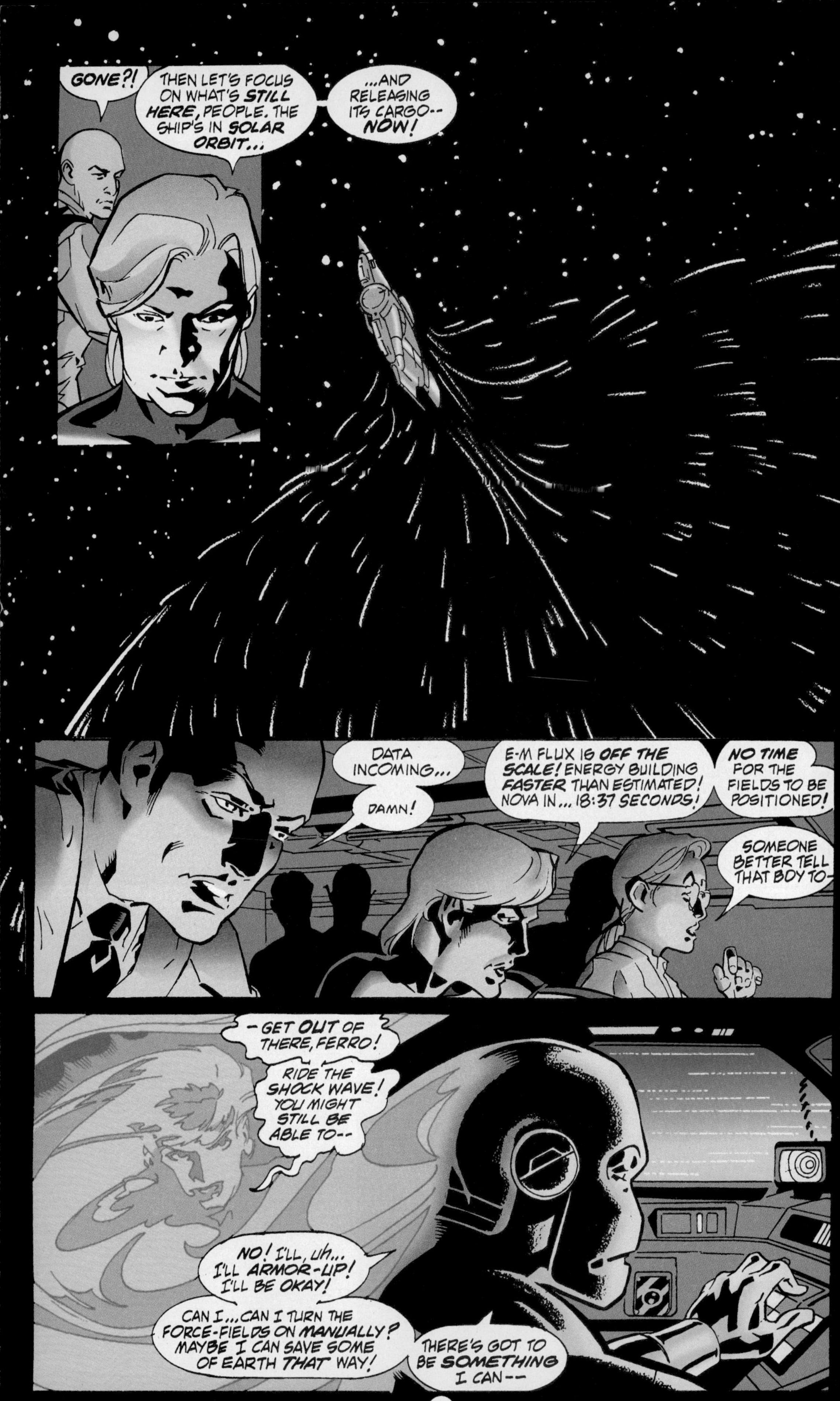
GONE?!
THEN LET'S FOCUS ON WHAT'S STILL HERE, PEOPLE. THE SHIP'S IN SOLAR ORBIT...
...AND RELEASING ITS CARGO-- NOW!
DATA INCOMING...
DAMN!
E-M FLUX IS OFF THE SCALE! ENERGY BUILDING FASTER THAN ESTIMATED! NOVA IN... 18:37 SECONDS!
NO TIME FOR THE FIELDS TO BE POSITIONED!
SOMEONE BETTER TELL THAT BOY TO-
-GET OUT OF THERE, FERRO!
RIDE THE SHOCK WAVE! YOU MIGHT STILL BE ABLE TO--
NO! I'LL, uh... I'LL ARMOR-UP! I'LL BE OKAY!
CAN I... CAN I TURN THE FORCE-FIELDS ON MANUALLY? MAYBE I CAN SAVE SOME OF EARTH THAT WAY!
THERE'S GOT TO BE SOMETHING I CAN--

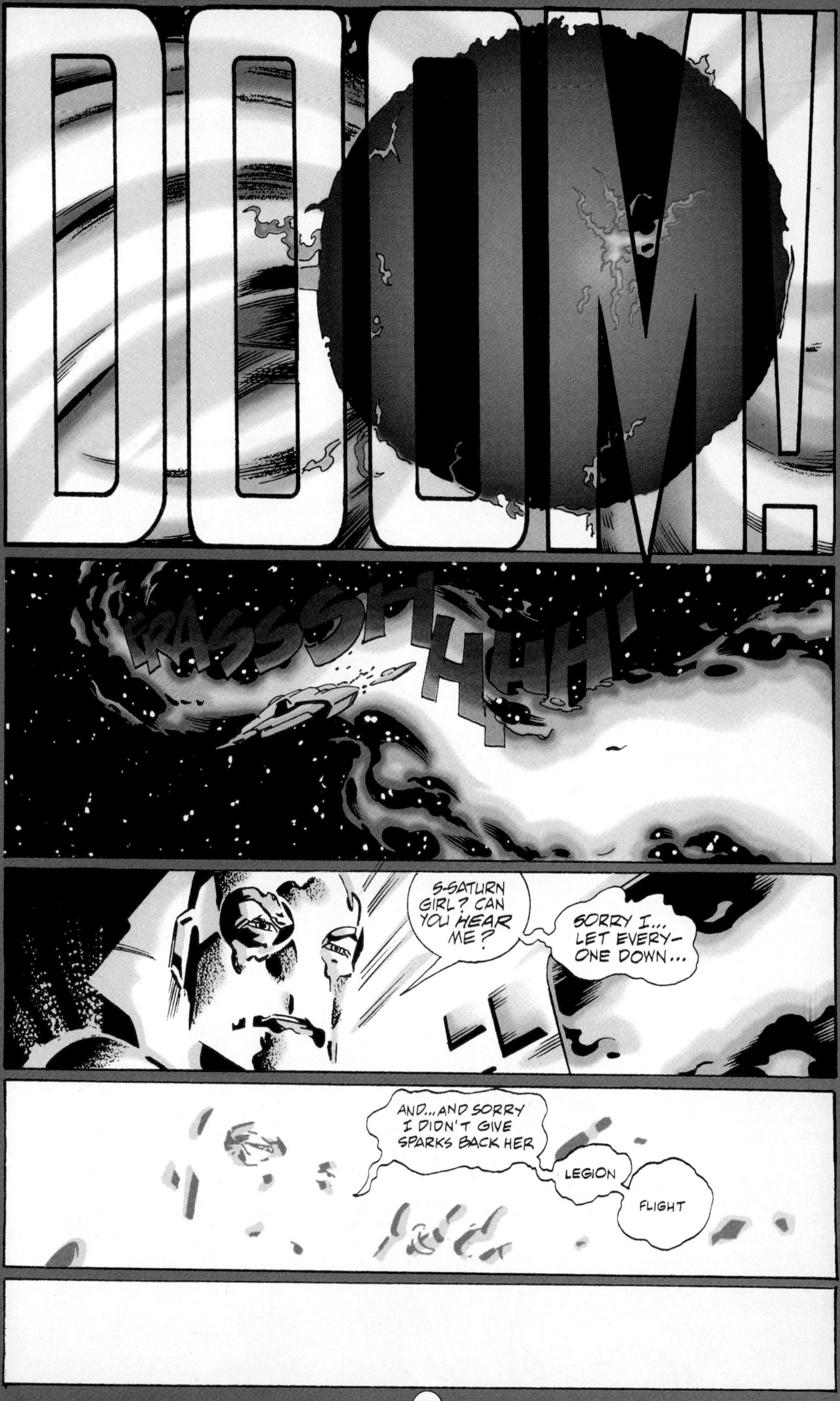
DOOM!
KRASSSHHHH!
S-SATURN GIRL? CAN YOU HEAR ME?
SORRY I... LET EVERY-ONE DOWN...
AND... AND SORRY I DIDN'T GIVE SPARKS BACK HER
LEGION
FLIGHT

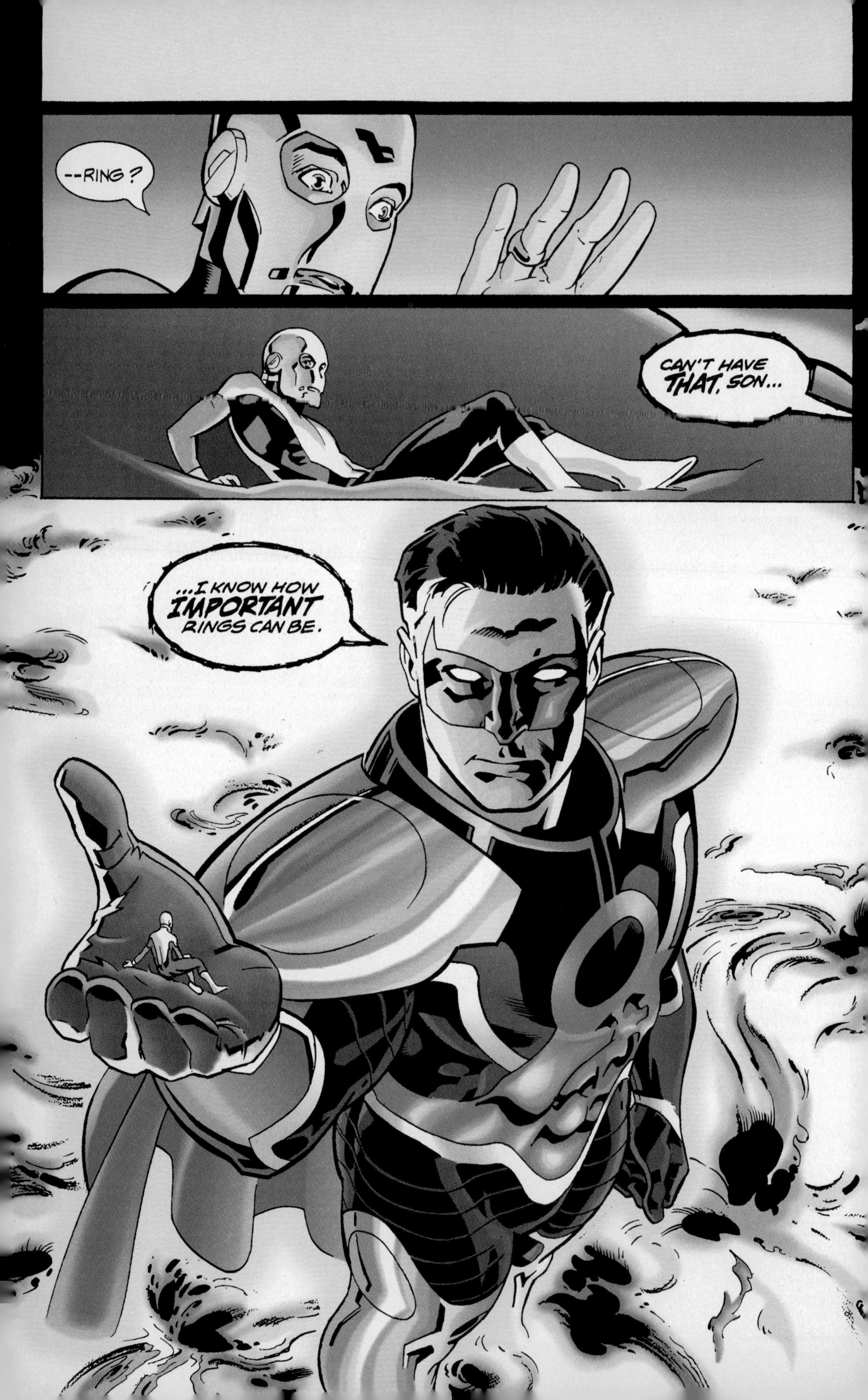
--RING?
CAN'T HAVE THAT, SON...
...I KNOW HOW IMPORTANT RINGS CAN BE.

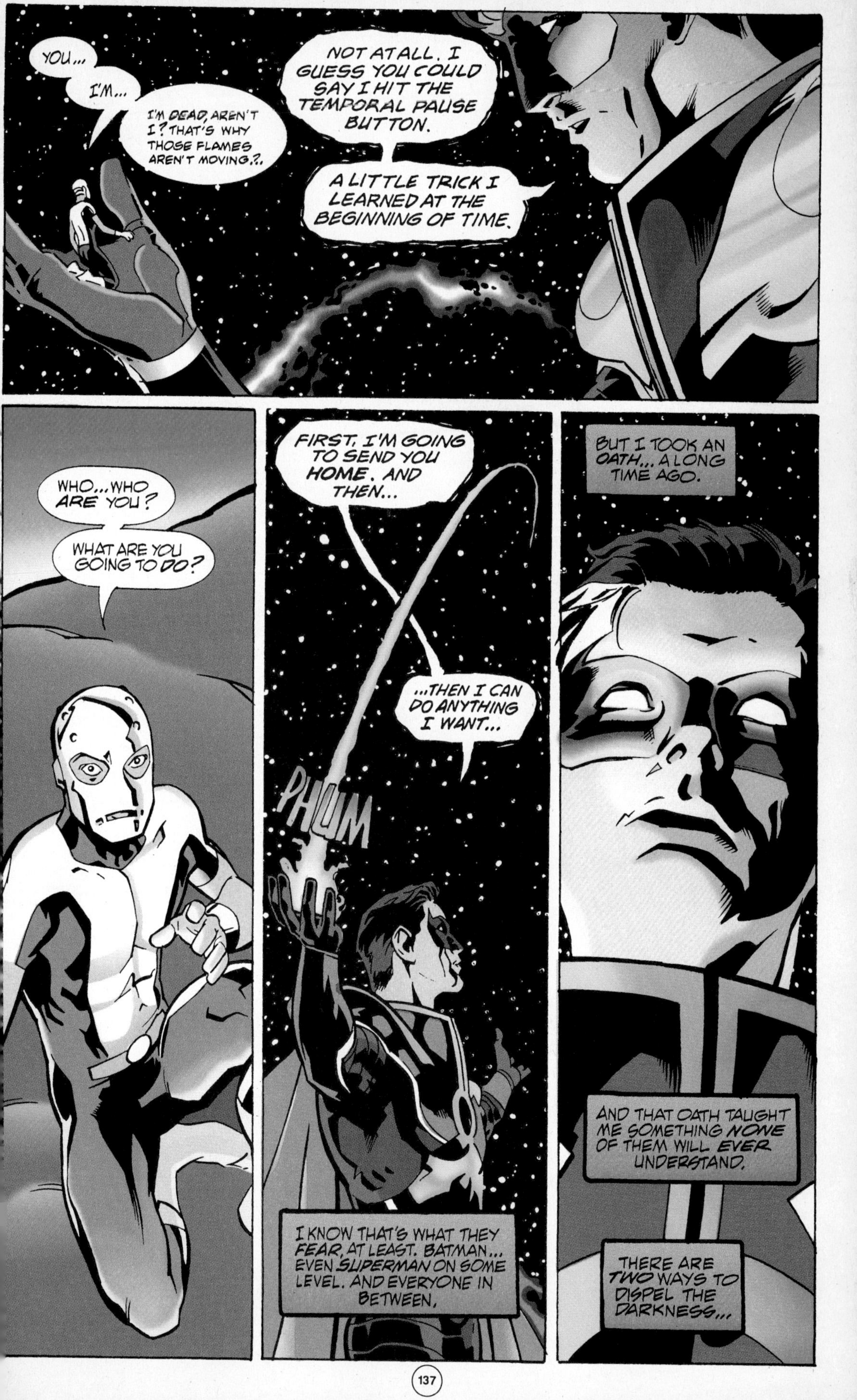
YOU...
I'M...
I'M DEAD, AREN'T I? THAT'S WHY THOSE FLAMES AREN'T MOVING.?.
NOT AT ALL. I GUESS YOU COULD SAY I HIT THE TEMPORAL PAUSE BUTTON.
A LITTLE TRICK I LEARNED AT THE BEGINNING OF TIME.
WHO...WHO ARE YOU?
WHAT ARE YOU GOING TO DO?
FIRST, I'M GOING TO SEND YOU HOME. AND THEN...
...THEN I CAN DO ANYTHING I WANT...
PHUM
I KNOW THAT'S WHAT THEY FEAR, AT LEAST. BATMAN... EVEN SUPERMAN ON SOME LEVEL. AND EVERYONE IN BETWEEN.
BUT I TOOK AN OATH... A LONG TIME AGO.
AND THAT OATH TAUGHT ME SOMETHING NONE OF THEM WILL EVER UNDERSTAND.
THERE ARE TWO WAYS TO DISPEL THE DARKNESS...

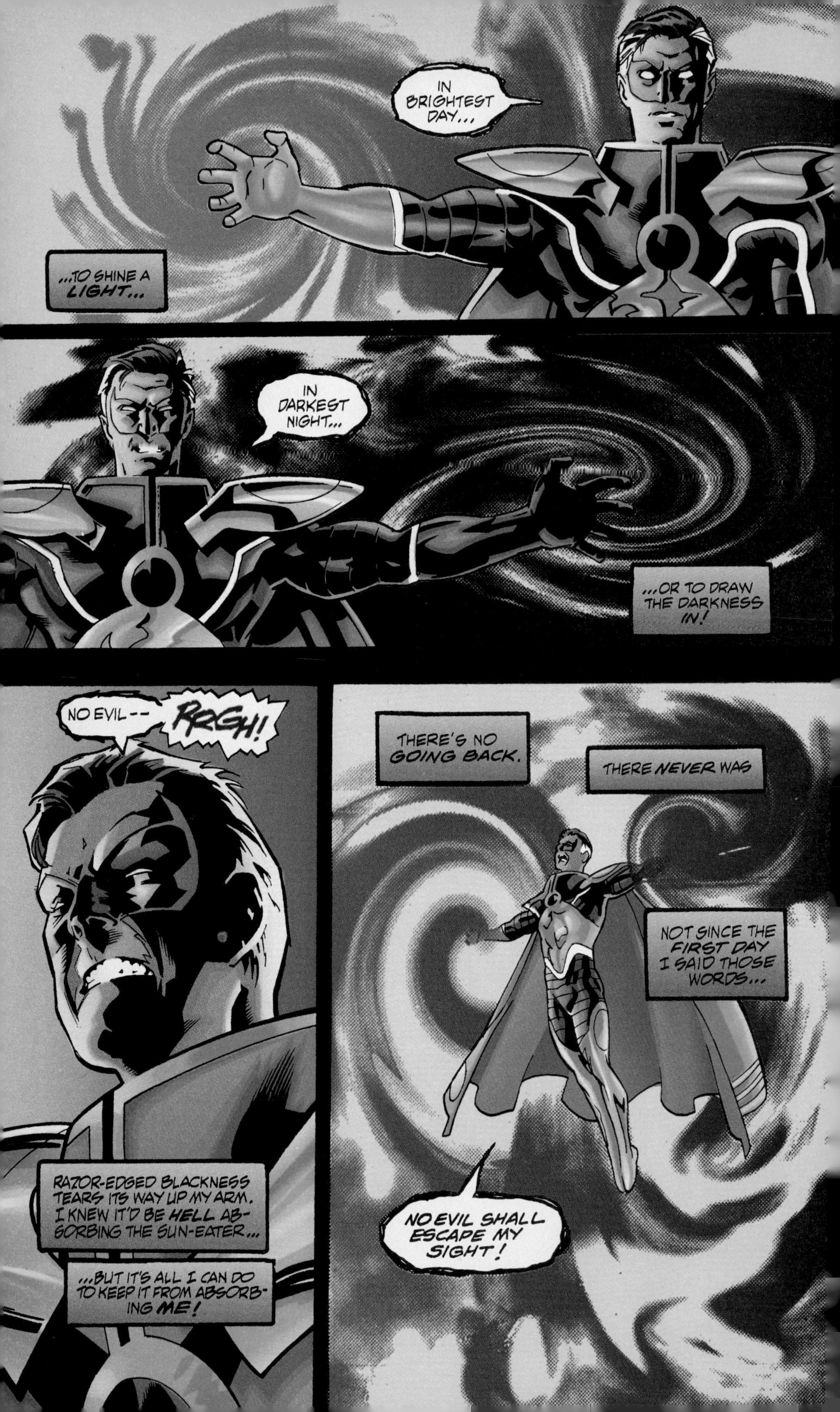
IN BRIGHTEST DAY...
...TO SHINE A LIGHT...
IN DARKEST NIGHT...
...OR TO DRAW THE DARKNESS IN!
NO EVIL--
RRGH!
RAZOR-EDGED BLACKNESS TEARS ITS WAY UP MY ARM. I KNEW IT'D BE HELL ABSORBING THE SUN-EATER...
...BUT IT'S ALL I CAN DO TO KEEP IT FROM ABSORBING ME!
THERE'S NO GOING BACK.
THERE NEVER WAS
NOT SINCE THE FIRST DAY I SAID THOSE WORDS...
NO EVIL SHALL ESCAPE MY SIGHT!

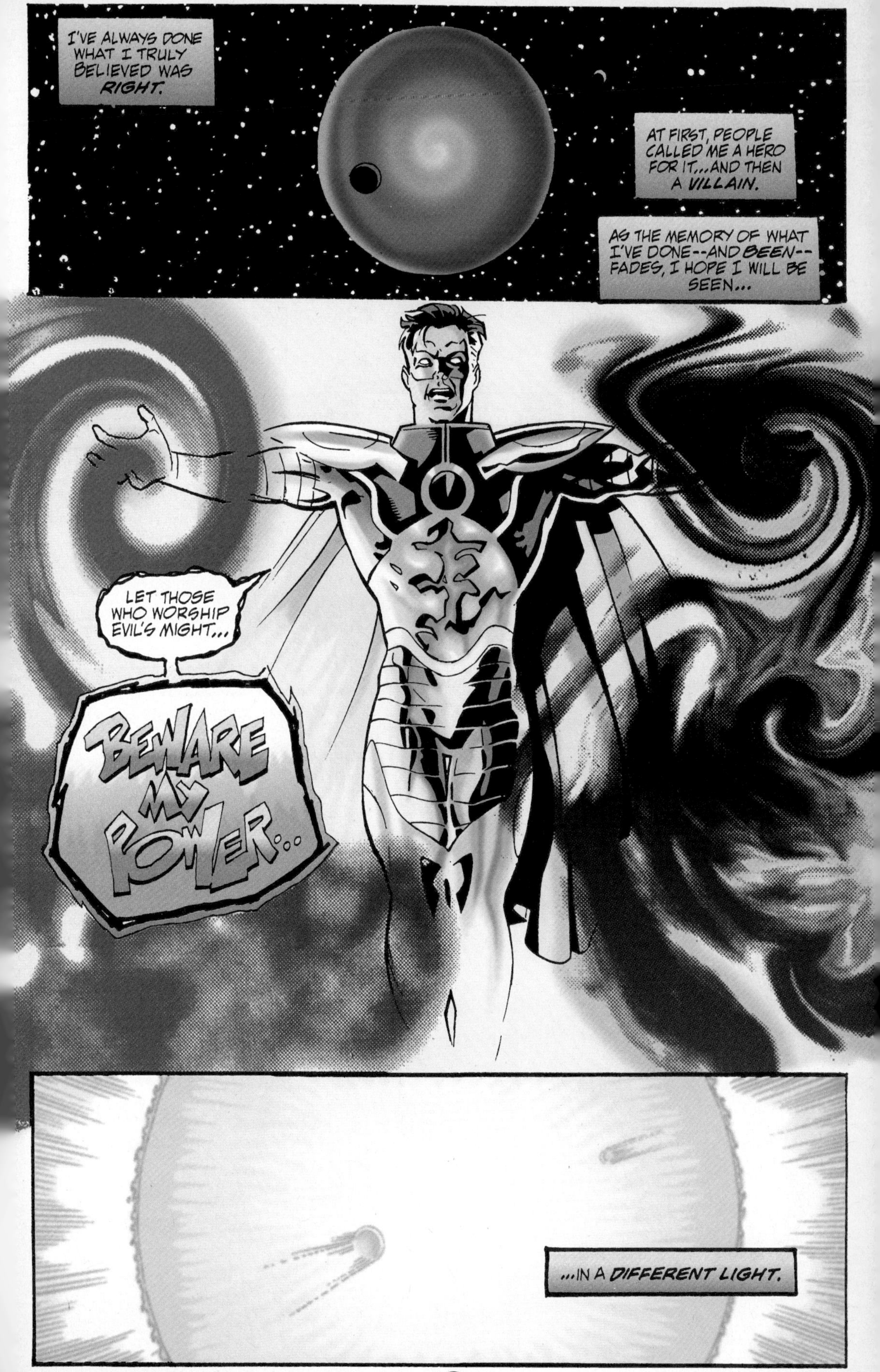

I'VE ALWAYS DONE WHAT I TRULY BELIEVED WAS RIGHT.
AT FIRST, PEOPLE CALLED ME A HERO FOR IT...AND THEN A VILLAIN.
AS THE MEMORY OF WHAT I'VE DONE--AND BEEN--FADES, I HOPE I WILL BE SEEN...
LET THOSE WHO WORSHIP EVIL'S MIGHT...
BEWARE MY POWER...
...IN A DIFFERENT LIGHT.

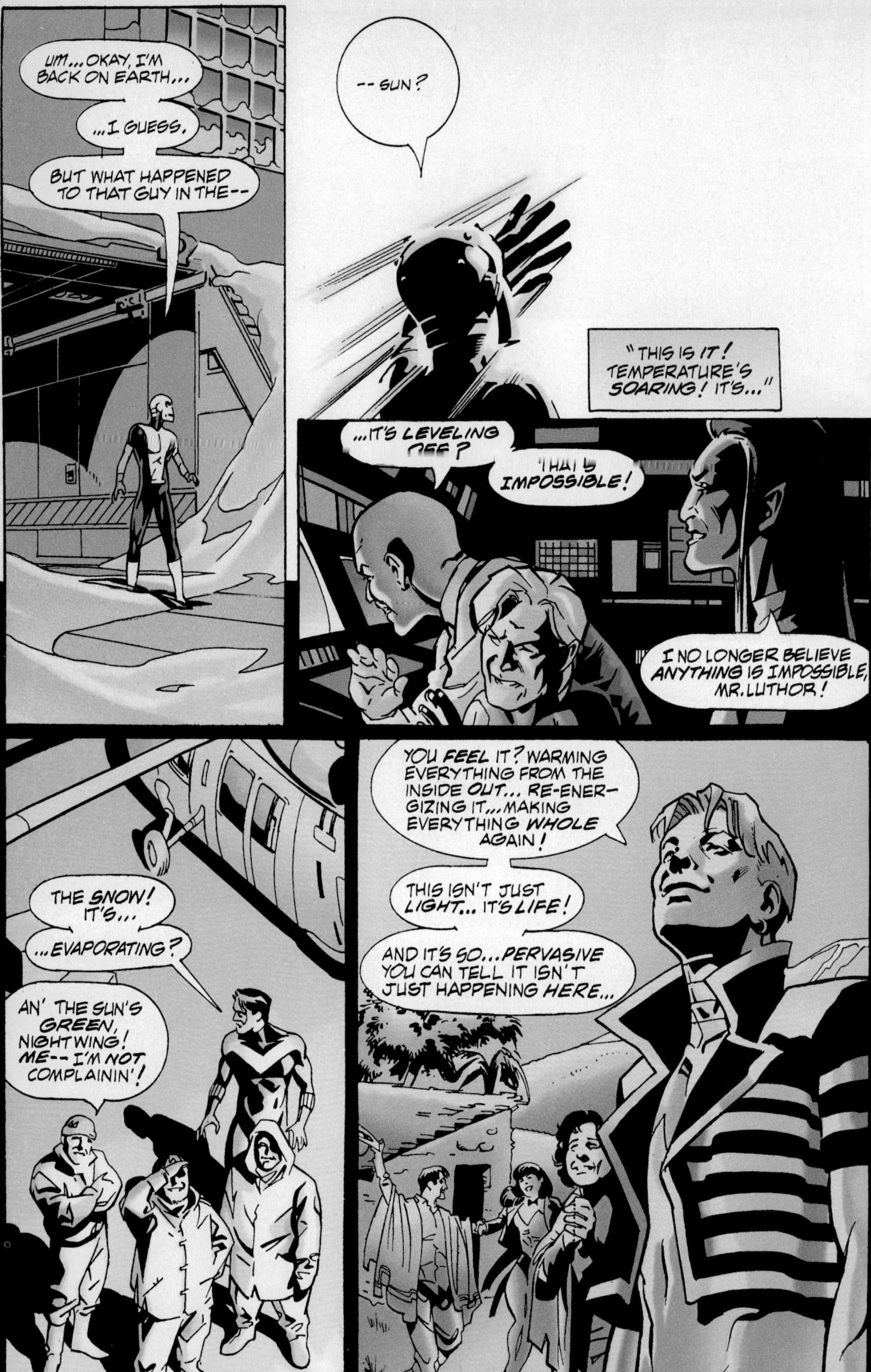
UM... OKAY, I'M BACK ON EARTH...
...I GUESS.
BUT WHAT HAPPENED TO THAT GUY IN THE--
-- SUN?
"THIS IS IT! TEMPERATURE'S SOARING! IT'S..."
...IT'S LEVELING OFF?
THAT'S IMPOSSIBLE!
I NO LONGER BELIEVE ANYTHING IS IMPOSSIBLE, MR. LUTHOR!
THE SNOW! IT'S...
...EVAPORATING?
AN' THE SUN'S GREEN, NIGHTWING! ME-- I'M NOT COMPLAININ'!
YOU FEEL IT? WARMING EVERYTHING FROM THE INSIDE OUT... RE-ENERGIZING IT... MAKING EVERYTHING WHOLE AGAIN!
THIS ISN'T JUST LIGHT... IT'S LIFE!
AND IT'S SO... PERVASIVE YOU CAN TELL IT ISN'T JUST HAPPENING HERE...

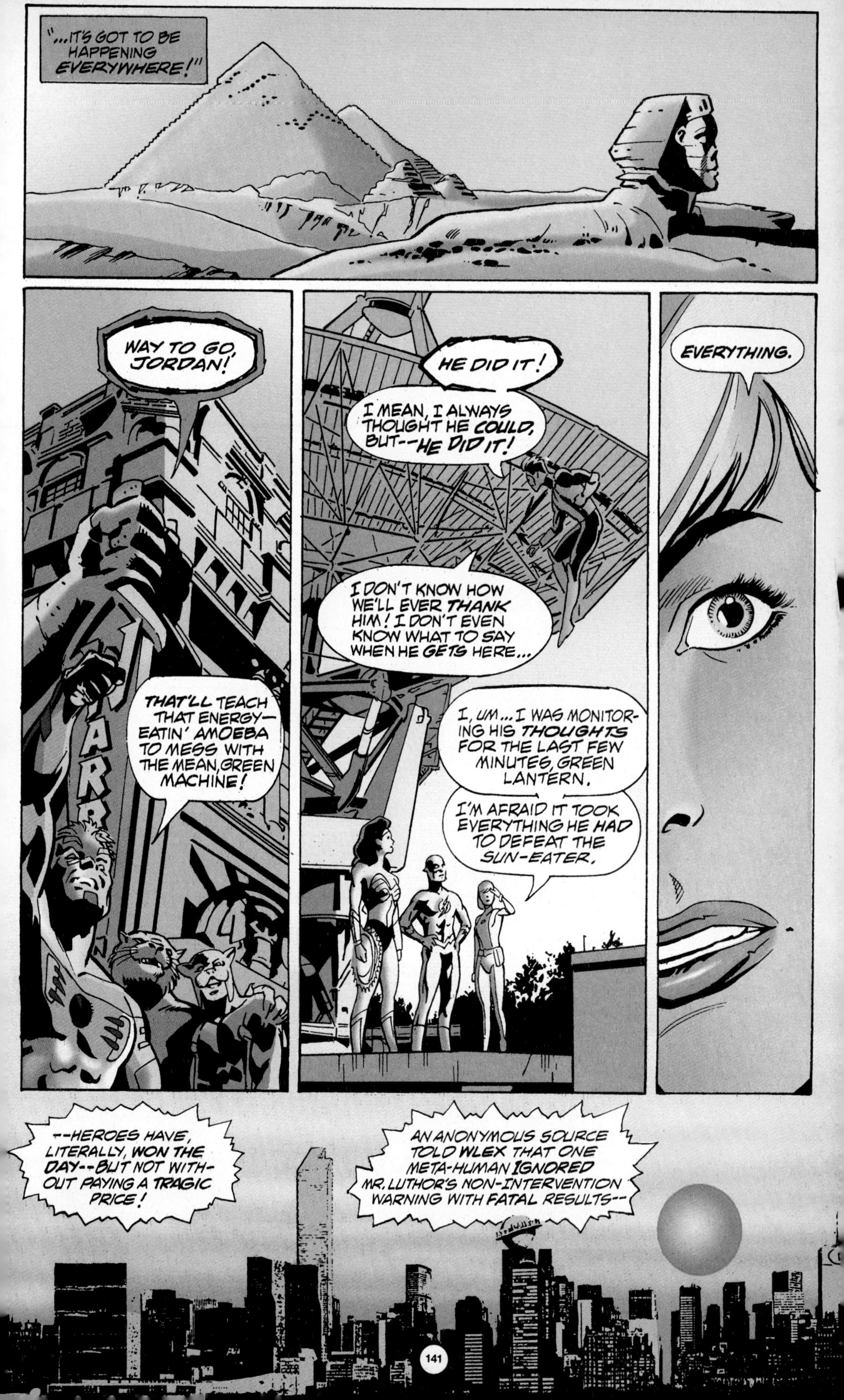
"...IT'S GOT TO BE HAPPENING EVERYWHERE!"
WAY TO GO, JORDAN!
THAT'LL TEACH THAT ENERGY— EATIN' AMOEBA TO MESS WITH THE MEAN, GREEN MACHINE!
HE DID IT!
I MEAN, I ALWAYS THOUGHT HE COULD, BUT--HE DID IT!
I DON'T KNOW HOW WE'LL EVER THANK HIM! I DON'T EVEN KNOW WHAT TO SAY WHEN HE GETS HERE...
I, UM... I WAS MONITORING HIS THOUGHTS FOR THE LAST FEW MINUTES, GREEN LANTERN.
I'M AFRAID IT TOOK EVERYTHING HE HAD TO DEFEAT THE SUN-EATER.
EVERYTHING.
--HEROES HAVE, LITERALLY, WON THE DAY--BUT NOT WITHOUT PAYING A TRAGIC PRICE!
AN ANONYMOUS SOURCE TOLD WLEX THAT ONE META-HUMAN IGNORED MR. LUTHOR'S NON-INTERVENTION WARNING WITH FATAL RESULTS--

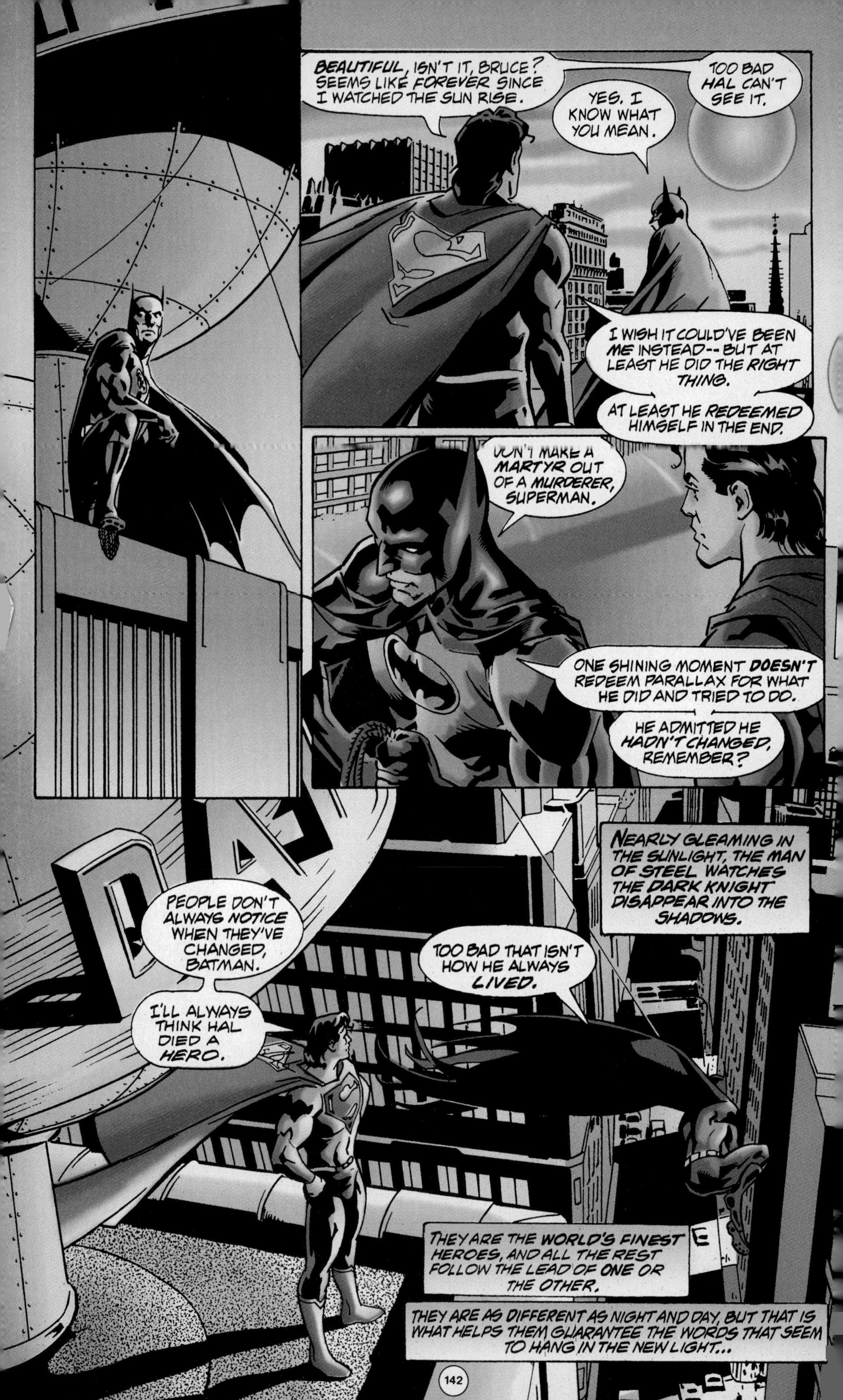
BEAUTIFUL, ISN'T IT, BRUCE? SEEMS LIKE FOREVER SINCE I WATCHED THE SUN RISE.
YES. I KNOW WHAT YOU MEAN.
TOO BAD HAL CAN'T SEE IT.
I WISH IT COULD'VE BEEN ME INSTEAD-- BUT AT LEAST HE DID THE RIGHT THING.
AT LEAST HE REDEEMED HIMSELF IN THE END.
DON'T MAKE A MARTYR OUT OF A MURDERER, SUPERMAN.
ONE SHINING MOMENT DOESN'T REDEEM PARALLAX FOR WHAT HE DID AND TRIED TO DO.
HE ADMITTED HE HADN'T CHANGED, REMEMBER?
NEARLY GLEAMING IN THE SUNLIGHT, THE MAN OF STEEL WATCHES THE DARK KNIGHT DISAPPEAR INTO THE SHADOWS.
PEOPLE DON'T ALWAYS NOTICE WHEN THEY'VE CHANGED, BATMAN.
I'LL ALWAYS THINK HAL DIED A HERO.
TOO BAD THAT ISN'T HOW HE ALWAYS LIVED.
THEY ARE THE WORLD'S FINEST HEROES, AND ALL THE REST FOLLOW THE LEAD OF ONE OR THE OTHER.
THEY ARE AS DIFFERENT AS NIGHT AND DAY, BUT THAT IS WHAT HELPS THEM GUARANTEE THE WORDS THAT SEEM TO HANG IN THE NEW LIGHT...

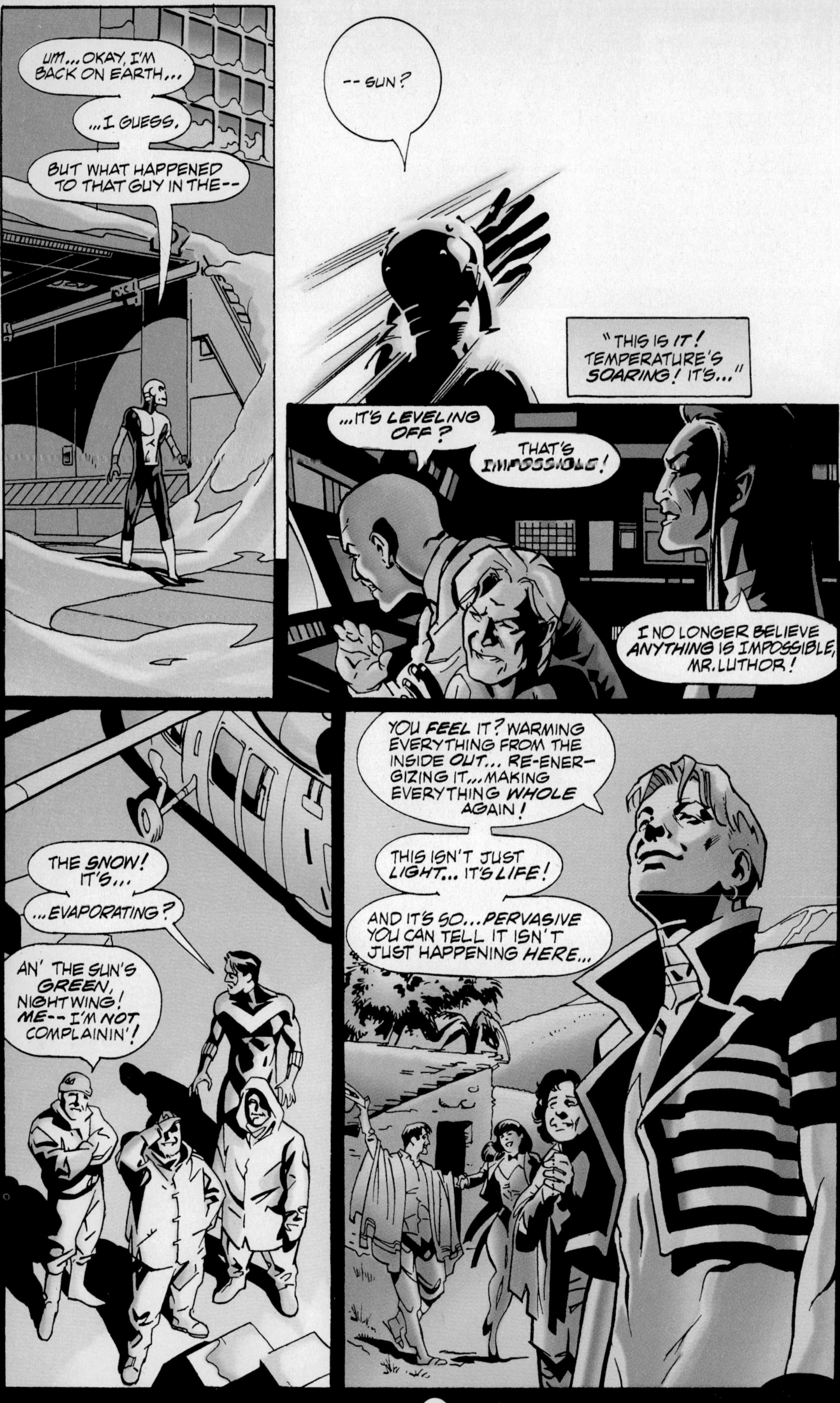
UM... OKAY, I'M BACK ON EARTH...
...I GUESS.
BUT WHAT HAPPENED TO THAT GUY IN THE--
-- SUN?
"THIS IS IT! TEMPERATURE'S SOARING! IT'S..."
...IT'S LEVELING OFF?
THAT'S IMPOSSIBLE!
I NO LONGER BELIEVE ANYTHING IS IMPOSSIBLE, MR. LUTHOR!
THE SNOW! IT'S...
...EVAPORATING?
AN' THE SUN'S GREEN, NIGHTWING! ME-- I'M NOT COMPLAININ'!
YOU FEEL IT? WARMING EVERYTHING FROM THE INSIDE OUT... RE-ENERGIZING IT... MAKING EVERYTHING WHOLE AGAIN!
THIS ISN'T JUST LIGHT... IT'S LIFE!
AND IT'S SO... PERVASIVE YOU CAN TELL IT ISN'T JUST HAPPENING HERE...

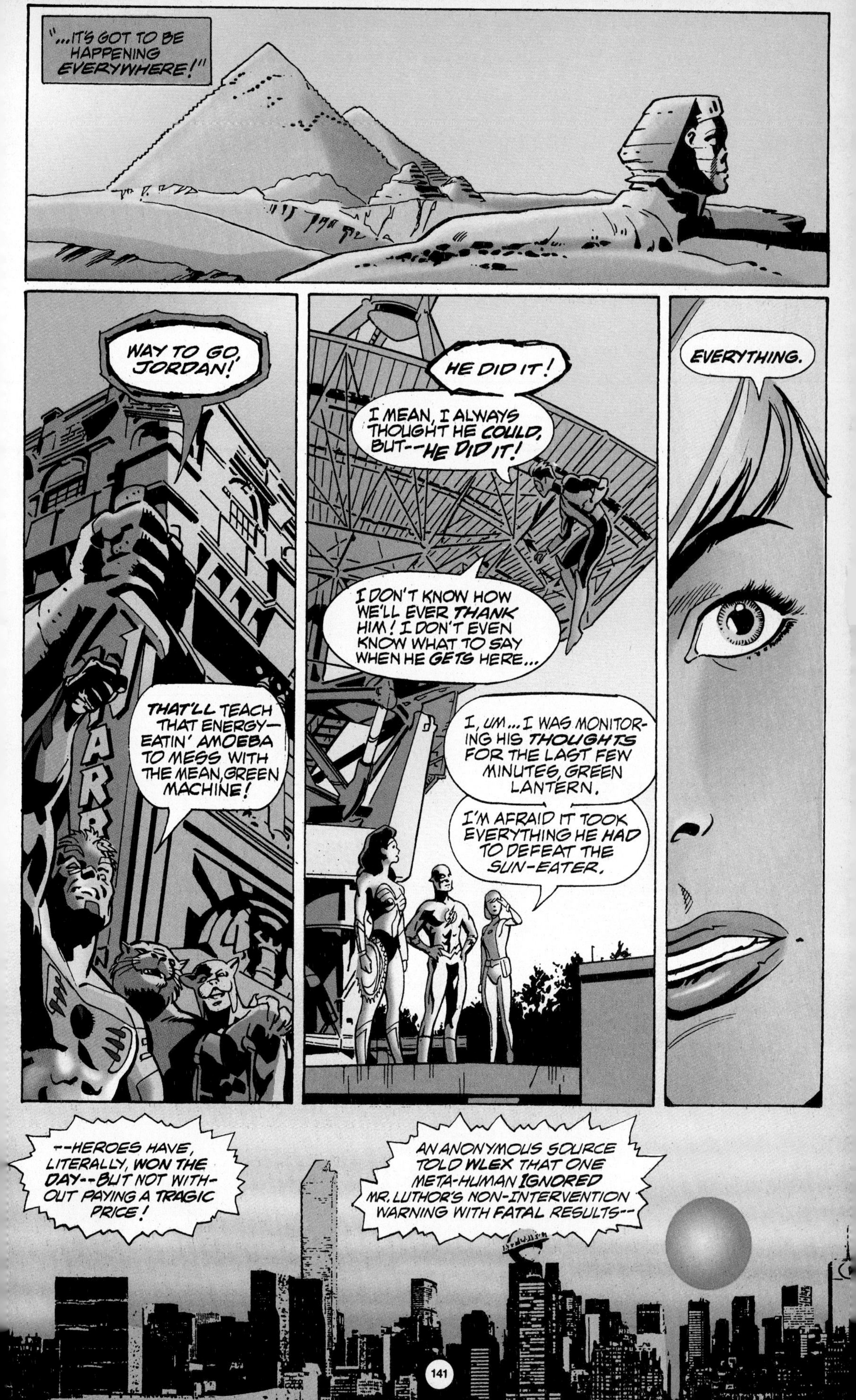
"...IT'S GOT TO BE HAPPENING EVERYWHERE!"
WAY TO GO, JORDAN!
THAT'LL TEACH THAT ENERGY-EATIN' AMOEBA TO MESS WITH THE MEAN, GREEN MACHINE!
HE DID IT!
I MEAN, I ALWAYS THOUGHT HE COULD, BUT--HE DID IT!
I DON'T KNOW HOW WE'LL EVER THANK HIM! I DON'T EVEN KNOW WHAT TO SAY WHEN HE GETS HERE...
I, UM... I WAS MONITORING HIS THOUGHTS FOR THE LAST FEW MINUTES, GREEN LANTERN.
I'M AFRAID IT TOOK EVERYTHING HE HAD TO DEFEAT THE SUN-EATER.
EVERYTHING.
--HEROES HAVE, LITERALLY, WON THE DAY--BUT NOT WITHOUT PAYING A TRAGIC PRICE!
AN ANONYMOUS SOURCE TOLD WLEX THAT ONE META-HUMAN IGNORED MR. LUTHOR'S NON-INTERVENTION WARNING WITH FATAL RESULTS--

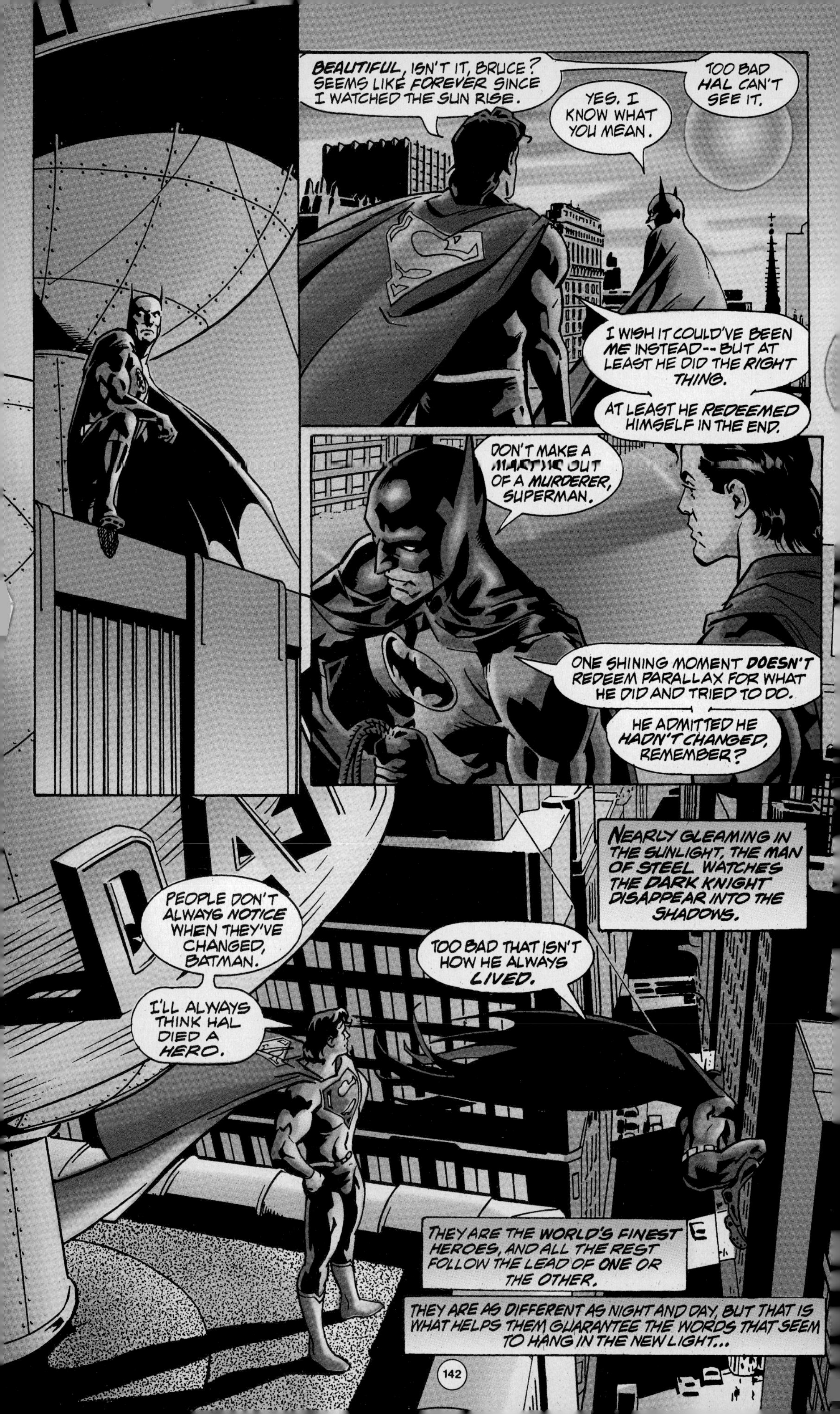
BEAUTIFUL, ISN'T IT, BRUCE? SEEMS LIKE FOREVER SINCE I WATCHED THE SUN RISE.
YES. I KNOW WHAT YOU MEAN.
TOO BAD HAL CAN'T SEE IT.
I WISH IT COULD'VE BEEN ME INSTEAD-- BUT AT LEAST HE DID THE RIGHT THING.
AT LEAST HE REDEEMED HIMSELF IN THE END.
DON'T MAKE A MARTYR OUT OF A MURDERER, SUPERMAN.
ONE SHINING MOMENT DOESN'T REDEEM PARALLAX FOR WHAT HE DID AND TRIED TO DO.
HE ADMITTED HE HADN'T CHANGED, REMEMBER?
NEARLY GLEAMING IN THE SUNLIGHT, THE MAN OF STEEL WATCHES THE DARK KNIGHT DISAPPEAR INTO THE SHADOWS.
PEOPLE DON'T ALWAYS NOTICE WHEN THEY'VE CHANGED, BATMAN.
I'LL ALWAYS THINK HAL DIED A HERO.
TOO BAD THAT ISN'T HOW HE ALWAYS LIVED.
THEY ARE THE WORLD'S FINEST HEROES, AND ALL THE REST FOLLOW THE LEAD OF ONE OR THE OTHER.
THEY ARE AS DIFFERENT AS NIGHT AND DAY, BUT THAT IS WHAT HELPS THEM GUARANTEE THE WORDS THAT SEEM TO HANG IN THE NEW LIGHT...

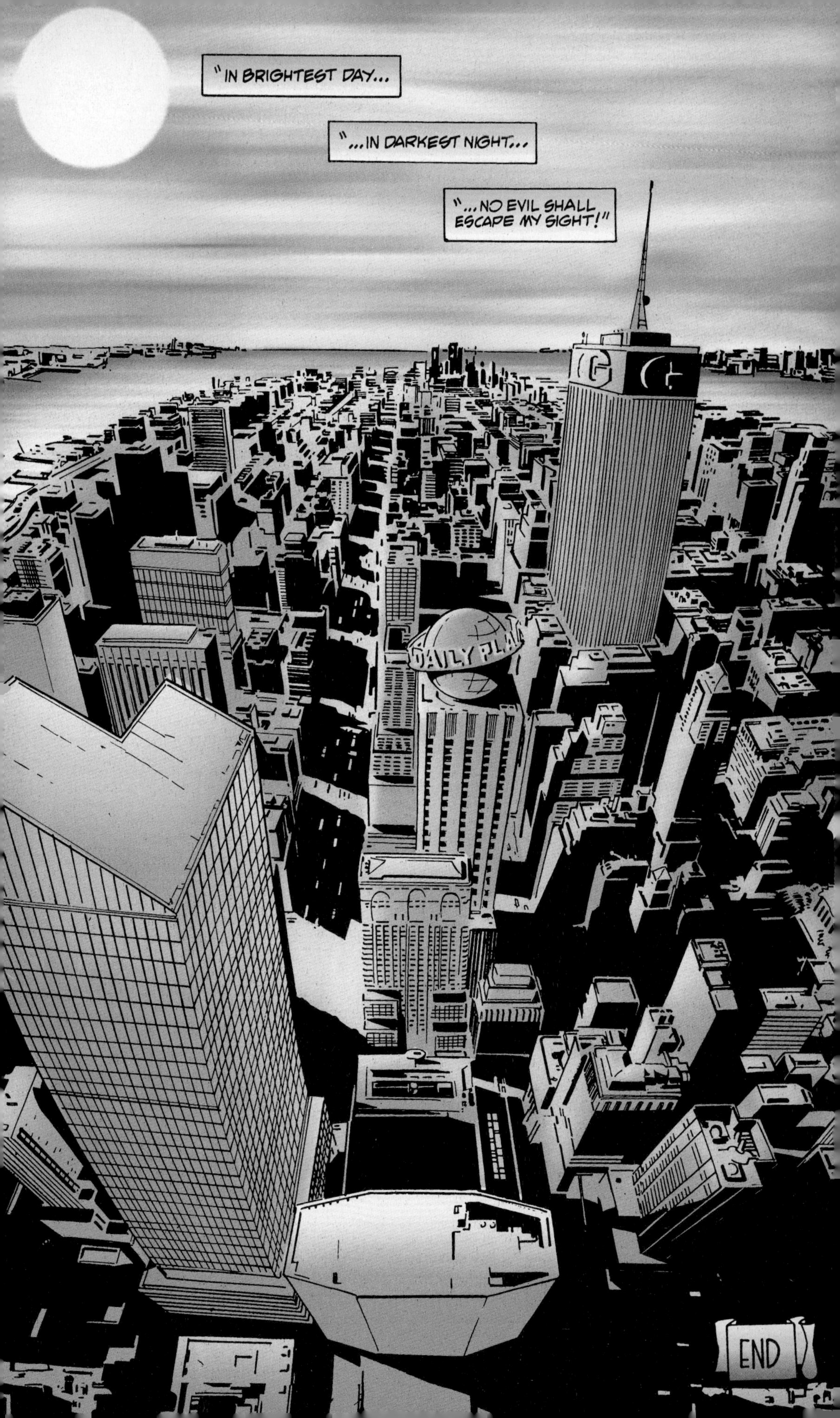
"IN BRIGHTEST DAY...
"...IN DARKEST NIGHT...
"...NO EVIL SHALL ESCAPE MY SIGHT!"
DAILY PLA
END

THE STARS OF THE DC UNIVERSE CAN ALSO BE FOUND IN THESE BOOKS:

GRAPHIC NOVELS

DARKSEID VS. GALACTUS: THE HUNGER
John Byrne

ENEMY ACE: WAR IDYLL
George Pratt

GREEN LANTERN: GANTHET'S TALE
Larry Niven/John Byrne

GREEN LANTERN/SILVER SURFER
Ron Marz/Darryl Banks/Terry Austin

JLA/WILDC.A.T.S: CRIME MACHINE
Grant Morrison/Val Semeiks/Kevin Conrad

JUSTICE RIDERS
Chuck Dixon/Anthony Williams/Mick Gray

THE POWER OF SHAZAM!
Jerry Ordway

TITANS: SCISSORS, PAPER, STONE
Adam Warren/Tom Simmons/Joe Rosas

COLLECTIONS

AQUAMAN: TIME & TIDE
Peter David/Kirk Jarvinen/Brad Vancata

THE AMALGAM AGE OF COMICS:
THE DC COMICS COLLECTION
Various writers and artists

DC VERSUS MARVEL/MARVEL VERSUS DC
Ron Marz/Peter David/Dan Jurgens/Claudio
Castellini/Josef Rubinstein/Paul Neary

THE FLASH: THE RETURN OF BARRY ALLEN
Mark Waid/Greg LaRocque/Ron Richardson

THE GOLDEN AGE
James Robinson/Paul Smith/Richard Ory

THE GREATEST 1950s STORIES EVER TOLD
Various writers and artists

THE GREATEST TEAM-UP STORIES EVER TOLD
Various writers and artists

HAWK & DOVE
Karl & Barbara Kesel/Rob Liefeld

HITMAN
Garth Ennis/John McCrea

IMPULSE: RECKLESS YOUTH
Mark Waid/Humberto Ramos/Wayne Faucher/various

JUSTICE LEAGUE: A MIDSUMMER'S NIGHTMARE
Mark Waid/Fabian Nicieza/Jeff Johnson/
Darick Robertson/John Holdredge/Hanibal Rodriguez

JUSTICE LEAGUE: A NEW BEGINNING
Keith Giffen/J. M. DeMatteis/Kevin Maguire

JUSTICE LEAGUE: NEW WORLD ORDER
Grant Morrison/Howard Porter/John Dell

KINGDOM COME
Mark Waid/Alex Ross

LEGENDS: THE COLLECTED EDITION
John Ostrander/Len Wein/John Byrne/Karl Kesel

LOBO'S GREATEST HITS
Various writers and artists

LOBO: THE LAST CZARNIAN
Keith Giffen/Alan Grant/Simon Bisley

LOBO'S BACK'S BACK
Keith Giffen/Alan Grant/Simon Bisley/
Christian Alamy

RETURN TO THE AMALGAM AGE OF COMICS:
THE DC COMICS COLLECTION
Various writers and artists

THE RAY: IN A BLAZE OF POWER
Jack C. Harris/Joe Quesada/Art Nichols

SOVEREIGN SEVEN
Chris Claremont/Dwayne Turner/Jerome Moore/
various

THE SPECTRE: CRIMES AND PUNISHMENTS
John Ostrander/Tom Mandrake

STARMAN: NIGHT AND DAY
James Robinson/Tony Harris/Wade von Grawbadger

STARMAN: SINS OF THE FATHER
James Robinson/Tony Harris/Wade von Grawbadger

WONDER WOMAN: THE CONTEST
William Messner-Loebs/Mike Deodato, Jr.

WONDER WOMAN: THE CHALLENGE OF ARTEMIS
William Messner-Loebs/Mike Deodato, Jr.

WONDER WOMAN: SECOND GENESIS
John Byrne

ZERO HOUR: CRISIS IN TIME
Dan Jurgens/Jerry Ordway

OTHER COLLECTIONS OF INTEREST

CAMELOT 3000
Mike W. Barr/Brian Bolland

RONIN
Frank Miller

WATCHMEN
Alan Moore/Dave Gibbons

ARCHIVE EDITIONS

ALL STAR COMICS ARCHIVES Volume 1
(ALL STAR COMICS 3-6)
Various writers and artists

ALL STAR COMICS ARCHIVES Volume 2
(ALL STAR COMICS 7-10)
Various writers and artists

ALL STAR COMICS ARCHIVES Volume 3
(ALL STAR COMICS 11-14)
Various writers and artists

THE FLASH ARCHIVES Volume 1
(The Scarlet Speedster's adventures from
FLASH COMICS 104, SHOWCASE 4, 8, 13, 14,
and THE FLASH 105-108)
John Broome/Robert Kanigher/
Carmine Infantino/Frank Giacoia/Joe Giella/
Joe Kubert

JUSTICE LEAGUE OF AMERICA ARCHIVES Volume 1
(THE BRAVE AND THE BOLD 28-30 and JUSTICE
LEAGUE OF AMERICA 1-6)
Gardner Fox/Mike Sekowsky/various

JUSTICE LEAGUE OF AMERICA ARCHIVES Volume 2
(JUSTICE LEAGUE OF AMERICA 7-14)
Gardner Fox/Mike Sekowsky/various

JUSTICE LEAGUE OF AMERICA ARCHIVES Volume 3
(JUSTICE LEAGUE OF AMERICA 15-22)
Gardner Fox/Mike Sekowsky/various

LEGION OF SUPER-HEROES ARCHIVES Volume 1
(The Legion of Super-Heroes' adventures from
ADVENTURE COMICS 247, 267, 282, 290, 293,
300-305, ACTION COMICS 267, 276, 287, 289,
SUPERBOY 86, 89, 98 and SUPERMAN 147)
Various writers and artists

LEGION OF SUPER-HEROES ARCHIVES Volume 2
(The Legion of Super-Heroes' adventures from
ADVENTURE COMICS 306-317 and SUPERMAN'S PAL,
JIMMY OLSEN 72)
Various writers and artists

LEGION OF SUPER-HEROES ARCHIVES Volume 3
(The Legion of Super-Heroes' adventures from
ADVENTURE COMICS 318-328, SUPERMAN'S PAL,
JIMMY OLSEN 76 and SUPERBOY 117)
Various writers and artists

LEGION OF SUPER-HEROES ARCHIVES Volume 4
(The Legion of Super-Heroes' adventures from
ADVENTURE COMICS 329-339 and
SUPERBOY 124-125)
Various writers and artists

LEGION OF SUPER-HEROES ARCHIVES Volume 5
(The Legion of Super-Heroes' adventures from
ADVENTURE COMICS 340-349)
Various writers and artists

LEGION OF SUPER-HEROES ARCHIVES Volume 6
(The Legion of Super-Heroes' adventures from
ADVENTURE COMICS 350-358)
Various writers and artists

LEGION OF SUPER-HEROES ARCHIVES Volume 7
(The Legion of Super-Heroes' adventures from
ADVENTURE COMICS 359-367 and SUPERMAN'S PAL,
JIMMY OLSEN #106)
Various writers and artists

**For the nearest comics shop carrying collected editions and monthly titles from
DC Comics, call 1-888-COMIC BOOK.**

971031